THE
HANDY
SUPREME COURT
ANSWER
BOOK

About the Author

David L. Hudson Jr. is an attorney-author who works as First Amendment Scholar for the First Amendment Center at Vanderbilt University. He writes regularly on the Supreme Court, as a contributing editor to the American Bar Association's *Preview of U.S. Supreme Court Cases*. He also teaches several classes at the Nashville School of Law, an introduction to law class at Middle Tennessee State University, and a First Amendment class at Vanderbilt Law School. He is the author of more than 16 books, including *The Rehnquist Court: Understanding Its Impact and Legacy* (Praeger, 2006). He is a graduate of Duke University and Vanderbilt Law School.

The Handy Answer Book Series®

The Handy Answer Book for Kids (and Parents)
The Handy Biology Answer Book
The Handy Geography Answer Book
The Handy Geology Answer Book
The Handy History Answer Book, 2nd Ed.
The Handy Math Answer Book
The Handy Ocean Answer Book
The Handy Physics Answer Book
The Handy Politics Answer Book
The Handy Presidents Answer Book
The Handy Religion Answer Book
The Handy Science Answer Book, Cent. Ed.
The Handy Sports Answer Book
The Handy Supreme Court Answer Book
The Handy Weather Answer Book

Please visit us at visibleink.com.

THE
HANDY
SUPREME
COURT
ANSWER
BOOK

David L. Hudson Jr.

Detroit

THE HANDY SUPREME COURT ANSWER BOOK

Copyright 2008 by Visible Ink Press®

This publication is a creative work fully protected by all applicable copyright laws, as well as by misappropriation, trade secret, unfair competition, and other applicable laws.

No part of this book may be reproduced in any form without permission in writing from the publisher, except by a reviewer who wishes to quote brief passages in connection with a review written for inclusion in a magazine or newspaper.

Visible Ink Press®
43311 Joy Road #414
Canton, MI 48187–2075

Visible Ink Press is a registered trademark of Visible Ink Press LLC.

Most Visible Ink Press books are available at special quantity discounts when purchased in bulk by corporations, organizations, or groups. Customized printings, special imprints, messages, and excerpts can be produced to meet your needs. For more information, contact Special Markets Director, Visible Ink Press, at www.visibleink.com or (734) 667-3211.

Art Director: Mary Claire Krzewinski
Typesetting: The Graphix Group

ISBN-13: 978-1-57859-196-1

Library of Congress Cataloging-in-Publication Data has been applied for.

Front cover images of Supreme Court Building courtesy of iStockPhoto; *Dred Scott* case and pro-choice rally courtesy of AP Images.

Back cover images of children reciting the Pledge of Allegiance courtesy of Mark Wilson/Getty and Fuller Court courtesy of the Library of Congress.

For Rich Brust, Deb Weiss, Larry Baker,
Chuck Williams, Tony Mauro, my wife, and my parents

Contents

Introduction

Abortion, affirmative action, capital punishment, medicinal usage of marijuana, religious freedom, treatment of captives during the War on Terror, and even a presidential election. All these pressing societal issues have been examined by a body of nine (since 1869) jurists in the so-called "Court of Last Resort." The U.S. Supreme Court has the final say in our judicial system. Our fourth (and perhaps greatest) chief justice—John Marshall—declared the power of judicial review for the U.S. Supreme Court and lower courts in *Marbury v. Madison* (1803) when he wrote that "it is emphatically the province and duty of the judicial department to say what the law is."

Like all other public institutions, sometimes the Court has performed miserably, as it did in *Dred Scott v. Sandford* (1857) when sanctioning slavery. At other times, the Court has led the way to a more just society, as it did when ruling unanimously that segregated public schools violated the Equal Protection Clause in *Brown v. Board of Education* (1954).

Yet, the Court remains a mystery to many citizens. Its hearings are not televised and some justices remain committed to keeping cameras out of the courtroom forever. When asked about the possibility of such coverage, Justice David Souter reportedly said, "Over my dead body!" Most people cannot name all the justices of the Supreme Court. Some may know Clarence Thomas from his contentious (and, at times, salacious) confirmation hearing in 1991; others knew Sandra Day O'Connor because of her gender-breaking role. However, the average person may not know the names of John Paul Stevens, Antonin Scalia, Anthony Kennedy, and the rest of the current justices.

The Handy Supreme Court Answer Book seeks to increase reader knowledge on this important public institution. It provides a comprehensive overview of the Court from its inception in 1789 to the present. There have been seventeen chief justices in the history of the Court—from John Jay to John G. Roberts Jr. This book examines all seventeen justices and their Courts, as well as many of the nearly one hundred associate justices who have served in this venerable institution.

Most of the book is divided into chapters based on the name of the particular chief justice. Some periods were much longer and more significant than others. For instance, Chief Justice Marshall served more than thirty years in his role as head of the Court. On the other hand, Chief Justice Harlan Fiske Stone served only five. Earl Warren presided over a Court from 1953 to 1969 that literally transformed American society. More recently, William H. Rehnquist presided over the Court from 1986 to 2005, ushering in a new era of federalism that recalibrated the balance between federal and state governments.

For each period, the book opens with interesting questions and answers regarding the justices on that particular Court. It then presents information regarding the Court's major decisions during that time period. Readers will learn about the landmark cases of *Marbury v. Madison* (1803), *Gibbons v. Ogden* (1824), *Dred Scott v. Sandford* (1857), the *Civil Rights Cases* (1883), *Powell v. Alabama* (1932), *Brown v. Board of Education* (1954), *Gitlow v. New York* (1925), *Miranda v. Arizona* (1966), *Roe v. Wade* (1973), and *Bush v. Gore* (2000). Readers also will read about many of the protagonists in these famous cases—the litigants, attorneys, and jurists who helped shape American law. For instance, *The Handy Supreme Court Answer Book* examines the landmark decision of *Gideon v. Wainwright* (1963), in which the Court ruled that the Sixth Amendment right of assistance of counsel (right to a lawyer) was extended to the states. Readers will learn about the plaintiff and former petty thief Clarence Earl Gideon, his lawyer (and future U.S. Supreme Court justice) Abe Fortas, and the justice who rendered the Court's opinion, Hugo Black—who stayed on the Court long enough to see his dissenting opinion from twenty-one years earlier in *Betts v. Brady* (1942) become the law of the land. Also covered are the Supreme Court cases involving such cultural celebrities as Larry Flynt, Jerry Falwell, and Anna Nicole Smith. Readers also discover how famous Court language such as "shouting fire in a theatre" contributed mightily to jurisprudence on the First Amendment—the first 45 words in our Bill of Rights.

For the most important opinions, the book provides key excerpts from the Court's opinions—not only the majority opinions but also from concurring and dissenting opinions. Sometimes justices on the Court—just like all of us in society—disagree on fundamental questions of law and policy. Some of these divisions are brought to life in the following pages.

Additionally, the book provides opening chapters on the origins of the Court, the structure of the American judicial system, and interesting trivia about the individuals (108 men and 2 women) who have donned the black robes in the so-called "Marble Palace." The author sincerely hopes that you find the book as informative while reading it, as he did in preparing it. Thank you for your interest in the Court!

David L. Hudson Jr.

Acknowledgments

The author thanks Visible Ink Press for the early development of the project, which involved Marty Connors, Roger Matuz, Mary Beth Perrot, Christa Gainor, and Terri Schell. Additional thanks are given to Roger Jänecke for marketing and managerial wisdom; Larry Baker for his project management and indexing skills; Robyn Young and Barry Puckett for their illustration work; Robert Huffman for his imaging and scanning expertise; Sarah Hermsen for her proofreading; Mary Claire Krzewinski for her always-solid book design; and Jake Di Vita of The Graphix Group for his seemingly 'round-the-clock typesetting.

The author would also like to thank the following individuals: Joan Biskupic, Richard Brust, Ronald Collins, Carla Hudson, David and Carol Hudson, Tony Mauro, Robert O'Neil, Gene Policinski, John Seigenthaler, John Vile, Eugene Volokh, and Artemus Ward.

ORIGINS OF THE FEDERAL COURT SYSTEM

CREATION OF THE COURT

How was the **U.S. Supreme Court created**?

Article III, Section 1, of the U.S. Constitution provided that "the judicial Power of the United States, shall be vested in one supreme Court, and in such inferior Courts as the Congress may from time to time ordain and establish." The Constitution was adopted in 1787 and ratified in 1788. However, the Constitution did not create the U.S. Supreme Court. Congress passed a law known as the Judiciary Act of 1789, which created the Court and established its jurisdiction. The Judiciary Act of 1789 called for six justices on the Court—a chief justice and five associate justices.

Does Article III call for a **chief justice**?

Ironically, Article III does not mention a chief justice at all. It only mentions that there will be "one supreme court." However, Article I, Section 3, mentions a "Chief Justice" when talking about the impeachment of a president. It reads: "When the President of the United States is tried, the Chief Justice shall preside."

Where was the **Constitution itself created**?

The U.S. Constitution was created during the summer of 1787 at a meeting of fifty-five delegates whose assigned job was to propose revisions to the Articles of Confederation, the authoritative document of the existing government, which did not provide enough power for a central government. The delegates actually went beyond their job duties and created an entire new Constitution during a process that author Catherine Drinker Bowen called "the Miracle at Philadelphia." This process culminated on September 17, 1787, when thirty-nine men signed the new docu-

Virginia delegate Edmund Randolph was instrumental in bringing forth a plan to create a federal judiciary branch in 1789. Randolph went on to become the nation's first attorney general. *Hulton Archive/Getty Images.*

ment. Various states then ratified the Constitution in 1787 and 1788 that put the Constitution into effect.

What is the **structure of the Constitution**?

The Constitution features seven sections, called articles. The first three articles deal with the powers of the three branches of government. Article I deals with the legislative branch (Congress), Article II deals with the executive branch (the president), and Article III deals with the judicial branch (the court system).

The Constitution features a system of separation of powers and checks and balances among the three branches of government. For example, Congress passes legislation but the president can veto (or stop) the legislation, which Congress can then override by a super-majoritarian vote of two-thirds. This means that if a president vetoes a piece of legislation, the law can still be enacted if two-thirds of the members of Congress vote to override the presidential action. However, the judicial branch can then declare a law unconstitutional if it determines that it is not compatible with the Constitution.

When did the framers consider a **separate judicial branch**?

Virginia delegate Edmund Randolph, later the nation's first attorney general, introduced the so-called Virginia Plan, which called for the creation of a federal judiciary, on May 29, 1787. The Virginia Plan called for Congress, not the executive branch, to appoint judges.

Under the Constitution, who **appoints Supreme Court justices**?

The Constitution provides that the president has the power to appoint "Judges of the Supreme Court." Article II, Section 2, says that the president "shall have Power … [to] nominate, and by and with the Advice and Consent of the Senate, shall appoint … Judges of the Supreme Court, and all other Officers of the United States, whose Appointments are not herein otherwise provided for." This means that the president nominates Supreme Court justices and the U.S. Senate then confirms (or denies) the selection.

Which framer first proposed **how justices would obtain their positions**?

Nathaniel Gorham, one of two members from Massachusetts who signed the Constitution at the 1787 Philadelphia Convention, first proposed the idea that the president should nominate the justices and the Senate should confirm them.

Were the framers in agreement on the **creation of lower federal courts**?

No, the framers disagreed over whether the Constitution should call for the creation of lower federal courts. For example, John Rutledge—who would later become the second chief justice of the U.S. Supreme Court—said that creating

Massachusetts delegate Nathaniel Gorham first proposed that the president should nominate the justices and the Senate should confirm them. *Hulton Archive/Getty Images.*

lower federal courts would constitute "an unnecessary encroachment" upon state courts. Maryland's Luther Martin warned that the creation of lower federal courts would cause "jealousies and oppositions in the State tribunals." However, Virginia's James Madison—the nation's future fourth president—argued that lower federal courts were necessary to ensure the fair administration of justice. He warned that state courts may not provide "unbiased" rulings.

JUDICIAL REVIEW AND JUDICIAL INDEPENDENCE

Did the framers agree on the **power of judicial review**?

No, the Founding Fathers did not agree on the power of judicial review—the power of the Supreme Court to review the constitutionality of laws and regulations. The Federalists believed in establishing a strong, central government. One such Federalist, Alexander Hamilton, the nation's first secretary of the Treasury, argued forcefully for the power of judicial review in one of his *Federalist Papers* (#78). The *Federalist Papers* were a series of essays published anonymously under the pen name "Publius" by Hamilton, James Madison, and John Jay to support the newly drafted Constitution and the new central government. In 1789, Madison argued for the addition of a Bill of Rights to the Constitution, and wrote that the Bill of Rights would give the judiciary a "check" on legislative encroachments on individual liberties.

3

Pro-Con: Judicial Review

Pro-Judicial Review (*Federalist Papers*): "It is far more rational to suppose, that the courts were designed to be an intermediate body between the people and the legislature, in order, among other things, to keep the latter within the limits assigned to their authority. The interpretation of the laws is the proper and peculiar province of the courts. A constitution is, in fact, and must be regarded by the judges, as a fundamental law. It therefore belongs to them to ascertain its meaning, as well as the meaning of any particular act proceeding from the legislative body."

Anti-Judicial Review (*Anti-Federalist Papers*): "The supreme court under this constitution would be exalted above all other power in the government, and subject to no control. The business of this paper will be to illustrate this, and to show the danger that will result from it. I question whether the world ever saw, in any period of it, a court of justice invested with such immense powers, and yet placed in a situation so little responsible. Certain it is, that in England, and in the several states, where we have been taught to believe the courts of law are put upon the most prudent establishment, they are on a very different footing."

Others, known as Anti-Federalists, believed that the new Constitution concentrated too much power in the new, federal government. They wanted to keep the power with the individual state governments. Robert Yates, a leader from New York, wrote a series of essays called the *Anti-Federalist Papers* under the pen name "Brutus." In one of these, he attacked the concept of judicial review as residing too much power in the judiciary.

Does the **Constitution explicitly give the power of judicial review to the judiciary**?

No, the U.S. Constitution does not mention the concept of judicial review. Many framers assumed that the Court would have the power to declare laws unconstitutional but it is not specifically mentioned in the Constitution. Several lower courts asserted the power of judicial review and, most famously, Chief Justice John Marshall clearly established the power for the judiciary when he wrote in *Marbury v. Madison* (1803) that "it is emphatically, the province of the judicial department, to say what the law is."

What **other provisions of the Constitution imply a power of judicial review** on the part of the courts?

The Supremacy Clause of the Constitution, at least to some historians and scholars, provides some justification for the principle of judicial review. Chief Justice John Marshall cited the Supremacy Clause in his famous *Marbury v. Madison* (1803) opinion, which declared that the judiciary had the power of judicial review. Marshall wrote:

> It is also not entirely unworthy of observation that in declaring what shall be the supreme law of the land, the constitution itself is first mentioned; and not the laws of the United States generally, but those only which shall be made in pursuance of the constitution, have that rank.

> Thus, the particular phraseology of the Constitution of the United States confirms and strengthens the principle, supposed to be essential to all written Constitutions, that a law repugnant to the Constitution is void; and that courts, as well as other departments, are bound by that instrument.

Chief Justice John Marshall referred to the Supremacy Clause when giving his opinion in the famous *Marbury v. Madison* trial in 1803. This case declared that that the judiciary had the power of judicial review. *Hulton Archive/Getty Images.*

What was the leading framer **James Madison's opinion of judicial review?**

Virginia delegate James Madison realized that too much power in any one branch could create problems when he wrote in the *Federalist Papers* (#47): "The accumulation of all powers, legislative, executive and judiciary, in the same hands, whether of one, a few or many, and where hereditary, self-appointed, or elective, may justly be pronounced the very definition of tyranny." Madison actually favored a system whereby the justices would join with members of the executive branch to form a "council of revision" that would review laws proposed by the U.S. Congress.

What were some **important precursors to *Marbury v. Madison*?**

Marbury v. Madison is rightfully considered the leading decision on judicial review since it was decided by the U.S. Supreme Court. However, it did not occur in a vacuum, as a few state courts had already assumed the power of judicial review to invalidate laws. These include *Rutgers v. Waddington* (1784), *Trevett v. Weeden* (1786), and *Bayard v. Singleton* (1787).

The *Rutgers* decision involved a British merchant named Waddington, who occupied the property of Rutgers under orders from the British military during the Revolutionary War. The legal issue concerned whether Waddington could be convicted of trespassing for invading the property of an American citizen. Alexander Hamilton defended Waddington, arguing that the New York trespass law must yield to a 1783 treaty between the United States and Great Britain that prohibited the punishment of British sympathizers (called Tories or Loyalists) for conduct during the war.

The *Trevett* decision concerned the prosecution of butcher James M. Varnum for violating a Rhode Island law that punished those who refused to accept paper money. The Rhode Island court struck down the state law, causing an outrage in the legislature. The legislature called the judges before its body to question them for their act of striking down a state law. The legislature even refused to reappoint four of the five judges.

In *Bayard,* Elizabeth Bayard sought to recover property confiscated because her father was a Loyalist. The owner of the property, a Mr. Singleton, had purchased the property from the state of North Carolina. The North Carolina court ruled in favor of Bayard, striking down the Confiscation Act, passed by the North Carolina General Assembly during the American Revolution. The judges determined that the confiscation law violated the North Carolina Constitution's provision for trial by jury and determined that Bayard should have the opportunity to present her case before a jury.

These three decisions served as key precedents on the road to *Marbury v. Madison.*

Who were the **attorneys in *Bayard v. Singleton*?**

Two future U.S. Supreme Court justices served as the attorneys in *Bayard v. Singleton.* James Iredell, one of the first six justices on the Supreme Court, argued the case for Elizabeth Bayard, while future justice Alfred Moore, appointed to the Court by President John Adams, argued the case for the defendant Singleton and the state.

What does **Article III** say about the **tenure of federal judges?**

Article III in effect provides life tenure for federal judges. It sets no time limit but says that federal judges "shall hold their Offices during good behavior." Article II, Section 4, provides for the removal of "all civil Officers of the United States ... on Impeachment for, and Conviction of, Treason, Bribery, or other high Crimes and Misdemeanors."

Why did the **Constitution give federal judges life tenure**?

The framers gave life tenure to federal judges to ensure an independent judiciary, a judiciary that would not bow to the political pressures of the day. Federal judges often have to make difficult decisions that a significant segment of the public may question quite critically. For this reason, Alexander Hamilton wrote in the *Federalist Papers* (#78) that "the complete independence of the courts of justice is peculiarly essential in a limited Constitution."

Founding Father Alexander Hamilton, the nation's first secretary of the Treasury, recommended that Supreme Court justices receive life tenure in order to ensure "complete independence of the courts." *Library of Congress.*

Alexander Hamilton stated (from #78): "If then the courts of justice are to be considered as the bulwarks of a limited constitution against legislative encroachments, this consideration will afford a strong argument for the permanent tenure of judicial offices, since nothing will contribute so much as this to that independent spirit of judges, which must be essential to the faithful performance of so arduous a duty."

Can federal judges be impeached?

Yes, federal judges can be impeached. The Constitution provides that federal judges "shall hold their Offices during good behavior." They can be impeached for "treason, Bribery or other high crimes and misdemeanors." This means that federal judges receive lifetime appointments but can be removed from office for bad conduct. The Constitution gives the U.S. House of Representatives the "sole power of impeachment" and the U.S. Senate "the sole Power to try all impeachments." It takes a two-thirds majority vote in the Senate for someone to be impeached and removed from office.

Have any federal judges been impeached?

Yes, several federal judges have been impeached by the House and many of those impeached by the House have been convicted in the Senate. The following federal judges have been impeached. Some resigned after the House voted to impeach, others were acquitted in the Senate and some were convicted by the Senate.

> **John Pickering (1803):** U.S. District Court for the District of New Hampshire (impeached by House and convicted by the Senate)

> **Samuel Chase (1804–5):** Associate Justice of the U.S. Supreme Court (impeached by the House in 1804 and acquitted by the Senate in 1805)

CourtSpeak: Modern View on Life Tenure of Supreme Court Justices

Chief Justice William Rehnquist (2004): "By guaranteeing judges life tenure during good behavior, the Constitution tries to insulate judges from the public pressures that may affect elected officials. The Constitution protects judicial independence not to benefit judges, but to promote the rule of law: judges are expected to administer the law fairly, without regard to public reaction....

"A natural consequence of life tenure should be the ability to benefit from informed criticism from legislators, the bar, academe, and the public. When federal judges are criticized for judicial decisions and actions taken in the discharge of their judicial duties, however, it is well to remember [a principle that has] long governed the tenure of federal judges.... Congress' authority to impeach and remove judges should not extend to decisions from the bench. That principle was established nearly 200 years ago in 1805, after a Congress dominated by Jeffersonian Republicans impeached Supreme Court Justice Samuel Chase.... The political precedent set by Chase's acquittal has governed the use of impeachment to remove federal judges from that day to this: a judge's *judicial* acts may not serve as a basis for impeachment. Congress's authority to impeach and remove judges should not extend to decisions from the bench...."

James H. Peck (1830): U.S. District Court for the District of Missouri (impeached by the House and acquitted by the Senate)

West H. Humphreys (1862): U.S. District Court for the Middle, Eastern and Western Districts of Tennessee (impeached by the House and convicted in the Senate)

Mark H. Delahay (1873): U.S. District Court for the District of Kansas (impeached by the House and resigned before trial in the Senate)

Charles Swayne (1904): U.S. District Court for the Northern District of Florida (impeached by the House and acquitted in the Senate)

Robert W. Archbald (1912): U.S. Commerce Court (impeached by the House and convicted by the Senate)

George W. English (1926): U.S. District Court for the Eastern District of Illinois (impeached by the House and resigned from office)

Harold Louderback (1933): U.S. District Court for the Northern District of California (impeached by the House and acquitted by the Senate)

Halsted L. Ritter (1936): U.S. District Court for the Southern District of Florida (impeached by the House and convicted by the Senate)

Harry E. Claiborne (1986): U.S. District Court for the District of Nevada (impeached by the House and convicted in the Senate)

Alcee L. Hastings (1988): U.S. District Court for the Southern District of Florida (impeached by the House and convicted in the Senate)

Walter L. Nixon (1989): U.S. District Court for the Southern District of Mississippi (impeached by the House and convicted by the Senate)

Only one U.S. Supreme Court justice, Samuel Chase, has ever been impeached by the House of Representatives. The Senate acquitted Chase in March 1803. In 1969, Justice Abe Fortas resigned from the U.S. Supreme Court after facing a threat of impeachment.

What happened with the **impeachment of Samuel Chase**?

Samuel Chase had a distinguished political history. He had signed the Declaration of Independence. He had served as the chief judge of Maryland's highest state court.

Samuel Chase is the only Supreme Court justice to be impeached by the House of Representatives. The Senate, however, acquitted him in March 1803. *Hulton Archive/Getty Images.*

However, Chase landed into trouble when he became a Supreme Court justice. His troubles occurred when he rode circuit and served as presiding judge in some key cases. For example, Chase apparently conducted himself in a very partisan manner during the sedition trial of James Callender. He also attacked President Thomas Jefferson, saying the president had engaged in "seditious attacks on the principles of the Constitution." The House of Representatives impeached Chase 72–32 on eight charges in March 1804. However, the Senate acquitted Chase in 1805. On one charge, the Senate voted 19–15 to convict Chase. But Chase was acquitted on even this charge because there needed to be a two-thirds vote for conviction (or 24 votes). Many view the acquittal of Justice Chase as essential to the principle of an independent judiciary.

JUDICIARY ACT OF 1789 AND THE LOWER FEDERAL COURTS

Why is the **Judiciary Act of 1789 so important**?

It is important because it created the federal judicial system in the United States. Justice Sandra Day O'Connor wrote in her book *The Majesty Of the Law: Reflections of a Supreme Court Justice* that the Judiciary Act of 1789 "stands as the single most important legislative enactment of the nation's founding years." The Judiciary Act is important because it created the federal court system. The U.S. Constitution called for the creation of a "supreme court" and the "inferior courts" but it was Congress that did the creating when it passed the Judiciary Act of 1789.

Who was the **principal author of the Judiciary Act of 1789**?

Oliver Ellsworth of Connecticut was the principal author of the Judiciary Act of 1789. A member of the Philadelphia Convention of 1787, Ellsworth became a U.S. senator when the Senate first convened in 1789. He was elected chair of the committee designed to follow the dictates of Article III of the new Constitution to create a federal judicial system. William Paterson from New Jersey, another member of the 1787 Convention and an original U.S. senator, also assisted in the drafting of the Judiciary Act of 1789. Both Ellsworth and Paterson later became justices on the U.S. Supreme Court. They both were classmates at the College of New Jersey (later Princeton College) before they entered politics.

What type of **federal court system did Congress create** in the Judiciary Act of 1789?

Congress passed the Federal Judiciary Act of 1789, which filled in many of the blanks in Article III of the Constitution. For example, Article III simply stated that there would be "one supreme court" and such "inferior courts" as Congress deemed necessary.

The Judiciary Act created a three-tiered system of federal courts, which still exists into the twenty-first century. The Act created a U.S. Supreme Court (of six justices), federal circuit courts, and federal district courts. There were 13 district courts, consisting of the districts of Maine, New Hampshire, Massachusetts, Connecticut, New York, New Jersey, Pennsylvania, Delaware, Maryland, Virginia, Kentucky, South Carolina, and Georgia. In each district, there would be a district court and a district judge that would hold four annual sessions.

The Judiciary Act also called for three circuit courts—the Eastern, Middle, and Southern Circuits. The Eastern Circuit consisted of the districts of Connecticut, Maine, Massachusetts, New Hampshire, and New York. The Middle Circuit consisted of the districts of Delaware, Kentucky, Maryland, New Jersey, Pennsylvania, and Virginia.

The Southern Circuit consisted of the districts of Georgia and South Carolina. Each circuit court would consist of panels of three judges—a local district court judge and two U.S. Supreme Court justices.

Who were the **original federal district court judges** in these thirteen districts?

The thirteen original federal district court judges were: Richard Law (District of Connecticut); David Sewall (District of Maine); John Lowell (District of Massachusetts); John Sullivan (District of New Hampshire); James Duane (District of New York); Gunning Bedford (District of Delaware); Harry Innes (District of Kentucky); William Paca (District of Maryland); David Brearley (District of New Jersey); Francis Hopkinson (District of Pennsylvania); Cyrus Griffin (District of Virginia); Nathaniel Pendleton (District of Georgia); and William Drayton (District of South Carolina).

What **three additional federal district courts** were created within two years of the Judiciary Act of 1789?

Congress added federal district courts in the states of North Carolina, Rhode Island, and Vermont. President George Washington nominated John Stokes for the District of North Carolina; Harry Marchant for the District of Rhode Island; and Nathaniel Chipman for the District of Vermont.

What part of the Judiciary Act of 1789 gives the **Supreme Court the power to review state laws?**

Section 25 of the Judiciary Act of 1789 provides that the U.S. Supreme Court can review state laws to determine whether they comport with the Constitution. The section reads that where "the validity" of a state law is questioned "on the ground of being repugnant to the constitution, treaties or laws of the United States," the U.S. Supreme Court has jurisdiction. This section originally caused great controversy, as many believed that the rights of the states were being invaded by the federal government and its courts.

What was **circuit duty**?

The Judiciary Act of 1789 created 13 lower federal courts called district courts. These district courts were divided into three circuits—the Eastern, the Middle, and the Southern. The circuit courts were composed of a district court judge and two justices of the U.S. Supreme Court. "Circuit duty," or "riding circuit," meant that U.S. Supreme Court justices had to travel across the country to hear cases across the country. An early U.S. Supreme Court justice, Thomas Johnson of Maryland, resigned after a little more than a year because of the difficulties caused by traveling to different circuit courts. In 1793, Congress passed a law that required circuit courts to consist of only one U.S. Supreme Court justice. Supreme Court justices "rode circuit" until 1891.

Section 25 of the Judiciary Act of 1789

"And be it further enacted, That a final judgment or decree in any suit, in the highest court of law or equity of a State in which a decision in the suit could be had, where is drawn in question the validity of a treaty or statute of, or an authority exercised under the United States, and the decision is against their validity; or where is drawn in question the validity of a statute of, or an authority exercised under any State, on the ground of their being repugnant to the constitution, treaties or laws of the United States, and the decision is in favour of such their validity, or where is drawn in question the construction of any clause of the constitution, or of a treaty, or statute of, or commission held under the United States, and the decision is against the title, right, privilege or exemption specially set up or claimed by either party, under such clause of the said Constitution, treaty, statute or commission, may be re-examined and reversed or affirmed in the Supreme Court of the United States upon a writ of error...."

When did Congress create **separate judges for the circuit courts**?

Congress established sixteen judgeships in six circuit courts in the Judiciary Act of 1801. The first five circuits would receive three judges each, while a single judge would man the Sixth Circuit. The outgoing administration of Federalist president John Adams wanted to strengthen the federal judicial system, particularly before the Democratic-Republican administration of incoming president Thomas Jefferson and a new Congress dominated by Jefferson's party took office. The Democratic-Republicans repealed the Judiciary Act of 1801 in the Judiciary Act of 1802. This new law kept the structure of the six circuits but abolished the separate judgeships.

Which **federal judges lost their jobs** because of the Judiciary Act of 1802?

The Judiciary Act of 1802 abolished the new judgeships created by the Judiciary Act of 1801. The following judges lost their jobs: First Circuit: Benjamin Bourne and Jeremiah Smith; Second Circuit: Egbert Benson, Samuel Hitchcock, and Oliver Wolcott; Third Circuit: Richard Bassett, William Griffith, and William Tilghman; Fourth Circuit: Philip Barton Key, Charles Magill, and George Keith Taylor; Fifth Circuit: Joseph Clay, Dominic Augustin Hall, and Edward Harris; and Sixth Circuit: William McClung.

What law **created the U.S. Courts of Appeals** that exists today?

Congress created nine circuit courts of appeals by the Judiciary Act of 1891, also called the Evarts Act, named after U.S. senator William Evarts of New York. These new circuit court of appeals featured three judges each. A court of appeals for the D.C. Circuit was added in 1893; a court of appeals for the Tenth Circuit was added in 1929; and the Eleventh Circuit was added in 1980 by dividing the existing Fifth Circuit into two parts. In 1982, the Court created the Federal Circuit, which hears specialized appeals in patent and civil personnel cases among others. The Evarts Act essentially established the basic model for the modern-day federal judicial system.

Who was **William Evarts**?

William Maxwell Evarts was one of the nation's leading lawyers. He also served in the U.S. Senate and sponsored the Judiciary Act of 1891. Evarts served as counsel

William Maxwell Evarts, best known for serving as President Andrew Johnson's counsel during his impeachment proceedings. He also was a U.S. senator and served in the Abraham Lincoln and Rutherford B. Hayes administrations. *Brady-Handy Photograph Collection/Library of Congress.*

for then-President Andrew Johnson during his impeachment proceedings. He also served as U.S. attorney for President Abraham Lincoln and as secretary of state for President Rutherford B. Hayes.

How does **the system created by the Founding Fathers** compare with the current federal court system?

The Judiciary Act of 1789 created the same three-tiered court system of federal district courts, federal circuits, and U.S. Supreme Court that exists today. The Evarts Act modernized the system by actually placing new judges on the circuit court appellate level, as opposed to staffing the circuit courts with district judges and U.S. Supreme Court justices. Now, there are ninety-four federal district courts, thirteen federal circuit courts of appeals, and one U.S. Supreme Court composed of nine justices. One major difference in the current system from the 1789 system is that now there are separate judges on the federal circuit courts of appeals. Another major difference is that the circuit courts of appeals are appellate courts; they no longer function as trial courts.

How many **judges on the Court of Appeals hear individual cases**?

Most cases that reach the federal appeals courts are heard by panels of three judges. Sometimes the panel consists of three federal appeals court judges and sometimes it is composed of two federal appeals court judges and a district court judge within that circuit.

The Current Federal Appeals Courts

There is one national federal appeals court, called the Federal Circuit, that hears specialized cases, such as patent and civil service personnel cases, that arise throughout the country.

There are also twelve regional courts of appeals based in various parts of the country. Each one hears cases coming through the federal court system from specific geographic regions of the country.

D.C. Circuit (located in the District of Columbia): covers the District of Columbia

First Circuit (Boston): Maine, Massachusetts, Rhode Island, and Puerto Rico

Second Circuit (New York City): Connecticut, New York, and Vermont

Third Circuit (Philadelphia): Delaware, New Jersey, Pennsylvania, and the Virgin Islands

Fourth Circuit (Richmond): Maryland, North Carolina, South Carolina, Virginia, and West Virginia

Fifth Circuit (New Orleans): Louisiana, Mississippi, and Texas

Sixth Circuit (Cincinnati): Kentucky, Michigan, Ohio, and Tennessee

Seventh Circuit (Chicago): Illinois, Indiana, and Wisconsin

Eighth Circuit (St. Louis): Arkansas, Iowa, Minnesota, Missouri, Nebraska, North Dakota, and South Dakota

Ninth Circuit (San Francisco): Alaska, Arizona, California, Hawaii, Idaho, Montana, Nevada, Oregon, Washington, Guam, and the Northern Mariana Islands

Tenth Circuit (Denver): Colorado, Kansas, New Mexico, Oklahoma, Utah, and Wyoming

Eleventh Circuit (Atlanta): Alabama, Florida, and Georgia

When a party loses a case before a three-judge panel, the losing party can then appeal for full-panel, or en banc, review. En banc review means that the full panel of non-retired members of the federal appeals court will sit and hear the case. This number generally ranges from eleven to fifteen. Federal Rules of Appellate Procedure, Rule 35, provides: "An en banc hearing or rehearing is not favored and ordinarily will not be granted unless: (1) en banc consideration is necessary to secure or maintain uniformity of the court's decisions; or (2) the proceeding involves a question of extreme importance." There is no exact science as to when a court might grant en banc review. But Rule 35 offers two possibilities—when the panel decision conflicts with an earlier panel decision or when the case is extremely important.

> ## U.S. Supreme Court's Original Jurisdiction
>
> "The Supreme Court shall have original and exclusive jurisdiction of all controversies between two or more States. (b) The Supreme Court shall have original but not exclusive jurisdiction of: (1) All actions or proceedings to which ambassadors, other public ministers, consuls, or vice consuls of foreign states are parties; (2) All controversies between the United States and a State; (3) All actions or proceedings by a State against the citizens of another State or against aliens."

JURISDICTION

What is **jurisdiction**?

Jurisdiction refers to the legal power and authority of a court to hear and decide a case. When a court is said to have jurisdiction, it means that the court is the proper forum to decide the legal controversy in question. Often, legal professionals use the term jurisdiction to mean the court's area of authority in geographic terms. For instance, the Sixth U.S. Circuit Court of Appeals is a federal appeals court that has jurisdiction over federal cases that arise in Tennessee, Kentucky, Ohio, and Michigan. The Sixth Circuit would not have jurisdiction over a federal case that arose in Illinois. That would be a decision within the control of the Seventh U.S. Circuit Court of Appeals.

What **types of jurisdiction** does the U.S. Supreme Court have?

The U.S. Supreme Court has both original jurisdiction and appellate jurisdiction. Original jurisdiction means that a case originates in that particular court. The U.S. Supreme Court has original jurisdiction in lawsuits between different states, some cases in which a state is a party, and cases involving foreign diplomats.

Appellate jurisdiction means that a higher court has the power to review judgments by a lower court. In other words, the losing party in a case can appeal to the U.S. Supreme Court, asking the high court to take the case. The U.S. Supreme Court has appellate jurisdiction over all decisions of the federal courts of appeals, decisions by the highest state courts (usually called state supreme courts) that involve a federal question (constitutional law), and decisions by special panels of three judges in federal district courts.

What is an **example of the Court's original jurisdiction**?

The U.S. Supreme Court exercised its original jurisdiction to settle a border dispute between the states of Virginia and Tennessee in *Virginia v. Tennessee* (1893).

15

Robert Bork is one of twelve men to be formally nominated as a Supreme Court justice, only to be rejected by the Senate. Bork was rejected in 1987 after President Ronald Reagan nominated him. *Hulton Archive/Getty Images.*

APPOINTMENT, CONFIRMATION, AND QUALIFICATIONS

How are **federal judges appointed to the federal bench**?

Article II, Section 2, provides that the president of the United States shall have the power to nominate "Judges of the Supreme Court." That same part of the Constitution also provides that the president shall have the power to nominate "all other Officers of the United States, whose Appointments are not herein otherwise provided for, and which shall be established by Law." This means that the president has the power to nominate all federal judges.

The Constitution also provides that the U.S. Senate shall provide "Advice and Consent." This means that the president's judicial nominees must be confirmed by the Senate.

What is the **confirmation process**?

After the president nominates a candidate to the U.S. Supreme Court, the U.S. Senate either confirms or denies the nominee. The Senate Judiciary Committee gathers extensive information about the nominee, holds hearings, and eventually votes on whether to move the candidate on for a full Senate vote. The confirmation process can

Prior Judicial Experience of the Current Justices

Chief Justice John Roberts Jr.: U.S. Court of Appeals for the District of Columbia, 2003–5

Justice Samuel Alito Jr.: U.S. Court of Appeals for the Third Circuit, 1990–2005

Justice Stephen Breyer: U.S. Court of Appeals for the First Circuit, 1980–94

Justice Ruth Bader Ginsburg: U.S. Court of Appeals for the D.C. Circuit, 1980–93

Justice Anthony Kennedy: U.S. Court of Appeals for the Ninth Circuit, 1975–87

Justice Antonin Scalia: U.S. Court of Appeals for the D.C. Circuit, 1982–86

Justice David Souter: Superior Court of New Hampshire, 1978–83; Supreme Court of New Hampshire, 1983–90; U.S. Court of Appeals for the First Circuit, 1990

Justice John Paul Stevens: U.S. Court of Appeals for the Seventh Circuit, 1970–75

Justice Clarence Thomas: U.S. Court of Appeals for the D.C. Circuit, 1990–91

---

be quite difficult and lengthy depending on how controversial the candidate is deemed to be by Congress, their constituents, and interested public interest groups. It only takes a majority vote for a candidate to win confirmation. However, twenty-six nominations by presidents have not been successful. The Senate rejected twelve appointments to the Court. Those twelve, and the Senate's rejection vote tally, were:

John Rutledge (1795): rejected 14–10 (as chief justice)
Alexander Wolcott (1811): rejected 24–9
John C. Spencer (1843): rejected 26–21
George W. Woodward (1845): rejected 29–20
Jeremiah Black (1860): rejected 26–25
Ebenezer R. Hoar (1870): rejected 33–24
William B. Hornblower (1893): rejected 30–24
Wheeler Peckham (1894): rejected 41–32
John J. Parker (1930): rejected 41–39
Clement F. Haynesworth Jr. (1969): rejected 55–45
G. Harrold Carswell (1970): rejected 51–45
Robert Bork (1987): rejected 58–42

What **qualifications must a federal judge possess**?

The Constitution provides no criteria or qualifications for federal judges. Technically, a non-lawyer with no legal experience could be appointed to the U.S. Supreme Court.

17

ABA Standing Committee on Federal Judiciary: "To merit a rating of 'Well Qualified,' the nominee must be at the top of the legal profession in his or her legal community; have outstanding legal ability, breadth of experience, and the highest reputation for integrity; and either demonstrate or exhibit the capacity for judicial temperament. The rating of 'Qualified' means that the nominee meets the Committee's very high standards with respect to integrity, professional competence and judicial temperament and that the Committee believes that the nominee will be able to perform satisfactorily all of the duties and responsibilities required by the high office of a federal judge.

"When a nominee is found 'Not Qualified,' the Committee, based on its investigation, has determined that the nominee does not meet the Committee's standards with regard to professional competence, judicial temperament or integrity."

Congress and the Department of Justice carefully review nominees to determine if they have the requisite degree of professional accomplishment and experience necessary for the lofty position. Most of the judges have a record of outstanding professional achievement, key political connections, and a history of public service in some capacity. Many appellate judges have had some prior judicial experience. For example, all nine justices of the U.S. Supreme Court previously had some form of judicial experience before they served on the U.S. Supreme Court.

What is the **role of the American Bar Association** in the Supreme Court nomination/confirmation process?

With more than 400,000 members, the American Bar Association is the largest professional trade association of lawyers. It has played a significant role in the U.S. Supreme Court (and lower federal courts) confirmation process. The ABA participates through its 15-member Standing Committee on Federal Judiciary.

From 1952 to 2001, the presidents of the United States would consult with the Standing Committee regarding proposed nominees. For example, President Gerald Ford sought the committee's views on numerous candidates before finally nominating Justice John Paul Stevens in 1976. Since 1948, the Committee has provided the U.S. Senate Judiciary Committee with evaluations of every federal judicial nominee.

In March 2001, President George W. Bush took a different stance. Alberto Gonzales, counsel to the president, wrote a letter to the ABA, saying that the White House

Size of the Court

1789–1807: 6 justices
1807–37: 7 justices
1837–63: 9 justices

1863–66: 10 justices
1866–69: 7 justices
1869–present: 9 justices

would no longer use the Standing Committee as a pre-screening mechanism before selecting judicial nominees. Gonzales wrote in part:

> The question, in sum, is not whether the ABA's voice should be heard in the judicial selection process. Rather, the question is whether the ABA should play a unique, quasi-official role and thereby have its voice heard before and above all others. We do not think that kind of preferential arrangement is either appropriate or fair.

> It would be particularly inappropriate, in our view, to grant a preferential, quasi-official role to a group, such as the ABA, that takes public positions on divisive political, legal, and social issues that come before the courts. This is not to suggest that the ABA should not adopt policy positions or express its views. But considerations of sound constitutional government suggest that the President not grant a preferential, quasi-official role in the judicial selection process to a politically active group.

However, the Senate Judiciary Committee asked the ABA Standing Committee on the Federal Judiciary to continue reviewing those nominated for federal judgeships. And the White House still used the ABA's recommendation of "highly qualified" for nominee Samuel Alito Jr. in arguing that he should be confirmed. The ABA's ratings of "highly qualified," "qualified," and "not qualified" still carry great weight in the legal profession.

When and how did the Court come to be composed of **nine justices**?

The Court's membership grew to nine members with the passage of the Judiciary Act of 1869. The thinking behind the legislation was to have a Supreme Court justice for every circuit court of appeals. Since there were nine circuit courts, it made sense to have nine justices on the Supreme Court.

The number of justices has fluctuated over the years from between five to ten. Since 1869, the number has remained at nine. However, in 1937, President Franklin D. Roosevelt introduced his "court-packing" plan that would have increased the Court's size to as many as fifteen justices. His proposal was not passed and the number has remained constant.

Salaries of the U.S. Supreme Court Justices

Year	Chief Justice	Associate Justices	Year	Chief Justice	Associate Justices
2006	$212,100	$203,000	1980	$92,400	$88,700
2005	$208,100	$199,100	1979	$84,700	$81,300
2004	$203,000	$194,300	1978	$79,100	$76,000
2003	$198,600	$193,000	1977	$75,000	$72,000
2002	$192.600	$184,400	1976	$68,800	$66,000
2001	$186,300	$178,300	1975	$65,600	$63,000
2000	$181,400	$173,600	1969	$62,500	$60,000
1998	$175,400	$167,900	1964	$40,000	$39,500
1993	$171,500	$164,100	1955	$35,500	$35,000
1992	$166,200	$159,000	1946	$25,500	$25,000
1991	$160,600	$153,600	1926	$20,500	$20,000
1990	$124,000	$118,600	1911	$15,000	$14,500
1987	$108,400	$104,100	1903	$13,000	$12,500
1986	$111,700	$107,200	1873	$10,500	$10,000
1985	$108,400	$104,100	1871	$8,500	$8,000
1984	$104,700	$100,600	1855	$6,500	$6,000
1982	$100,700	$96,700	1819	$5,000	$4,500
1981	$96,800	$93,000	1789	$4,000	$3,500

What is the compensation of the Supreme Court justices and other federal judges?

The chief justice makes $212,100 per year, while the associate justices make $203,000 per year. This has risen dramatically since the time of the first Supreme Court justices when the chief made $4,000 a year and the associate justices $3,500 a year. Federal law, 28 U.S.C. Section 5 provides: "The Chief Justice and each associate justice shall each receive a salary at annual rates determined under section 225 of the Federal Salary Act of 1967 (2 U.S.C. 351–361), as adjusted by section 461 of this title."

Federal appeals court judges make $175,100 a year, while federal district court judges make $162,500 a year.

SUPREME COURT RULES, PRACTICES, AND TRADITIONS

THE BUILDING

Where did the **U.S. Supreme Court first meet**?

The U.S. Supreme Court first met in the Royal Exchange Building on Broad Street in New York City on February 2, 1790. The Court met on the second floor of the building in the afternoons, as the New York state legislature met there during the morning hours. A year later, the Court convened in Philadelphia, the new national capital. The U.S. Supreme Court did not meet in Washington, D.C., until February 2, 1801.

In what **other places did the U.S. Supreme Court meet**?

The Court met in Philadelphia from February 1791 until it moved to Washington, D.C., in 1801. The Court met in two places in Philadelphia—first, in the State House, and then for the rest of the decade in the Philadelphia City Hall building. The Supreme Court shared its physical location with the Mayor's Court. If the Court's schedule conflicted with the local court, the Court would often move upstairs to a room occupied by the Common Council.

In February 1801, the Court moved to Washington, D.C., where it met in an unfinished committee room in the Capitol building until 1809. In 1808 and 1809, the Capitol building underwent major remodeling, which forced the Court to move to several locations, including a nearby tavern in 1809.

In 1810, the Court began meeting in the basement of the Capitol. That changed when the British burned the building to the ground in August 1814 during the War of 1812. The justices met for approximately two years in a rented house near the Capitol building. That house later became known as Bell Tavern. In 1817, the Court returned to the Capitol to a room described as "little better than a dungeon." In 1819, the Court

A view of the Philadelphia State House, the second home of the U.S. Supreme Court, after it moved there from New York City. *Library of Congress.*

returned to its courtroom where it remained until 1860 when it moved upstairs to the Old Supreme Court Chamber. The Court remained in this location until it finally received its own building in 1935.

When did the **U.S. Supreme Court get its own building**?

Surprisingly, the U.S. Supreme Court did not receive its own building until 1935. The Court had met for more than 145 years in other locations before it moved into the Supreme Court Building, located at First and East Capitol Streets NE, in Washington, D.C. In 1929, Chief Justice William Howard Taft (a former president of the United States) managed to convince Congress to fund a building for the U.S. Supreme Court.

What is the **nickname of the Supreme Court Building**?

The nickname of the building is the Marble Palace, because white marble represents the primary material used in the building. According to the Supreme Court's own Web site, $3 million worth of marble was used in its construction. Famous attorney and scholar John Paul Frank published a book about the U.S. Supreme Court in 1958 entitled *Marble Palace: The Supreme Court in American Life.*

What famous case did **John Frank argue before the Court**?

In addition to being a Supreme Court scholar, John Frank was a first-rate attorney. He represented Ernesto Miranda in the famous *Miranda v. Arizona* case decided by the Warren Court in 1966. He also argued for the State of Arizona in the lawyer-advertising case *Bates v. State Bar of Arizona* (1977).

The Supreme Court Building in Washington, D.C., home of the highest court in the land since 1935. *iStockphoto*.

Who was the **architect of the new Supreme Court Building**?

Cass Gilbert, who also designed the Customs House and the U.S. Chamber of Commerce Building in Washington, D.C., was the architect of the new Supreme Court Building. Unfortunately, Gilbert died before the completion of the building, which was then handled by his son, Cass Gilbert Jr.

THE TERM

When does the **U.S. Supreme Court meet**?

The U.S. Supreme Court convenes the first Monday of October for the start of its new term. The Court's term usually ends at the end of June. Federal law, codified at 28 U.S.C. section 2 provides: "The Supreme Court shall hold at the seat of government a term of court commencing on the first Monday in October of each year and may hold such adjourned or special terms as may be necessary."

When did the Court first begin its terms on the **first Monday of October**?

The U.S. Supreme Court first began its term on the first Monday in October 1917. Congress had passed a law effectuating such a change in a 1916 statute. In the mid-nineteenth century, the Court was beginning its term in December and meeting through March. However, the Court's docket exploded in growth, as it was hearing many more cases. To accommodate the expanding docket, Congress allowed the Court in 1866 to set its own

23

starting point for its terms. The Court moved its starting time until October. In 1873, Congress formalized this development by passing a law that moved the Court's term from the first Monday of December to the second Monday in October. It remained there until 1917.

When did the **Court originally begin its new terms**?

The Judiciary Act of 1789 provided that the Court's terms shall begin "the first Monday of February" and "the first Monday of August." The first meeting of the Court occurred on February 2, 1790.

Does the Court ever **meet outside of its traditional term time**?

Yes, the Court sometimes holds special sessions in important cases. For example, the Court held a special session on July 19, 1942, to hear the case of *Ex Parte Quirin* to determine whether alleged German saboteurs were entitled to a federal habeas corpus review of their military commission convictions. More recently, the Court called a special session to hear the case of *McConnell v. Federal Election Commission* in September 2003. The case involved a major First Amendment challenge to the Bipartisan Campaign Reform Act, a federal law restricting "soft money" spending and other funding restrictions in political elections.

PROCESSES

How is a **case brought to the U.S. Supreme Court**?

The U.S. Supreme Court has discretionary jurisdiction over the vast majority of cases, at least since 1925 when Congress passed the Judiciary Act of 1925. This means that most cases originate in the lower courts and the U.S. Supreme Court does not have to review the lower court's decision unless it decides to grant certiorari, or review.

In more than 90 percent of the Court's cases, the party asking the Court to hear the case—the petitioner—petitions the court for review in a document called a petition for writ of certiorari. The opposing party—the respondent—then responds in a document asking the court not to accept the case for review. The Court then decides whether the case is "certworthy," or acceptable for review.

What determines if the U.S. Supreme Court will hear a case?

The Supreme Court has discretionary jurisdiction, which means that in the vast majority of cases the Court has discretion whether or not it will hear a particular case. The Court only hears eighty out of eight thousand cases each term so the chances for review in any particular case are extremely small.

However, the Court has provided "consideration" for cases that it might take in Rule 10 of its Supreme Court Rules.

CourtSpeak: Rule 10 of the Rules of the Supreme Court

Considerations governing review on writ of certiorari: "Review on a writ of certiorari is not a matter of right, but of judicial discretion. A petition for a writ of certiorari will be granted only for compelling reasons. The following, although neither controlling nor fully measuring the Court's discretion, indicate the character of the reasons the Court considers:

(a) a United States court of appeals has entered a decision in conflict with the decision of another United States court of appeals on the same important matter; has decided an important federal question in a way that conflicts with a decision by a state court of last resort; or has so far departed from the accepted and usual course of judicial proceedings, or sanctioned such a departure by a lower court, as to call for an exercise of this Court's supervisory power;

(b) a state court of last resort has decided an important federal question in a way that conflicts with the decision of another state court of last resort or of a United States court of appeals;

(c) a state court or a United States court of appeals has decided an important question of federal law that has not been, but should be, settled by this Court, or has decided an important federal question in a way that conflicts with relevant decisions of this Court.

A petition for a writ of certiorari is rarely granted when the asserted error consists of erroneous factual findings or the misapplication of a properly stated rule of law."

What is the importance of **circuit splits**?

Even experienced Court observers warn there is no way to predict with great accuracy when the U.S. Supreme Court will agree to hear a case. However, one of the best predictors is when a case presents an issue that divides the lower federal appeals courts. This is called a circuit split. Rule 10(a) of the Rules of the Supreme Court identifies as an important consideration when a federal appeals court decision conflicts with another federal appeals court decision.

For example, in 2005 the U.S. Supreme Court heard the case of *Cutter v. Wilkinson* to determine the constitutionality of a federal law called the Religious Land Use and Institutionalized Persons Act (RLUIPA). The high court agreed to hear this case in part because the Sixth U.S. Circuit Court of Appeals had ruled the act violated the Establishment Clause of the First Amendment. Several other circuits, including the Fourth, Seventh, and Ninth, had ruled that RLUIPA did *not* violate the Establishment Clause. The U.S. Supreme Court took the case to resolve the circuit split on the constitutionality of this federal law, which it did by upholding the law.

What are **circuit assignments**?

Sometimes litigants will seek an immediate stay of a lower court ruling before a particular Supreme Court justice. The circuits are divided among the nine justices for them to consider these emergency applications. As of February 1, 2006, the circuit assignments for the current Court are:

Chief Justice John Roberts Jr.	District of Columbia, Federal and Fourth Circuits
Justice John Paul Stevens	Sixth and Seventh Circuits
Justice Antonin Scalia	Fifth Circuit
Justice Anthony Kennedy	Ninth Circuit
Justice David Souter	First and Third Circuits
Justice Clarence Thomas	Eleventh Circuit
Justice Ruth Bader Ginsburg	Second Circuit
Justice Stephen Breyer	Tenth Circuit
Justice Samuel A. Alito Jr.	Eighth Circuit

What is the **discuss list**?

The discuss list refers to a group of cases that the justices, primarily the chief justice, determine are cases worthy of discussion in the Court's conference meetings, which are held on Wednesdays and Fridays. If a case makes the "discuss list," it has a far better chance of being accepted for review.

What is the **rule of four**?

The rule of four refers to a Supreme Court practice that the Court will hear a case if four justices agree the case is certworthy, or worthy of being reviewed. The practice has been in existence since at least 1924.

> ## CourtSpeak: Rule 28—Oral Argument
>
> "Oral Argument should emphasize and clarify the written arguments in the briefs on the merits. Counsel should assume that all Justices have read the briefs before oral argument. Oral argument read from a prepared text is not favored....
>
> Unless the Court directs otherwise, each side is allowed one-half hour for argument. Counsel is not required to use all the allotted time....
>
> Regardless of the number of counsel participating in oral argument, counsel making the opening argument shall present the case fairly and completely and not reserve points of substance for rebuttal."

Where do the justices decide whether to accept a case for review?

The justices decide which cases they will decide in their weekly meetings in conference. These meetings take place in the "Conference Room" in the Supreme Court building. Only the nine justices attend these conference meetings; law clerks and other personnel are not allowed to attend. If someone knocks on the door, the most junior justice must answer the door.

The chief justice normally begins the meetings by bringing up the cases on the "discuss list." The chief justice then speaks about particular cases and whether he or she believes the case should be reviewed. The customary practice is that each of the justices speaks in order of seniority.

When the Court decides to hear a case, what happens next?

The Court informs the Clerk of the Court, who must then schedule oral argument. Under Rule 25, the petitioner then must draft a written document called a brief (a bit of a misnomer because briefs can be up to fifty pages long) within forty-five days of the Court's order that it has accepted the case. The respondent then has thirty days from the date of the petitioner's filing to file its response brief. The petitioner may then file a reply brief as long as it is filed more than one week before oral argument.

What is oral argument?

Oral argument is the process by which attorneys come before the U.S. Supreme Court and present their case. The attorneys face questioning about the case from the individual justices. Rule 28 provides that generally each side is given thirty minutes for argument. The petitioner presents first and then the respondent follows. The petitioner can reserve some time for rebuttal after the respondent's argument. Oral argument is

An artist's sketch shows attorney John Gibbons presenting an oral argument in front of the Supreme Court justices in April 2004. *Dana Verkouteren/AP Images.*

important because it offers the advocates the only time with which to interact with the justices and persuade them to their points of view.

The justices vary in how much they question the attorney-advocates. Justice Antonin Scalia is known for being quite vocal at oral argument, firing many questions at the attorneys. Justice Clarence Thomas, on the other hand, is normally quite reticent at oral argument. In most cases, he does not ask a single question.

What **types of attorneys argue cases** before the U.S. Supreme Court?

Most lawyers never argue a case before the U.S. Supreme Court. Some attorneys practice regularly before the U.S. Supreme Court as members of the Supreme Court Bar. The great Daniel Webster, a U.S. congressman and attorney from Massachusetts who lived from 1782 to 1852, argued nearly 250 cases before the U.S. Supreme Court. He was involved in many landmark decisions, such as *Dartmouth College v. Woodward* (1819), *Gibbons v. Ogden* (1824), and *Charles River Bridge v. Warren Bridge* (1837). John William Davis, who lived from 1873 to 1955, argued 140 cases before the U.S. Supreme Court, including *Youngstown Sheet and Tube Co. v. Sawyer* (1952) and *Brown v. Board of Education* (1954).

In the present-day, Tom Goldstein of Akin Gump Strauss Hauer & Feld LLP has argued sixteen cases before the U.S. Supreme Court by the time he was in his early 30s. His practice consists nearly entirely of U.S. Supreme Court cases. Other lawyers may argue one case before the U.S. Supreme Court, as they represented the litigant from the beginning of the case.

Those who serve as solicitor general, a position appointed by the president to argue for the United States, naturally argue many more cases than even those members of the Supreme Court Bar who regularly argue cases.

When does the **Court hear oral arguments**?

The Court generally hears oral arguments two weeks of every month from October through April. During the weeks of oral argument, the Court hears cases from 10:00 AM to 12:00 PM E.S.T. on Monday, Tuesday, and Wednesday.

One of America's greatest attorneys, Daniel Webster, argued nearly 250 cases before the U.S. Supreme Court. *Brady-Handy Photograph Collection/Library of Congress.*

After oral argument, when does the Court decide the case?

The Court meets in conference to discuss their initial votes in the case. The Court discusses the cases argued on Monday in its Wednesday afternoon conference meeting. For the cases argued on Tuesday and Wednesday, the Court discusses them in its Friday conference meeting.

The chief justice opens the discussions, outlining the applicable law and facts and his or her views of the case. This practice extends to all the justices in order of seniority. The justices also discuss how they plan to decide the case. The chief justice announces the vote. If the chief justice is in the majority, he or she assigns who will write the majority opinion for the Court. If the chief justice is in the minority, the most senior justice in the majority makes the opinion assignments.

There is no specific timetable for when the Court will issue its opinions, though in nearly all cases, the Court will issue a decision by the end of June. In a few cases, however, the Court will not issue an opinion and ask for re-argument. For example, the Roberts Court ordered re-argument in 2006 in the case of *Garcetti v. Ceballos,* a highly watched case involving the free-speech rights of public employees.

If the majority opinion becomes the law of the land, **are concurring and dissenting opinions important**?

Yes, concurring and even dissenting opinions can be important. Sometimes, the law will develop such that a concurring opinion will actually become the guidepost for future deci-

Types of Opinions

Unanimous opinion: An opinion in which all justices vote with the majority.

Majority opinion: This opinion, which must have five votes, is the ruling of the Court. It stands as precedent for future cases.

Plurality opinion: The main opinion of the Court but one that fails to command a majority of the justices. For instance, a case may have four justices agreeing with one opinion, two justices who file concurring opinions but not joining the other four, and three justices in dissent. In this 4–2–3 split, there is no majority opinion.

Concurring opinion: An opinion that agrees with the result but not the reasoning of the majority or main opinion of the Court. A justice who writes a concurring opinion may want to emphasize particular points of law or simply indicate that the main opinion reached the right result by taking the wrong path.

Dissenting opinion: An opinion that disagrees with the result of the majority opinion.

Per curiam opinion: An opinion rendered by the Court, or a majority of the Court, collectively instead of a single justice.

sions in the area. A classic example was Justice John Marshall Harlan's concurring opinion in the Fourth Amendment case *Katz v. United States* (1967). While Justice Potter Stewart wrote the Court's majority opinion, Harlan's concurring opinion and "reasonable expectation of privacy" test has become the opinion relied on by the majority of lower courts.

Similarly, dissenting opinions can be important, particularly if the U.S. Supreme Court overrules itself in a particular area of the law. A classic example of a dissenting opinion that became the law of the land was Justice Hugo Black's dissenting opinion in the Sixth Amendment right to counsel case of *Betts v. Brady* (1942). The majority in *Betts* ruled that state courts did not have to provide an attorney to all indigent defendants charged with felonies in non-death penalty cases. However, the Court overruled that decision twenty-one years later in *Gideon v. Wainwright* (1963) and, in a remarkable irony, Justice Black had the honor of writing the unanimous opinion for the Court, taking the same position that he took in dissent in *Betts*.

Has the oral argument rule always provided for **thirty minutes to each side**?

No, the oral argument has not always been thirty minutes. In fact, oral arguments used to take several days in some cases. Many of the justices chafed under the process

> ## CourtSpeak: Rule 37, Rules of the Supreme Court
>
> "An amicus curiae brief that brings to the attention of the Court relevant matter not already brought to its attention by the parties may be of considerable help to the Court. An amicus curiae brief that does not serve this purpose burdens the Court, and its filing is not favored."

of hearing lawyers give speeches hour upon hour. In 1849, the Court adopted Rule 53, which set the time limit for each attorney at two hours each. If attorneys wished to argue longer than two hours, they had to petition for special permission. In 1925, the Court limited the argument time to one hour on each side. The Court said this change was "due to the crowded calendar of the Court." In 1970, the Court changed its rules again, limiting each side to the present-day requirement of thirty minutes each.

What are **amicus briefs**?

Amicus, or friend of the court, briefs are briefs filed by interested non-parties who wish to emphasize particular aspects of a case and stress its importance to the Court. Amicus briefs are a regular staple of U.S. Supreme Court practice, particularly in important, high-profile decisions. For example, approximately ninety amicus briefs were filed before the Court in the affirmative action in education cases of *Grutter v. Bollinger* and *Gratz v. Bollinger.*

Sometimes, the justices seem to consider certain amicus briefs as very significant and persuasive. For example, Chief Justice William Rehnquist cited the amicus brief of the Association of American Editorial Cartoonists written by attorney Rosalyn Mazer in his unanimous opinion for the Court in the celebrated First Amendment decision in *Hustler Magazine v. Falwell* (1988).

PERSONNEL

Who is the **reporter** of the Supreme Court?

The reporter of decisions is the individual responsible for compiling the U.S. Supreme Court decisions into the *United States Reports,* the official compilation of U.S. Supreme Court opinions. There have been sixteen reporters in the history of the Court. They include:

Alexander Dallas	1790–1800
William Cranch	1801–15
Henry Wheaton	1816–27

31

Richard Peters	1828–42
Benjamin Howard	1843–60
Jeremiah Black	1861–62
John Wallace	1863–74
William Otto	1875–83
John Davis	1883–1902
Charles Butler	1902–16
Ernest Knaebel	1916–44
Walter Wyatt	1946–63
Henry Putzel Jr.	1964–79
Henry Curtis Lind	1979–89
Frank D. Wagner	1989–present

Who is the **Clerk of the Court**?

The Clerk of the Court is the person who oversees the administration of the Court's docket and caseload. The position of clerk is established by federal law, 28 U.S.C. section 671, which provides in part: "The Supreme Court may appoint and fix the compensation of a clerk and one or more deputy clerks. The clerk shall be subject to removal by the Court. Deputy clerks shall be subject to removal by the clerk with the approval of the Court or the Chief Justice of the United States."

There have been nineteen Clerks of the U.S. Supreme Court in its history, including:

John Tucker	1790–91
Samuel Bayard	1791–1800
Elias B. Caldwell	1800–25
William Griffith	1826–27
William T. Carroll	1827–63
D. W. Middleton	1863–80
James H. McKenney	1880–1913
James Maher	1913–21
William R. Stansbury	1921–27
Charles Elmore Copley	1927–52
Harold B. Willey	1952–56
John T. Fey	1956–58
James Browning	1958–61
John F. Davis	1961–70
E. Robert Seaver	1970–72
Michael Rodak	1972–81
Alexander Stevas	1981–85
Joseph F. Spaniol Jr.	1985–91
William K. Suter	1991–present

The nineteenth Clerk of the Court, William Suter, is seen in this artist's sketch reading a document as John Roberts (foreground) is about to be sworn in as chief justice on October 3, 2005. The sitting justices are on the left and Attorney General Alberto Gonzales, President George W. Bush, and Roberts's family are seated on the far right. *Dana Verkouteren/AP Images.*

Who are **law clerks**?

Each U.S. Supreme Court hires several law clerks to assist in the screening of cases in the certiorari pool, writing of memoranda on legal issues, drafting of opinions, and other legal matters. Most of the justices hire four law clerks. Many of the law clerks are recent graduates of prestigious law schools such as Harvard or Yale. Many of the law clerks serve for a U.S. Supreme Court justice after having clerked for a federal circuit court of appeals judge. Most clerks work for a justice for one year, though some will work on two-year terms.

What Supreme Court justice **started the practice of hiring a law clerk**?

Justice Horace Gray instituted the practice of law clerks in 1882 when he joined the Court. When he was a member of the Supreme Judicial Court of Massachusetts, Gray had started the practice there as well, hiring future Supreme Court justice Louis Brandeis. Gray paid for the clerk out of his own pocket. The practice became formalized when Congress passed a 1922 law that allowed each justice to hire one law clerk for a salary of $3,600.

33

What **functions do law clerks serve**?

Law clerks often serve as an initial screener of the thousands of cases that are appealed to the U.S. Supreme Court. They will often write memos explaining to the justices which cases are "certworthy," or worthy of their attention. Nearly all of the justices (except Justice John Paul Stevens) pool their clerks together in a "cert pool" to examine the thousands of petitions that come to the Court each year. Justice Lewis Powell proposed the idea of the cert pool in 1972 to save time and increase efficiency. Critics charge that it gives too much power to the law clerks. Justice Stevens does not participate and his law clerks review all petitions that are filed before the Court. The two newest members of the Supreme Court, Chief Justice John G. Roberts and Justice Samuel Alito are in the cert pool, despite Roberts's criticism of the cert pool phenomenon in 1997. Some experts have predicted that Chief Justice Roberts may reform the cert pool practice.

The law clerks also write research memoranda and draft opinions for the justices. The responsibility of law clerks obviously depends upon each particular justice.

Who are some of the more **famous law clerks**?

There have been many Supreme Court law clerks who have achieved great prominence in the legal profession. Here are just a few of the many:

Kenneth Starr: Former federal appeals court and independent counsel who investigated President Bill Clinton (leading to his impeachment); clerked for Chief Justice Warren Burger.

Richard Posner: Longtime judge on the Seventh U.S. Circuit Court of Appeals and author of more than forty books; clerked for Justice William Brennan.

Robert O'Neil: Former president of the University of Virginia and the founder of the Thomas Jefferson Center for the Protection of Free Expression; clerked for Justice William Brennan.

Kenneth Starr, center, began his law career as the law clerk for Supreme Court justice Warren Burger; Starr became well known as the independent counsel who investigated President Bill Clinton prior to his impeachment. *Luke Frazza/AFP/Getty Images.*

Alan Dershowitz: Harvard Law professor and well-known author/legal commentator; clerked for Justice Arthur Goldberg.

Laura Ingraham: Popular syndicated radio host, author, and political analyst; clerked for Justice Clarence Thomas.

What is the Supreme Court **Fellows Program**?

In 1973, Chief Justice Warren Burger established the Supreme Court Fellows Program to provide assistance to the Court, the Federal Judicial Center, the Administrative Office of the United States Courts, and the U.S. Sentencing Commission. The fellows are similar to law clerks—they help with workload and write reports and memoranda. Since the 2000–2001 term, the chief justice has selected four individuals to serve as Supreme Court Fellows. One goes with the Supreme Court, one with the Federal Judicial Center, one with the Administrative Office of the Courts, and one with the Sentencing Commission.

Who is the **marshal** of the U.S. Supreme Court?

The marshal of the U.S. Supreme Court is the person who oversees the security, maintenance, and operation of the Supreme Court Building. Federal law, 28 U.S.C. section 672, has provided for this position since 1867. There have been ten head marshals of the Supreme Court, including:

The Inaugural Supreme Court Fellows

The inaugural Supreme Court Fellows class of 1973–74 consisted of three individuals: Gordon Gee, who is now president of Ohio State University in Columbus; Russell Wheeler, who now serves as deputy director of the Federal Judicial Center in Washington, D.C.; and Howard R. Whitcomb, who is an emeritus professor of political science at Lehigh University in Pennsylvania.

Richard C. Parsons	1867–72
John Nicolay	1872–87
John M. Wright	1888–1915
Frank Key Green	1915–38
Thomas E. Waggaman	1938–52
T. Perry Lippitt	1952–72
Frank M. Hepler	1972–76
Alfred M. Wong	1976–94
Dale E. Bosley	1994–2001
Pamela Talkin	2001–present

What is the **Office of Legal Counsel**?

The Office of Legal Counsel is an administrative unit under the control of the chief justice of the U.S. Supreme Court. It consists of two attorneys who help the Court in cases involving petitions for extraordinary writs and cases in which the Court's original jurisdiction is invoked.

What was the **original oath** that federal judges had to take?

Section 8 of the Judiciary Act of 1789 provides that Supreme Court and district judges had to take the following oath:

> I, [justice's name], do solemnly swear or affirm, that I will administer justice without respect to persons, and do equal right to the poor and to the rich, and that I will faithfully and impartially discharge and perform all the duties incumbent on me as [type of judge] according to the best of my abilities and understanding, agreeable to the Constitution and laws of the United States. So help me God.

The oath was amended in 1990 by replacing "according to the best of my abilities and understanding, agreeable to the Constitution" with the words "under the Constitution."

STATE COURTS

What types of **cases do state courts handle**?

State courts handle virtually every kind of case imaginable. In fact, most cases in the country are brought in one type of state court or another. Divorces, child custody, personal injury, criminal, employment, contract disputes, will contests, and juvenile cases are just some of the types of cases regularly filed in state courts.

What is the **structure of state court systems**?

The structure of state court systems varies widely from state to state. The lowest courts are courts of limited jurisdiction—sometimes called inferior courts—that hear only particular types of cases. These are called small claims, general session, municipal, justice-of-the-peace, juvenile, and magistrate courts. For example, a citizen who contests a traffic ticket will likely appear in a general sessions court.

The courts of general jurisdiction are often organized along the same three-tiered pattern found in the federal system of (1) trial courts, (2) intermediate appellate courts, and (3) final appellate courts. For example, Tennessee trial courts consist of circuit courts, chancery courts, probate courts, and criminal courts. The intermediate appellate courts are the Tennessee Court of Appeals and the Tennessee Court of Criminal Appeals, while the final appellate court is the Tennessee Supreme Court.

Some state court systems have only two level of courts. For example, South Dakota has circuit courts and a supreme court. The nomenclature of the courts can also differ quite greatly. In most states, the final appellate court is called the Supreme Court, but in Maryland and New York the highest court is called the Court of Appeals.

The National Center for State Courts provides an excellent overview of the structure of every state's court system at http://www.ncsconline.org/D_Research/Ct_Struct/.

What determines whether a **case is filed in federal or state court**?

Often times, the question of whether a case is filed in federal or state court depends on which court has jurisdiction, or the ability to hear a case. Because state courts have broad jurisdiction, the most common question is whether the federal court has jurisdiction. An exception is bankruptcy cases, which are heard in federal court. Sometimes, cases—such as employment discrimination cases—can be filed in either state or federal court. The question then becomes one of legal strategy.

State High Courts

State	Highest State Court	# of Justices
Alabama	Alabama Supreme Court	9
Alaska	Alaska Supreme Court	5

State High Courts (cntd.)

State	Highest State Court	# of Justices
Arizona	Arizona Supreme Court	5
Arkansas	Arkansas Supreme Court	7
Colorado	Colorado Supreme Court	7
Connecticut	Connecticut Supreme Court	7
Delaware	Delaware Supreme Court	5
District of Columbia	D.C. Court of Appeals	9
Florida	Florida Supreme Court	7
Georgia	Georgia Supreme Court	7
Hawaii	Hawaii Supreme Court	5
Idaho	Idaho Supreme Court	5
Illinois	Illinois Supreme Court	7
Indiana	Indiana Supreme Court	5
Iowa	Iowa Supreme Court	7
Kansas	Kansas Supreme Court	7
Kentucky	Kentucky Supreme Court	7
Louisiana	Louisiana Supreme Court	7
Maine	Maine Supreme Judicial Court	7
Maryland	Maryland Court of Appeals	7
Massachusetts	Massachusetts Supreme Judicial Court	7
Michigan	Michigan Supreme Court	7
Minnesota	Minnesota Supreme Court	7
Mississippi	Mississippi Supreme Court	9
Missouri	Missouri Supreme Court	7
Montana	Montana Supreme Court	7
Nebraska	Nebraska Supreme Court	7
Nevada	Nevada Supreme Court	7
New Hampshire	New Hampshire Supreme Court	5
New Jersey	New Jersey Supreme Court	7
New Mexico	New Mexico Supreme Court	5
New York	New York Court of Appeals	7
North Carolina	North Carolina Supreme Court	7
North Dakota	North Dakota Supreme Court	5
Ohio	Ohio Supreme Court	7
Oklahoma	Oklahoma Supreme Court (civil cases)	9
	Oklahoma Court of Criminal Appeals (criminal cases)	5
Oregon	Oregon Supreme Court	7
Pennsylvania	Pennsylvania Supreme Court	7
Rhode Island	Rhode Island Supreme Court	5
South Carolina	South Carolina Supreme Court	5
South Dakota	South Dakota Supreme Court	5

State High Courts (cntd.)

State	Highest State Court	# of Justices
Tennessee	Tennessee Supreme Court	5
Texas	Texas Supreme Court (civil cases)	9
	Texas Court of Criminal Appeals (criminal cases)	9
Utah	Utah Supreme Court	5
Vermont	Vermont Supreme Court	5
Virginia	Virginia Supreme Court	7
Washington	Washington Supreme Court	9
West Virginia	West Virginia Supreme Court	5
Wisconsin	Wisconsin Supreme Court	7
Wyoming	Wyoming Supreme Court	5

SUPREME COURT TRIVIA

SUPREME COURT
FIRSTS AND BEGINNINGS

Who were the **first six justices** on the U.S. Supreme Court?

The first six justices nominated to the U.S. Supreme Court were John Jay (as chief justice), John Rutledge, William Cushing, James Wilson, John Blair, and Robert H. Harrison. The Senate confirmed all the nominees, but Harrison, a judge from Maryland, declined the nomination because of poor health. In his place, President George Washington nominated James Iredell of North Carolina.

Which Supreme Court justices attended the **Constitutional Convention of 1787** in Philadelphia?

Five Supreme Court justices attended the Constitutional Convention of 1787, during which the U.S. Constitution was created. These included John Rutledge from South Carolina, Oliver Ellsworth from Connecticut, William Paterson from New Jersey, James Wilson from Pennsylvania, and John Blair from Virginia. They were among the fifty-five delegates that attended the famous Philadelphia Convention that created the U.S. Constitution. Justice Gabriel Duvall was chosen to be one of Maryland's four delegates to the Convention but he, along with the other delegates from Maryland, never attended.

When did the **Supreme Court initially meet**?

The U.S. Supreme Court initially met in February 1790. The Judiciary Act of 1789 provided that the Court would hold two sessions annually, beginning the first Mondays of February and August.

Levi Woodbury was the first U.S. Supreme Court justice to attend law school. *Daguerreotype Collection/Library of Congress.*

Who was the **first law school student** to go on to become a U.S. Supreme Court justice?

Levi Woodbury, who studied law at Tapping Reeve Law School in 1810 after earning his undergraduate degree from Dartmouth College, went on to become a U.S. Supreme Court justice. He left the law school to serve an apprenticeship. Woodbury served on the Court from 1846 to 1851.

Which justice hired the **first female law clerk**?

Justice William O. Douglas hired Lucille Loman in 1944. Although she became the Court's first female law clerk, she also served as Douglas's personal secretary.

Which justice hired the **first African American law clerk**?

Justice Felix Frankfurter hired William T. Coleman Jr. in 1948. Coleman was the first African American to serve on the *Harvard Law Review*'s board of editors.

CAREERS AWAY FROM THE COURT

How many Supreme Court justices were **former state governors**?

Nine justices were former state governors. These included John Jay, New York governor from 1795 to 1801 after he served on the U.S. Supreme Court; John Rutledge, South Carolina governor from 1779 to 1782; Thomas Johnson, Maryland governor (its first) from 1777 to 1779; William Paterson, New Jersey governor from 1790 to 1793; Levi Woodbury, New Hampshire governor from 1823 to 1824; Salmon P. Chase, Ohio governor from 1856 to 1860; Frank Murphy, Michigan governor from 1937 to 1939; James Francis Byrnes, South Carolina governor from 1951 to 1955, after his short stay on the U.S. Supreme Court (1941–42); and Chief Justice Earl Warren, California governor from 1943 to 1953.

Which justices were **former veterans**?

Six justices served in the Revolutionary War: Chief Justice John Marshall fought in battles such as Great Bridge and Germantown; Alfred Moore served in the North Carolina Regiment; Thomas Johnson briefly served in the Maryland state militia (as first brigadier-general); Henry Livingston served as a commissioned captain in the Continental Army; Bushrod Washington, the nephew of George Washington, served in the Continental Army; and Thomas Todd enlisted when he was only 14 years old.

Two justices served in the War of 1812: James Moore Wayne served in a volunteer Georgia militia unit and John Catron served under General Andrew Jackson.

Five justices served in the Civil War: Lucius Quintus Cincinnatus Lamar served in the Confederate Army as a colonel for the Eighteenth Mississippi Regiment; Edward Douglass White and Horace Lurton served in the Confederate Army; Oliver Wendell Holmes served in the Union Army and was wounded three times during combat; and William Burnham Woods fought for the Union in Ohio, rising to the rank of brevet major general.

Four justices served in World War I: Earl Warren and Frank Murphy served in the Army; Tom C. Clark served in the National Guard; and Harold Burton served in the Army, receiving a Purple Heart.

Five justices served in World War II: Potter Stewart and Byron White served in the Navy; William Brennan served in the Army; William Rehnquist served in the Air Force; and John Paul Stevens served in the Navy, earning a Bronze Star.

Which U.S. Supreme Court justices served as **federal appeals court judges on the U.S. Court of Appeals for the District of Columbia Circuit**?

Four of the current members of the U.S. Supreme Court have served on the D.C. Circuit, which is why some pundits have referred to it as the second most important federal court in the American legal system. Chief Justice John G. Roberts served on the D.C. Circuit from 2003 to 2005; Justice Antonin Scalia was on the D.C. Circuit from 1982 to 1986; Clarence Thomas served from 1990 to 1991; and Ruth Bader Ginsburg served from 1980 to 1993.

Which former justices were **newspaper editors or reporters**?

John McLean, who served from 1830 to 1862, published the *Western Star* newspaper in Lebanon, Ohio. Henry Baldwin, who served from 1830 to 1844, published with his law partners a newspaper called *The Tree of Liberty*. Stanley Matthews, who served from 1881 to 1889, edited the weekly *Tennessee Democrat* and later the *Cincinnati Morning Herald*. Melville Fuller, who served as chief justice from 1888 to 1910, was an editor of *The Age,* a daily newspaper. John Clarke, who served from 1916 to 1922, was publisher of *The Vindicator* in Youngstown, Ohio. William Howard Taft, who served as chief jus-

U.S. Supreme Court justice Samuel Freeman Miller, who served from 1862 to 1890, was also a practicing medical doctor. He received his medical degree from Transylvania University. *Brady-Handy Photograph Collection/Library of Congress.*

tice from 1921 to 1930, was a reporter for the *Cincinnati Commercial* during his law school days. James Byrnes, who served from 1941 to 1942, was the owner and editor of the *Aiken Journal and Review* in Aiken, South Carolina.

Which U.S. Supreme Court justices formerly served as **U.S. attorney general**?

Nine justices had formerly served as U.S. attorney general before becoming a member of the U.S. Supreme Court. These justices were Roger B. Taney, Nathan Clifford, Joseph McKenna, William Moody, James C. McReynolds, Harlan Fiske Stone, Frank Murphy, Robert Jackson, and Tom C. Clark.

Which U.S. Supreme Court justices formerly served as **U.S. solicitor general**?

Five Supreme Court justices formerly served as solicitor generals at some point in their careers before ascending to the U.S. Supreme Court. They include William Howard Taft (1890–92), Charles Evans Hughes (1929–30), Stanley Reed (1935–38), Robert H. Jackson (1938–40), and Thurgood Marshall (1965–67).

What former justice was a **practicing medical doctor**?

Samuel Freeman Miller, who served on the Court from 1862 to 1890, graduated from Transylvania University in 1838 with a degree in medicine. He practiced medicine for 12 years in Knox County, Kentucky, before going into the practice of law. Justice Noah Haynes Swayne also studied medicine in his youth before turning to the study of law. Justice Hugo Black attended Birmingham Medical School for one year.

Which **chief justices were associate justices** before their elevation to the top post?

There have been five associate justices who later ascended to the post of chief justice.
They are John Rutledge, Edward White, Charles Evans Hughes, Harlan Fiske Stone,

and William Rehnquist. Rutledge served as associate justice from February 15, 1790 (the first date the Court ever met), to March 5, 1791, when he resigned to serve as chief judge of the South Carolina Court of Common Pleas. President George Washington then appointed Rutledge to the position of chief justice in August 1795. Washington made a recess appointment, meaning an appointment is made when the Senate is not in session. The nominee can take his or her seat but must be confirmed to remain on the bench. Rutledge served for only a few months as chief justice because the Senate rejected his nomination 15–10 in December 1795. White served as an associate justice from 1894 to 1910. President William Howard Taft nominated him for chief justice in 1910 and he served in that capacity until his death in 1921. Hughes served as an associate justice from 1910 to 1916. He resigned to run for president but lost to Woodrow Wilson. President Herbert Hoover then nominated Hughes for chief justice, a position he served from 1930 to 1941. Stone served as associate justice from 1925 until 1941. Then, President Franklin D. Roosevelt elevated Stone to chief justice in 1941, where he served until his death in 1946. Rehnquist served as an associate justice from 1972 to 1986, when President Ronald Reagan nominated him to serve as the nation's sixteenth chief justice, a post in which he remained until his death in 2005.

Which U.S. Supreme Court justices were former **Supreme Court clerks**?

Byron White clerked for Chief Justice Fred Vinson in 1946–47. William Rehnquist clerked for Justice Robert Jackson in 1951–52. John Paul Stevens clerked for Justice Wiley Rutledge in 1947–48. Stephen Breyer clerked for Justice Arthur Goldberg in 1964–65. John Roberts clerked for Rehnquist in 1980–81.

Which two U.S. Supreme Court justices **never held a position of public office or official governmental position** until their Supreme Court nominations?

Justice Joseph Bradley and his replacement on the Supreme Court, Justice George Shiras Jr., never held positions of public office until they were nominated to the U.S. Supreme Court—Bradley in 1870 and Shiras in 1892. Bradley ran for Congress in 1862 but lost. In 1881, Shiras declined the nomination of the Pennsylvania state legislature to be senator. He had a very successful private law practice in Pittsburgh for more than thirty years.

Who is the only justice to have **served both as a federal district court and a federal appeals court judge** before his elevation to the U.S. Supreme Court?

Charles Evans Whittaker served as a federal district court judge in Missouri from 1954 to 1956 and as a federal appeals court judge (Eighth Circuit) from 1956 to 1957.

FAMILY AFFAIRS

Which justice had the **most marriages**?

Justice William O. Douglas, who served on the Court for more than thirty-six years, was married four times. His first three marriages—to Mildred Riddle, Mercedes Hester Davison, and Joan Martin—ended in divorce. He then married Cathleen Ann Heffernan in 1966; they were married until his death in 1980.

Which Supreme Court justice had the **most siblings**?

John Marshall, the Court's fourth chief justice, was the oldest of fifteen children of Thomas and Mary Randolph Marshall. Marshall and his wife Polly continued the trend of a large family, as they had ten children.

Which Supreme Court justice **married a sixteen-year-old**?

Oliver Ellsworth, the nation's third chief justice of the U.S. Supreme Court and the chief architect of the Judiciary Act of 1789, married sixteen-year-old Abigail Wolcott in 1771.

Which two justices **married cousins**?

Chief Justice Morrison Waite married his second cousin Amelia C. Warner, while Justice Henry Baldwin married his third cousin Marianna Norton.

Which justice **married a childhood friend**?

Harlan Fiske Stone married a childhood playmate, Agnes Harvey, in 1899 after a nine-year engagement.

Which justice was **tutored by Horatio Alger**?

As a child, Justice Benjamin Cardozo was tutored by author Horatio Alger.

Which justice later became a brother-in-law to the **author of the "Star-Spangled Banner"**?

Chief Justice Roger Taney was the brother-in-law to another Maryland-based attorney, Francis Scott Key, who became famous for writing the words to the "Star-Spangled Banner."

Which justice was a **descendant of John Cotton,** the great sixteenth-century Puritan theologian and author?

William Cushing, one of the Court's first six justices, was related to John Cotton, who was famous for writing *The Way of the Churches of Christ in New England* (1645), among other books.

Which justice married a **sister of first lady Dolley Madison**?

Thomas Todd married Lucy Payne, sister of first lady Dolley Madison. They were married on President James Madison's plantation.

Which justice had a **twin**?

Justice Benjamin Cardozo had a twin sister named Emily.

Which U.S. Supreme Court justices were **lifelong bachelors**?

"Star-Spangled Banner" author Francis Scott Key (above) was the brother-in-law of Chief Justice Roger Taney. *Hulton Archive/Getty Images.*

There were five justices who never married. They include: William Henry Moody (served on the Court, 1906–10); James McReynolds (1914–41); John Hessin Clarke (1916–22); Benjamin Cardozo (1932–38); and Frank Murphy (1940–49). As of 2007, Supreme Court Justice David Souter, who ascended to the bench in 1990, also has never married.

Which justice **had the most children**?

Benjamin Robert Curtis had twelve children, five with his first wife Eliza, three with second wife Nancy, and four with third wife Malleville. Robert Trimble, who served from 1826 to 1828, had eleven children with his wife Nancy. John Marshall had ten children.

Which justice left nearly his **entire estate to charities**?

Justice James C. McReynolds, known for his rude behavior toward Jewish justice Louis Brandeis and to women in general, surprised many by leaving nearly his entire estate

47

Felix Frankfurter, shown here in his office in November 1957, was one of six U.S. Supreme Court justices who was not born in the United States. He was born in Vienna, Austria. *AP Images*.

to charities, including a children's hospital. He had supported thirty-three children injured by a Nazi attack in World War II.

BIRTH, DEATH, AND TENURE

Which U.S. Supreme Court justices were **not born in the United States**?

Six justices were not born in the United States. James Wilson, who served on the Court from 1789 to 1798, was born in Caskardy, Scotland, in 1742. James Iredell, who served from 1790 to 1799, was born in Lewes, England. William Paterson, who served from 1793 to 1806, was born in County Antrim, Ireland. David Brewer, who served from 1889 to 1910, was born in Asia Minor (present-day Turkey). George Sutherland, who served from 1922 to 1938, was born in Buckingshire, England. Felix Frankfurter, who served from 1939 to 1962, was born in Vienna, Austria.

In what **four states have the most justices been born**?

Twelve justices have been born in New York: John Jay, Henry Brockhurst Livingston, Smith Thompson, Samuel Nelson, Joseph Bradley, Ward Hunt, Samuel Blatchford, Rufus Peckham, Charles Evans Hughes, Benjamin Cardozo, Ruth Bader Ginsburg, and John Roberts. Ten justices have been born in Virginia: John Blair, Bushrod Washington, John Marshall, Thomas Todd, Robert Trimble, Philip Barbour, John McKinley, Peter Daniel, Noah Swayne, and Lewis Powell. Nine justices have been born in Massachusetts: William Cushing, Joseph Story, Benjamin Curtis, Horace Gray, Henry Billings Brown, Oliver Wendell Holmes, William Henry Moody, Harold Burton, and David Souter. Kentucky, the Bluegrass State, was home to eight justices. They are John Marshall Harlan, Samuel Miller, Horace Lurton, James McReynolds, Louis Brandeis, Stanley Reed, Wiley Rutledge, and Fred Vinson.

Which Supreme Court justices **shared the same birthday**?

Lucius Quintus Cincinnatus Lamar (who served from 1888 to 1893), Warren Burger (1969–86), and David Souter (1990–) all were born on September 17. Owen Roberts (1930–45) and James Byrnes (1941–42) were both born on May 2. Roger Brooke Taney (1836–64) and Pierce Butler (1922–39) were both born on March 17. David Davis (1862–77) and Samuel Blatchford (1882–93) were both born on March 9. Thomas Todd (1807–1826) and Potter Stewart (1958–91) were both born on January 23.

Which two justices **died on the same day**?

Retired chief justice William Howard Taft and Justice Edward Sanford each died on March 8, 1930. Taft died of heart failure while Sanford died unexpectedly of uremic poisoning.

Which justices **lived to at least the age of 90**?

The U.S. Supreme Court's eight nanogenarians were Stanley Reed (95), Oliver Wendell Holmes (93), George Shiras Jr. (92), James F. Byrnes (92), Gabriel Duvall (91), William Brennan (91), Lewis Powell (90), and Harry Blackmun (90). Holmes is the only one of the eight who continued to serve on the Court while he was in his 90s.

Which justice **did not live to see his fiftieth birthday**?

Justice James Iredell, who served from 1790 to 1799, died at the age of 48. He is the only justice to die before the age of 50.

How many justices have **served at least thirty years on the Court**?

Twelve members of the U.S. Supreme Court have served at least thirty years on the U.S. Supreme Court. They are: William O. Douglas (36 years), Stephen J. Field (34), John Marshall (34), Joseph Story (34), John Marshall Harlan (34), Hugo Black (34), William Brennan (33), William Rehnquist (33), John McLean (32), James Wayne (32), William Johnson (30), and current (as of 2007) justice John Paul Stevens (31).

Which U.S. Supreme Court justices **served the shortest and longest terms** on the bench respectively?

Thomas Johnson served the shortest time on the U.S. Supreme Court, from November 1791 to February 1793. William O. Douglas served the longest time on the Court—36 years and seven months—from April 1939 to November 1975.

Who were the **youngest justices** upon nomination to the U.S. Supreme Court?

Joseph Story and William Johnson were both appointed to the U.S. Supreme Court at age 32, though Story was younger by a few months.

Who was the **youngest chief justice**?

John Jay, the nation's first chief justice, was only 44 years old upon his appointment by President George Washington in 1789.

Who was the **oldest justice** appointed to the Court?

The oldest person appointed as a new justice to the Court was Horace Lurton, who was 65 when President William Howard Taft nominated him in 1909. The oldest person to become chief justice was 68-year-old Harlan Fiske Stone. He had spent the previous sixteen years as an associate justice before being nominated by President Franklin D. Roosevelt in 1941.

HAIL TO THE CHIEF

Which **presidents appointed the most justices** to the U.S. Supreme Court?

George Washington elevated eleven men to the U.S. Supreme Court. Franklin Delano Roosevelt appointed nine. Of course, Washington, as the first president, had to nominate a group of men (six) to populate the very first Supreme Court. And Roosevelt, elected to four terms, had more opportunity—twelve years—to nominate justices.

Which **presidents made no Supreme Court appointments**?

Neither William Henry Harrison nor Zachary Taylor served as president long enough to be afforded the opportunity to nominate a Supreme Court justice. Harrison died in 1841, after only one month in office; Taylor died during his sixteenth month in office in 1850. Andrew Johnson, who served nearly a full term (1865–69), following the assassination of Abraham Lincoln in April 1865, also did not make a selection for the high court. The only full-term president who made no Supreme Court appointments was Jimmy Carter, who served from 1977 to 1981.

Which **president served two full terms and made only one appointment** to the U.S. Supreme Court?

James Monroe served eight years and appointed only Smith Thompson to the bench in 1823.

Which U.S. Supreme Court justice was **former president of the United States**?

William Howard Taft served as president of the United States from 1909 to 1913. In 1921—eight years after leaving office—he was nominated as chief justice of the U.S. Supreme Court by President Warren G. Harding.

What **future U.S. president** was offered a position on the U.S. Supreme Court?

John Quincy Adams was offered a position on the U.S. Supreme Court by then-President James Madison. Adams declined. He later served as secretary of state, president, and U.S. representative from Massachusetts, and also argued several cases before the U.S. Supreme Court in his capacity as a distinguished lawyer. For example, he argued on behalf of a group of African men captured into slavery in the famous *Amistad* case in 1841, while he was still a member of the U.S. House of Representatives.

Have any **presidents nominated justices of another political party** to the U.S. Supreme Court?

Yes, but it is the exception rather than the rule. Seven Republican presidents nominated Democratic justices: Abraham Lincoln nominated Stephen Field; Benjamin Harrison nominated Howell E. Jackson; Warren G. Harding nominated Pierce Butler; Herbert Hoover nominated Benjamin Cardozo; William Howard Taft nominated Associate Justice Edward White to chief justice and also nominated Horace Lurton and Joseph R. Lamar; Dwight D. Eisenhower nominated William J. Brennan; and Richard Nixon nominated Lewis Powell. Two Democratic presidents nominated Republican justices: Franklin D. Roosevelt nominated Harlan Fiske Stone; and Harry S. Truman nominated Harold H. Burton.

Which justices, who were **recess appointments,** actually served on the Court before the Senate voted on their confirmations?

Five justices served on the bench before Senate confirmation. They are: John Rutledge, Benjamin R. Curtis, Earl Warren, William Brennan, and Potter Stewart. Of these five, only Rutledge was not confirmed. There have been ten other justices who were recess appointments, but they did not take their seats until after confirmation. They are: Thomas Johnson, Bushrod Washington, Alfred Moore, Henry Brockholst Livingston, John McKinley, Levi Woodbury, David Davis, John Marshall Harlan, and Oliver Wendell Holmes.

Future president John Quincy Adams was offered a position as U.S. Supreme Court justice by President James Madison. Adams, shown here in 1843, went on to become secretary of state, president, and U.S. representative from Massachusetts. He also represented a group of Africans in the famous *Amistad* case in 1841. *Hulton Archive/Getty Images.*

William Rehnquist was one of two U.S. Supreme Court chief justices to preside over a presidential impeachment trial. Here, Rehnquist listens to testimony in the Senate chamber during the impeachment trial of President Bill Clinton on February 12, 1999. *AP Images.*

Which two Supreme Court chief justices presided over trials involving **impeached presidents**?

In 1868, Chief Justice Salmon P. Chase oversaw the trial in the U.S. Senate in which impeached president Andrew Johnson was acquitted, allowing him to remain as the nation's embattled leader. In 1999, impeached president Bill Clinton, was likewise acquitted, following a trial presided over by Chief Justice William Rehnquist.

EDUCATION

Which U.S. Supreme Court justice **graduated from college at age 14**?

Justice John Archibald Campbell graduated from the University of Georgia at age 14. A child prodigy, he entered college at the age of 11. He served on the U.S. Supreme Court from 1853 to 1861. He resigned his Court seat at the start of the Civil War and became the Confederate government's assistant secretary of war. He eventually established a successful law practice in New Orleans and argued numerous cases before the U.S. Supreme Court, including the famous *Slaughter House Cases* in 1873. Samuel Blatchford also attended college as a youngster; he entered Columbia College when he was 14 and later graduated first in his class.

Which justice was the first to **graduate from a law school**?

Justice Benjamin Curtis graduated from Harvard Law School in 1832. He also earned his undergraduate degree from Harvard in 1829.

Which five U.S. Supreme Court justices served as **law school deans**?

The five former law school deans were: Horace Lurton, Vanderbilt University School of Law; Harlan Fiske Stone, Columbia University Law School; William Howard Taft, the University of Cincinnati Law School; Owen Roberts, the University of Pennsylvania Law School; and Wiley Rutledge, the University of Iowa Law School.

Who is the only U.S. Supreme Court justice to **teach law school while serving on the U.S. Supreme Court**?

Justice Joseph Story taught at Harvard Law School beginning in 1829. He taught at Harvard while he served on the Court until 1845.

Which twentieth century U.S. Supreme Court justices **never received a high school diploma**?

Amazingly, Justice Charles Evans Whittaker, who served on the Court from 1957 to 1962, never graduated from high school or college. He obtained entrance to Kansas City Law School based on high test scores. Similarly, Justice James Francis Byrnes also never graduated from high school. He dropped out of school at age 14 to work as a law clerk.

Which justices who served entirely during the twentieth century **never obtained a law degree**?

Justice Robert Jackson, who served from 1941 to 1954, attended Albany Law School but did not graduate. He was admitted to the bar after attending only one year of law school. Justice Stanley Reed, who served from 1938 to 1957, studied law at both the University of Virginia and Columbia University, but did not graduate. He also studied international law at the Sorbonne in Paris, France. Pierce Butler, who served from 1922 to 1939, did not attend law school. He learned the practice of law under a St. Paul law firm. George Sutherland, who served from 1922 to 1938, attended the University of Michigan Law School but did not graduate. John Hessin Clarke, who served from 1916 to 1922, did not attend law school, learning law from his father. Mahlon Pitney, who served from 1912 to 1922, did not graduate and also learned law from his father. Joseph Rucker Lamar, who served from 1911 to 1916, attended Washington and Lee University in 1877 but did not graduate. William Rufus Day, who served from 1903 to 1922, attended the University of Michigan law school but did not graduate. William

Henry Moody, who served from 1906 to 1910, attended Harvard Law School in 1876–1877 but did not graduate.

Which justice **left his high school after a fight**?

Justice Joseph Story left Marblehead Academy after being severely disciplined for a fight. Story then went to Harvard.

Which future chief justices were **expelled from college**?

Future associate and chief justice Harlan Fiske Stone was expelled from Massachusetts Agricultural College for pushing a teacher. Oliver Ellsworth, who was the third chief justice, was dismissed from Yale after his sophomore year.

Which U.S. Supreme Court justices have **law schools named after them**?

Three justices have law schools named after them: Chief Justice John Marshall (two John Marshall Law Schools—one in Chicago and another in Atlanta—and the Marshall-Wythe School of Law at William and Mary in Virginia), Justice Louis Brandeis (the Brandeis School of Law at the University of Louisville), and Justice Thurgood Marshall (the Thurgood Marshall School of Law at Texas Southern University).

SPORTS AND GAMES

Which Supreme Court justice was once known as **"Whizzer"**?

Justice Byron White obtained the nickname "Whizzer" as an All-American running back at the University of Colorado. He played professional football with the Pittsburgh Pirates (now Steelers) and, later, the Detroit Lions. In 1938, his rookie season, he led the National Football League in rushing. Long after his football days were over, a waitress once asked White, "Are you Whizzer White?" He answered, "I was." It was widely known that he disliked the nickname.

Which justice participated in both **football and wrestling** in high school?

Chief Justice John Roberts captained his high school football team at La Lumiere High School in La Porte, Indiana. He also was a star wrestler, attaining a record of 24–3.

What **type of court** is found in the Supreme Court Building?

On its top (fourth) floor, the U.S. Supreme Court contains a basketball court for Court employees, law clerks, and even the justices. It is referred to as "the highest court in the land."

Byron "Whizzer" White, star running back for the University of Colorado. He later played for the Pittsburgh Pirates (now Steelers) and Detroit Lions before going into law. He served as a U.S. Supreme Court justice from 1962 to 1993. *Hulton Archive/Getty Images.*

What justice did former **NBA great Charles Barkley** visit in 2004?

Charles Barkley, the former perennial NBA all-star and current NBA television analyst, stopped by the Supreme Court in 2004 to dine with his friend Justice Clarence Thomas in the Court cafeteria.

Which U.S. Supreme Court justice is an **expert bridge player**?

Justice John Paul Stevens has played in many bridge tournaments in the Washington, D.C., area. He is a life-master bridge player, the highest ranking in the American Contract Bridge League.

MISCELLANEOUS TRIVIA

Who are the only Supreme Court justices to **sign the Declaration of Independence**?

James Wilson and Samuel Chase are the only justices to sign the Declaration of Independence. Both were members of the Continental Congress—Wilson from Pennsylvania, and Chase from Maryland. Edward Rutledge, brother of Justice John Rutledge, also signed the famous document.

Which **justice tried to drown himself** after the Senate failed to confirm his nomination for chief justice?

John Rutledge, a former associate justice whom President George Washington nominated as chief justice in 1795 as a recess appointment, tried to drown himself after hearing news of his rejection by the Senate. He was saved by a couple of slaves.

Which **future Supreme Court justices met each other in a state court case**?

Future chief justice of the U.S. Supreme Court Roger B. Taney tried his first case before future justice Gabriel Duvall, then a state judge in Maryland, in 1799.

Which justice **killed a man in a duel**?

Justice Henry Brockholst Livingston, who served on the Court from 1807 to 1823, killed a man in a duel in 1798. Livingston, who had switched from the Federalist Party to the Democratic-Republican Party, had written an article mocking the Federalists. An angry Federalist reportedly punched Livingston, which led to the duel. Some sources report that Livingston was actually involved in several duels and was prone to violence.

57

Which former U.S. Supreme Court justice **prosecuted alleged ax-murderer Lizzie Borden**?

William Moody, who served on the Court from 1906 to 1910, prosecuted Lizzie Borden when he was a district attorney in Massachusetts. Borden was immortalized in the famous verse: "Lizzie Borden took an axe / And gave her mother forty whacks. / And when she saw what she had done, / She gave her father forty-one."

Borden allegedly killed her father and stepmother with an ax in Fall River, Massachusetts. Moody assisted in the prosecution even though the crime took place outside the Eastern District of Massachusetts, where he was district attorney. Borden was acquitted.

Which Supreme Court justices have been **Catholic**?

The first Catholic appointed to the Court was Chief Justice Roger Taney, nominated to the Court by President Andrew Jackson in 1835. The other Catholic justices are: Edward D. White, Joseph McKenna, Pierce Butler, Frank Murphy, William Brennan, Anthony Kennedy, Antonin Scalia, Clarence Thomas, John Roberts, and Samuel Alito.

Which U.S. Supreme Court justices have been **Jewish**?

The first Jewish justice was Louis Brandeis, nominated to the Court by President Woodrow Wilson in 1916. The other Jewish justices are Benjamin Cardozo, Felix Frankfurter, Arthur J. Goldberg, Abe Fortas, Ruth Bader Ginsburg, and Stephen Breyer.

Who was the **tallest** U.S. Supreme Court justice?

Horace Gray, who served on the Court from 1882 to 1902, was the tallest justice at six feet six inches tall. Gray reached this height at the age of thirteen.

Who was the **shortest** U.S. Supreme Court justice?

Alfred Moore, who served on the Court from 1800 to 1804, was the smallest justice at less than five feet tall and weighing less than 90 pounds.

Which justice was **disbarred twice**?

Justice Stephen Field was disbarred twice while serving in an administrative position in Marysville, California. He was also jailed for contempt of court. The setbacks proved to be temporary as Field later served six years on the California Supreme Court before his thirty-four-year tenure on the U.S. Supreme Court.

Who is the only Supreme Court justice to **play the role of a justice in a movie**?

Justice Harry Blackmun starred as Justice Joseph Story in the movie *Amistad* in 1997. The Steven Spielberg–directed movie was popular with audiences and garnered four Academy Award nominations.

Which U.S. Supreme Court justice has made more than one **singing appearance at the Washington Opera**?

Justice Ruth Bader Ginsburg participated with Justice Antonin Scalia as an extra in 1994 for a production of *Ariadne auf Naxos*. In 2003, Ginsburg, Stephen Breyer, and Anthony Kennedy served as extras for a 2003 production of *Die Fledermaus*. Ginsburg had said that if she could pick any career, it would be an opera singer.

U.S. Supreme Court justice Ruth Bader Ginsburg, a lover of opera, has appeared as a singing extra in two different productions. *Getty Images*.

Which justice participated in a **National Public Radio trivia quiz**?

In 2007, Justice Stephen Breyer participated in National Public Radio's news quiz show, "Wait Wait … Don't Tell Me!" He was asked three rock-n-roll questions—relating to David Bowie, Iggy Pop, and Ozzy Osbourne—and missed them all.

THE JAY, RUTLEDGE, AND ELLSWORTH COURTS (1789–1800)

Who were the **nation's first three chief justices**?

The first three chief justices of the U.S. Supreme Court were John Jay, John Rutledge, and Oliver Ellsworth. Jay served from 1789 to 1795. Rutledge, who had served as an associate justice from 1789 to 1791, served as chief justice for only five months in 1795. He was a recess appointment and the Senate rejected his nomination. Ellsworth served from 1796 to 1800 after sitting associate justice William Cushing became the second chief justice nominee of President George Washington to be rejected by the Senate in 1796.

Which **justices served on these first three courts**?

Twelve justices served on the courts of John Jay, John Rutledge (who also served as an associate justice), and Oliver Ellsworth. Besides the chief justices themselves, the justices were William Cushing, James Wilson, John Blair, James Iredell, Thomas Johnson, William Paterson, Samuel Chase, Bushrod Washington, and Alfred Moore.

What positions did Jay, Rutledge, and Ellsworth hold **before serving as chief justice**?

John Jay had a distinguished political career in his home state of New York, including serving as a delegate at the Continental Congress and later becoming president of that colonial governmental body. He also served as chief justice of the New York state court, minister to Spain, and secretary of foreign affairs under President George Washington. He acted as a special envoy to Great Britain while serving as chief justice of the Supreme Court, which led to the adoption of a treaty between the two nations called the Jay Treaty.

John Rutledge also had a distinguished political career from his home state of South Carolina. He served as a member of the South Carolina Commons House of

Assembly, acting South Carolina attorney general, a member of the Continental Congress, president of the South Carolina General Assembly, governor of South Carolina, judge of the Chancery Court of South Carolina, and chief member of the South Carolina delegation to the Philadelphia Convention (which formed the U.S. Constitution). Rutledge also served as an associate justice on the Court for seventeen months.

Oliver Ellsworth had an impressive political career in his home state of Connecticut, serving as a member of the Connecticut General Assembly, the Hartford County state attorney, a member of the Continental Congress, a judge on the Connecticut Superior Court, a delegate to the Philadelphia Convention, and U.S. senator. He also served as commissioner to France while he served as chief justice.

What **position did President George Washington first offer to Jay**?

President Washington first offered Jay the position of secretary of state, which Jay declined. Then, Washington made him the nation's first chief justice of the U.S. Supreme Court.

Why did these **chief justices leave the Court**?

Jay left the Court to become governor of New York, a position he coveted more than the chief justice of the Supreme Court. The Court in those early days was not considered a top position, as many early justices left for state positions or state judgeships.

Rutledge first served as one of the Court's original six associate justices, though he never actually heard a case on the Court due to illness. Rutledge did hear some cases in his capacity of "riding circuit," as the Judiciary Act of 1789 required Supreme Court justices to serve as circuit court judges. Rutledge left the Court as an associate justice for what he considered a better position—chief justice of the South Carolina Supreme Court.

In July 1795, President Washington appointed Rutledge to the position of chief justice while Congress was in recess (a so-called recess appointment). However, Rutledge had to leave the Court after the U.S. Senate failed to confirm him by a vote of 14–10. Many senators opposed Rutledge's nomination because of political reasons, mainly his opposition to the Jay Treaty, named after the Court's first chief justice, John Jay. President Washington enlisted Jay, while he was still chief justice, to negotiate with the British over several issues that were causing conflict between the two nations. Many Americans were upset with the British for their capture and seizure of American ships. Many believed that Jay was not forceful enough in his negotiations and did not obtain enough concessions from the British for their unlawful behavior. Rutledge called the Jay Treaty a "prostitution of the dearest rights of free men." This did not sit well with several members of the U.S. Senate, who denied him the chief justice position. Rutledge did not take the rejection well, as he apparently tried to drown himself.

Ellsworth left the position as chief justice because of poor health.

Oliver Ellsworth, the nation's third U.S. Supreme Court chief justice. *Hulton Archive/Getty Images.*

John Rutledge, the nation's second U.S. Supreme Court chief justice. Rutledge was a recess appointment who served for only five months as chief justice before the U.S. Senate rejected him, 14–10. *Hulton Archive/Getty Images.*

Who were the **first six justices nominated** for the U.S. Supreme Court?

The first six justices nominated to the U.S. Supreme Court were Chief Justice John Jay and Justices John Rutledge, William Cushing, James Wilson, John Blair, and Robert H. Harrison. The Senate confirmed all the nominees, but Harrison, a judge in Maryland, declined the nomination because of poor health. In his place, Washington nominated James Iredell of North Carolina.

How many of the **first six justices had state court judicial experience**?

Five of the first six justices—John Jay, John Rutledge, William Cushing, John Blair, and James Iredell—had prior judicial experience. Only James Wilson of the original six had never served as a judge.

Jay had been chief justice of the New York State Court, Rutledge had been judge of the Court of Chancery of South Carolina, Cushing had been a member of the Supreme Judicial Court of Massachusetts, Blair had been chief justice of the Virginia Court of Appeals, and Iredell had been a judge on the Superior Court of North Carolina.

Which justice had the **most judicial experience**?

By far, Justice William Cushing had the most prior judicial experience. He had been a judge in Massachusetts for nearly twenty years. He served as a probate judge for two years in 1760–61, on the Superior Court of Massachusetts for five years, and on the Supreme Judicial Court of Massachusetts for twelve years.

What exactly was **"riding circuit"**?

Riding circuit referred to the practice established in the Judiciary Act of 1789 of having the justices of the U.S. Supreme Court also serve on the circuit courts. At the time, the three circuits were the Southern Circuit (consisting of South Carolina, Georgia, and North Carolina), the Middle Circuit (consisting of Delaware, Maryland, New Jersey, Pennsylvania, and Virginia) and the Eastern Circuit (consisting of Connecticut, Massachusetts, New Hampshire, New York, Rhode Island, and Vermont). Riding circuit refers to the fact that the judges would often have to log thousands of miles to attend courts in various states to hear different cases.

What early court justice **served on the court for only a little more than one year** because of circuit riding?

Justice Thomas Johnson, nominated by President George Washington in 1791, took office in November 1791 but did not last long because he detested the practice of riding circuit. Because of this onerous task, he resigned in February 1793. He has the

Thomas Johnson served only 15 months on the bench, the shortest time of any Supreme Court justice. *Hulton Archive/Getty Images.*

distinction of serving the shortest time on the Court, writing only one opinion during his short time on the bench.

What federal law is perhaps **Ellsworth's greatest achievement**?

Oliver Ellsworth was the principal draftsman of the Judiciary Act of 1789, the law that created the U.S. Supreme Court and the federal court system. Ellsworth served on the chair of the committee in charge of the bill and he wrote much of the bill by his own hand. Justice Sandra Day O'Connor wrote in her 2003 book *The Majesty of the Law:* "The Judiciary Act stands as the single most important legislative enactment of the nation's founding years."

What other early Supreme Court justice **participated in the writing of the Judiciary Act of 1789**?

Justice William Paterson helped his Princeton classmate, Oliver Ellsworth, draft the Judiciary Act of 1789 when both served in the U.S. Senate. Paterson is perhaps best known in history for coming up with the New Jersey Plan, which would have provided for a one-house Congress, during the Philadelphia Convention.

Which Supreme Court justices **attended the Constitutional Convention of 1787** in Philadelphia to create the U.S. Constitution?

Five future Supreme Court justices attended the Constitutional Convention of 1787: John Rutledge from South Carolina, Oliver Ellsworth from Connecticut, William Paterson from New Jersey, James Wilson from Pennsylvania, and John Blair from Virginia. They were among the fifty-five delegates attending the famous Philadelphia Convention who created the U.S. Constitution. Future justice Gabriel Duvall was chosen to be one of Maryland's four delegates to the Convention but he, along with the other delegates from Maryland, never attended.

What **famous documents did John Jay help write**?

John Jay, along with future president James Madison and future Treasury secretary Alexander Hamilton, wrote the *Federalist Papers,* a series of essays designed to arouse public support for the new U.S. Constitution. Madison and Hamilton were the primary authors of the eighty-five-essay set; Jay wrote about five essays.

U.S. general and future first president George Washington presides over the Constitutional Convention in Philadelphia in 1787. *Hulton Archive/Getty Images.*

Which member of the early court **served time in jail for his debts**?

Associate Justice James Wilson, one of the most prominent figures at the Philadelphia Convention, served time in jail in Burlington, New Jersey, for not paying his debts. He was later jailed a second time. The money problems often prevented Wilson from fulfilling his judicial duties.

What early Supreme Court justice was **related to President George Washington**?

Justice Bushrod Washington was a nephew of President George Washington. Justice Washington's father, John Augustine Washington, was the president's brother. President John Adams nominated Bushrod Washington in December 1798. He served for thirty years until his death in 1829.

What was the **initial salary** of the Supreme Court justices?

Congress passed a law on September 23, 1789, called the Compensation Act, that provided for the salaries of federal officials. The associate justices received $4,000 per year, while the chief justice received $4,500 per year.

When did the **Supreme Court initially meet**?

The U.S. Supreme Court initially met in February 1790. The Judiciary Act of 1789 provided that the Court would hold two sessions annually, beginning the first Mondays of February and August.

How many **decisions did the U.S. Supreme Court make during its first three terms?**

The Court heard no cases during its first three terms in February 1790, August 1790, and February 1791. There were no cases before the Court in those original terms and the justices handled administrative matters at the high court. Soon, though, the justices were busy with the burdens of riding circuit—serving in the lower federal circuit courts.

DECISIONS

What **famous decision** in the 1790s led to a **constitutional amendment?**

The Court decided 4–1 in *Chisholm v. Georgia* (1793) that the state of Georgia could be sued by a South Carolina citizen. This decision caused great uproar and led to the Congressional passage of the Eleventh Amendment, which generally prohibits states from being hauled into court by individuals (at least for monetary damages).

The case arose because the state of Georgia did not pay for supplies to South Carolina merchant Robert Farquhar. The state refused to pay Farquhar because he was a Loyalist (loyal to England). Georgia made the legal argument that it was immune from suit because it was a state that could not be sued by a citizen of another state. After Farquhar died, the executor of his estate, Alexander Chisholm (who also was from South Carolina), then sued the state in federal court for nearly $70,000. Georgia, believing it had immunity from a suit by a South Carolina citizen, argued that the federal court did not have jurisdiction.

The Court ruled 4–1 that Georgia could be sued. The justices in the majority focused on the explicit language in Article III of the Constitution, which provides that "the judicial power of the United States shall extend to controversies between a state and citizens of another state."

Congress adopted the Eleventh Amendment in 1795 and it was ratified in 1798. It provides: "The Judicial power of the United States shall not be construed to extend to any suit in law or equity, commenced or prosecuted against one of the United States by Citizens of another State, or by Citizens or Subjects of any Foreign State."

Who **argued the case for Alexander Chisholm?**

Remarkably, U.S. attorney general Edmund Randolph argued the case as a private attorney on behalf of Alexander Chisholm. In those days, government attorneys could supplement their income by taking private cases. Randolph was unopposed by the state of Georgia. The Supreme Court reporter, Alexander Dallas, submitted a written response from the state's lawyers but no one personally appeared to argue on the state's behalf.

CourtSpeak: *Chisholm v. Georgia* State vs. State Case (1793)

Chief Justice John Jay (majority): "If we attend to the words, we find them to be express, positive, free from ambiguity, and without room for such implied expressions: 'The judicial power of the United States shall extend to controversies between a state and citizens of another state.' If the Constitution really meant to extend these powers only to those controversies in which a State might be Plaintiff, to the exclusion of those in which citizens had demands against a State, it is inconceivable that it should have attempted to convey that meaning in words, not only so incompetent, but also repugnant to it; if it meant to exclude a certain class of these controversies, why were they not expressly excepted; on the contrary, not even an intimation of such intention appears in any part of the Constitution. It cannot be pretended that where citizens urge and insist upon demands against a State, which the State refuses to admit and comply with, that there is no controversy between them. If it is a controversy between them, then it clearly falls not only within the spirit, but the very words of the Constitution."

Justice John Blair (majority): "It seems to me, that if this Court should refuse to hold jurisdiction of a case where a State is a Defendant, it would renounce part of the authority conferred, and consequently, part of the duty imposed on it by the Constitution; because it would be a refusal to take cognizance of a case where a State is a party."

Justice James Wilson (majority): "'The judicial power of the United States shall extend to controversies, between a state and citizens of another State.' Could the strictest legal language; could even that language, which is peculiarly appropriated to an art, deemed, by a great master, to be one of the most honorable, laudable, and profitable things in our law; could this strict and appropriated language, describe, with more precise accuracy, the cause now depending before the tribunal?"

Justice William Cushing (majority): "Upon the whole, I am of the opinion, that the Constitution warrants a suit against a State, by an individual citizen of another State."

Justice James Iredell (dissenting): "I believe there is no doubt that neither in the State now in question, nor in any other in the Union, any particular Legislative mode, authorizing a compulsory suit for the recovery of money against a State, was in being either when the Constitution was adopted, or at the time the judicial act was passed."

John Jay, the nation's first U.S. Supreme Court chief justice. *Hulton Archive/Getty Images.*

CourtSpeak: *Calder v. Bull* Ex Post Facto Law Case (1798)

Justice Samuel Chase (unanimous ruling): "I will state what laws I consider ex post facto laws, within the words and the intent of the prohibition. 1st. Every law that makes an action, done before the passing of the law, and which was innocent when done, criminal; and punishes such action. 2nd. Every law that aggravates a crime, or makes it greater than it was, when committed. 3rd. Every law that changes the punishment, and inflicts a greater punishment, than the law annexed to the crime, when announced. 4th. Every law that alters the legal rules of evidence, and receives less, or different, testimony, than the law required at the time of the commission of the offence, in order to convict the offender."

Justice William Paterson: "The words ex post facto, when applied to a law, have a technical meaning, and, in legal phraseology, refer to crimes, pains, and penalties.... Here the meaning, annexed to the terms ex post facto laws, unquestionably refers to crimes, and nothing else."

Justice James Iredell: "The policy, the reason and humanity, of the prohibition, do not, I repeat, extend to civil cases, to cases that merely affect the private property of citizens. Some of the most necessary and important acts of Legislation are, on the contrary, founded upon the principle, that private rights must yield to public exigencies."

Justice William Cushing: "The case appears to me to be clear of all difficulty, taken either way. If the act is a judicial act, it is not touched by the Federal Constitution; and, if it is a legislative act, it is maintained and justified by the ancient and uniform practice of the state of Connecticut."

In what case did the Supreme Court define **ex post facto laws**?

The U.S. Supreme Court first defined ex post facto laws in *Calder v. Bull* (1798), a case examining whether the Connecticut legislature violated the rights of heirs (Calder and his wife) when it passed a law ordering a new hearing in a probate court. After the new hearing, the probate court ruled in favor of other heirs (Bull and his wife). The Calders argued that the Connecticut legislature's act of ordering a new hearing in probate court constituted an ex post facto law. An ex post facto law is one that makes conduct a crime even though the conduct was not a crime when it originally occurred. In other words, an ex post facto law criminalizes conduct retroactively.

The U.S. Supreme Court unanimously ruled 4–0 that the Connecticut law was not an ex post facto law because it affected only civil law, not criminal law. Ex post facto laws, according to the justices, referred to laws that retroactively increased punishment for crimes or made certain innocent conduct a crime.

71

The four justices hearing the case—Samuel Chase, William Paterson, James Iredell, and William Cushing—all wrote separate opinions, though Cushing's was very short. This conformed with the Court's existing practice of issuing seriatim opinions, or a series of opinions—each justice issuing his own separate opinion. Chief Justice Oliver Ellsworth and James Wilson did not participate. In the late 1790s, Wilson was beset with financial problems, including being jailed twice for his debts.

In what decision did the Court address **direct and indirect taxes**?

The Court unanimously ruled 3–0 in *Hylton v. United States* (1796) that Congress had the power to tax carriages without apportioning the taxes among the various states. Daniel Hylton was cited for not paying taxes on his 125 stipulated carriages. He contended that the tax was unconstitutional because Article II, Section 9, of the U.S. Constitution provides that no direct taxes "shall be laid, unless in Proportion to the Census or Enumeration herein before directed to be taken." This provision means that direct taxes could not be imposed unless they were apportioned among the states based on population. Interestingly, at the Constitutional Convention of 1787, a delegate had asked for a definition of a direct tax and no one answered. This meant that the definition of a direct tax was unclear. The Supreme Court reasoned that the tax on carriages was an indirect tax not subject to the apportionment requirement. The Court reasoned that if a tax could not easily be apportioned among the states, then it was most likely an indirect tax. Because the Court held that a tax on carriages was not a direct tax, it concluded that the tax could be imposed lawfully.

CourtSpeak: *Ware v. Hylton* State Law vs. U.S. Treaty Case (1796)

Justice Samuel Chase (unanimous ruling): "It is the declared will of the people of the United States that every treaty made, by the authority of the United States, shall be superior to the Constitution and laws of any individual State; and their will alone is to decide. If a law of a State, contrary to a treaty, is not void, but voidable only by a repeal, or nullification by a State Legislature, this certain consequence follows, that the will of a small part of the United States may controul or defeat the will of the whole. The people of America have been pleased to declare, that all treaties made before the establishment of the National Constitution, or laws of any of the States, contrary to a treaty, shall be disregarded."

Justice William Paterson: "No act of any state legislature, and no payment made under such act into the public coffers, shall obstruct the creditor in his course of recovery against his debtor. The act itself is a lawful impediment, and therefore is repealed; the payment under the act is also a lawful impediment, and therefore is made void."

Justice James Wilson: "But even if Virginia had the power to confiscate, the treaty annuls the confiscation. The fourth article is well expressed to meet the very case: it is not confined to debts existing at the time of making the treaty; but is extended to debts heretofore contracted. It is impossible by any glossary, or argument, to make the words more perspicuous, more conclusive, than by a bare recital."

Justice William Cushing: "A State may make what rules it pleases; and those rules must necessarily have place within itself. But here is a treaty, the supreme law, which overrules all State laws upon the subject, to all intents and purposes; and that makes the difference."

What did the Court say about the **power of the Court to strike down unconstitutional federal law**?

Justice Samuel Chase addressed the question of whether the Court could strike down an unconstitutional federal law. He intimated that the Court had the power to strike down such laws but that it would be done very rarely. Referring to *Hylton v. United States,* Chase explained: "As I do not think the tax on carriages is a direct tax, it is unnecessary, at this time, for me to determine, whether this court, constitutionally possesses the power to declare an act of Congress void, on the ground of its being made contrary to, and in violation of, the Constitution; but if the court have such power, I am free to declare, that I will never exercise it, but in a very clear case."

In what case did the Court rule that **Virginia law had to take a backseat to a treaty**?

U.S. Supreme Court justice William Cushing joined his fellow justices in ruling unanimously that a U.S. treaty takes precedent over a state law. "Here is a treaty, the supreme law, which overrules all State laws," said Cushing. *Hulton Archive/Getty Images.*

The U.S. Supreme Court ruled 4–0 in *Ware v. Hylton* (1796) that a 1777 Virginia law allowing Revolutionary War–era debtors to pay a reduced amount of money to the state treasury rather than paying British creditors was invalid because it conflicted with a treaty signed by the United States with Great Britain in 1783. This so-called Treaty of Paris provided that British creditors should be able to recover the debts that were owed to them before and during the war. The treaty provided: "It is agreed, that creditors on either side, shall meet with no legal impediment to the recovery of the full value in sterling money, of all bona fide debts heretofore contracted."

The Court determined that this treaty trumped the Virginia state law. Justice Samuel Chase explained that "it is the declared duty of the State Judges to determine any Constitution, or laws of any State, contrary to that treaty (or any other) made under the authority of the United States, null and void. National or Federal Judges are bound by duty and oath to the same conduct."

In *Ware v. Hylton* and *Hylton v. United States,* **is Hylton the same person**?

Yes, Daniel Lawrence Hylton, a prosperous Virginia merchant, is the same person who was a litigant in both famous cases. The U.S. government wanted a test case on the carriage tax law and agreed to pay all of Hylton's legal expenses in *Hylton v. United States.*

What **famous person represented Hylton** before the U.S. Supreme Court?

John Marshall represented Daniel Hylton before the U.S. Supreme Court in *Ware v. Hylton.* Though he lost the case, five years later Marshall would become chief justice of the Court for thirty-four years and in the estimation of most historians become the Court's greatest chief justice.

In what case did the **justices decline to review pension benefits of soldiers**?

The U.S. Supreme Court first examined this question in *Hayburn's Case* (1792) and then in other cases collectively called the Invalid Pension Act cases. Congress had passed a law that provided that federal judges would review disability pension claims by soldiers and settlement claims of dead soldiers' wives and orphans. One of these individuals was veteran William Hayburn. The law also provided that the judges' decisions would be reviewed by the secretary of war. A group of federal judges, including five U.S. Supreme Court justices, wrote letters to President George Washington, declining the appointments because they believed it violated separation of powers principles. To the justices, it was inconsistent with separation of powers principles to have their decisions reviewed by an executive branch official.

The three-judge circuit court for the district of New York, which included Chief Justice John Jay and Justice William Cushing, issued an opinion to President Washington, explaining their opposition to the law. "That neither the legislative nor the executive branches, can constitutionally assign to the judicial any duties, but such as are properly judicial, and to be performed in a judicial matter," they wrote.

The three-judge circuit court for the district of Pennsylvania, which included Justices James Wilson and John Blair, wrote a letter to President Washington. They wrote that the law was "radically inconsistent with the independence of that judicial power which is vested in the courts; and consequently, with that important principle which is so strictly observed by the constitution of the United States."

Finally, the two-judge circuit court for the district of North Carolina, which included Justice James Iredell, also objected to the practice by letter to President Washington. The judges noted that the law "subjects the decision of the court to a mode of revision, which we consider to be unwarranted by the constitution." Congress responded to *Hayburn's Case* by passing a new law dealing with veterans' pensions.

Why is *Hayburn's Case* important?

The case was important because it helped establish the principle of judicial independence: the executive and legislative branches could not place the federal courts, including U.S. Supreme Court justices, in a subservient role when it comes to interpreting the law.

In what case did the U.S. Supreme Court assert jurisdiction over admiralty disputes involving captured ships?

The U.S. Supreme Court, under the leadership of Chief Justice John Jay, ruled in *Glass v. The Sloop Betsey* (1794) that federal courts in the United States have jurisdiction over captured vessels taken into American ports even if the ships involved are not American. The issue arose after a French ship, the *Citizen Genet,* captured a Swedish vessel called the *Sloop Betsey* and sent the vessel into Baltimore. The French captain, Pierre Arcade Johannene, asserted that France had the right to set up its own prize court, a court specifically designed to hear admiralty disputes, in the United States to hear this dispute.

The U.S. Supreme Court determined that "no foreign power can of right institute, or erect, any court of judicature of any kind, within the jurisdiction of the United States." The Court also determined that "every District Court in the United States, possesses all the powers of a court of Admiralty."

Why is the **captured ship decision important**?

The *Glass v. The Sloop Betsey* case is important for at least two reasons. One, it established that the Court had jurisdiction to hear admiralty and prize disputes, involving the capture and detainment of various ships and vessels. This became a source of many cases for the Court in the early years. Second, the case is perhaps even more important because it established the United States as an independent power willing to stand up to other countries, such as France, and assert itself in the international arena.

THE MARSHALL COURT (1801–35)

How many and which justices **served on the Marshall Court**?

Sixteen justices served on the Marshall Court, including Chief Justice John Marshall and Justices William Cushing, William Paterson, Samuel Chase, Bushrod Washington, Alfred Moore, William Johnson, Henry Brockholst Livingston, Thomas Todd, Gabriel Duvall, Joseph Story, Smith Thompson, Robert Trimble, John McLean, Henry Baldwin, and James M. Wayne.

What is **noteworthy about the tenure of several of the Marshall Court justices**?

From 1812 to 1824, Chief Justice John Marshall and Justices Washington, Johnson, Todd, Duvall, Story, and Thompson served the longest tenure of any sitting justices in the Court's history.

What **government positions did Marshall have** before serving as chief justice?

Marshall served many terms in the Virginia House of Delegates, beginning in 1782. He also served as a delegate to the Virginia state convention for ratification of the U.S. Constitution, minister to France in 1797–98, a U.S. representative in 1799–1800, and the secretary of state under President John Adams in 1800–1801.

Why is Marshall considered the **greatest of the chief justices**?

In his 1996 biography of Marshall, author Jean Edward Smith referred to the chief justice as "the Definer of the Nation." Marshall's opinions gave the U.S. Supreme Court and the judicial branch the power and respect that they deserved. He did this in many ways. For example, he persuaded his colleagues to drop the practice of in sepiatim opinions, where each justice

U.S. Supreme Court chief justice John Marshall. *AP Images.*

would speak and issue his opinion. Under Marshall, the Court often spoke in one, unified voice—many times through the chief justice. He also established the principle of judicial review in *Marbury v. Madison* (1803), which gave the judiciary the power to review the constitutionality of legislation and regulations. Supreme Court justice Sandra Day O'Connor wrote in her book *The Majesty of the Law:* "It is no overstatement to claim that Chief Justice Marshall fulfilled the Constitution's promise of an independent federal judiciary."

Another factor of Marshall's greatness is that he was the first chief justice to serve for any length of time. (He served for thirty-four years; the first chief justice, John Jay, had previously served the longest—six years.) Justice Oliver Wendell Holmes, who served from 1902 to 1932, believed part of Marshall's greatness lay in his "being there" during the formative period of the nation. But Marshall was more than just an accidental force of history; he had great leadership abilities that enabled him to guide the Court during his lengthy term.

Whom did **John Marshall believe should be chief justice**?

Marshall advised President John Adams that the appointment of chief justice should go to associate justice William Paterson, one of the drafters of the Judiciary Act of 1789 and a leading framer at the 1787 Philadelphia Convention that created the Constitution. However, President Adams did not offer the position to Paterson in part because Paterson was a close friend of Alexander Hamilton, with whom Adams did not see to eye to eye. Actually, Adams first offered the position to John Jay, the nation's first chief justice, who had resigned in 1795 after serving nearly six years to become governor of New York. When Jay declined the appointment, many advised the president to select Paterson, the associate justice with the most seniority. Adams decided instead to nominate Marshall. When Marshall's name was first proposed, many Federalist members of the Senate delayed his confirmation because they wanted Adams to nominate Paterson.

What **significant proposal did William Paterson make** at the Constitutional Convention of 1787?

New Jersey delegate Paterson opposed the Virginia Plan, which called for the creation of two houses of congress that would be composed of representatives chosen on the basis of population. This proposal did not favor the states with smaller populations, such as Paterson's New Jersey, which would have fewer representatives in Congress. Paterson then proposed the so-called New Jersey Plan, or Paterson Plan, which called for one house of Congress that would be filled with the same number of members from each state. Paterson basically proposed what became the U.S. Senate.

What member of the Marshall Court **faced impeachment proceedings**?

Justice Samuel Chase, a partisan Federalist, faced impeachment proceedings for his conduct during several sedition prosecutions, including a trial involving James Callender in

Richmond. Callender, as editor of the *Richmond Examiner,* was charged with sedition for his harsh comments about President John Adams. Callender wrote that Adams was "mentally deranged" and a "hideous hermaphroditical character, which has neither the force of a man, nor the gentleness and sensibility of a woman." Chase presided over Callender's trial in a biased manner, keeping all Anti-Federalists off the jury and making other rulings favorable to the prosecution.

Chief Justice Marshall expressed concern that the politically motivated impeachment would threaten the independence of the judiciary. He testified as a witness in the trial presided over by Vice President Aaron Burr. Attorney General John Randolph failed to obtain the necessary two-thirds majority on any of the impeachment charges for conviction. In fact, many Democratic-Republicans joined their Federalist counterparts and voted for acquittal on several of the charges.

President John Adams was the subject of a sedition trial in front of the U.S. Supreme Court. A newspaper editor made disparaging remarks about the president, leading to a trial in which Chief Justice Samuel Chase—like Adams, a Federalist—was accused of behaving in a biased manner favorable to the prosecution. Chase faced impeachment proceedings as a result of his conduct. *Time & Life Pictures/Getty Images.*

Over what **impeachment trial did Marshall preside**?

Marshall presided over the impeachment trial of Vice President Aaron Burr in 1807 in his capacity as a circuit judge. Marshall's rulings in the case effectively nullified the prosecution's treason charges against Burr. His rulings also increased the antagonism of President Thomas Jefferson, a Democratic-Republican, who was not an ally of Marshall, a Federalist. The two had clashed through the years and the *Marbury* case only served to exacerbate tensions between the two political rivals.

Whose attacks in the press caused Marshall to write **anonymous replies under the name "A Friend of the Constitution?"**

Spencer Roane, a jurist on the Virginia Supreme Court, attacked the Marshall Court for several of its rulings. Roane's attacks intensified in 1819 after the Court's decision in *McCullough v. Maryland,* which Roane viewed as yet another attack on state sovereignty. Roane and friend William Brockenbrough wrote essays in the *Richmond Enquirer,* heavily criticizing the Court's decision. Marshall responded with a series of newspaper editorials signed as either "A Friend of the Union" or "A Friend to the Constitution."

Which justice was considered the **greatest scholar on the Marshall Court**?

Without a doubt, Justice Joseph Story was the greatest scholar on the Marshall Court and arguably the greatest scholar in the history of the U.S. Supreme Court. He wrote a three-volume work entitled *Commentaries on the Constitution,* which was read by law students and lawyers across the country. He also published many other volumes on other areas of the law. He also helped found and taught law at Harvard University. It is rumored that Chief Justice Marshall once said to Story upon handing over an opinion: "This is the law; now you find the precedents."

U.S. Supreme Court justice William Johnson was known as the "first great dissenter." *Hulton Archive/Getty Images.*

Which justice is often referred to as the **"first great dissenter?"**

Justice William Johnson, President Thomas Jefferson's first appointment to the Court, is called the Court's "first great dissenter," or first dissenter, because he was the first justice to disagree with opinions issued by Chief Justice Marshall. He founded the practice of filing dissenting opinions. Johnson filed thirty-four dissents during his more than thirty years on the Court. While this seems minor by today's standards, the commanding practice of the Marshall Court was unanimity.

Which justice's **bizarre behavior** negatively impacted the Marshall Court at times?

Justice Henry Baldwin's bizarre behavior became an issue on the Marshall Court. He disrupted conferences and became very disagreeable with his fellow justices. Baldwin suffered from a mental illness that caused his erratic behavior. His behavior deteriorated to the point that he was hospitalized for "lunacy" in 1833. Some sources say that

81

Baldwin suffered from a type of obsessive compulsive disorder. He returned to the bench and served until his death in 1844.

Which Marshall Court justice was **related by marriage to John Jay**?

Henry Brockholst Livingston was the brother-in-law of former Supreme Court chief justice John Jay. Jay had married Livingston's sister, Sarah Van Brugh Livingston, in 1774.

DECISIONS

In which case did Marshall proclaim that the **Supreme Court has the power of judicial review**?

The Marshall Court established the power of judicial review in the famous case of *Marbury v. Madison* (1803). Chief Justice Marshall proclaimed that "it is emphatically the province and duty of the judicial department to say what the law is."

What were the **underlying facts of *Marbury v. Madison***?

Federalist John Adams was leaving the presidency, having been defeated by his vice president, Democratic-Republican Thomas Jefferson. The Federalist Congress quickly passed a new judiciary act that created many new judgeships, including forty-five justice-of-the-peace positions. Adams's secretary of state—none other than John Marshall himself—then had to sign the commissions for these "midnight justices" for them to take office.

Unfortunately, Marshall did not have time to deliver all the commissions before the new Jefferson administration took over the White House. Seventeen justices of the peace, including William Marbury, did not receive their commissions before the new president was in office. Marbury sued Jefferson's secretary of state, James Madison, asking the Court to issue a writ of mandamus forcing Madison to deliver Marbury his commission.

What did the **Court actually rule in *Marbury v. Madison***?

John Marshall, now chief justice of the Supreme Court, noted that Marbury was entitled to his commission, as he had been appointed by the president, confirmed by the Senate and otherwise qualified for the position. The Court also determined that Secretary of State James Madison wrongfully withheld Marbury's commission from him.

However, Marshall also ruled that Marbury's suit must fail because Section 13 of the Judiciary Act of 1789, which authorized the Court to issue a writ of mandamus, was unconstitutional. Marshall reasoned that Section 13 conflicted with Article III of the U.S. Constitution, which provided that the Supreme Court did not have original jurisdiction of Marbury's case, only appellate jurisdiction. In other words, Marshall reasoned that Section 13 was unconstitutional because it attempted to confer original

CourtSpeak: Section 13 of the Judiciary Act of 1789

"SEC. 13. *And be it further enacted,* That the Supreme Court shall have exclusive jurisdiction of all controversies of a civil nature, where a state is a party, except between a state and its citizens; and except also between a state and citizens of other states, or aliens, in which latter case it shall have original but not exclusive jurisdiction. And shall have exclusively all such jurisdiction of suits or proceedings against ambassadors, or other public ministers, or their domestics, or domestic servants, as a court of law can have or exercise consistently with the law of nations; and original, but not exclusive jurisdiction of all suits brought by ambassadors, or other public ministers, or in which a consul, or vice consul, shall be a party. And the trial of issues in fact in the Supreme Court, in all actions at law against citizens of the United States, shall be by jury. The Supreme Court shall also have appellate jurisdiction from the circuit courts and courts of the several states, in the cases herein after specially provided for; and shall have power to issue writs of prohibition to the district courts, when proceeding as courts of admiralty and maritime jurisdiction, and writs of *mandamus,* in cases warranted by the principles and usages of law, to any courts appointed, or persons holding office, under the authority of the United States."

jurisdiction to litigants like William Marbury, but the Constitution provided that the Court only had appellate jurisdiction, meaning the suit had to be filed in the lower courts. Marshall explained that "the jurisdiction had to be appellate, not original."

Whatever happened to **William Marbury**?

Marbury never became a justice of the peace, though he did become a prominent and successful banker in Washington, D.C.

The Marshall Court **upheld a federal bankruptcy law** in what decision?

The Marshall Court ruled in *United States v. Fisher* (1805) that Congress had the authority to pass the Bankruptcy Act of 1801, which gave the federal government first priority to obtain monies from debtors in insolvency cases vis-à-vis other creditors. Chief Justice Marshall explained that the measure was justified by the Necessary and Proper Clause and the Supremacy Clause in the U.S. Constitution.

What are the **historical coincidences** associated with this case?

Chief Justice Marshall actually was one of the primary sponsors of the bankruptcy law when he was a U.S. representative from Virginia. The other coincidence was that one of the

83

other chief sponsors of the legislation, U.S. congressman Robert Goodloe Harper of South Carolina, represented Fisher, the person challenging the constitutionality of the law.

The Marshall Court **struck down a state law for the first time** in what decision?

The Marshall Court, by a vote of 4–1, invalidated a state law for the first time in *Fletcher v. Peck* (1810) in a case that involved questionable land deals. In 1795, the state of Georgia sold more than 30 million acres of land in the Yazoo area (located in present-day Alabama and Mississippi) to several Northern land companies. These companies in turn sold the land to third parties at much higher prices. It was revealed that many Georgia legislators received bribes for their votes in approving the land sales. In the next round of elections, these legislators were voted out of office and the new legislature passed a law in 1796 that annulled the original sale contracts.

This cancellation presented a problem for innocent third-parties who purchased the land without knowledge of the shady origins of how the land was first acquired. In what some think was a contrived lawsuit—many believe plaintiff and defendant planned the lawsuit together—Robert Fletcher of New Hampshire sued John Peck of Massachusetts in 1803 to "quiet," or establish, his title to ensure that he had a valid claim to the land.

The Court ruled that the Georgia law invalidating the Yazoo land sales was unconstitutional because it violated the Constitution's Contract Clause, preventing states from impairing the obligations of contracts. Chief Justice Marshall reasoned that the new law could negatively impact innocent, third-party purchasers, such as Fletcher. "If the original transaction was infected with fraud, these purchasers did not partici-

> ## CourtSpeak: *Fletcher v. Peck* Land Deal Case (1810)
>
> Chief Justice John Marshall (majority): "When, then, a law is in its nature a contract, when absolute rights have vested under that contract, a repeal of the law cannot devest those rights; and the act of annulling them, if legitimate, is rendered so by a power applicable to the case of every individual in the community....
>
> "Since, then, in fact, a grant is a contract executed, the obligation of which still continues, and since the Constitution uses the general term 'contract' without distinguishing between those which are executory and those which are executed, it must be construed to comprehend the latter as well as the former. A law annulling conveyances between individuals, and declaring that the grantors should stand seised of their former estates, notwithstanding those grants, would be as repugnant to the Constitution as a law discharging the vendors of property from the obligation of executing their contracts by conveyances. It would be strange if a contract to convey was secured by the Constitution, while an absolute conveyance remained unprotected."

pate in it, and had no notice of it," he wrote. "They were innocent." Marshall ruled that Fletcher had "vested rights" in the land that he had innocently purchased.

What **famous men represented Peck** before the U.S. Supreme Court?

The case was argued twice before the U.S. Supreme Court. In 1809, future president John Quincy Adams represented Peck and future U.S. Supreme Court justice Joseph Story represented Peck in the reargument.

What **famous man represented Fletcher in both arguments** before the Court?

Luther Martin, a Maryland delegate to the U.S. Constitutional Convention in 1787, represented Fletcher both times. Martin allegedly showed up drunk to the first argument and the Court had to adjourn until he became sober. Martin was Maryland's first attorney general and served as a defense counsel for Supreme Court justice Samuel Chase and Vice President Aaron Burr during their impeachment trials.

In what **Contract Clause case** did the U.S. Supreme Court **rule in favor of a college**?

The Marshall Court ruled in *Dartmouth College v. Woodward* (1819) that the state of New Hampshire violated the Constitution's Contract Clause by changing the status of Dartmouth College and altering the internal functioning of the college. The governor of the

Dartmouth College, subject of the Supreme Court trial *Dartmouth College v. Woodward,* in which the Court ruled that the state of New Hampshire violated the Constitution's Contract Clause by changing the school's status from a private college to a state-controlled public university. *Hulton Archive/Getty Images.*

state, William Plumer, was a diehard Democratic-Republican who wished to change the Federalist-dominated Board of Trustees. He sought to change the private college into a state-controlled public university. The college's trustees battled him in court. They argued that the school's 1769 charter from the king of England and subsequently the New Hampshire government (before Plumer took office) gave it vested rights to its private status.

Chief Justice John Marshall agreed, writing that the college's private charter was a contract protected by the Contract Clause. "The opinion of the Court, after mature deliberation, is that this is a contract, the obligation of which cannot be impaired without violating the Constitution of the United States."

What **attorney argued the case for Dartmouth College**?

Former U.S. representative Daniel Webster of New Hampshire (and future U.S. representative and senator from Massachusetts) successfully argued the case for Dartmouth College. He was particularly passionate in his argument, because he had graduated from Dartmouth in 1801.

The Supreme Court **upheld the National Bank** in what famous case?

The Marshall Court unanimously ruled in *McCullough v. Maryland* (1819) that Congress had the power to create a national bank and that the state of Maryland could not tax a

CourtSpeak: *Dartmouth College v. Woodward* Contract Clause Case (1819)

Chief Justice John Marshall (thoughts on a corporation): "A corporation is an artificial being, invisible, intangible, and existing only in contemplation of law. Being the mere creature of law, it possesses only those properties which the charter of its creation confers upon it, either expressly, or as incidental to its very existence. These are such as are supposed best calculated to effect the object for which it was created. Among the most important are immortality, and, if the expression may be allowed, individuality; properties, by which a perpetual succession of many persons are considered as the same, and may act as a single individual. They enable a corporation to manage its own affairs, and to hold property, without the perplexing intricacies, the hazardous and endless necessity, of perpetual conveyances for the purpose of transmitting it from hand to hand. It is chiefly for the purpose of clothing bodies of men, in succession, with these qualities and capacities, that corporations were invented, and are in use. By these means, a perpetual succession of individuals are capable of acting for the promotion of the particular object, like one immortal being. But this being does not share in the civil government of the country, unless that be the purpose for which it was created. Its immortality no more confers on it political power, or a political character, than immortality would confer such power or character on a natural person. It is no more a state instrument, than a natural person exercising the same powers would be."

branch of the National Bank located in Maryland. The state of Maryland levied a tax on all banks not chartered by the state. This tax applied only to the National Bank. James McCullough, the National Bank's cashier, refused to pay the state tax, leading to the lawsuit.

What did Chief Justice Marshall say about the **"Necessary and Proper" Clause of the Constitution**?

Marshall reasoned that Congress had the power to create the National Bank based on its powers under the "Necessary and Proper" Clause of the Constitution, which provides: "To make all Laws which shall be necessary and proper for carrying into Execution the foregoing Powers, and all other Powers vested by this Constitution in the Government of the United States, or in any Department or Officer thereof."

How **long were oral arguments** in the *McCullough* case?

Oral arguments in *McCullough v. Maryland* lasted nine days—between February 22 and March 3, 1819.

What **famous lawyers argued the** *McCullough* **case?**

Daniel Webster, who argued nearly 250 cases before the Court in his illustrious career, was one of the lawyers for the United States in the case. Luther Martin, whether drunk or sober, argued the case for the state of Maryland.

In what two decisions involving the **confiscation of Loyalist property** did the Supreme Court establish its authority over state courts?

One of the controversial issues arising with the early Marshall Court concerned the confiscation of property from those loyal to the British government—individuals often called Loyalists. At issue in *Fairfax's Devise v. Hunter's Lessee* was the legality of the state of Virginia's confiscation of the estate of the late Lord Thomas Fairfax, including a stretch of land called the Northern Neck of Virginia.

Lord Fairfax had instructed that, upon his death, the property would be bequeathed to his nephew, the Reverend Denny Martin. However, state officials confiscated the land and sold the land to investor David Hunter. The Virginia courts determined that the property belonged to Hunter, reasoning that its state laws dealing with the confiscation of property were constitutional. The U.S. Supreme Court reversed the Virginia court's decision, with Justice Joseph Story reasoning that the land should go to Fairfax's heirs. Story also noted that under the unpopular Jay Treaty with the British, the confiscation of Loyalist land was illegal.

On remand, the Virginia Supreme Court thumbed its nose at the U.S. Supreme Court, questioning the authority of the Court under Section 25 of the Judiciary Act of 1789, which gave the Court the jurisdiction to hear appeals from state courts. The Virginia Supreme Court jurists, such as the well-known Spencer Roane, criticized the Court's opinion. Roane believed that the federal government was encroaching upon the sovereign authority of the state of Virginia.

The Virginia Supreme Court essentially ignored the U.S. Supreme's Court commands, turning a title dispute over land into a major constitutional battle between a state supreme court and the U.S. Supreme Court. The case returned to the U.S. Supreme Court under the name *Martin v. Hunter's Lessee,* as the living heir of Lord

CourtSpeak: *Martin v. Hunter's Lessee* Property Confiscation Case (1816)

Justice Joseph Story (majority): "The constitution unavoidably deals in general language. It did not suit the purposes of the people, in framing this great charter of our liberties, to provide for minute specifications of its powers, or to declare the means by which those powers should be carried into execution. It was foreseen that this would be a perilous and difficult, if not an impracticable, task. The instrument was not intended to provide merely for the exigencies of a few years, but was to endure through a long lapse of ages, the events of which were locked up in the inscrutable purposes of Providence. It could not be foreseen what new changes and modifications of power might be indispensable to effectuate the general objects of the charter; and restrictions and specifications, which, at the present, might seem salutary, might, in the end, prove the overthrow of the system itself. Hence its powers are expressed in general terms, leaving to the legislature, from time to time, to adopt its own means to effectuate legitimate objects, and to mould and model the exercise of its powers, as its own wisdom, and the public interests, should require."

Fairfax was Denny Martin's younger brother, Thomas Bryan Martin, who was also a nephew of Lord Fairfax. In this decision, Justice Story rebuked the Virginia Supreme Court and affirmed the constitutionality of Section 25 of the Judiciary Act of 1789.

What exactly did the **Virginia Supreme Court say about what it perceived to be the U.S. Supreme Court's lack of jurisdiction**?

The Virginia Supreme Court wrote: "The court is unanimously of opinion that the appellate power of the supreme court of the United States does not extend to this court under a sound construction of the constitution of the United States; that so much of the 25th section of the act of congress, to establish the judicial courts of the United States, as extends the appellate jurisdiction of the supreme court to this court, is not in pursuance of the constitution of the United States. That the writ of error in this cause was improvidently allowed under the authority of that act; that the proceedings thereon in the supreme court were coram non judice [not in the presence of a judge] in relation to this court, and that obedience to its mandate be declined by the court."

How did Justice Story respond to this **flagrant disregard to U.S. Supreme Court authority**?

Story responded by writing an opinion that clearly established the power of the U.S. Supreme Court to review state supreme court decisions. He upheld the constitutional-

89

ity of Section 25 of the Judiciary Act of 1789, writing that "the appellate power of the United States must ... extend to state tribunals." Jean Edward Smith, in his biography of Chief Justice Marshall, entitled *John Marshall: Definer of a Nation,* writes: "*Martin v. Hunter's Lessee* provided the rationale for the supremacy of the Union."

Why did Chief Justice **Marshall not participate in *Martin v. Hunter's Lessee?***

Marshall did not participate because his brother James actually owned a portion of the land in question. James Marshall had purchased land directly from Denny Martin in the 1790s. Fearing a conflict of interest, Chief Justice Marshall recused himself.

In what famous decision did Marshall broadly define **Congress's interstate commerce powers**?

The Marshall Court broadly defined commerce in its 1824 decision in *Gibbons v. Ogden* in a battle of steamboat entrepreneurs. The state of New York granted an exclu-

Steamboats, similar to Robert Fulton's *Clermont,* shown here in the New York harbor, were the focus of the *Gibbons v. Ogden* interstate commerce case in 1824. *Getty Images.*

sive license to Robert Livingston and Robert Fulton, the inventor of the steamboat, to operate steamboats in the New York Harbor and the Hudson River. Livingston and Fulton then licensed Aaron Ogden to operate steamboats from New York City to Elizabethtown, New Jersey.

Ogden's former business partner, Thomas Gibbons, wanted to break up this monopoly. He had acquired a federal permit to operate steamboats between New York and New Jersey. Gibbons contended that because he had a federal permit, he did not need to obtain permission from the state of New York. Ogden sued Gibbons, arguing that Gibbons's activities were infringing on Ogden's exclusive monopoly from the state of New York. Ogden sought an injunction, ordering Gibbons to cease infringing on his exclusive privilege.

Gibbons, backed by the wealthy Cornelius Vanderbilt, fought back in court by hiring perhaps the best lawyer in America—Daniel Webster. The U.S. Supreme Court ruled that Ogden's exclusive monopoly was invalid because it infringed on Congress's Commerce Clause powers. Marshall broadly defined the powers of Congress's commerce powers, writing: "Commerce, undoubtedly, is traffic, but it is something more: it is intercourse. It describes the commercial intercourse between nations, and parts of nations, in all its branches, and is regulated by prescribing rules for carrying on that intercourse." The decision was important because it was an example of the U.S. Supreme Court broadly defining Congress's Commerce Clause powers.

CourtSpeak: *Gibbons v. Ogden* Interstate Commerce Case (1824)

Chief Justice John Marshall (on navigation as a form of commerce): "If commerce does not include navigation, the government of the Union has no direct power over that subject, and can make no law prescribing what shall constitute American vessels, or requiring that they shall be navigated by American seamen. Yet this power has been exercised from the commencement of the government, has been exercised with the consent of all, and has been understood by all to be a commercial regulation. All America understands, and has uniformly understood, the word 'commerce,' to comprehend navigation. It was so understood, and must have been so understood, when the constitution was framed. The power over commerce, including navigation, was one of the primary objects for which the people of America adopted their government, and must have been contemplated in forming it. The convention must have used the word in that sense, because all have understood it in that sense; and the attempt to restrict it comes too late."

Marshall (on the broad scope of Congress's commerce powers): "We are now arrived at the inquiry—What is this power? It is the power to regulate; that is, to prescribe the rule by which commerce is to be governed. This power, like all others vested in Congress, is complete in itself, may be exercised to its utmost extent, and acknowledges no limitations, other than are prescribed in the constitution. These are expressed in plain terms, and do not affect the questions which arise in this case, or which have been discussed at the bar. If, as has always been understood, the sovereignty of Congress, though limited to specified objects, is plenary as to those objects, the power over commerce with foreign nations, and among the several States, is vested in Congress as absolutely as it would be in a single government, having in its constitution the same restrictions on the exercise of the power as are found in the constitution of the United States. The wisdom and the discretion of Congress, their identity with the people, and the influence which their constituents possess at elections, are, in this, as in many other instances, as that, for example, of declaring war, the sole restraints on which they have relied, to secure them from its abuse. They are the restraints on which the people must often they solely, in all representative governments.

"The power of Congress, then, comprehends navigation, within the limits of every State in the Union; so far as that navigation may be, in any manner, connected with 'commerce with foreign nations, or among the several States, or with the Indian tribes.' It may, of consequence, pass the jurisdictional line of New York, and act upon the very waters to which the prohibition now under consideration applies."

What was the **impact of the *Gibbons v. Ogden* decision**?

The decision was significant because it further established the power of the federal government over the states. It also spurred the national economy by ensuring that Congress had broad Commerce Clause powers and by eliminating certain state-centered monopolies that negatively impacted interstate commerce.

How personal was the **conflict between Gibbons and Ogden**?

The two men and former partners had a heated personal conflict. Gibbons went so far as to challenge Ogden to a duel. Ogden refused and later sued Gibbons for trespassing, winning a court judgment of $5,000.

What **political positions did Ogden hold**?

Ogden had a long and illustrious career in politics. He served as governor of New Jersey and as a U.S. senator. He also was a presidential elector in the 1796 election.

Besides both being involved in the steamboat business, what **occupation did Gibbons and Odgen share**?

Both Ogden and Gibbons were trained lawyers but only dabbled in the practice of law.

What famous case involving the **selling of lottery tickets** established the power of federal courts to review state laws?

The case that resolved an important question of the power and jurisdiction of federal courts was *Cohens v. Virginia* (1821), a case involving the selling of lottery tickets. Jacob Cohen started Cohen's Lottery and Exchange Office of Baltimore and brothers Philip and Mendes Cohen managed the Norfolk branch. The Cohen brothers sold national lottery tickets, an activity approved by the federal government and administered by officials from the District of Columbia.

The problem was that the state of Virginia wanted to promote its own lottery. The state passed a law in 1820 that prohibited the sale of out-of-state lottery tickets. State officials charged the Cohens with violating this law because they were selling District of Columbia lottery tickets. While the Cohens were only fined $100, the case was important to them because it affected the vitality of their business. The case is important historically because it involved an important question of federal judicial power.

Convicted in a local state court, the Cohens appealed to the U.S. Supreme Court, contending that the national lottery was a federal institution that the states could not regulate. The state of Virginia argued that the U.S. Supreme Court did not have jurisdiction to hear an appeal in this state court conviction under a state law. The state of

CourtSpeak: Supremacy of the Federal Judiciary in *Cohens v. Virginia* (1821)

Chief Justice John Marshall: "The constitution and laws of a state so far as they are repugnant to the constitution and laws of the United States, are absolutely void. These States are constituent parts of the United States. They are members of one great empire—for some purposes sovereign, for some purposes subordinate. In a government so constituted, is it unreasonable that the judicial power should be competent to give efficacy to the constitutional laws of the legislature? That department can decide on the validity of the Constitution or law of a State, if it be repugnant to the Constitution or to a law of the United States. Is it unreasonable that it should also be empowered to decide on the judgment of a State tribunal enforcing such unconstitutional law? Is it so very unreasonable as to furnish a justification for controlling the words of the Constitution?

"We think it is not. We think that, in a government acknowledgedly supreme, with respect to objects of vital interest to the nation, there is nothing inconsistent with sound reason, nothing incompatible with the nature of government, in making all its departments supreme so far as respects those objects and so far as is necessary to their attainment. The exercise of the appellate power over those judgments of the State tribunals which may contravene the Constitution or laws of the United States is, we believe, essential to the attainment of those objects."

Virginia also argued that the Supreme Court could not hear the case because of the Eleventh Amendment, which generally provides for state immunity from lawsuits by private individuals. Chief Justice John Marshall's opinion established the supremacy of the federal judiciary. He ruled that the Eleventh Amendment had no application and that Section 25 of the Judiciary Act of 1789 gave the U.S. Supreme Court the jurisdiction to review state laws alleged to be repugnant to the U.S. Constitution.

In what decision did the Marshall Court rule that the **president has the ultimate authority to call out the militia** and such orders cannot be reviewed by the judiciary?

The Marshall Court ruled unanimously in *Martin v. Mott* (1827) that Jacob Mott could not challenge his punishment for a court martial for refusing to join the militia when called during the War of 1812. Mott had been fined $96 and faced a one-year imprisonment. The Court, in an opinion written by Justice Joseph Story, said there could be no judicial review of the decision to call out the militia and determine whether it was the proper course of action. "While subordinate officers or soldiers are pausing to consider whether they ought to obey, or are scrupulously weighing the evidence of the facts

> **CourtSpeak: *Martin v. Mott***
> **Presidential Authority over Militia Case (1827)**
>
> Justice Joseph Story (unanimous): "Is the President the sole and exclusive judge whether the exigency has arisen, or is it to be considered as an open question, upon which every officer to whom the orders of the President are addressed, may decide for himself, and equally open to be contested by every militia-man who shall refuse to obey the orders of the President? We are all of opinion, that the authority to decide whether the exigency has arisen, belongs exclusively to the President, and that his decision is conclusive upon all other persons. We think that this construction necessarily results from the nature of the power itself, and from the manifest object contemplated by the act of Congress."

upon which the commander in chief exercises the right to demand their services, the hostile enterprise may be accomplished without the means of resistance," Story wrote.

In what decision did the Marshall Court rule that **a state can release debtors from prison**?

The Marshall Court ruled in *Mason v. Haile* (1827) that the state of Rhode Island constitutionally could prohibit debtors from being imprisoned without violating the U.S. Constitution. Writing for the majority of the Court, Justice Smith Thompson reasoned that "we are not aware that such a power in the States has ever been questioned." He stated that release debtors do "not take away the entire remedy, but only so far as imprisonment forms a part of such remedy."

Justice Bushrod Washington filed the Court's lone dissent. He believed the case was controlled by *Sturges v. Crowninshield* (1819) in which the Court ruled that a state could not relieve a debtor from bankruptcy if the original contract was made before the passage of the bankruptcy law. "If the principle which governs the two cases can be reconciled with each other, the course of reasoning by which it is to be effected is quite too subtle for my mind to comprehend it," Washington wrote frankly.

In what decision did the Marshall Court reject a federal common-law claim of **seditious libel**?

The Marshall Court ruled in *United States v. Hudson and Goodwin* (1812) that the federal courts cannot exercise jurisdiction in a common-law criminal seditious libel case. The case arose after the federal government charged Barzillai Hudson and George Goodwin for publishing in the *Connecticut Currant* that the president and the U.S. Congress gave French emperor Napoleon Bonaparte $2 million to make a treaty with Spain. Justice William John-

President Andrew Jackson, above, disagreed with the Marshall Court's ruling in *Worcester v. Georgia,* which favored the Cherokee Nation. Jackson eventually instituted a policy that forced the Cherokee to leave their land and move west in what became known as the "Trail of Tears." *Hulton Archive/Getty Images.*

son wrote that "the legislative authority of the Union must first make an act a crime, affix a punishment for it, and declare the Court that shall have jurisdiction of the offence."

What Marshall Court **decision did President Andrew Jackson openly defy**?

The Marshall Court ruled 5–1 in *Worcester v. Georgia* (1831) that the state of Georgia could not punish Samuel Worcester, a congregational minister, for living on Cherokee lands. The state of Georgia had passed a law requiring any white person to secure a license before living on Cherokee land. The Court ruled that this law violated the sovereign authority of the Cherokee nation.

President Andrew Jackson reportedly said: "John Marshall has made his decision; now let him enforce it." Jackson instituted a policy of uprooting the Cherokee and forcing them west to a reservation. This travel was called the "Trail of Tears."

What was the only **major constitutional decision in which Chief Justice Marshall was on the dissenting side**?

The only major decision that Chief Justice Marshall found himself in dissent was the Court's 1827 in *Ogden v. Saunders.* The Court was asked to decide whether a state bankruptcy law violated the Contract Clause for contracts that were entered after the passage of the law. The Court ruled 4–3 that state bankruptcy laws were constitutional as applied to contracts passed after the legislation. The case involved George Ogden, a New Yorker, who sought to discharge his debt to John Saunders of Kentucky. The

> ## CourtSpeak: *Worcester v. Georgia*
> ## Cherokee Sovereign Authority Case (1831)
>
> Chief Justice John Marshall (majority): "The Cherokee Nation, then, is a distinct community, occupying its own territory, with boundaries accurately described, in which the laws of Georgia can have no force, and which the citizens of Georgia have no right to enter but with the assent of the Cherokees themselves or in conformity with treaties and with the acts of Congress. The whole intercourse between the United States and this nation is, by our Constitution and laws, vested in the government of the United States."

majority of four believed that a state had the power to pass a bankruptcy law and that such a law did not violate the Contract Clause for contracts passed after the bankruptcy law. All four justices in the majority wrote separate opinions.

In what decision did the Marshall Court refuse to apply the **Fifth Amendment protection of just compensation to the states**?

The Marshall Court ruled in *Barron v. Baltimore* (1833) that the Fifth Amendment only protected individuals from the federal government, not state and local governments. The case arose after John Barron claimed that excavating by the city had destroyed his family's wharf. Barron sued in state court, claiming that the city should pay him for the damage. He argued that he was protected by the Fifth Amendment Clause, which provides that "private property [shall not] be taken, without just compensation." A jury awarded him $4,500 but the state supreme court reversed.

Barron appealed to the U.S. Supreme Court, where Chief Justice Marshall ruled that the Fifth Amendment did not extend to the states. He wrote that if the Founders had wanted the Bill of Rights to extend to the states, "they would have declared this purpose in plain and intelligible language." The Fifth Amendment right to just compensation, like the vast majority of other provisions in the Bill of Rights, was eventually extended to apply to the states by the adoption of the Fourteenth Amendment in 1868 and a series of later U.S. Supreme Court decisions. The Fourteenth Amendment contains the Due Process Clause, which provides that "no state shall deny any person life, liberty or property without due process of law." Thus, Barron would have a Fifth Amendment claim today but he did not in 1833 when there was no Fourteenth Amendment.

Who was the **attorney for the city of Baltimore**?

Roger B. Taney represented the city of Baltimore in the *Barron* case. A few years later, Taney would succeed Marshall as chief justice of the U.S. Supreme Court.

CourtSpeak: *Ogden v. Saunders*
Contract Clause and Bankruptcy Case (1827)

Justice Bushrod Washington (majority): "It is thus most apparent, that, which ever way we turn, whether to laws affecting the validity, construction, or discharges of contracts, or the evidence or remedy to be employed in enforcing them, we are met by this overruling and admitted distinction, between those which operate retrospectively, and those which operate prospectively. In all of them, the law is pronounced to be void in the first class of cases, and not so in the second."

Justice William Johnson (majority): "The right, then, of the creditor, to the aid of the public arm for the recovery of contracts, is not absolute and unlimited, but may be modified by the necessities or policy of societies. And this, together with the contract itself, must be taken by the individual, subject to such restrictions and conditions as are imposed by the laws of the country. The right to pass bankrupt laws is asserted by every civilized nation in the world."

Justice Smith Thompson (majority): "It is admitted, and has so been decided by this Court, that a State law, discharging insolvent debtors from their contracts, entered into antecedent to the passing of the law, falls within this clause in the constitution, and is void. In the case now before the Court, the contract was made subsequent to the passage of the law; and this, it is believed, forms a solid ground of distinction, whether tested by the letter, or the spirit and policy of the prohibition. It was not denied on the argument, and, I presume, cannot be, but that a law may be void in part and good in part; or, in other words, that it may be void, so far as it has a retrospective application to past contracts, and valid, as applied prospectively to future contracts."

Justice Robert Trimble (majority): "As, in a state of nature, the natural obligation of a contract consists in the right and potential capacity of the individual to take, or enforce the delivery of the thing due to him by the contract, or its equivalent; so, in the social state, the obligation of a contract consists in the efficacy of the civil law, which attaches to the contract, and enforces its performance, or gives an equivalent in lieu of performance. From these principles it seems to result as a necessary corollary, that the obligation of a contract made within a sovereign State, must be precisely that allowed by the law of the State, and none other."

Chief Justice John Marshall (dissenting): "If one law enters into all subsequent contracts, so does every other law which relates to the subject. A legislative act, then, declaring that all contracts should be subject to legislative control, and should be discharged as the legislature might prescribe, would become a component part of every contract, and be one of its conditions."

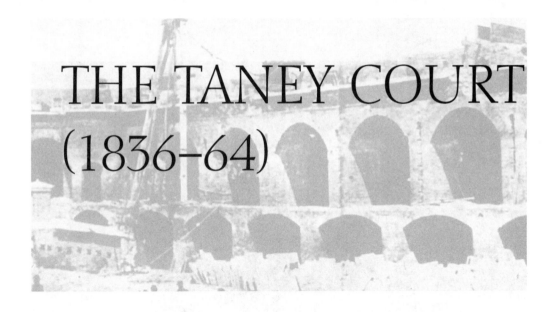

THE TANEY COURT (1836–64)

How many and which **justices served on the Taney Court**?

Twenty justices served on the Taney Court, including Chief Justice Roger Taney and Justices Joseph Story, Smith Thompson, John McLean, Henry Baldwin, James M. Wayne, Philip Barbour, John Catron, John McKinley, Peter Daniel, Samuel Nelson, Levi Woodbury, Robert C. Grier, Benjamin Curtis, John Campbell, Nathan Clifford, Noah H. Swayne, Samuel F. Miller, David Davis, and Stephen Field.

What **government positions did Chief Justice Taney hold** before coming to the Court?

He served in the Maryland House of Delegates and the Maryland Senate. Later, he held the positions of Maryland attorney general, U.S. attorney general, and U.S. secretary of the treasury.

In what position did the **Senate reject Taney**?

When Congress was in recess in September 1833, President Andrew Jackson appointed Taney as U.S. secretary of the Treasury. Nine months later, after disagreements over banking issues, the U.S. Senate rejected his appointment and Taney was out of office. Jackson then appointed Taney to replace Justice Gabriel Duvall but a Senate vote was postponed. It served to Taney's advantage, however, because when Chief Justice John Marshall died, President Jackson then nominated Taney to fill the position of chief justice. The Senate confirmed Taney by a 29–15 vote.

What **famous person was related** to Taney?

Attorney Francis Scott Key, author of the "Star Spangled Banner," was the brother of Taney's wife, Anne Phoebe Carlton Key.

U.S. Supreme Court chief justice Roger Taney. *Hulton Archive/Getty Images.*

Which justice on the Taney Court gave a copy of his **dissenting opinion to a newspaper before official publication**?

Justice Benjamin Curtis provided a Boston newspaper with a copy of his dissenting opinion in the *Dred Scott* case before it was officially released. Curtis's action greatly upset Chief Justice Taney.

Which member of the Taney Court was **a Quaker**?

Justice Noah Swayne, nominated by President Abraham Lincoln in 1862, was born to Quaker parents in Virginia. He moved to the free state of Ohio in large part because he detested the practice of slavery. Swayne was the only Quaker to ever serve on the U.S. Supreme Court.

Which two former justices on the Taney Court **returned to the Supreme Court several times to argue cases**?

Benjamin Curtis and John Campbell both left the Court and established very successful law practices. On numerous occasions, they presented arguments before the U.S. Supreme Court. Curtis argued more than fifty cases before the U.S. Supreme after he resigned in 1857. Some of the more notable cases he argued included *Paul v. Virginia* (1869), *Hepburn v. Griswold* (1870), and *The Potomac* (1869). He also served as a key member of President Andrew Johnson's defense team during his impeachment trial in the Senate in 1868.

Campbell resigned from the Court in 1861 after his home state of Alabama seceded from the Union. He rebounded personally to establish a very successful law practice in his own right. He argued a number of times before the U.S. Supreme Court, in such trials as the Slaughterhouse Cases (1873), *Chaffraix v. Shiff* (1875), and *Ketchum v. Duncan* (1877).

Which member of the Taney Court later **joined the Confederate government**?

The aforementioned Justice John Campbell joined the Confederate government as assistant secretary of war. He was in charge of enlisting men to fight in the war. After the war, Campbell was imprisoned for four months in Fort Pulaski, Georgia. President Andrew Johnson ordered his release, but Campbell was destitute upon his release. Campbell traveled to New Orleans and rebounded by establishing a very successful law practice. He once again became one of the country's leading lawyers, arguing regularly before the U.S. Supreme Court.

Which justice on the Taney Court was **disowned by his home state during the Civil War**?

Justice James Wayne, nominated by President Andrew Jackson in 1835, refused to leave the bench when the South and his home state of Georgia seceded from the Union. The

Several years before he became a U.S. Supreme Court justice, John A. Campbell served as assistant secretary of war for the Confederate government. *Brady-Handy Photographic Collection/Library of*

Georgia press and others harshly criticized Wayne for his refusal to resign from the Court, as Justice John Campbell, an Alabama native, had done. Wayne not only refused to resign, but actually ruled in favor of President Lincoln's blockading of Confederate city ports in the *Prize Cases*.

Which member of the Taney Court was a **former high school teacher**?

Justice Robert Cooper Grier, nominated by President James K. Polk in 1846, taught Latin and Greek at his father's school, Northumberland Academy, in his home state of Pennsylvania. When his father died, Grier succeeded him as the school's headmaster before moving on to a career in law.

DECISIONS

In what infamous decision did the Supreme Court **regard blacks as mere slaves**?

The Taney Court issued the most criticized decision in U.S. Supreme Court history when it ruled in *Scott v. Sandford* (1857) that former slave Dred Scott was not free even when he was residing in free territory. Taney referred to African Americans as "that unfortunate race" who were "so far inferior, that they had no rights which the white man was bound to respect." Some historians have even cited the decision as one of the catalysts for the horrific Civil War.

Who was **Dred Scott**?

Dred Scott was a slave owned by Peter Blow in Alabama. Scott moved with Blow when he moved to Missouri, another state that authorized slavery. After Blow died, his executor sold Scott to Dr. John Emerson, a St. Louis–based army doctor. Emerson then moved his family—and Scott—to Illinois, which was a free state. Emerson eventually moved back to St. Louis and died. Scott and his wife Harriet filed a lawsuit in Missouri courts, arguing that they were freed when Emerson had moved to the free state of Illinois. Emerson's widow and her brother, John Sanford (court records misspelled his name as Sandford), contested Scott's suit, leading to *Scott v. Sandford* case.

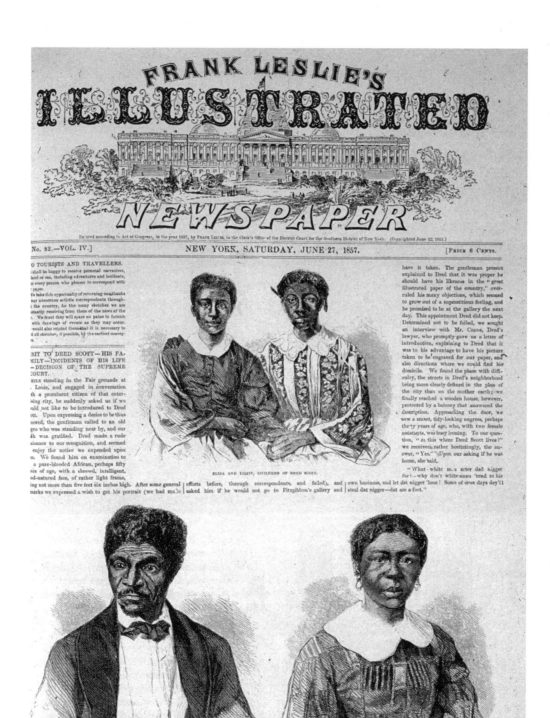

The front page of *Frank Leslie's Illustrated Newspaper* shows coverage of the *Dred Scott* case. The U.S. Supreme Court ruled that a slave entering a non-slave state could not gain freedom. *Hulton Archive/Getty Images.*

Why did many believe that **Dred Scott had a valid claim**?

Scott believed he had a valid claim because some courts had adhered to the doctrine of "once free, always free." This meant that if a slave reached free territory legally, then he or she was free because slavery was outlawed in those jurisdictions. The Missouri courts and the U.S. Supreme Court did not accept that argument, however.

How did the U.S. Supreme Court reject the Declaration of Independence's **"All men are created equal" principle for Scott**?

Chief Justice Roger Taney reasoned that it was clear that the Founders did not believe this applied to members of the African race when they wrote the Declaration of Independence. Taney wrote that "it is too clear for dispute, that the enslaved African race were not intended to be included, and formed no part of the people who framed and adopted this declaration."

Slaves reach freedom via the so-called Underground Railroad. An operator of the railroad, who harbored a slave, was sued by a slaveowner who claimed that the Fugitive Slave Act of 1793 was constitutional. In *Jones v. Van Zandt*, the U.S. Supreme Court agreed. *Charles H. Phillips/Time & Life Pictures/Getty Images.*

What about the **Missouri Compromise of 1820,** which provided that there could be no slavery in many states?

Chief Justice Taney actually ruled that this law was unconstitutional, writing: "It is the opinion of the court that the act of Congress which prohibited a citizen from holding and owning property of this kind in the territory of the United States north of the line therein mentioned, is not warranted by the Constitution."

Which **two justices dissented in the *Scott* case?**

Justices John McLean and Benjamin Curtis were the Court's only two dissenters. Both believed that the majority ignored the reality that African Americans were free men in many states of the Union and that Dred Scott was free after living in Illinois for years.

Which justice was so **upset by the *Scott* case that he resigned?**

Curtis was so upset by the Court's decision in the *Dred Scott* case that he resigned from the bench shortly thereafter. The *Scott* decision was issued on March 6, 1857; Curtis left on September 30.

The Taney Court **upheld the Fugitive Slave Act of 1793** in what decision?

The Taney Court unanimously ruled in *Jones v. Van Zandt* (1847) that the Fugitive Slave Act of 1793 was constitutional. John Van Zandt, an operator of the so-called

CourtSpeak: *Jones v. Van Zandt* (1847) Slavery Case

Justice Levi Woodbury (unanimous): "Before concluding, it may be expected by the defendant that some notice should be taken of the argument, urging on us a disregard of the constitution and the act of Congress in respect to this subject, on account of the supposed inexpediency and invalidity of all laws recognizing slavery or any right of property in man. But that is a political question, settled by each State for itself; and the federal power over it is limited and regulated by the people of the States in the constitution itself, as one of its sacred compromises, and which we possess no authority as a judicial body to modify or overrule. Whatever may be the theoretical opinions of any as to the expediency of some of those compromises, or of the right of property in persons which they recognize, this court has no alternative, while they exist, but to stand by the constitution and laws with fidelity to their duties and their oaths. Their path is a strait and narrow one, to go where that constitution and the laws lead, and not to break both, by travelling without or beyond them."

Underground Railroad, was sued by Kentucky slaveowner Wharton Jones for harboring a male slave named Andrew. The Taney Court, in an opinion written by Justice Levi Woodbury, upheld the constitutionality of the law. The Court determined that slavery was a "political question settled by each State for itself."

In what decision did the Court rule that **Ohio did not have to release a suspected criminal to Kentucky**?

The Taney Court unanimously ruled in *Kentucky v. Dennison* (1861) that the governor of Ohio, William Dennison, did not have to release an Ohio man who helped a female slave escape from Kentucky to Ohio. Willis Lago, a free African American man, helped a female slave named Charlotte escape from the slave state of Kentucky to the free state of Ohio.

Kentucky governor Beriah Magoffin asked Ohio governor Salmon Chase, the future chief justice of the U.S. Supreme Court, to return Lago for prosecution. Chase, an abolitionist, refused to comply. When Chase left office, his successor, Dennison, also refused to comply. Magoffin then sued in the U.S. Supreme Court for a court order forcing Ohio to comply with the extradition order. The U.S. Supreme Court had original jurisdiction to hear the case because it was a case between two states, Kentucky and Ohio.

The U.S. Supreme Court ruled that while Dennison may have a moral duty to obey the law, the Court could not enforce him to comply. Taney wrote that Dennison should comply with the order but "if the Governor of Ohio refuses to discharge this duty, there is no power delegated to the General Government, either through the Judicial Department or any other department, to use any coercive means to compel him."

In what celebrated decision did the Taney Court **affirm the release of Africans enslaved by Spaniards**?

In *The Amistad* (1841), the U.S. Supreme Court affirmed a lower court judgment that forty-three African slaves who washed ashore in Connecticut on the Spanish ship *The Amistad* should be returned to their native land free from the shackles of slavery by their Spanish captors.

The celebrated case occurred when the Spanish ship sailed from Havana, Cuba, to Porte Principe, another town in Cuba. The Africans revolted and killed the ship's captain, Ramon Ferrer and a few other members of the crew. Two crew members, Jose Ruiz and Pedro Montes, momentarily escaped but were captured. The Africans did not kill Ruiz and Montes. Apparently, the two Spaniards promised to sail the ship back to Africa, but instead headed for America. The ship was discovered by Lieutenant Thomas Gedney of the U.S. Coast Guard and by sea captains Henry Green and Peletiah Fordham.

Ruiz and Montes told authorities of the African mutiny, which led to the imprisonment of the Africans. The Spanish men, Gedney, Green, and Fordham all filed claims for either all or part of the ship and its cargo's value. Meanwhile, President Martin Van Buren pressured the U.S. attorney in Connecticut to file a claim on behalf of the Spanish government. The Africans—the so-called Amistads—were placed on trial for murder.

The civil claims took predominance as the courts had to sort out whether the slaves were property and if so, who owned them. A federal trial court judge determined that the Amistads were free men who were unlawfully transported by the Spanish and should be returned to their native land. The United States appealed the decision to Circuit Judge Smith Thompson, who affirmed. Then, the United States appealed to the U.S. Supreme Court.

What was the **ruling in *The Amistad* case**?

In a unanimous ruling, the U.S. Supreme Court determined in an opinion written by Justice Joseph Story that "these negroes never were the lawful slaves of Ruiz or Montes, or of any other Spanish subjects." The government attorney argued that the Amistads should still be returned to Spain pursuant to the obligations of a treaty between the two nations. Story rejected that argument, noting that the Africans were aboard the ship on a fraud in violation of even Spanish law. He added that the Africans have just as much rights as the Spanish subjects.

What **attorneys argued on behalf of the Amistads** before the U.S. Supreme Court?

The Amistads were represented by Roger Baldwin, the future governor of Connecticut, and John Quincy Adams, the former president of the United States.

107

A newspaper clipping shows the death of *Amistad* captain Ferrer. The *Amistad* was the source of a U.S. Supreme Court trial involving African slaves held captive by the crew of a Spanish ship. *Hulton Archive/Getty Images.*

Who was the **only justice to dissent in *The Amistad* case**?

The erratic and mentally unstable Henry Baldwin dissented but did not write an opinion to provide his rationale.

In what decision did the Taney Court **uphold the Fugitive Slave Act of 1793**?

The U.S. Supreme Court upheld the constitutionality of the federal Fugitive Slave Act of 1793 in *Prigg v. Pennsylvania* (1842), while striking down a Pennsylvania state "personal liberty" law that conflicted with the Fugitive Slave law. The case involved professional slavecatcher Edward Prigg, who tracked down former slave Margaret Morgan and returned her to her Maryland owner, Margaret Ashmore.

Prigg returned Morgan to Maryland without obtaining the required certificate under federal law because a Pennsylvania state judge refused to issue him one. Pennsylvania authorities then charged Prigg with kidnapping. The two states fast-tracked the litigation and it reached the U.S. Supreme Court.

In his opinion, Justice Story wrote: "Upon these grounds, we are of opinion, that the act of Pennsylvania upon which this indictment is founded, is unconstitutional and void. It purports to punish as a public offence against that state, the very act of seizing and removing a slave, by his master, which the constitution of the United States was designed to justify and uphold."

CourtSpeak: *The Amistad* Slavery Case (1841)

Justice Joseph Story (majority): "It is also a most important consideration in the present case, which ought not to be lost sight of, that, supposing these African negroes not to be slaves, but kidnapped, and free negroes, the treaty with Spain cannot be obligatory upon them; and the United States are bound to respect their rights as much as those of Spanish subjects. The conflict of rights between the parties under such circumstances, becomes positive and inevitable, and must be decided upon the eternal principles of justice and international law …. The treaty with Spain never could have intended to take away the equal rights of all foreigners of the protection given them by other treaties, or by the general law of nations. Upon the merits of the case, then, there does not seem to us to be any ground for doubt, that these negroes ought to be deemed free; and that the Spanish treaty interposes no obstacle to the just assertion of their rights."

In what decision did the Taney Court **strike down a provision in a state constitution**?

The Taney Court ruled 6–3 in *Dodge v. Woolsey* (1856) that the provision of the Ohio Constitution that increased taxes on banks violated the Contract Clause of the U.S. Constitution, which provides: "No State shall … pass any … Law impairing the Obligation of Contracts." The Court majority, in an opinion written by Justice James Wayne, reasoned that the Ohio Constitutional provision in 1851 and subsequent statute in 1853 impaired the contractual obligation that the state had with banks pursuant to an 1845 law that provided for a lesser tax.

In other words, the Court determined that the state of Ohio impaired its contractual obligation with banks in 1845 by passing a new law that raised taxes. Justice John Campbell dissented, arguing that the Court had invaded the province of state governments.

In what case did the Taney Court have to **decide between two bridge-builders**?

The Taney Court ruled 4–3 in *Charles River Bridge v. Warren Bridge* (1837) that the Massachusetts legislature could contract with the Warren Bridge Company to build a new bridge between Boston and Charlestown. The Warren Bridge businessmen convinced the legislature it would be a better deal for the public and the state, as they would not charge tolls after their construction costs were recovered. The problem was that years earlier the state legislature had granted a charter to the Charles River Bridge Company for the construction of the existing Charles River Bridge between the two cities. The Charles River Bridge officials did not want the construction of a new bridge to compete with them, as the tolls they had received over the years had proven quite profitable.

CourtSpeak: *Charles River Bridge v. Warren Bridge* Construction Case (1837)

Chief Justice Roger Taney (majority): "The object and the end of all government is, to promote the happiness and prosperity of the community by which it is established; and it can never be assumed, that the government intended to diminish its power of accomplishing the end for which it was created; and in a country like ours, free, active and enterprising, continually advancing in numbers and wealth, new channels of communication are daily found necessary both for travel and trade; and are essential to the comfort, convenience and prosperity of the people. A state ought never to be presumed to surrender this power."

Justice Joseph Story (dissenting): "No man will hazard his capital in any enterprise, in which, if there be a loss, it must be borne exclusively by himself; and if there be success, he has not the slightest security of enjoying the rewards of that success, for a single moment. If the government means to invite its citizens to enlarge the public comforts and conveniences, to establish bridges, or turnpikes, or canals, or railroads, there must be some pledge, that the property will be safe; that the enjoyment will be co-extensive with the grant; and that success will not be the signal of a general combination to overthrow its rights and to take away its profits. The very agitation of a question of this sort is sufficient to alarm every stockholder in every public enterprise of this sort, throughout the whole country."

The Charles River Bridge Company sued, seeking an injunction to prevent the building of a new bridge by the Warren Bridge Company. The Charles River Bridge Company argued that the state legislature violated the Contract Clause by impairing the original contract it had with the state. However, the Warren Bridge Company countered that the important public interests at stake trumped whatever private property rights Charles River Bridge had. The majority of the Court was concerned that if the monopoly was upheld, then improvements in transportation that would benefit the public at large could only take place at the whim of the private property owner.

The Taney Court ruled 4–3 in favor of the new bridge and the Warren Bridge Company. Chief Justice Taney reasoned that exclusive grants must be construed narrowly and must take into account the underlying public interests. "In charters of this description, no rights are taken from the public, or given to the corporation, beyond those which the words of the charter, by their natural and proper construction, purport to convey."

What was the **significance of the bridge-builders decision**?

The chief importance of the decision was that the Supreme Court was now considering the public interest as paramount when reviewing Contract Clause claims. The Court established that the state government has a police power to pass legislation that furthers the interests of the public. Some allege the decision actually helped business by promoting competition and innovation.

Who were the **attorneys who argued the case**?

The case was argued by some of the country's finest lawyers. Daniel Webster argued on behalf of the Charles River Bridge Company, while Simon Greenleaf and John Davis represented the Warren Bridge Company.

What other Taney Court decision involved the **height of a bridge**?

The Taney Court ruled 7–2 in *Pennsylvania v. Wheeling and Belmont Bridge Co.* (1852) that the state of Pennsylvania had a valid claim against a company's bridge that was built so low that it negatively impacted interstate commerce. The Virginia legislature chartered the company to build the Wheeling Bridge across the Ohio River into Pennsylvania. The Court ruled that it impeded interstate commerce and ordered the bridge either removed or raised.

What **happened to the bridge**?

Congress did not agree with the Court's decision and subsequently passed a federal law mandating that the original height of the bridge was proper. The law read: "That the bridges across the Ohio River at Wheeling, in the State of Virginia, and at Bridgeport, in the State of Ohio, abutting on Zane's Island, in said river, are hereby declared to be lawful structures in their present positions and elevations, and shall be so held and taken to be any thing in the law or laws of the United States to the contrary notwithstanding." It was the first time that Congress had legislatively overruled a Supreme Court decision. The case went back up to the U.S. Supreme Court, which ruled the bridge did not impede interstate commerce.

In what decision did the Taney Court say that a **corporation has diversity jurisdiction**?

The Taney Court ruled unanimously in *Louisville Railroad Co. v. Letson* (1844) that a New York citizen could sue in federal court a railroad corporation that was chartered in South Carolina because the federal court had diversity jurisdiction, which permits a federal court to entertain suits between parties (litigants) from different states. The Court determined that the railroad company was deemed to be a citizen in the state in

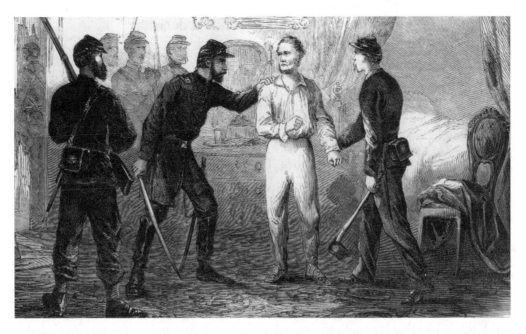

Civil War critic and former U.S. representative Clement Vallandigham is arrested in his Dayton, Ohio, home on May 5, 1863, for declaring sympathy for the enemy. In *Ex Parte Vallandigham,* the U.S. Supreme Court ruled that it could not review a military court decision. *Hulton Archive/Getty Images.*

which it was chartered. The decision made it easier for corporations to sue and be sued in the federal courts.

What were the **License Cases**?

The License Cases were a trio of cases—*Thurlow v. Massachusetts, Fletcher v. Rhode Island,* and *Peirce v. New Hampshire*—in which the Taney Court unanimously upheld state laws that taxed alcoholic beverages imported into the state. The laws were designed to favor local retailers. The local retailers convinced the state legislatures that they needed an advantage over out-of-state merchants. Individuals who sold out-of-state beverages without a license challenged the constitutionality of the state laws, arguing that the laws infringed on the federal government's control of interstate commerce. Instead, the justices determined that the statutes were justified by the state's police powers. "Every State … may regulate its own internal traffic, according to its own judgment and upon its own views of the interest and well-being of its citizens," Chief Justice Taney wrote.

In what case did the Taney Court rule it **could not review a military court decision**?

The Taney Court ruled that it could not conduct a habeas corpus review of the military trial of outspoken Civil War critic and former U.S. representative Clement Val-

Fort Sumter flies under a Confederate flag on April 4, 1861. President Abraham Lincoln issued an order to block Confederate ports despite the lack of a formal declaration of war by Congress. The U.S. Supreme Court ruled in *The Prize Cases* that the president had the constitutional authority to do that. *Hulton Archive/Getty Images.*

landigham of Ohio in *Ex Parte Vallandigham* (1864). In the spring of 1863, General Ambrose Burnside, without consulting President Abraham Lincoln, had arrested Vallandigham for publicly expressing sympathies for the enemy. At a speech in Mount Vernon, Ohio, Vallandigham said that "the present war was a wicked, cruel, and unnecessary war, one not waged for the preservation of the Union, but for the purpose of crushing out liberty and to erect a despotism."

In May 1863, military officials tried and convicted Vallandigham. Instead of throwing him in jail, President Lincoln ordered him moved to Murfreesboro, Tennessee, in the Confederacy. Vallandigham appealed to the U.S. Supreme Court; it ruled in February 1864 that it did not have jurisdiction to entertain a review of the military court ruling. "The Supreme Court of the United States has no power to review by certiorari the proceedings of a military commission ordered by a general officer of the United States Army, commanding a military department," Justice James Wayne wrote for the Court.

What happened to **Vallandigham after his banishment to the South**?

The Confederates treated him well; he wound up in Bermuda, then sailed to Canada. Having been nominated in July 1863 for governor of Ohio, he ran in absentia but   113

Justice Robert Grier (majority): "This greatest of civil wars was not gradually developed by popular commotion, tumultuous assemblies, or local unorganized insurrections. However long may have been its previous conception, it nevertheless sprung forth suddenly from the parent brain, a Minerva in the full panoply of war. The President was bound to meet it in the shape it presented itself, without waiting for Congress to baptize it with a name; and no name given to it by him or them could change the fact."

Justice Samuel Nelson (dissenting): "Now, in one sense, no doubt this is war, and may be a war of the most extensive and threatening dimensions and effects, but it is a statement simply of its existence in a material sense, and has no relevancy or weight when the question is what constitutes war in a legal sense, in the sense of the law of nations, and of the Constitution of the United States? For it must be a war in this sense to attach to it all the consequences that belong to belligerent rights...

"Congress alone can determine whether war exists or should be declared; and until they have acted, no citizen of the State can be punished in his person or property, unless he has committed some offence against a law of Congress passed before the act was committed, which made it a crime, and defined the punishment. The penalty of confiscation for the acts of others with which he had no concern cannot lawfully be inflicted."

lost. He returned to Ohio in 1864 where many cheered him as a hero. Not wanting to create a martyr, Lincoln ignored him and did not arrest him. Vallandigham also ran unsuccessfully for the U.S. Senate in 1869 and then had great success as a trial lawyer. Unfortunately, as an attorney for the defendant in a murder trial, Vallandigham accidentally shot himself to death while demonstrating how the victim had been shot.

In what famous case did the Court narrowly uphold the **president's power to order a blockade**?

The U.S. Supreme Court ruled 5–4 in *The Prize Cases* (1863) that President Lincoln had the constitutional authority to block Confederate ports even though Congress had not yet made a formal declaration of war. Lincoln issued the order in April 1861 after the Confederates fired upon Fort Sumter, South Carolina—thereby beginning the Civil War—but before Congress ratified all of Lincoln's war-related activities in August.

What were the **captured ships involved in *The Prize Cases*?**

The ships involved included the U.S. ships *Amy Warwick* and the *Crenshaw,* the British ship *Hiawatha,* and the Mexican ship *Brilliante.*

Why was this case known as ***The Prize Cases*?**

The word "prize" is a legal term referring to the capture and detention at sea of a ship or vessel and the goods taken from the vessel. In England, courts that dealt with these controversies were called prize courts.

In what decision did the Taney Court address the meaning of **"due process of law"**?

The Taney Court first addressed the meaning of due process in *Murray's Lessee v. Hoboken Land & Improvement Co.* (1856). In the unanimous decision, the Court reasoned that the federal government could issue distress warrants, an administrative, nonjudicial procedure, to recover monies embezzled by Samuel Swartwout, a New York customs official appointed by President Andrew Jackson.

In the Court's opinion, Justice Benjamin Curtis wrote that the government's process did not violate due process. "The words, 'due process of law,' were undoubtedly intended to convey the same meaning as the words, 'by the law of the land,' in Magna Carta," Curtis wrote.

THE CHASE COURT (1864–73)

How many and which **justices served on the Chase Court**?

Thirteen justices served on the Chase Court, including Chief Justice Salmon P. Chase and Justices James Wayne, John Catron, Samuel Nelson, Robert Grier, Nathan Clifford, Noah H. Swayne, Samuel F. Miller, David Davis, Stephen Field, William Strong, Joseph Bradley, and Ward Hunt.

What **government positions did Salmon Chase hold** before becoming chief justice?

Salmon Chase had a distinguished career of public service. The Ohioan served in the U.S. Senate from 1849 to 1955 and then again in 1860–61. He also was Ohio's governor from 1856 to 1860 and President Abraham Lincoln's secretary of the Treasury from 1861 to 1864.

What **views made Chase well-known** before his elevation to the U.S. Supreme Court?

Chase was known for his antislavery views, believing that the "peculiar institution" was a moral abomination. Chase defended many abolitionists who had harbored fugitive slaves from the South. His defense of abolitionists earned him the moniker the "attorney general for runaway negroes." Chase's antislavery views caused him to join the Liberty Party and then the Free Soil Party.

How **long did it take for Chase to be confirmed** as chief justice?

The U.S. Senate confirmed Chase by voice vote the same day he was nominated by President Lincoln on December 6, 1864.

U.S. Supreme Court chief justice Salmon P. Chase. *Hulton Archive/Getty Images.*

What **case did attorney Chase argue** before joining the Court?

Salmon Chase argued the case of *Jones v. Van Zandt* (1847) before the U.S. Supreme Court on behalf of John Van Zandt, who helped slaves escape to free territory. Kentucky slaveowner Wharton Jones sued Van Zandt for harboring a 32-year-old male slave named Andrew. The Court upheld the constitutionality of the Fugitive Slave Act of 1793, rejecting Chase's arguments that slavery was incompatible with the Bill of Rights, the Declaration of Independence, and the Northwest Ordinance of 1787, which forbade slavery in many locations, such as Chase's home state of Ohio.

What was most unusual in Supreme Court history about the **number of justices on the Chase Court**?

In the early days of the Chase Court, in 1864 and 1865, there were ten justices on the Court. They were Chief Justice Chase and Justices Wayne, Catron, Nelson, Grier, Clifford, Swayne, Miller, Davis, and Field. Since 1869, when Congress passed the Judiciary Act of 1869, the maximum number of justices allowed has remained at nine.

In what decision did the Chase Court say that a **person suspected of treason could not be tried by a military court**?

In perhaps its most noteworthy decision, the Chase Court ruled in *Ex Parte Milligan* (1866) that Langdon Milligan could not be tried by a military tribunal instead of fully-functioning civil courts. Milligan and several other individuals in the Order of American Knights were arrested on charges of conspiring to steal firearms at a federal arsenal and free Confederate prisoners in Indiana. Milligan was arrested and sentenced to death by a military tribunal. Milligan petitioned a federal court for habeas corpus, asking it to rule that a military tribunal did not have the authority to try Milligan.

The Court unanimously ruled that Milligan should have been tried in a civilian, instead of military, court. In his majority opinion, Justice David Davis reasoned that civil courts were the proper forum when a defendant's constitutional rights to trial by jury, grand jury indictment, and other protections are present. "Martial rule can never exist where the courts are open, and in the proper and unobstructed exercise of their jurisdiction," he wrote.

Justice Salmon Chase filed a concurring opinion joined by three other justices that agreed with the result but applied different reasoning. Chase reasoned that Milligan should be released based on statutory, not constitutional, grounds. He wrote that the Habeas Corpus Act of 1863 provided that the proper forum for Milligan's trial was a civil, not military, court. "The act of Congress of March 3d, 1863, comprises all the legislation which seems to require consideration in this connection," Chase wrote.

U.S. Supreme Court justice Stephen J. Field. *Hulton Archive/Getty Images.*

What were the violations of which **Milligan was accused**?

Military authorities charged Milligan with the following violations: "(1) Conspiracy against the Government of the United States; (2) Affording aid and comfort to rebels against the authority of the United States; (3) Inciting insurrection; (4) Disloyal practices; and (5) Violation of the laws of war."

How did the Court rule in *Ex Parte Milligan* with regard to a **president and habeas corpus**?

No. In his opinion, Justice Davis specifically stated that in times of war and emergency, a president may have to suspend habeas corpus. Davis explained: "It is essential to the safety of every government that, in a great crisis, like the one we have just passed through, there should be a power somewhere of suspending the writ of habeas corpus…. In the emergency of the times, an immediate public investigation according to law may not be possible; and yet, the peril to the country may be too imminent to suffer such persons to go at large."

What attorney in *Ex Parte Milligan* was a **relative of a sitting Supreme Court justice**?

One of Milligan's attorneys before the U.S. Supreme Court was prominent New York–based practitioner David Dudley Field, the brother of U.S. Supreme Court justice Stephen Field. Judicial ethics were not as rigid as they are today, so there was little talk of Justice Field recusing himself.

The Chase Court **invalidated loyalty oaths** in what two decisions?

The Chase Court ruled 5–4 in *Cummings v. Missouri* and *Ex Parte Garland* (1867), collectively called the Test Oath Cases, that loyalty oaths requiring individuals to swear they did not support the Confederacy were unconstitutional. In the *Missouri* case, Father John Cummings, a young priest, challenged a Missouri law requiring various persons in many occupations to swear they had not supported the Confederacy. The Missouri Loyalty Oath was as follows:

> ## CourtSpeak: *Ex Parte Milligan* Habeas Corpus Case (1866)
>
> Justice David Davis (majority): "The Constitution of the United States is a law for rulers and people, equally in war and in peace, and covers with the shield of its protection all classes of men, at all times, and under all circumstances. No doctrine, involving more pernicious consequences, was ever invented by the wit of man than that any of its provisions can be suspended during any of the great exigencies of government. Such a doctrine leads directly to anarchy or despotism, but the theory of necessity on which it is based is false; for the government, within the Constitution, has all the powers granted to it, which are necessary to preserve its existence; as has been happily proved by the result of the great effort to throw off its just authority."
>
> Justice Salmon P. Chase (concurring): "We cannot doubt that, in such a time of public danger, Congress had power, under the Constitution, to provide for the organization of a military commission, and for trial by that commission of persons engaged in this conspiracy. The fact that the Federal courts were open was regarded by Congress as a sufficient reason for not exercising the power; but that fact could not deprive Congress of the right to exercise it. Those courts might be open and undisturbed in the execution of their functions, and yet wholly incompetent to avert threatened danger, or to punish, with adequate promptitude and certainty, the guilty conspirators."

I...do solemnly swear that I am well acquainted with the terms of the third section of the second article of the Constitution of the State of Missouri, adopted in the year eighteen hundred and sixty-five, and have carefully considered the same; that I have never, directly or indirectly, done any of the acts in said section specified; that I have always been truly and loyally on the side of the United States against all enemies thereof, foreign and domestic; that I will bear true faith and law of the land, any law or ordinance of any State to the contrary notwithstanding; that I will, to the best of my ability, protect and defend the Union of the United States, and not allow the same to be broken up and dissolved, or the government thereof to be destroyed or overthrown, under any circumstances, if in my power to prevent it; that I will support the Constitution of the State of Missouri; and that I make this oath without any mental reservation of evasion, and hold it to be binding on me.

In *Ex Parte Garland*, Augustus Hill Garland, an attorney and former Confederate senator from Arkansas, challenged the constitutionality of a federal law that required attorneys to take a similar oath to practice in the federal courts.

The majority reasoned that both statutes were unconstitutional because they were ex post facto laws and bills of attainder. Justice Stephen Field reasoned that the oaths

121

Attorney Augustus Hill Garland, subject of the *Ex Parte Garland* Supreme Court case. Garland challenged the constitutionality of a federal law that required lawyers to swear they had not supported the Confederacy. Garland was a former Confederate senator from Arkansas. *Hulton Archive/Getty Images.*

were ex post facto laws because they criminalized conduct that was not a crime when committed. He also reasoned that they were bills of attainder because they punished a certain class of person without a trial.

What **famous attorney represented Father Cummings** before the U.S. Supreme Court?

Once again, Justice Field's brother, David Dudley Field, represented Father Cummings before the U.S. Supreme Court. Justice Field wrote the majority opinion in favor of Cummings.

In what decision did the Chase Court rule that it **could not stop the president from enforcing the Reconstruction Acts**?

The Chase Court unanimously ruled in *Mississippi v. Johnson* (1867) that it could not stop President Andrew Johnson from enforcing the Reconstruction Acts of 1867, which divided most Southern states into five military districts and required them to write new constitutions and give blacks the right to vote. Mississippi filed a motion in the courts, seeking a court order enjoining the enforcement of the Reconstruction Acts.

Writing for the Court, Chief Justice Chase reasoned that the Court did not have the power to restrain the president in the exercise of his discretionary duties. "An attempt on the part of the judicial department of the government to enforce the performance of such duties by the President might be justly characterized, in the language of Chief Justice Marshall, as 'an absurd and excessive extravagance,'" he wrote.

What was ironic about **President Johnson's battle with the state of Mississippi** about the Reconstruction Acts?

It was ironic that President Johnson asserted his authority to enforce the Reconstruction Acts because he had initially opposed and even vetoed the very acts.

CourtSpeak: *Cummings v. Missouri* Loyalty Oath Case (1867)

Justice Stephen Field (majority): "The clauses in question subvert the presumptions of innocence, and alter the rules of evidence, which heretofore, under the universally recognized principles of the common law, have been supposed to be fundamental and unchangeable. They assume that the parties are guilty; they call upon the parties to establish their innocence; and they declare that such innocence can be shown only in one way—by an inquisition, in the form of an expurgatory oath, into the consciences of the parties."

Justice Samuel Miller (dissenting): "In the discussion of these cases, I have said nothing, on the one hand, of the great evils inflicted on the country by … the voluntary action of many of those persons affected by the laws under consideration, nor, on the other hand, of the hardships which they are now suffering much more as a consequence of that action than of any laws which Congress can possibly frame. But I have endeavored to bring to the examination of the grave questions of constitutional law involved in this inquiry those principles alone which are calculated to assist in determining what the law is, rather than what, in my private judgment, it ought to be."

The acts became law because Congress overrode his veto and Johnson was not pleased when the state of Mississippi challenged his executive authority to enforce the law.

In what decision did the Court allow Congress to **take away the Court's appellate jurisdiction**?

The Chase Court unanimously ruled in *Ex Parte McCardle* (1869) that it no longer had jurisdiction over habeas corpus appeals because Congress had amended the Habeas Corpus Act of 1867 to eliminate the Court's appellate jurisdiction.

The case must be understood in light of a continuing battle between Congress and the Court over legislation passed during the time of Reconstruction. The defendant in *McCardle* asserted that he was being detained in violation of his constitutional rights. He appealed to the U.S. Supreme Court under a provision in the Habeas Corpus Act of 1867. However, Congress, fearful the Court might invalidate the Reconstruction Acts, amended the Habeas Corpus law to eliminate the Court's jurisdiction.

Chief Justice Chase wrote succinctly: "It is quite clear, therefore, that this court cannot proceed to pronounce judgment in this case, for it has no longer jurisdiction of the appeal."

Some have criticized the Court for bowing to Congress in this case. However, Chief Justice William Rehnquist may have summed it up best in a 2003 speech about judicial independence when he said: "Undoubtedly, it could have ruled differently in the *McCardle* case, but it may be that the Court's apparent decision to live to fight another day was the best conceivable one under the circumstances."

Who was the **defendant in *Ex Parte McCardle*?**

The defendant was William McCardle, a Vicksburg, Mississippi, newspaper editor who attacked Union occupation of his state after the Civil War.

President Andrew Johnson's enforcement of the Reconstruction Acts of 1867 was upheld by the U.S. Supreme Court in *Mississippi v. Johnson. Hulton Archive/Getty Images.*

In what decision did the Chase Court rule that Texas could recover **securities sold by its confederate government when it seceded from the union?**

The Chase Court ruled in *Texas v. White* (1869) that the state of Texas could sue in federal court to recover bonds that it had been issued in 1851, a decade before it had seceded from the Union. After readmission into the Union, the state sued to recover state-owned securities sold by its Confederate government. Chief Justice Chase ruled in favor of the state, reasoning that Texas never really left the Union, and that the acts of the Confederate government were unlawful. "The legislature of Texas, at the time of the repeal, constituted one of the departments of a State government, established in hostility to the Constitution of the United States," Chase explained. "It cannot be regarded, therefore, in the courts of the United States, as a lawful legislature, or its acts as lawful acts." Thus, Texas was entitled to recover its securities.

In what two cases did the Chase Court **change positions with respect to greenbacks?**

Two of the more important Chase Court decisions—*Hepburn v. Griswold* (1870) and the *Legal Tender Cases* (1871)—dealt with whether the Legal Tender Act of 1862 was

CourtSpeak: *Legal Tender Cases:* Paper Money vs. Gold (1871)

Justice William Strong (majority): "It would be difficult to overestimate the consequences which must follow our decision. They will affect the entire business of the country, and take hold of the possible continued existence of the government. If it be held by this court that Congress has no constitutional power, under any circumstances, or in any emergency, to make treasury notes a legal tender for the payment of all debts (a power confessedly possessed by every independent sovereignty other than the United States), the government is without those means of self-preservation which, all must admit, may, in certain contingencies, become indispensable, even if they were not when the acts of Congress now called in question were enacted. It is also clear that if we hold the acts invalid as applicable to debts incurred, or transactions which have taken place since their enactment, our decision must cause, throughout the country, great business derangement, widespread distress, and the rankest injustice. The debts which have been contracted since February 25th, 1862, constitute, doubtless, by far the greatest portion of the existing indebtedness of the country."

Chief Justice Salmon P. Chase (dissenting): "The present majority of the court say that legal tender notes 'have become the universal measure of values,' and they hold that the legislation of Congress, substituting such measures for coin by making the notes a legal tender in payment, is warranted by the Constitution. But if the plain sense of words, if the contemporaneous exposition of parties, if common consent in understanding, if the opinions of courts avail anything in determining the meaning of the Constitution, it seems impossible to doubt that the power to coin money is a power to establish a uniform standard of value, and that no other power to establish such a standard, by making notes a legal tender, is conferred upon Congress by the Constitution."

constitutional. The Legal Tender Act enabled the government to force creditors to accept paper money instead of gold coins for debts.

The first time the issue came before the Court, it ruled 4–3 in *Hepburn v. Griswold* against the constitutionality of the Legal Tender Act as applied to preexisting contracts. Before the passage of the Legal Tender Act, Susan Hepburn borrowed $11,250 from Henry Griswold. Hepburn then sought to pay the debt back in paper money instead of coin. Griswold sued to recover the debt in gold and silver coin, as gold was worth more than paper money. The Court narrowly ruled 4–3 in Griswold's favor, determining that the Legal Tender Act could not be applied retroactively to preexisting contracts.

U.S. Supreme Court justice William Strong. *Hulton Archive/Getty Images.*

After this decision, President Ulysses S. Grant appointed two new members to the U.S. Supreme Court, William Strong and Joseph Bradley. This shifted the balance of power and led to a reversal of *Hepburn v. Griswold.*

In two cases, *Knox v. Lee* and *Parker v. Davis* (collectively called the *Legal Tender Cases*), the U.S. Supreme Court ruled 5–4 that debtors could repay creditors in paper money instead of coin. The Court also ruled the Legal Tender Act constitutional.

THE WAITE COURT (1874–88)

How many and which **justices served on the Waite Court**?

Fifteen justices served on the Waite Court, including Chief Justice Morrison Waite and Justices Nathan Clifford, Noah H. Swayne, Samuel F. Miller, Stephen J. Field, William Strong, Joseph P. Bradley, Ward Hunt, John Marshall Harlan, William B. Woods, Stanley Matthews, Horace Gray, Samuel Blatchford, and Lucius Q. C. Lamar.

What **government positions did Morrison Waite hold** before his elevation to the Supreme Court?

Waite served as a member of the Ohio General Assembly for two years, from 1850 to 1852. He ran for the U.S. Congress twice but lost both elections. He served as a representative at the Geneva Convention in 1871 and served as president of the Ohio Constitutional Convention in 1873–74.

Was **Waite President Grant's first choice** as chief justice?

No, Waite was President Ulysses S. Grant's seventh choice—at least—for the job. Grant first chose U.S. senator Roscoe Conkling of New York, who turned down the position. Allegedly, Grant's secretary of state, Hamilton Fish, and two other U.S. senators, Timothy Howe of Wisconsin and Oliver Morton of Indiana, also turned down the offer. Grant then nominated Attorney General George H. Williams for the position but his nomination collapsed when it was revealed that Williams had used Justice Department funds for personal use, including the purchase of an expensive carriage. Grant sent Caleb Cushing's name to the U.S. Senate, thinking the former head of the Geneva Convention would be an excellent nomination. However, opposition to Cushing surfaced when it was revealed that he had ties to disgraced Confederate leader Jefferson Davis.

It became a national embarrassment that President Grant could not fill the position of chief justice. Waite entered the picture because he had no negative political baggage

U.S. Supreme Court chief justice Morrison Waite. *Brady-Handy Photographic Collection/Library of Congress.*

and because he, like Cushing, had earned a measure of respect for his participation in the successful Geneva Convention meeting. Waite was an unexpected choice even to Waite himself, who believed it a joke when he first received the telegram with the offer of chief justice.

Which members of the Waite Court served on the **commission that ultimately selected the winner of the 1876 presidential election**?

Justices Nathan Clifford, Stephen Field, Samuel Miller, William Strong, and Joseph Bradley served on the electoral commission that decided the outcome of the 1876 presidential election.

The 1876 presidential election between the Democratic candidate, New York governor Samuel Tilden, and his Republican opponent, Ohio governor Rutherford B. Hayes, was probably the messiest in U.S. history, when disputes rose over which candidate had more electoral votes. Congress put together a 15-member commission made up of five Republican congressmen, five Democratic congressman,

An electoral commission made up of five Republican congressmen, five Democratic congressmen, and five U.S. Supreme Court justices (from the Waite Court) selected Ohio governor Rutherford B. Hayes (above) as president following the controversial 1876 presidential election. *Underwood and Underwood/ Time & Life Pictures/Getty Images.*

and five U.S. Supreme Court justices. The first four justices would consist of two Republicans and two Democrats and those four justices would selected the fifth justice.

Congress chose Democratic justices Clifford and Field and Republicans Miller and Strong. Many believed that Justice David Davis, a Republican who may have favored Tilden, would be the decisive fifth justice. However, Davis resigned to become a member of the U.S. Senate. Justice Joseph Bradley, a staunch Republican, was selected as the fifth justice on the electoral commission. Predictably, all members voted along party lines and the commission selected Hayes as the winner by a narrow 8–7 vote.

Why did the Waite Court hear so many **Fourteenth Amendment cases**?

The Waite Court heard many Fourteenth Amendment cases because of timing. The Fourteenth Amendment, as part of Reconstruction, had been ratified in 1868, a few years before the beginning of the Waite Court. Thus, the justices had to explain the meaning of due process and equal protection, as well as determine whether the Fourteenth Amendment extended certain protections in the Bill of Rights to the states.

RACIAL DISCRIMINATION/CIVIL RIGHTS

The Waite Court **invalidated the Civil Rights Act of 1875** in what group of cases?

The Waite Court ruled in the *Civil Rights Cases* (1883) that Congress exceeded its constitutional authority in the Civil Rights Act of 1875 by outlawing private acts of discrimination. According to the Court, the Thirteenth and Fourteenth Amendments, which outlawed slavery and gave all persons rights of citizenship, only extended to protect individuals from unlawful governmental, or state, action. The Civil Rights Act of 1875, by contrast, extended to protect African Americans from private wrongs. The Act outlawed racial discrimination in places of public accommodation, such as inns and railroads. "It would be running the slavery argument into the ground to make it apply to every act of discrimination," Justice Joseph Bradley wrote for the Court. He added that at some point African Americans "cease to be the special favorites of the laws."

What were the collection of cases that collectively became known as the *Civil Rights Cases*?

The cases came from five states: Kansas, California, Missouri, New York, and Tennessee. The case from Kansas, *United States v. Stanley,* involved Murray Stanley, an inn proprietor who denied African American Bird Gee the opportunity to eat a meal at his inn. In the California case, *United States v. Ryan,* Michael Ryan denied African American George Tyler the opportunity to view a theater show in San Francisco. In the Missouri case, *United States v. Nichols,* inn owner Samuel Nichols denied a room to African American W. H. R. Agee. In the New York case, *United States v. Singleton,* a Mr. Singleton denied entry to an African American to the Grand Opera House. In the Tennessee case, *Robinson v. Memphis & Charleston Railroad Co.,* the railroad company allegedly refused to allow African American Sallie J. Robinson to board the defendant's train in Grand Junction, Tennessee.

What did the **1875 Civil Rights Act prohibit**?

The 1875 Civil Rights Act sought to prohibit unlawful discrimination in places of public accommodation, including inns, hotels, railroads, and theaters. Section 1 of the law provided: "That all persons within the jurisdiction of the United States shall be entitled to the full and equal enjoyment of the accommodations, advantages, facilities, and privileges of inns, public conveyances on land or water, theaters, and other places of public amusement; subject only to the conditions and limitations established by law, and applicable alike to citizens of every race and color, regardless of any previous condition of servitude."

How did Congress justify the **Civil Rights Act of 1875**?

The Thirty-Ninth Congress justified the passage of the Civil Rights Act of 1875 as a necessary law to stamp out the incidents and badges of slavery and involuntary servitude imposed upon African Americans. Congress believed the law would help enforce two recently enacted constitutional amendments—the Thirteenth Amendment, which outlawed slavery, and the Fourteenth Amendment, which attempted to give recently freed slaves the same general rights as white citizens.

Why did the Court **strike down the Civil Rights Act of 1875**?

The Court invalidated the Civil Rights Act of 1875 because it determined that the law reached beyond Congress's power under the Thirteenth and Fourteenth Amendments. The majority believed that Congress did not have the power to prohibit simple private wrongs, as opposed to wrongs committed by governmental actors. Justice Joseph P. Bradley explained:

> In this connection it is proper to state that civil rights, such as are guarantied by the constitution against state aggression, cannot be impaired by the wrongful acts of individuals, unsupported by state authority in the shape of laws, customs, or judicial or executive proceedings. The wrongful act of an individual, unsupported by any such authority, is simply a private wrong, or a crime of that individual; an invasion of the rights of the injured party, it is true, whether they affect his person, his property, or his reputation; but if not sanctioned in some way by the state, or not done under state authority, his rights remain in full force, and may presumably be vindicated by resort to the laws of the state for redress.

Who was the Court's **lone dissenter in the *Civil Rights Cases*?**

Justice John Marshall Harlan, a former slave owner from the state of Kentucky, established his reputation as "the Great Dissenter" with his lone dissent in the *Civil Rights Cases*. He wrote that "the substance and spirit of the recent amendments of the Constitution have been sacrificed by a subtle and ingenious verbal criticism."

He also noted that the state had a role in providing its citizens protection in places of public accommodation:

> In every material sense applicable to the practical enforcement of the Fourteenth Amendment, railroad corporations, keepers of inns, and managers of places of public accommodation are agents or instrumentalities of the State,

131

> ## CourtSpeak: *Civil Rights Cases:*
> ## Government's Role in Private Discrimination (1875)
>
> Justice Joseph P. Bradley (majority): "When a man has emerged from slavery and with the aid of beneficient legislation has shaken off the inseparable concomitants of that state, there must be some stage in the progress of his elevation when he takes the rank of a mere citizen, and ceases to be a special favorite of the laws, and when his rights as a citizen, or a man are to be protected in the ordinary modes by which other men's rights are protected."
>
> Justice John Marshall Harlan (dissenting): "My brethren say that when a man has emerged from slavery, and by the aid of beneficient legislation has shaken off the inseparable concomitants of that state, there must be some stage in the progress of his elevation when he takes the rank of a mere citizen, and ceases to be the special favorite of the laws, and when his rights as a citizen, or a man, are to be protected in the ordinary modes by which other men's rights are protected. It is, I submit, scarcely just to say that the colored race has been the special favorite of the laws.... Today, it is the colored race which is denied, by corporations and individuals wielding public authority, rights fundamental in their freedom and citizenship. At some future time, it may be that some other race will fall under the ban of race discrimination."

because they are charged with duties to the public, and are amenable, in respect of their duties and functions, to governmental regulation.

What case arose after a **massacre of African Americans in Louisiana**?

The Court's decision in *U.S. v. Cruikshank* (1876) arose from an election dispute in Colfax, Louisiana, that erupted into violence when a group of angry white men stormed a local courthouse being protected by a local sheriff and many black Republicans. On Easter Sunday in 1873, the band of whites murdered at least fifty blacks, though some estimates rank the number of casualties as much higher.

Federal investigators charged more than ninety white men, including William Cruikshank, with violation of the Ku Klux Klan Act of 1870. That law made it illegal to "injure, oppress, threaten, or intimidate any citizen with intent to prevent or hinder his free exercise and enjoyment of any right or privilege granted or secured to him by the constitution or laws of the United States, or because of his having exercised the same." Cruikshank was accused of terrorizing African Americans Levi Nelson and Alexander Tillman and not allowing them to exercise their constitutional rights of peaceable assembly. Cruikshank and others could not be prosecuted for killing Nelson and Tillman because only state authorities could prosecute them for murder (which they did not).

CourtSpeak: *U.S. v. Cruikshank*
Law Enforcement Domain Case (1876)

Chief Justice Morrison R. Waite (unanimous): "The government of the United States is one of delegated powers alone. Its authority is defined and limited by the Constitution. All powers not granted to it by that instrument are reserved to the States or the people. No rights can be acquired under the constitution or laws of the United States, except such as the government of the United States has the authority to grant or secure. All that cannot be so granted or secured are left under the protection of the States."

Why did *Cruikshank* prevail before the U.S. Supreme Court?

The Court essentially ruled that the responsibility of law enforcement in this matter lay with state and local government officials, rather than federal investigators. The Court, in a unanimous opinion written by Chief Justice Waite, reasoned that the indictments "do not contain charges of a criminal nature made indictable under the laws of the United States."

The Waite Court convicted a man of violating federal law designed to ensure voting rights in what decision?

The Waite Court unanimously ruled in *Ex Parte Yarbrough* (1884)—often called the Ku Klux Klan cases—that Jasper Yarbrough and other Ku Klux Klan members could be convicted of violating federal law when they beat and wounded Barry Saunders, an African American, to keep him from voting in a federal election.

The Court, in unusually strong language, affirmed Congress's power to pass laws designed to ensure voting in federal elections. "If this government is anything more than a mere aggregation of delegated agents of other states and governments, each of which is superior to the general government, it must have the power to protect the elections on which its existence depends, from violence and corruption," wrote Justice Samuel Miller. "If it has not this power, it is left helpless before the two great natural and historical enemies of all republics, open violence and insidious corruption."

The Waite Court protected African American rights to serve on a jury in what famous decision?

The Waite Court ruled 7–2 in *Strauder v. West Virginia* (1880) that a state law limiting jury service to whites violated the Equal Protection Clause of the Fourteenth Amendment. The law limited jury service to "all white male persons." Tyler Strauder, an African Ameri-

133

Two members of the Ku Klux Klan (KKK) from after the Civil War. In the so-called Ku Klux Klan cases of 1884, the Waite Court unanimously ruled that KKK members could be convicted of violating federal law when they beat an African American to keep him from voting in an election. *Hulton Archive/Getty Images.*

can convicted of murder by an all-white jury, contended that he should have a new trial because his constitutional rights were violated by a system that ensured he was not tried by a jury of his peers. The Court determined that the Equal Protection Clause was designed to "protect an emancipated race and to strike down all possible legal discriminations" against African Americans.

Writing for the majority, Justice William Strong said, "That the West Virginia statute respecting juries—the statute that controlled the selection of the grand and petit jury in the case of the plaintiff in error—is such a discrimination ought not to be doubted. Nor would it be if the persons excluded by it were white men. If in those States where the colored people constitute a majority of the entire population a law should be enacted excluding all white men from jury service, thus denying to them the privilege of participating equally with the lacks in the administration of justice, we apprehend no one would be heard to claim that it would not be a denial to white men of the equal protection of the laws. Nor if a law should be passed excluding all naturalized Celtic Irishmen, would there be any doubt of its inconsistency with the spirit of the amendment. The very fact that colored people are singled out and expressly denied by a statute all right to participate in the administration of the law, as jurors, because of their color, though they are citizens, and may be in other respects fully qualified, is practically a brand upon them, affixed by the law, an assertion of their inferiority, and a stimulant to that race prejudice which is an impediment to securing to individuals of the race that equal justice which the law aims to secure to all others."

In what decision did the Waite Court **affirm the conviction of a judge who excluded blacks from juries**?

In *Ex Parte Virginia* (1879), the Waite Court ruled that Virginia judge J. D. Coles could be punished for refusing to allow African Americans to serve on juries in the Pittsylvania County Courthouse in Chatham, Virginia. "We do not perceive how holding an office under a State, and claiming to act for the State, can relieve the holder from obligation to obey the Constitution of the United States, or take away the power of Congress to punish his disobedience," Justice William Strong wrote for the Court.

U.S. Supreme Court justice Stanley Matthews (above), in writing the Court's opinion on *Yick Wo v. Hopkins,* said that discrimination against Chinese launderers was illegal and that "no reason for it exists except hostility to the race and nationality to which the petitioners belong, and which, in the eye of the law, is not justified. *Hulton Archive/Getty Images.*

In what decision involving **laundries** did the Waite Court establish **important equal protection principles**?

The U.S. Supreme Court ruled unanimously in *Yick Wo v. Hopkins* (1896) that San Francisco officials violated the equal-protection rights of Chinese laundry operators Yick Wo and Wo Lee by subjecting them to more onerous regulation than white laundry owners. The city passed a law that provided: "It shall be unlawful, from and after the passage of this order, for any person or persons to establish, maintain, or carry on a laundry, within the corporate limits of the city and county of San Francisco, without having first obtained the consent of the board of supervisors, except the same be located in a building constructed either of brick or stone."

The evidence established that two hundred Chinese laundry owners, most of whom had wooden structures, were denied operating permits, while seventy-nine of eighty Caucasian laundry operators were granted permits. According to the Court, this overwhelming pattern of discrimination violated the Equal Protection Clause of the Fourteenth Amendment.

Writing for the Court, Justice Stanley Matthews concluded: "The fact of this discrimination is admitted. No reason for it is shown, and the conclusion cannot be resisted that no reason for it exists except hostility to the race and nationality to which the petitioners belong, and which, in the eye of the law, is not justified. The discrimination is therefore illegal, and the public administration which enforces it is a denial of the equal protection of the laws, and a violation of the Fourteenth Amendment of the Constitution."

The case is important because it established that a law can violate the Equal Protection Clause even thought it is race-neutral on its face as long as proof can be established showing a discriminatory pattern of operation.

VOTING RIGHTS

The Waite Court **rejected women's rights** to vote in what decision?

The Waite Court unanimously ruled in *Minor v. Happersett* (1874) that the state of Missouri did not violate the constitutional rights of Virginia Louise Minor when a state official named Reese Happersett denied her the right to vote. Minor contended that denying her the right to vote infringed upon her rights under the Fourteenth Amendment.

The Court, in an opinion written by Chief Justice Waite, rejected her constitutional claim, looking at the tradition of women's exclusion from voting. "Women were excluded from suffrage in nearly all the States by the express provision of their constitutions and laws," he wrote. "If the law is wrong, it ought to be changed; but the power for that is not with us. The arguments addressed to us bearing upon such a view of the subject may perhaps be sufficient to induce those having the power, to make the alteration, but they ought not to be permitted to influence our judgment in determining the present rights of the parties now litigating before us. No argument as to woman's need of suffrage can be considered. We can only act upon her rights as they exist. It is not for us to look at the hardship of withholding. Our duty is at an end if we find it is within the power of a State to withhold."

The Waite Court refused to enforce the Fifteenth Amendment in what decision?

The Waite Court ruled 8–1 in *United States v. Reese* (1876) that federal charges against Kentucky election official Hiram Reese should be dismissed even though Reese had prevented African American William Garner from voting. Reese would not allow Garner to vote unless Garner showed his receipt for paying a poll tax, but apparently other election officials would not allow Garner to pay the poll tax. The Court had a clear opportunity to enforce the Fifteenth Amendment, which prohibited the denial of the right to vote based on race. The Court, however, determined that one section of the Kentucky statute went too far by prohibiting actions by election officials that had nothing to do with race. The net effect of the decision was that it embolded state officials, particularly in Southern states, to evade the requirements of the Fifteenth Amendment by couching their objections to would-be African American voters in terms of poll taxes and literary requirements.

COMMERCE

The Waite Court **upheld state power to regulate private business** in what famous decision?

The Waite Court ruled 7–2 in *Munn v. Illinois* (1877) that the state of Illinois could regulate the rates set by Illinois grain elevator operators in the city of Chicago, the only city in the state with a population of more than one hundred thousand. The state had convicted Ira Munn, the owner of Munn & Scott, the largest grain storage company in the state, because Munn had avoided paying the proper storage rates.

The case eventually reached the U.S. Supreme Court and Munn's lawyers argued that the state law was unconstitutional because it infringed on the U.S. Congress's Commerce Clause powers and unlawfully impacted their property rights in violation of the Fourteenth Amendment Due Process Clause.

Chief Justice Waite, writing for the majority, rejected all constitutional challenges to the law. He reasoned that the law was a valid exercise of a state's police powers, writing that "when private property is devoted to a public use, it is subject to public regulation." He also rejected the notion that the law exceeded Congress's commerce powers, writing that any effect on interstate commerce was incidental.

Why did Justices **Field and Strong dissent**?

Justices Stephen Field and William Strong dissented in an opinion authored by Field. He questioned vigorously the majority's conclusion that the Illinois statute did not violate the due process rights of the company who had their property interest impacted by the legislation. He wrote in oft-cited language: "If this be sound law, if there be no protection, either in the principles upon which our republican government is founded, or in the prohibitions of the Constitution against such invasion of private rights, all property and all business in the State are held at the mercy of a majority of its legislature."

CourtSpeak: *Munn v. Illinois*
Private Business Regulation Case (1877)

Justice Stephen Field (dissenting): "The warehouses of these plaintiffs in error are situated and their business carried on exclusively within the limits of the State of Illinois. They are used as instruments by those engaged in State as well as those engaged in inter-state commerce, but they are no more necessarily a part of commerce itself than the dray or the cart by which, but for them, grain would be transferred from one railroad station to another. Incidentally they may become connected with inter-state commerce, but not necessarily so. Their regulation is a thing of domestic concern, and, certainly, until Congress acts in reference to their inter-state relations, the State may exercise all the powers of government over them, even though in so doing it may indirectly operate upon commerce outside its immediate jurisdiction. We do not say that a case may not arise in which it will be found that a State, under the form of regulating its own affairs, has encroached upon the exclusive domain of Congress in respect to inter-state commerce, but we do say that, upon the facts as they are represented to us in this record, that has not been done."

The Court **invalidated a state antidiscrimination law based on the Commerce Clause** in what decision?

The Waite Court unanimously ruled in *Hall v. DeCuir* (1878) that an African American woman denied entry to a statesroom on a vessel traveling between Louisiana and Mississippi could not recover damages because the application of the statute infringed on Congress's interstate commerce powers. Josephine DeCuir sued Mr. Hall, the operator of a Mississippi steamboat, under an 1869 Louisiana law that prohibited racial discrimination in public transportation. However, the Waite Court, in an opinion written by the chief justice, reasoned that the statute burdened interstate commerce by imposing a Louisiana law on a vessel that traveled in interstate commerce amongst states other than Louisiana.

Chief Justice Waite wrote:

> "But we think it may safely be said that State legislation which seeks to impose a direct burden upon inter-state commerce, or to interfere directly with its freedom, does encroach upon the exclusive power of Congress. The statute now under consideration, in our opinion, occupies that position. It does not act upon the business through the local instruments to be employed after coming within the State, but directly upon the business as it comes into the State from without or goes out from within. While it purports only to control the carrier when engaged within the State, it must necessarily influence his conduct to some extent in the management of his business through-

> ### CourtSpeak: *Hurtado v. California* Grand Jury Rights Case (1884)
>
> Justice Stanley Matthews (majority): "We are unable to say that the substitution for a presentment or indictment by a grand jury of the proceeding by information after examination and commitment by a magistrate, certifying to the probable guilt of the defendant, with the right on his part to the aid of counsel, and to the cross-examination of the witnesses produced for the prosecution, is not due process of law."
>
> Justice John Marshall Harlan (dissenting): "Does not the fact that the people of the original states required an amendment of the national constitution, securing exemption from prosecution for a capital offense, except upon the indictment or presentment of a grand jury, prove that, in their judgment, such an exemption was essential to protection against accusation and unfounded prosecution, and therefore was a fundamental principle in liberty and justice?"

out his entire voyage. His disposition of passengers taken up and put down within the State, or taken up within to be carried without, cannot but affect in a greater or less degree those taken up without and brought within, and sometimes those taken up and put down without. A passenger in the cabin set apart for the use of whites without the State must, when the boat comes within, share the accommodations of that cabin with such colored persons as may come on board afterwards, if the law is enforced."

CRIMINAL JUSTICE

In what decision did the Waite Court rule that **state courts do not have to proceed with a grand jury indictment in murder cases**?

The Fifth Amendment of the Bill of Rights provides that "No person shall be held to answer for a capital, or otherwise infamous crime, unless on presentment or indictment of a Grand Jury." However, the California Constitution of 1879 provided that "Offenses heretofore required to be prosecuted by indictment, shall be prosecuted by information, after examination and commitment by a magistrate."

Defendant Joseph Hurtado challenged his conviction in the California courts for the murder of Jose Antonio Stuardo. Hurtado contended his conviction was invalid because he did not have the benefit of a grand jury to review the prosecutor's contentions. Instead, the prosecutor proceeded with an information to a magistrate.

Hurtado contended that the Fifth Amendment right to a grand jury in death-penalty cases was extended to the states via the Fourteenth Amendment Due Process

Clause. The Waite Court rejected this contention by a 8–1 vote in *Hurtado v. California* (1884). The majority, in an opinion written by Justice Stanley Matthews, believed that Hurtado's due-process rights were not violated because the procecutor proceeded by information instead of a grand jury indictment.

John Marshall Harlan was the Court's lone dissenter, believing that the Fourteenth Amendment incorporated the Fifth Amendment's grand jury indictment requirement to the states.

U.S. Supreme Court justice John Marshall Harlan was the Court's lone dissenter in *Hurtado v. California*. *Brady-Handy Photographic Collection/Library of Congress*.

What **landmark privacy decision** involved both the Fourth and Fifth Amendments?

The Waite Court's decision in *Boyd v. United States* (1886) established that forcing an individual to produce his or her personal papers against his or her will violates both the Fourth and Fifth Amendments. The case arose after customs officials sought to determine whether the head of E. A. Boyd & Sons imported plate glass without paying the requisite custom duties.

A federal prosecutor obtained a court order to force Boyd to produce his invoices showing the purchase of the plates of glass. This led to a judicial determination that Boyd had violated the customs law and must forfeit the goods. On appeal, it was argued that this compulsory production of business records violated both the Fourth and Fifth Amendments.

The Waite Court unanimously ruled against the government, establishing a ruling that served as a key precedent for individual privacy. It is also the first case in which the U.S. Supreme Court spoke for any length about the Fourth Amendment.

In what decision did the Waite Court **refuse to extend the Second Amendment right to bear arms to the states**?

The Waite Court unanimously ruled in *Presser v. Illinois* (1886) that the Second Amendment "right to bear arms" did not provide protection to a man who led a group of four hundred men in an armed procession. An Illinois statute limited persons, other

> ## CourtSpeak: *Boyd v. United States* Privacy Case (1886)
>
> Justice Joseph Bradley (unanimous): "We have already noticed the intimate relation between the two amendments. They throw great light on each other. For the 'unreasonable searches and seizures' condemned in the fourth amendment are almost always made for the purpose of compelling a man to give evidence against himself, which in criminal cases is condemned in the fifth amendment; and compelling a man 'in a criminal case to be a witness against himself,' which is condemned in the fifth amendment, throws light on the question as to what is an 'unreasonable search and seizure' within the meaning of the fourth amendment. And we have been unable to perceive that the seizure of a man's private books and papers to be used in evidence against him is substantially different from compelling him to be a witness against himself. We think it is within the clear intent and meaning of those terms."

than the regular organized volunteer militia, from gathering together in a drill or parade with firearms without a license from the governor.

Harold Presser led his group of armed men without obtaining a permit and was convicted for violating the Illinois law. The Court reasoned that Presser could not rely on the Second Amendment in part because the amendment did not extend to the states. The Court, in an opinion written by Justice William Woods, stated: "We think it clear that the sections under consideration, which only forbid bodies of men to associate together as military organizations, or to drill or parade with arms in cities and towns unless authorized by law, do not infringe the right of the people to keep and bear arms. But a conclusive answer to the contention that this amendment prohibits the legislation in question lies in the fact that the amendment is a limitation only upon the power of congress and the national government, and not upon that of the state."

In what decision did the Waite Court rule that **American federal courts could not assert jurisdiction over a Sioux Indian accused of murder**?

The Waite Court unanimously ruled 9–0 in *Ex Parte Crow Dog* (1883) that a federal territorial court did not have jurisdiction over a Sioux Indian who allegedly killed another Indian on tribal lands. Crow Dog allegedly killed Spotted Tail and federal officials sought the death penalty against Crow Dog for his murderous act. Crow Dog was tried, convicted and sentenced to death. However, Sioux tribal law prohibited the death penalty but provided that Crow Dog would have to support the surviving family members of Spotted Tail.

The Court concluded that the federal court did not have jurisdiction; instead, the Sioux tribe had jurisdiction over the matter. The Court said that the tribe had the

Representatives of the U.S. Department of Indian Affairs meet with Sioux leaders in the Dakota Territory in the mid-1880s. In 1883, the Waite Court ruled unanimously in *Ex Parte Crow Dog* that federal courts did not have jurisdiction over the Sioux tribe in legal issues. *Hulton Archive/Getty Images.*

right to "the maintenance of order and peace among their own members by the administration of their own laws and customs."

The decision caused much outrage and led to the Indian Major Crimes Act in 1885, giving federal courts jurisdiction over murders on tribal lands.

In strong language, Justice Stanley Matthews wrote:

"It is a case of life and death. It is a case where, against an express exception in the law itself, that law, by argument and inference only, is sought to be extended over aliens and strangers; over the members of a community, separated by race, by tradition, by the instincts of a free though savage life, from the authority and power which seeks to impose upon them the restraints of an external and unknown code, and to subject them to the responsibilities of civil conduct, according to rules and penalties of which they could have no previous warning; which judges them by a standard made by others, and not for them, which takes no account of the conditions which should except them from its exactions, and makes no allowance for their inability to understand it. It tries them not by their peers, nor by the customs of their people, nor the law of their land, but by superiors of a different race, according to the law of a social state of which they have an imperfect conception, and which is opposed to the traditions of their history, to the habits of their lives, to the strongest prejudices of their savage nature; one which measures the red man's revenge by the maxims of the white man's morality."

In what decision did the Waite Court **uphold a fornication law with increased penalties for interracial associations**?

The Waite Court unanimously upheld a state fornication law in *Pace v. Alabama* (1883) that was designed to prevent interracial associations. The law in question provided that those who live together in fornication could be punished with a $100 fine and six months in jail. However, if the fornicating individuals were black and white, then the penalties were substantially increased to between two and seven years in prison.

Tony Pace, a black man, and Mary Cox, a white woman, were charged with violating the law. Pace challenged his conviction, arguing that the statute violated equal protection by discriminating on the basis of race.

The Waite Court ruled that the statute did not violate equal protection because it punished both the white and black offender who engaged in interracial associations equally. This decision was not overruled until the Warren Court's decisions in *McLaughlin v. Florida* (1964) and *Loving v. Virginia* (1967), which struck down a ban on interracial marriage.

MISCELLANEOUS DECISIONS

What Waite Court decision **rejected a First Amendment challenge to polygamy laws**?

The Waite Court unanimously ruled in *Reynolds v. United States* (1878) that an antibigamy law in the territory of Utah (which was not a state yet) did not violate the First Amendment rights of a Mormon man named George Reynolds who had more than one wife.

The law in question provided: "Every person having a husband or wife living, who marries another, whether married or single, in a Territory, or other place over which the United States have exclusive jurisdiction, is guilty of bigamy, and shall be punished by a fine of not more than $500, and by imprisonment for a term of not more than five years."

Reynolds contended that he could not be convicted of a crime for exercising his religious beliefs. Chief Justice Waite responded that while a person may not be punished for their religious beliefs, they may be punished for their actions that violate the criminal laws. In other words, there is no defense to illegal conduct by claiming it was inspired by religious beliefs. "Can a man excuse his practices to the contrary because of his religious belief?" Waite wrote. "To permit this would be to make the professed doctrines of religious belief superior to the law of the land, and in effect to permit every citizen to become a law unto himself. Government could exist only in name under such circumstances."

143

What Waite Court decision **affirmed convictions for several Baltimore election judges**?

The Waite Court ruled 6–2 in *Ex Parte Siebold* (1880) that five Baltimore election judges—Albert Siebold, Walter Tucker, Martin C. Burns, Lewis Coleman, and Henry Bowers—could be punished for violation of federal election law for allegedly stuffing ballot boxes during a federal election.

The state officials contended that their convictions should be reversed because the federal law invaded the province of the states, as the elections dealt with state regulations. The Court, in an opinion written by the chief justice, determined that when there is "concurrent authority" of federal and state governments, the federal government has jurisdiction. Waite wrote that it is "almost absurd" to suggest that the federal government doesn't have control over regulations of federal elections.

In what decision did the Waite Court rule that a **state can prohibit lotteries under its police powers**?

The Waite Court ruled 8–0 (Justice Ward Hunt did not participate) in *Stone v. Mississippi* (1880) that the state of Mississippi could retroactively ban lotteries by constitutional amendment and apply that law against a company that had previously been

granted a contract to conduct a lottery for twenty-five years.

CourtSpeak: *Ex Parte Siebold* **Ballot Box Stuffing Case (1880)**

Chief Justice Morrison R. Waite (majority): "It is objected that Congress has no power to enforce State laws or to punish State officers, and especially has no power to punish them for violating the laws of their own State. As a general proposition, this is undoubtedly true; but when, in the performance of their functions, State officers are called upon to fulfill duties which they owe to the United States as well as to the State, has the former no means of compelling such fulfillment? Yet that is the case here. It is the duty of the States to elect representatives to Congress. The due and fair election of these representatives is of vital importance to the United States. The government of the United States is no less concerned in the transaction than the State government is. It certainly is not bound to stand by as a passive spectator, when duties are violated and outrageous frauds are committed. It is directly interested in the faithful performance, by the officers of election, of their respective duties. Those duties are owed as well to the United States as to the State. This necessarily follows from the mixed character of the transaction,—State and national. A violation of duty is an offence against the United States, for which the offender is justly amenable to that government. No official position can shelter him from this responsibility. In view of the fact that Congress has plenary and paramount jurisdiction over the whole subject, it seems almost absurd to say that an officer who receives or has custody of the ballots given for a representative owes no duty to the national government which Congress can enforce; or that an officer who stuffs the ballot-box cannot be made amenable to the United States."

In 1867, the state government had granted a contract to a corporation run by John Stone to conduct a lottery for twenty-five years. However, a year later, the state adopted a new constitution outlawing lotteries. Stone asserted that the state could not prohibit him from running a lottery since the state had previously contracted with him. The Waite Court disagreed, with Chief Justice Waite writing that "no legislature can bargain away the public health or the public morals."

In what decision did the Waite Court rule that **Congress improperly interrogated a private citizen**?

The Waite Court unanimously ruled in *Kilbourn v. Thompson* (1881) that the U.S. House improperly investigated and interrogated Hallett Kilbourn regarding a bankrupt real estate venture in Washington D.C., of which the government was a creditor. John Thompson, the sergeant-at-arms of the House, had brought Kilbourn to the House for questioning. When Kilbourn refused to produce documents and answer questions, he was imprisoned in a District of Columbia jail for forty-five days for contempt.

The Court ruled that Congress could not punish Kilbourn because it had conducted an improper investigation into private matters, not future legislation. Chief Justice Waite wrote that "the House of Representatives not only exceeded the limit of its own authority, but assumed a power which could only be properly exercised by another branch of the government, because it was in its nature clearly judicial."

THE FULLER COURT (1888–1910)

How many and which **justices served on the Fuller Court**?

Twenty justices served on the Fuller Court, which lasted from 1888 to 1910. These justices included: Chief Justice Melville Fuller and Justices Samuel Miller, Stephen Field, Joseph Bradley, John Marshall Harlan, Stanley Matthews, Horace Gray, Samuel Blatchford, Lucius C. Q. Lamar, David Brewer, Henry Billings Brown, George Shiras, Howell Jackson, Edward White, Rufus Peckham, Joseph McKenna, Oliver Wendell Holmes, William Day, William Moody, and Horace Lurton.

What **governmental positions did Melville Fuller hold** before becoming chief justice?

Fuller was an accomplished lawyer but did not have many government positions before serving on the Court. He served as a city solicitor for Augusta, Maine, for one year and then served two years in the Illinois House of Representatives. He had never held any federal office before President Grover Cleveland nominated him to the position of chief justice.

Fuller participated actively in what **famous campaign**?

Fuller managed popular Illinois senator Stephen Douglas's 1858 campaign against challenger Abraham Lincoln, best known for the famous Lincoln-Douglas debates. Douglas won the senatorial election but Lincoln won the presidential nomination and the presidency two years later.

Was Fuller President Cleveland's **first choice**?

No, President Cleveland first asked Illinois Supreme Court justice John Scholfield, who declined. Cleveland then asked Fuller, who had previously turned down an offer to be solicitor general.

U.S. Supreme Court chief justice Melville Fuller. *Hulton Archive/Getty Images.*

CourtSpeak: *Plessy v. Ferguson*
"Separate but Equal" Accommodations Case (1896)

Justice Henry Billings Brown (majority): "We consider the underlying fallacy of the plaintiff's argument to consist in the assumption that the enforced separation of the two races stamps the colored race with a badge of inferiority.... If the two races are to meet upon terms of social equality, it must be the result of each other's merits, and a voluntary consent of individuals.... If one race be inferior to the other socially, the Constitution of the United States cannot put them on the same plane."

Justice John Marshall Harlan (dissenting): "But in view of the Constitution, in the eye of the law, there is in this country no superior, dominant ruling class of citizens. There is no caste here. Our Constitution is color-blind and neither knows nor tolerates classes among citizens. In respect of civil rights, all citizens are equal before the law. The humblest is the peer of the most powerful. The law regards man as man, and takes no account of his surroundings or of his color when his civil rights as guaranteed by the supreme law of the land are involved."

Why was **law not a surprising career** for Melville Fuller?

Fuller's father and two grandfathers were both lawyers, so it was a family tradition. His maternal grandfather, Nathan Weston, served on the Maine Supreme Court from 1834 to 1841, while his paternal grandfather, Henry Weld Fuller, was also a successful lawyer and later a judge. Fuller's father was a judge in Augusta, Maine.

Which **two justices on the Fuller Court were related**?

Justice Stephen Field was David Brewer's uncle. The two served together eight years, from 1889 to 1897. It is the only time in Supreme Court history that relatives served together on the Court.

RACIAL DISCRIMINATION

The Fuller Court upheld the **"separate but equal" doctrine** in what infamous decision?

The Fuller Court upheld the infamous "separate but equal" doctrine in *Plessy v. Ferguson* (1896), which upheld an 1890 Louisiana law providing for separate accommodations for different races. Homer Plessy, who was an "octoroon," an unflattering term for a person who was one-eighth black, was arrested in 1892 for boarding a whites-only coach.

Rodolphe Desdunes, the leader of the New Orleans' American Citizens' Equal Rights Association, had recruited his friend Plessy for the specific purpose of challenging the law. Plessy and Desdunes took the case all the way to the U.S. Supreme Court.

The Court, in an opinion written by Justice Henry Billings Brown, reasoned that the law did not violate the Fourteenth Amendment Equal Protection Clause because the law provided separate but equal facilities. Separate facilities, according to Brown, "do not necessarily imply the inferiority of either race to the other."

Who was the Court's **lone dissenter in *Plessy v. Ferguson*?**

John Marshall Harlan was the only justice to dissent and it is largely this dissent that earned him the name "the Great Dissenter." Harlan wrote that "our Constitution is color-blind and neither knows nor tolerates classes among citizens." He warned his colleagues that their decision would be "as pernicious as the decision" in *Dred Scott*.

In what decision did the Fuller Court uphold a law that **barred Chinese laborers who left the United States from returning?**

The U.S. Supreme Court decided a series of cases in the 1880s and 1890s known collectively as the Chinese Exclusion cases. One of the more important was *Chae Chan Ping v. United States* (1889), in which the Court upheld an 1888 law, called the Scott Act, which prohibited Chinese laborers from reentering the United States even if they had previously obtained a reentry certificate. The effect of this law was to abolish the certificates of reentry.

Chae Chan Ping was a Chinese laborer who lived in San Francisco for twelve years from 1875 to 1887. He left the United States and then sailed back to San Francisco in 1888. He was denied reentry based on the 1888 law.

The U.S. Supreme Court unanimously upheld the 1888 law, reasoning the government has broad powers in restricting the rights of aliens to enter the country. "That the government of the United States, through the action of the legislative department, can exclude aliens from its territory is a proposition which we do not think open to controversy," Justice Stephen Field wrote for the Court. "Jurisdiction over its own territory to that extent is an incident of every independent nation." He added that the government could revoke at any time reentry certificates to aliens "at its pleasure."

The Fuller Court **relaxed its stance toward Chinese persons born in America** in what decision?

The case was *U.S. v. Wong Kim Ark* (1898). The Fuller Court had begun in a time of extreme hostility toward persons of Chinese descent, as the Chinese Exclusion cases showed. However, the justices softened their stance in a decision involving Wong Kim

> ## CourtSpeak: *Chae Chan Ping v. United States* Reentry Case (1889)
>
> Justice Stephen Field (majority): "Whatever license, therefore, Chinese laborers may have obtained, previous to the act of October 1, 1888, to return to the United States after their departure, is held at the will of the government, revocable at any time, at its pleasure. Whether a proper consideration by our government of its previous laws, or a proper respect for the nation whose subjects are affected by its action, ought to have qualified its inhibition, and made it applicable only to persons departing from the country after the passage of the act, are not questions for judicial determination."

Ark, a man born to Chinese parents in San Francisco. The issue began when Ark left San Francisco to visit China and then sought to reenter the United States.

A customs inspector denied Ark reentry to the United States based on the Chinese Exclusion cases, such as *Chae Chan Ping v. United States* (1889). A lower federal court ruled that Ark could not be denied entrance to the United States because he was born there. The government appealed to the U.S. Supreme Court, which affirmed the lower court in *U.S. v. Wong Kim Ark.*

The Court relied on the explicit language of the Fourteenth Amendment, which states: "All persons born or naturalized in the United States, and subject to the jurisdiction thereof, are citizens of the United States and of the state wherein they reside." The Court wrote that this amendment "affirms the ancient and fundamental rule of citizenship by birth within the territory, in the allegiance and under the protection of the country, including all children born of resident aliens."

What **distinction did the Court make between the Chinese Exclusions cases and the *Wong Kim Ark* case**?

The Court recognized a distinction between Wong Kim Ark and the Chinese Exclusion Cases based on place of birth. The persons denied reentry to the United States in the Chinese Exclusion cases were not born in the United States. The Court pointed out that while Congress may pass laws limiting the status of aliens, the Fourteenth Amendment explicitly provides that all persons born in the United States are citizens.

Which **two justices dissented** and ruled against Wong Kim Ark?

Chief Justice Melville Fuller and Justice John Marshall Harlan, the lone dissenter in *Plessy v. Ferguson,* ruled against Wong Kim Ark. They focused on the fact that the Fourteenth Amendment was passed largely to ensure citizenship for recently freed African Americans. They wrote that "the subjects of the emperor of China … have never been allowed by our laws to acquire our nationality, and, except in sporadic instances, do not appear ever to have desired to do so."

LABOR

In what famous, oft-criticized decision did the Fuller Court **strike down a 10-hour workday for New York bakers**?

The Fuller Court ruled 5–4 in *Lochner v. New York* that a state law limiting employers to a 10-hour workday and a 60-hour workweek for their employees violated an employer's liberty of contract rights under the Fourteenth Amendment. The dispute arose after Utica-based bakery owner Joseph Lochner allegedly worked employee Aman Schmitter longer than 60 hours a week.

This violated an 1897 New York law that imposed the work-hour limitations to protect the health and safety of workers, many of whom toiled in less than savory conditions. A sharply divided Court struck down the law, finding it a violation of the employer's liberty of contract: "There is no reasonable ground for interfering with the liberty or person or the right of free contract, by determining the hours of labor, in the occupation of a baker." The Court majority, in an opinion written by Justice Rufus Peckham, reasoned that the state had failed to show that the measure was necessary to further the health and safety of the workers: "There is, in our judgment, no reasonable foundation for holding this to be necessary or appropriate as a health law to safeguard the public health, or the health of the individuals who are following the trade of a baker."

CourtSpeak: *Lochner v. New York* Work-Hours Limitation Case (1905)

Justice Rufus Peckham (majority): "It is manifest to us that the limitation of the hours of labor as provided for in this section of the statute under which the indictment was found, and the plaintiff in error convicted, has no such direct relation to, and no such substantial effect upon, the health of the employee, as to justify us in regarding the section as really a health law. It seems to us that the real object and purpose were simply to regulate the hours of labor between the master and his employees ... in a private business, not dangerous in any degree to morals, or in any real and substantial degree to the health of the employees. Under such circumstances the freedom of master and employee to contract with each other in relation to their employment, and in defining the same, cannot be prohibited or interfered with, without violating the Federal Constitution."

Justice Oliver Wendell Holmes (dissenting): "The Fourteenth Amendment does not enact Mr. Herbert Spencer's Social Statics.... Some of these laws embody convictions or prejudices which judges are likely to share. Some may not. But a Constitution is not intended to embody a particular economic theory, whether of paternalism and the organic relation of the citizen to the state or of laissez faire. It is made for people of fundamentally different views, and the accident of our finding certain opinions natural and familiar, or novel, and even shocking, ought not to conclude our judgment upon the question whether statutes embodying them conflict with the Constitution of the United States."

Justice John Marshall Harlan (dissenting): "Upon this point there is no room for dispute; for the rule is universal that a legislative enactment, Federal or state, is never to be disregarded or held invalid unless it be, beyond question, plainly and palpably in excess of legislative power."

Why was the *Lochner* decision criticized so much?

Many believed that the Court was substituting its own judgment for that of the legislature and imposing its own laissez-faire economic theory to the Constitution. Many criticized the decision because they believed that the Court's expansive interpretation of the Due Process Clause would enable it to strike down any state laws that conflicted with its pro-business, economic theory.

Which justices dissented in the *Lochner* case?

Justices Oliver Wendell Holmes and John Marshall Harlan both authored dissenting opinions. Holmes criticized the majority for reading its own economic theories into the Constitution. He said the law should not be struck down unless it could be shown that it was irrational and did not further the state's legitimate interest in health. Jus-

Women workers line up with baskets of dirty clothes at a commercial laundry. In *Muller v. Oregon,* the Fuller Court unanimously upheld a 10-hour work day limit for women workers. *Chaloner Woods/Hulton Archive/Getty Images.*

tice Harlan believed that the majority gave too short shrift to the state's police powers and to the presumption that legislation is constitutional.

Who ironically switched sides in the controversy over limiting bakers' hours?

As a member of the Journeyman Bakers' Union, Henry Weisman urged the New York legislature to pass the law protecting bakery employees. However, he switched sides years later and actually represented Lochner before the U.S. Supreme Court. Weisman served as counsel to the State Association of Master Bakers, which had funded Lochner's appeal to the U.S. Supreme Court. Weisman had become a master baker and claimed that he later saw that the law was unfair to bakery employers, particularly during "busy seasons" such as holidays.

The Court upheld a 10-hour limit for women workers in what decision?

The Fuller Court unanimously ruled 9–0 in *Muller v. Oregon* that an Oregon law providing that women working in mechanical establishments, factories, and laundries could not work more than 10 hours a day was constitutional. The case began when it was alleged that Joe Haselbeck, a foreman at Grand Laundry in Portland, required Mrs. Elmer Gotcher to work more than ten hours on September 4, 1905.

Curt Muller, the owner of the laundry, was convicted for violating the law. He

challenged his conviction, contending that the law violated the Fourteenth Amend-

---

CourtSpeak: *Muller v. Oregon* Women's Working Hours Case (1908)

Justice David Brewer (majority): "The two sexes differ in structure of body, in the functions to be performed by each, in the amount of physical strength, in the capacity for long continued labor, particularly when done standing, the influence of various health upon the future well-being of the race, the self-reliance which enables one to assert full rights, and in the capacity to maintain the struggle for subsistence. This difference justifies a difference in legislation, and upholds that which is designed to compensate for some of the burdens which rest upon her."

---

ment Due Process and Equal Protection clauses. His attorneys relied largely on the Fuller Court's decision in *Lochner,* which struck down a 10-hour work day for New York bakeries.

The U.S. Supreme Court relied in part on a paternalistic description of women to rule against Muller and in favor of the state law. "That women's physical structure and the performance of maternal functions place her at a disadvantage in the struggle for subsistence is obvious," Justice David Brewer wrote.

What **future Supreme Court justice represented the state** in this case?

Three attorneys represented the state before the U.S. Supreme Court, including Boston-based attorney Louis D. Brandeis. He authored a brief of more than 115 pages, the vast majority compiled of various social science data and literature that documented the damaging health effects on women from working long hours. The U.S. Supreme Court recognized Brandeis by name in its opinion, which is quite unusual: "In the brief filed by Mr. Louis D. Brandeis for the defendant in errors is a very copious collection of all these matters, an epitome of which is found in the margin." Brandeis's heavy reliance on social science and other non-legal data formed part of the basis of what became known as "Brandeis briefs."

In what decision did the Court uphold a **Utah law limiting the hours of miners**?

The Fuller Court ruled in *Holden v. Hardy* (1898) that a Utah statute limiting miners to 8-hour work days was constitutional. Albert Holden, convicted for violating the statute, challenged his conviction in federal court, suing Salt Lake County sheriff Harvey Hardy. The Court determined that the state's interests in ensuring public health and safety justified this law. The Court focused on the dangerous working conditions in mines in support of the statute.

155

A coal miner stands below ground. In *Holden v. Hardy*, the Fuller Court ruled that a Utah statute limiting miners to 8-hour work days was constitutional. *Hulton Archive/Getty Images.*

In what decision did the Court strike down a federal law protecting railroad workers from being fired for union activity?

The Fuller Court ruled 7–2 in *Adair v. United States* (1908) that a federal law prohibiting railroads from discriminating against employees for union activities violated the liberty of contract found in the Fifth Amendment's Due Process Clause and exceeded Congress's power under the Commerce Clause because there was "no legal or logical connection" between union activities and interstate commerce.

The law prohibited an employer from threatening "any employee with loss of employment, or ... unjustly discriminat[ing] against any employee because of his membership in such a labor corporation, association, or organization." Allegedly, William Adair, master mechanic for the Louisville & Nashville Railroad Company, discriminated against employee O. B. Coppage because of his union membership. (Adair was Coppage's supervisor.)

The majority, in an opinion written by Justice John Marshall Harlan, reasoned that the law invaded the liberty of contract between employer and employee. Harlan reasoned that the employment setting was generally one of equality, as either employer or employees could terminate the relationship at will. Relying on this at-will employment doctrine, Harlan reasoned that just as Coppage could leave his employment at any time or for any reason, the railroad boss "was at liberty, in his discretion, to discharge Coppage from service without giving any reason for so doing." Harlan also rejected the

> ### CourtSpeak: *Holden v. Hardy* Miners' Working Hours Case (1898)
>
> Justice Henry Billings Brown (majority): "While the general experience of mankind may justify us in believing that men may engage in ordinary employments more than eight hours per day without injury to their health, it does not follow that labor for the same length of time is innocuous when carried on beneath the surface of the earth, where the operative is deprived of fresh air and sunlight, and is frequently subjected to foul atmosphere and a very high temperature, or to the influence of noxious gases generated by the processes of refining or smelting."

notion that Congress could justify this law based on its commerce powers, asking: "But what possible legal or logical connection is there between an employee's membership in a labor organization and the carrying on of interstate commerce?"

In what decision did the Fuller Court strike down a state statute regulating **railway rates**?

The Fuller Court unanimously ruled 7–0 (Justices Fuller and McKenna did not participate) in *Smyth v. Ames* (1898) that a Nebraska statute regulating the rates of railways was unconstitutional. The Court determined that "the basis of all calculations as to the reasonableness of rates to be charged by a corporation maintaining a highway under legislative sanction must be the fair value of the property being used by it for the convenience of the public."

Looking at the evidence presented, the Court determined that the rates mandated by the Nebraska law were too low and "would deprive the railroad companies of the compensation they were legally entitled to receive." The Court established the precedent that the courts had the power to review rates by public utilities. This law remained in good standing until the Court overruled it in *Federal Power Commission v. Hope Natural Gas Co.* (1944).

In what case involving a railroad company did the Court extend the **Fifth Amendment protection of just compensation to the states**?

The Fuller Court ruled in *Chicago, Burlington & Quincy Railroad Company v. Chicago* (1897) that the Fifth Amendment protection of just compensation was extended to the states via the Fourteenth Amendment's Due Process Clause. This marked the first time that the U.S. Supreme Court ever extended a provision in the federal Bill of Rights to the states. The Court concluded: "Due process of law, as applied to judicial proceedings instituted for the taking of private property for public use, means, therefore, such process as recognizes the right of the owner to be compensated if his prop-

157

erty be wrested from him and transferred to the public." All the justices agreed that the Fourteenth Amendment Due Process Clause included the Fifth Amendment right to just compensation when the government takes private property. Justice David Brewer's opinion is labeled a dissent only because he did not believe, under the facts of the case, that the railroad company received just compensation.

What was the **railway company's underlying claim in the case** and what "just compensation" did it receive?

The city of Chicago decided to widen Rockwell Street, which forced the city to condemn certain parcels of land, including some owned by the Chicago, Burlington & Quincy Railroad Company. The city filed a petition for the condemnation of the land and asked for a determination of the just compensation to be paid to the railroad company for its loss of a right of way. A jury determined that the railroad company should be paid a total of $1 for the loss of its right of way (railroad track). Incidentally, Justice David Brewer wrote that the railroad company's receipt of $1 dollar amounted to nominal, rather than just, compensation. "The abundant promises of the forepart of the opinion vanish into nothing when the conclusion is reached," Brewer wrote.

> ## CourtSpeak: *Allgeyer v. Louisiana* Liberty of Contract Case (1897)
>
> Justice Rufus Peckham (unanimous): "The 'liberty' mentioned in that amendment means, not only the right of the citizen to be free from the mere physical restraint of his person, as by incarceration, but the term is deemed to embrace the right of the citizen to be free in the enjoyment of all his faculties; to be free to use them in all lawful ways; to live and work where he will; to earn his livelihood by any lawful calling; to pursue any livelihood or avocation; and for that purpose to enter into all contracts which may be proper, necessary, and essential to his carrying out to a successful conclusion the purposes above mentioned."

In what decision did the Fuller Court find a **Fourteenth Amendment right to make contracts**?

The Fuller Court unanimously ruled 9–0 in *Allgeyer v. Louisiana* (1897) that a state law prohibiting its residents from entering into insurance contracts with out-of-state companies was unconstitutional. The Court reasoned that such a restriction infringed on individuals' rights to enter into contracts without governmental infringement. The decision's elevation of the right to enter into contracts into the Fourteenth Amendment served as a key precedent when the Court began to strike down other state statutes as violative of the liberty of contract.

In what decision did the Fuller Court rule that a **state could ban the manufacture of alcohol**?

The Fuller Court ruled 8–0 in *Kidd v. Pearson* (1888) that the state of Iowa could ban the manufacture and sale of "intoxicating liquors" unless the alcohol is used for "mechanical, medicinal, culinary or sacramental purposes." A distillery owned by J. S. Kidd challenged the constitutionality of the statute, arguing that it infringed on the powers of the U.S. Congress, which regulates interstate commerce. The distillery argued that the banning of the manufacturing of liquor negatively impacted interstate commerce because it limited the flow of alcohol to other states.

The Fuller Court rejected this argument, finding that the statute affected in-state manufacturing, not interstate commerce. The Court explained that the state's broad police powers enabled it to control the manufacture and sale of alcohol. With respect to the interstate commerce argument, it explained: "It does not follow that, because the products of a domestic manufacture may ultimately become the subjects of interstate commerce, at the pleasure of the manufacturer the legislation of the state respecting such manufacture is an attempted exercise of the power to regulate commerce exclusively conferred upon congress."

159

> ## CourtSpeak: *Kidd v. Pearson* Interstate Commerce Alcohol Case (1888)
>
> Justice Lucius C. Q. Lamar (unanimous): "No distinction is more popular to the common mind, or more clearly expressed in economic and political literature, than that between manufactures and commerce. Manufacture is transformation—the fashioning of raw materials into a change of form for use. The functions of commerce are different. The buying and selling and the transportation incidental thereto constitute commerce; and the regulation of commerce in the constitutional sense embraces the regulation at least of such transportation."

In what Fuller Court decision did Justice Oliver Wendell Holmes advocate the **"stream of commerce" theory**?

Justice Oliver Wendell Holmes advocated the "stream of commerce" theory in the Court's unanimous decision in *Swift & Co. v. United States* (1905). The Court ruled that a group of meatpacking houses engaged in a variety of activities, including fixing and bidding up prices, that violated the Sherman Antitrust law. The meatpacking houses contended that their activities were intrastate in nature, but the Court noted that the sale of cattle resembled a "current of commerce" that was interstate in nature. Holmes wrote: "When cattle are sent for sale from a place in one state, with the expectation that they will end their transit, after purchase, in another, and when in effect they do so, with only the interruption necessary to find a purchaser at the stock yards, and when this is a typical, constantly recurring course, the current thus existing is a current of commerce among the states, and the purchase of the cattle is a part and incident of such commerce."

In what decision did the Fuller Court rule that **aliens can recover property** in the United States?

The Fuller Court ruled 8–0 in *De Geofroy v. Riggs* (1890) that French citizens can inherit property in the District of Columbia. The issue arose after T. Law-rason Riggs, a U.S. citizen, died without a will in the District of Columbia. Several of his nieces and nephews were French citizens. The issue arose because a dispute arose as to whether the nieces and nephews could recover because they were aliens or whether the entirety of the deceased's estate would go to his American siblings. The nieces and nephews petitioned for a share of the estate. Lower courts denied their claims, saying they could not recover because they were not U.S. citizens.

On appeal, the U.S. Supreme Court phrased the legal question as: "Can citizens of France take land in the District of Columbia by descent from citizens of the United States?" The Court, in an opinion written by Justice Stephen Field, answered yes, relying

Workers wash and tag freshly killed lamb at Swift's Packing House in Chicago in the early 1900s. In *Swift & Co. v. United States* (1905), the Fuller Court ruled that a group of meatpacking houses engaged in activities, including fixing and bidding up prices, that violated the Sherman Antitrust law. *Library of Congress.*

on an 1853 treaty between the United States and France that provided in part: "In all the states of the Union whose existing laws permit it, so long and to the same extent as the said laws shall remain in force, Frenchmen shall enjoy the right of possessing personal and real property by the same title, and in the same manner, as the citizens of the United States." The treaty further provided that in those states that do not allow French citizens to inherit property, "the President engages to recommend to them the passage of such laws" as are necessary to entitle French persons to inherit such property.

One problem remained for the French nieces and nephews: their uncle's estate was located in the District of Columbia, which is not a state. The U.S. Supreme Court addressed that problem by reasoning that the intent of the treaty was to provide French citizens the right to inherit property throughout the entire United States, of which the District of Columbia most certainly was a part.

What Fuller Court decision led to the adoption of a **Constitutional Amendment dealing with taxation**?

The Fuller Court's controversial decision in *Pollock v. Farmers' Loan & Trust Co.* (1895), striking down most of an 1894 federal income tax law, led to the eventual passage of the Sixteenth Amendment in 1913, which provides: "The Congress shall have power to lay and collect taxes on incomes, from whatever source derived, without apportionment among the several States and without regard to any census or enumeration."

Why were there **two decisions in *Pollock***?

The U.S. Supreme Court first issued its decision in *Pollock* on April 8, 1895, but split 4–4 on the question of whether a general income tax was constitutional. There were only eight justices participating because Justice Howell Jackson was afflicted with tuberculosis. After he recovered, the Court heard rearguments in early May and ruled 5–4 that the tax law was unconstitutional. The majority, in an opinion written by Chief

CourtSpeak: *Pollock v. Farmers' Loan & Trust Co.*
General Income Tax Case (1895)

Chief Justice Melville Fuller (majority): "The power to tax real and personal property and the income from both, there being an apportionment, is conceded; that such a tax is a direct tax in the meaning of the Constitution has not been, and, in our judgment, cannot be, successfully denied, and yet we are thus invited to hesitate in the enforcement of the mandate of the Constitution, which prohibits Congress from laying a direct tax on the revenue from property of the citizen without regard to state lines, and in such manner that the States cannot intervene by payment in regulation of their own resources lest a government of delegated powers should be found to be, not less powerful, but less absolute, than the imagination of the advocate had supposed."

Justice John Marshall Harlan (dissenting): "It thus appears that the primary object of all taxation by the general government is to pay the debts and provide for the common defence and general welfare of the United States, and that, with the exception of the inhibition upon taxes or duties on articles exported from the States, no restriction is in terms imposed upon national taxation except that direct taxes must be apportioned among the several States on the basis of numbers (excluding Indians not taxed), while duties, imposts and excises must be uniform throughout the United States."

Justice Henry Billings Brown (dissenting): "But, however this may be, I regard it as very clear that the clause requiring direct taxes to be apportioned to the population has no application to taxes which are not capable of apportionment according to population.... While I have no doubt that Congress will find some means of surmounting the present crisis, my fear is that, in some in moment of national peril, this decision will rise up to frustrate its will and paralyze its arm. I hope it may not prove the first step toward the submergence of the liberties of the people in a sordid despotism of wealth."

Justice Howell Jackson (dissenting): "The most natural and practical test by which to determine what is a direct tax in the sense of the Constitution is to ascertain whether the tax can be apportioned among the several States according to their respective numbers, with reasonable approximation to justice, fairness, and equality to all the citizens and inhabitants of the country who may be subject to the operation of the law. The fact that a tax cannot be so apportioned without producing gross injustice and inequality among those required to pay it should settle the question that it was not a direct tax within the true sense and meaning of those words as they are used in the Constitution."

Justice Fuller, reasoned that the law violated Article II, Section 9, of the Constitution, which provides: "No Capitation, or other direct, Tax shall be laid, unless in Proportion to the Census or Enumeration herein before directed to be taken." The argument was that the tax was unconstitutional because it was a direct tax that must be apportioned to the states according to their population, instead of being applied generally and uniformly to all those across the country with incomes greater than $4,000.

Justice Henry Billings Brown and three others dissented. Brown wrote: "The decision involves nothing less than a surrender of the taxing power to the moneyed class. Even the spectre of socialism is conjured up to frighten Congress from laying taxes upon the people in proportion to their ability to pay them."

In what decision did the Court uphold **broad use of the taxing power as a regulatory measure**?

The Fuller Court ruled 6–3 in *McCray v. United States* that Congress could impose taxes on the production of oleomargarine, a butter substitute, without invading the authority of the state's police powers. Licensed retail dealer Leo McCray challenged the federal law that imposed such a tax on the butter substitute after he was fined $50 for violating the law. He contended that the law was unconstitutional because Congress imposed the tax not to raise revenue but to regulate the manufacture of oleomargarine to favor the production of butter.

Writing for the Court, Justice Edward White found no constitutional problem with the statute. He reasoned that Congress has the constitutional power to issue excise taxes

CourtSpeak: *United States v. E. C. Knight* Antitrust Case (1895)

Chief Justice Melville Fuller (majority): "Contracts, combinations, or conspiracies to control domestic enterprise in manufacture, agriculture mining, production in all its forms, or to raise or lower prices or wages, might unquestionably tend to restrain external as well as domestic trade, but the restraint would be an indirect result, however inevitable, and whatever its extent, and such result would not necessarily determine the object of the contract, combination, or conspiracy."

Justice John Marshall Harlan (dissenting): "If this combination, so far as its operations necessarily or directly affect interstate commerce, cannot be restrained or suppressed under some power granted to congress, it will be cause for regret that the patriotic statesmen who framed the constitution did not foresee the necessity of investing the national government with power to deal with gigantic monopolies holding in their grasp, and injuriously controlling in their own interest, the entire trade among the states in food products that are essential to the comfort of every household in the land."

and to pass laws designed to prevent consumer fraud. It was common knowledge that oleomargarine was made to look just like butter. Justice White reasoned that if the states could prohibit the manufacture of oleomargarine because it deceived the public into buying it for butter, then surely the federal government had the power to tax the product. Chief Justice Fuller and Justices Brown and Peckham dissented without an opinion.

What was the **Lottery Case**?

The Fuller Court issued a 5–4 ruling in *Champion v. Ames* (1903), a case more commonly known as the Lottery Case, that Congress had the power to regulate the trafficking of lottery tickets. The majority reasoned: "We are of the opinion that lottery tickets are subjects of traffic, and therefore are subjects of commerce, and the regulation of the carriage of such tickets from state to state, at least by independent carriers, is a regulation of commerce among the several states." The case is important because it recognized a broad federal police power to enact legislation to prevent harmful effects upon the public.

What was the Fuller Court's first decision in which it applied the **Sherman Antitrust Act**?

The Fuller Court first considered a Sherman antitrust action in its famous *United States v. E. C. Knight* (1895) decision, which dealt with the government's action against the American Sugar Refining Company. The firm had acquired virtually all of

The Fuller Court ruled in *In Re Debs* (1895) that famed labor organizer Eugene Debs (above) could be cited for criminal contempt for refusing to obey a court injunction prohibiting the leading of a railway strike. *Hulton Archive/Getty Images.*

the sugar refining interests in the country, triggering the government's contention that the company had built a monopoly and restrained trade. The Court determined the antitrust law did not enable Congress to regulate the manufacture of products in individual states even if those products eventually reached into commerce and traveled into other states. The Court drew a sharp distinction between manufacturing and commerce, which limited Congress's power. "Commerce succeeds to manufacture and is not a part of it," wrote Chief Justice Fuller. "The fact that an article is manufactured for export to another state does not of itself make it an article of interstate commerce, and the intent of the manufacturer does not determine the time when the article or product passes from the control of the state and belongs to commerce."

Only Justice John Marshall Harlan dissented, reasoning that Congress must have the power to deal with "gigantic monopolies."

In what case did the U.S. Supreme Court sanction the use of injunctions against striking railroad workers?

The U.S. Supreme Court ruled in *In Re Debs* (1895) that famed labor organizer Eugene Debs could be cited for criminal contempt for refusing to obey a court injunction prohibiting the leading of a strike of Pullman railway cars and other railroads. "The strong arm of the National Government may be put forth to brush away all obstructions to the freedom of interstate commerce or the transportation of the mails," wrote Justice David Brewer. "If the emergency arises, the army of the Nation, and all its militia, are at the service of the Nation to compel obedience to its laws." The Court reasoned that the injunction was necessary to deal with the violence associated with the striking workers. Debs went to prison for six months and later became even better known as a Socialist Party candidate for president. He actually received more than one million votes in the 1912 and 1920 elections.

What famous **attorney represented Eugene Debs**?

Clarence Darrow, one of the country's most famous attorneys, defended Eugene Debs in *In Re Debs* when he was arrested for contempt of court for refusing to obey the court injunction regarding the railway strike. Ironically, Darrow had been an attorney for the railway but changed his allegiance in belief of the unfairness against the striking railroad workers.

What Fuller Court decision outlawed **secondary boycotts by unions**?

The Fuller Court unanimously ruled 9–0 in *Loewe v. Lawlor* (1908) that the union activities of the United Hatters of North America and the American Federation of Labor violated the Sherman Antitrust law because it impeded interstate commerce and restrained trade. The individual members of the Hatters union in Connecticut, where the suit originated, contended that they were not subject to the

Attorney Clarence Darrow (above) represented Eugene Debs in *In Re Debs* (1895). *Hulton Archive/Getty Images.*

Sherman antitrust acts because their conduct was intrastate in nature and only affected activities in Connecticut. The Fuller Court unanimously disagreed in an opinion written by Chief Justice Fuller. He wrote that the individual members were part of a broader union effort in various states that affected interstate commerce and trade. The ruling was a major victory for manufacturers and forced labor to petition Congress for statutory exemption from the labor laws.

CRIMINAL JUSTICE

In what decision did the Fuller Court define the meaning of the **"Cruel and Unusual Punishment Clause"** in the Eighth Amendment?

The Fuller Court ruled in *Weems v. United States* (1910) that Coast Guard officer Paul Weems's sentence of 15 years in the Philippine courts for falsifying official documents was excessive enough to violate the Eighth Amendment's ban on "cruel and unusual punishment." The Philippines, then a U.S. territory, had fashioned its Philippine Bill **167** of Rights after the U.S. Bill of Rights and, indeed, included a ban on cruel and unusual punishments.

The Court ruled 4–2 (Justices Lurton and Moody did not participate and Justice Brewer's replacement had not yet been named) that the sentence was excessive. Justice McKenna noted for the Court that a litany of more serious offenses in the United States provided less severe punishments than what Weems received, including some "degrees of homicide, misprision of treason, inciting rebellion, conspiracy to destroy the government by force … robbery, larceny, and other crimes."

In which case did the Fuller Court rule that **death by electrocution was not cruel and unusual**?

The Court ruled unanimously in *In Re Kemmler* (1890) that the state of New York could execute convicted murderer William Kemmler by a relatively new method of execution called electrocution. Attorneys for Kemmler argued that the punishment violated the Eighth Amendment because this punishment certainly was unusual. The Court noted that while the punishment could be classified as unusual because it was so new, it was not cruel. The Court noted that the New York legislature had the authority to pass a law allowing this new form of execution, writing: "The enactment of this statute was, in itself, within the legitimate sphere of the legislative power of the state, and in the observance of those general rules prescribed by our systems of jurisprudence; and the legislature of the state of New York determined that it did not inflict cruel and unusual punishment, and its courts have sustained that determination. We cannot perceive that the state has thereby abridged the privileges or immunities of the petitioner, or deprived him of due process of law."

What is the origin of the word **"electrocution"**?

The word "electrocution" comes from the combination of the words "execution" and "electricity." This form of death-penalty punishment is still used by some states.

> ## CourtSpeak: *Twining v. New Jersey* Self-Incrimination Case (1908)
>
> Justice William Moody (majority): "Even if the historical meaning of due process of law and the decisions of this court did not exclude the privilege from it, it would be going far to rate it as an immutable principle of justice which is the inalienable possession of every citizen of a free government.... The wisdom of the exemption has never been universally assented to since the days of [Jeremy] Bentham [a famous nineteenth-century English philosopher who generally argued in favor of individual freedom], many doubt it today, and it is best defended not as an unchangeable principle of universal justice, but as a law proved by experience to be expedient."
>
> Justice John Marshall Harlan (dissenting): "The Fourteenth Amendment would have been disapproved by every state in the Union if it had saved or recognized the right of a state to compel one accused of crime, in its courts, to be a witness against himself. We state the matter in this way because it is common knowledge that the compelling of a person to incriminate himself shocks or ought to shock the sense of right and justice to everyone who loves liberty. Indeed, this court has not hesitated thus to characterize the star chamber method of compelling an accused to be a witness against himself."

In what decision did the Fuller Court refuse to extend the **Fifth Amendment privilege against self-incrimination to the states**?

The Fuller Court ruled 8–1 in *Twining v. New Jersey* (1908) that the Fifth Amendment privilege against self-incrimination did not apply to the states. This meant that a New Jersey trial judge did not violate the constitutional rights of defendants Albert Twining and David Cornell when he instructed the jury to consider the fact that the two men refused to take the stand to defend themselves. The trial judge gave a jury instruction, which stated in part: "Because a man does not go upon the stand you are not necessarily justified in drawing an inference of guilt. But you have a right to consider the fact that he does not go upon the stand where a direct accusation is made against him."

After the two men, who were bank officials, were convicted of passing false information to a state banking examiner, they appealed their conviction to the U.S. Supreme Court.

In an opinion written by Justice William Moody, the Court ruled that New Jersey was free to adopt a privilege against self-incrimination but was not compelled to do so by the Federal Constitution. Moody noted that only four of the original thirteen states had incorporated a privilege against self-incrimination in their states. He added that the right against self-incrimination was not so fundamental a right that its absence

169

would constitute a violation of due process. According to Moody, the essential elements of the Due Process Clause were notice of the charges and an opportunity to be heard.

Who was the Court's **lone dissenter in the *Twining* case**?

Once again, Justice John Marshall Harlan was the Court's lone dissenter. He wrote that the Fourteenth Amendment protected individuals from incriminating themselves. He wrote: "Certainly it is, that when the present government of the United States was established it was the belief of all liberty-loving men in America that real, genuine freedom could not exist in any country that recognized the power of government to compel persons accused of crimes to be witnesses against themselves."

Is *Twining* still good law today?

No, defendants in state and federal courts cannot be forced to testify against themselves. Instead, they may assert their Fifth Amendment privilege against self-incrimination. The U.S. Supreme Court finally overruled *Twining* in its 1964 decision *Malloy v. Hogan*.

What **town was named after Twining**?

A New Mexico copper mining town was named Twining because the New Jersey banker financed it in the early 1900s. After his conviction for embezzlement, Twining sold his interest in the town. The town of Twining, located in Taos County, is a ghost town now; a ski resort exists on the former site.

What Fuller Court decision **upheld a state criminal conviction with only eight jurors**?

The Fuller Court ruled 8–1 in *Maxwell v. Dow* (1900) that Utah courts did not violate the constitutional rights of defendant Charles Maxwell when he was convicted by an 8-member jury instead of a 12-member jury used in the federal courts. Maxwell alleged that his Fifth Amendment rights were violated because he was prosecuted by an information instead of a grand jury indictment. In an information, a prosecutor submits the evidence to a judge for an initial threshold determination as to whether the prosecutor can proceed with the criminal charges.

The Court, in an opinion written by Justice Rufus Peckham, rejected Maxwell's constitutional claims, reasoning that these rights were not extended to state court defendants via the Fourteenth Amendment. Peckham recognized that "a jury composed, as at common law, of twelve jurors was intended by the Sixth Amendment to the Federal Constitution, there can be no doubt." However, Justice Peckham said that the Fourteenth Amendment did not extend the Sixth Amendment to the states and states could convict defendants with an 8-member jury.

CourtSpeak: *Maxwell v. Dow* Fourteenth Amendment Case (1900)

Justice Rufus Peckham (majority): "It appears to us that the questions whether a trial in criminal cases not capital shall be by a jury composed of eight instead of twelve jurors, and whether, in case of an infamous crime, a person shall only be liable to be tried after presentment or indictment of a grand jury, are eminently proper to be determined by the citizens of each State for themselves, and do not come within the clause of the amendment under consideration so long as all persons within the jurisdiction of the State are made liable to be proceeded against by the same kind of procedure and to have the same kind of trial, and the equal protection of the laws is secured to them."

Justice John Marshall Harlan (dissenting): "It does not meet the case to say that a trial by eight jurors is as much a trial by jury as if there were twelve jurors; for if a citizen charged with crime can be subjected to trial by a less number of jurors than that prescribed by the Constitution, the number may be reduced to three. Indeed, under the interpretation now given to the amendment, it will, I think, be impossible to escape the conclusion that a state may abolish trial by jury altogether in a criminal case, however grave the offense charged, and authorize the trial of a case of felony before a single judge. I cannot assent to this interpretation, because it is opposed to the plain words of the Constitution, and defeats the manifest object of the Fourteenth Amendment."

Who was the Court's **lone dissenter in the *Maxwell* case**?

Once again, Justice John Marshall Harlan filed the Court's only dissenting opinion. He believed that the Fourteenth Amendment's "Privileges and Immunities" Clause extended the protections in the first eight amendments in the Bill of Rights to the states. He also wrote that "the trial of the accused for the crime charged against him by a jury of eight persons was not consistent with the 'due process of law' prescribed by the Fourteenth Amendment."

In what famous decision did the Fuller Court **reject the equal protection claim of an African American defendant convicted by an all-white jury**?

The Fuller Court unanimously ruled 9–0 in *Williams v. Mississippi* (1898) that defendant Henry Williams's equal-protection rights were not violated when he was convicted by an all-white jury. Williams, an African American, asserted that his conviction violated the principles of equal protection because Mississippi's jury system effectively prevented blacks from serving on juries and led to an all-white jury. The state had

171

passed literacy and poll test requirements as an impediment for blacks that kept them from voting. The Court concluded that the Mississippi voting laws "do not on their face discriminate between the races, and it has not been shown that their actual administration was evil; only that evil was possible under them."

Associate Justice Rufus Peckham wrote on behalf of the Fuller Court in its decision allowing a state criminal conviction with only eight jurors, rather than the typical twelve. *Hulton Archive/Getty*

In what decision did the Fuller Court reverse the conviction of an **African American defendant who alleged discrimination in the Texas grand jury system**?

The Fuller Court unanimously ruled in *Carter v. Texas* (1900) that the conviction of Seth Carter, an African American male, must be set aside because the state court did not allow Carter sufficient opportunity to present evidence and because the grand jury system under which he was indicted was discriminatory because it did not allow for the inclusion of African Americans. The Court concluded that "the defendant has been denied a right duly set up and claimed by him under the Constitution and laws of the United States." The Court reasoned that the state court could not simply ignore the allegations and must address them in some fashion.

What decision gave **broad Fifth Amendment protection to grand jury witnesses**?

The Fuller Court unanimously ruled 9–0 in *Counselman v. Hitchcock* (1892) that Charles Counselman was entitled to invoke the protections of the Fifth Amendment when he was a grand jury witness. The government contended that Counselman was not entitled to invoke the Fifth Amendment because he was called as a witness, not as the focus of the criminal inquiry. However, the Court disagreed, emphasizing that it applied when a person was a "witness in any investigation."

What bizarre case involved a **U.S. marshal imprisoned for protecting a U.S. Supreme Court justice**?

The U.S. Supreme Court case with the most bizarre set of facts may well be *In Re Neagle* (1890). The issue concerned whether U.S. marshal David Neagle was entitled to federal habeas corpus relief after he killed a man who was trying to harm U.S. Supreme

---

CourtSpeak: *Counselman v. Hitchcock* **Fifth Amendment Case (1892)**

Justice Samuel Blatchford (unanimous): "It is impossible that the meaning of the constitutional provision can only be that a person shall not be compelled to be a witness against himself in a criminal prosecution against himself. It would doubtless cover such cases; but it is not limited to them. The object was to insure that a person should not be compelled, when acting as a witness in any investigation, to give testimony which might tend to show that he himself had committed a crime. The privilege is limited to criminal matters, but it is as broad as the mischief against which it seeks to guard."

Court justice Stephen Field. California prosecutors had charged Neagle with the murder of David Terry, a former chief justice of the California Supreme Court.

The underlying facts begin with an unstable woman named Sarah Hill, who was a mistress to U.S. senator William Sharon of Nevada. Hill claimed that she was married to Sharon and she hired prominent California lawyer David Terry, who had served with Justice Field on the California Supreme Court. Terry sued on her behalf, claiming she was married to Sharon. A trial court denied her claim to marriage. She then appealed to an appeals court. The presiding appeals court judge was Justice Field.

Field denied Hill's appeal, enraging attorney Terry. When Field ruled against Hill, she went berserk in the courtroom. The marshals attempted to subdue her, but Terry rose to defend Hill, whom he had married while the case was on appeal. Terry punched one marshal and pulled out his Bowie knife to face others. Several marshals, including David Neagle, subdued Terry. Justice Field then sentenced both Terry and Hill to jail time for contempt of court.

In jail, Terry and Hill made threats against Justice Field, causing the U.S. attorney to appoint a marshal to protect Justice Field. The attorney selected Neagle to protect Justice Field. With Neagle at his side, Field then traveled by train to California. Hill and Terry were also on the train. When Hill saw Field, she ran to get her gun and Terry slapped Field twice in the face. Neagle confronted Terry and ordered him to quit assaulting the Supreme Court justice. Neagle shot and killed Terry on the train, as Terry appeared to pull open his jacket to brandish his own weapon.

Hill sought an arrest warrant against Neagle and Field. San Joaquin County sheriff Thomas Cunningham arrested both Neagle and Field, charging them both with murder, even though only Neagle fired the pistol. Neagle was jailed, but Field was released and the charges were dropped against him, presumably because he did not fire the pistol.

Neagle later filed a petition in federal court, seeking his release from the California jail. He prevailed before a lower federal court, prompting Sheriff Cunningham to appeal to the U.S. Supreme Court.

What did the **U.S. Supreme Court rule in the *Neagle* case**?

The U.S. Supreme Court ruled 6–2 (Justice Field did not participate for obvious reasons) that Neagle should be free of the charges because he was acting in his capacity as a U.S. marshal providing protection to a federal judge. In his majority opinion, Justice Samuel Miller noted the unusual circumstances, writing: "The occurrence which we are called upon to consider was of so extraordinary a character that it is not to be expected that many cases can be found to cite as authority upon the subject." The Court determined that Neagle was entitled to federal habeas relief because he was acting under the authority of the U.S. government. "Why do we have marshals at all, if they cannot physically lay their hands on persons and things in the performance of their proper duties?" Miller wrote. "What functions can they perform, if they cannot use force?"

Justice Lucius Lamar and Chief Justice Fuller dissented, though not on any "conviction as to the guilt or innocence" of Neagle. These justices reasoned that the federal courts did not have jurisdiction over this situation.

What is **interesting about Neagle's background**?

Neagle served as a town marshal and deputy sheriff in Tombstone, Arizona, in the early 1880s, after the infamous OK Corral Gunfight allegedly involving "Doc" Holliday and Wyatt Earp.

What landmark decision on the Eleventh Amendment sanctioned the **jailing of a state attorney general**?

The Fuller Court ruled 8–1 in *Ex Parte Young* (1908) that a federal court could issue a contempt citation against Minnesota attorney general Edward T. Young for violating a

CourtSpeak: *Patterson v. Colorado* Unfavorable Cartoon Case (1907)

Justice Oliver Wendell Holmes (majority): "A publication likely to reach the eyes of a jury, declaring a witness in a pending cause a perjurer, would be none the less a contempt that it was true. It would tend to obstruct the administration of justice, because even a correct conclusion is not to be reached or helped in that way, if our system of trials is to be maintained. The theory of our system is that the conclusions to be reached in a case will be induced only by evidence and argument in open court, and not by any outside influence, whether of private talk or public print."

Justice John Marshall Harlan (dissenting): "I go further and hold that the privileges of free speech and of a free press, belonging to every citizen of the United States, constitute essential parts of every man's liberty, and are protected against violation by that clause of the 14th Amendment forbidding a state to deprive any person of his liberty without due process of law. It is, I think, impossible to conceive of liberty, as secured by the Constitution against hostile action, whether by the nation or by the states, which does not embrace the right to enjoy free speech and the right to have a free press."

federal court order temporarily preventing him from enforcing new state laws that limited railroad rates. The state of Minnesota had passed a law that controlled the rates of railroads. Several railways responded by suing in federal court, challenging the constitutionality of this state law. They argued that the new law deprived the companies of their property rights in violation of the Due Process Clause.

Attorney General Young ignored the federal court's temporary injunction and the next day proceeded to enforce the new railway rate laws in state court. The federal court then ordered Young to show cause why he should not be jailed for contempt of court for ignoring the federal court order. Young argued that, as the attorney general of Minnesota, he was entitled to immunity under the Eleventh Amendment, which generally protects states from lawsuits by citizens.

The U.S. Supreme Court ruled against Young in an opinion written by Justice Rufus Peckham, who reasoned that state officials are not entitled to Eleventh Amendment immunity if they attempt to enforce laws that violate the Constitution. In such cases, the official is "stripped of his official or representative character and is subjected in his person to the consequences of his individual conduct." Peckham concluded: "The state cannot ... impart to the official immunity from the responsibility to the supreme authority of the United States."

Why is the *Ex Parte Young* decision important?

The decision is important because it enables citizens and others to file lawsuits in federal court, challenging the constitutionality of state legislation. It means that citizens can sue in federal court to obtain an injunction, preventing the enforcement of laws that violate the Constitution.

In what decision did the Fuller Court uphold a **contempt citation for a newspaper for publishing unfavorable cartoons**?

The Fuller Court ruled 7–2 in *Patterson v. Colorado* (1907) that Thomas Patterson, owner of both the *Rocky Mountain News* and the *Denver Times,* could be punished for contempt for published articles and cartoons highly critical of the Colorado Supreme Court. The Court, in an opinion written by Justice Oliver Wendell Holmes, did not extend the First Amendment protections of freedom of the press to the states via the Fourteenth Amendment. Holmes also noted that the primary purpose of the Free Press Clause was to prevent prior restraints on speech, rather than subsequent punishments for expression.

THE WHITE COURT (1910–21)

How many and which **justices served on the White Court**?

Thirteen justices served on the White Court, including: Chief Justice Edward White and Justices John Marshall Harlan, Joseph McKenna, Oliver Wendell Holmes, William Rufus Day, Horace H. Lurton, Charles Evans Hughes, Willis Van Devanter, Joseph R. Lamar, Mahlon Pitney, James McReynolds, Louis D. Brandeis, and John H. Clarke.

What was **unusual about Justice White becoming chief justice**?

Edward White was the first associate justice to be promoted to chief justice. White had served on the U.S. Supreme Court since 1894 on the Fuller Court before being elevated to chief justice after the retirement of Chief Justice Melville Fuller. The other unusual aspect was that it was the first time a president of one political party nominated someone for chief justice from another political party. President William Howard Taft, a Republican, nominated White, who was a Democrat.

What **government positions did White hold** before becoming a Supreme Court justice?

Edward White served for one year as a Louisiana state senator, two years on the Louisiana Supreme Court, and three years as a U.S. senator from Louisiana.

What was **noteworthy about White's background**?

During the Civil War, White was a Confederate soldier who was captured in Port Hudson, Louisiana, where he remained for the rest of the war.

U.S. Supreme Court chief justice Edward White. *Frances Benjamin Johnston Collection/Library of Congress.*

Was White President Grover Cleveland's **first choice** for the Supreme Court as an associate justice?

No, President Cleveland had first nominated William B. Hornblower and then Wheeler Peckham (the brother of future Supreme Court justice Rufus Peckham) to replace Justice Samuel Blatchford. Cleveland chose Hornblower and Peckham in part because they were from New York, the same state as Blatchford. However, the Senate rejected Hornblower 30–24 and Peckham 41–32. Cleveland then selected White, who was confirmed on February 19, 1894, the very day he was nominated.

Why did President **William Howard Taft select White as chief justice**?

Some speculate that President Taft selected White as a result of his advanced age (67) because Taft himself hoped to be appointed to the Supreme Court in the future. This theory posits that Taft did not appoint the other contender for the position, future Supreme Court justice Charles Evans Hughes, because he was much younger. Others believe Taft selected White primarily because he was from the South and was a Catholic, factors that Taft may have thought would help him in his reelection bid.

RACIAL DISCRIMINATION

In what decision did the White Court **invalidate a state law that limited voting on Fifteenth Amendment grounds**?

The White Court unanimously ruled in *Guinn v. United States* (1915) that an Oklahoma voting law violated the Fifteenth Amendment, which protects the right of suffrage. The Oklahoma law provided that no person could vote unless he could read and write any section of the Oklahoma Constitution. The law also provided, however, that this literacy provision did not apply to those who were eligible to vote before January 1, 1866, the date the Fifteenth Amendment was passed. This "grandfather" clause essentially meant that illiterate whites could vote but not blacks.

The White Court ruled that this provision "re-creates and perpetuates the very conditions which the Amendment was intended to destroy"—the right to vote based on race. The Court, in an opinion by Chief Justice White, deemed it repugnant to base eligibility to vote on a person's status, or that of their ancestors, in 1866.

In what decision did the White Court strike down a **residential segregation law**?

The White Court unanimously ruled in *Buchanan v. Warley* (1917) that white real estate agent Charles H. Buchanan could sell a house to William Warley, the African American head of Louisville's NAACP branch and the editor of the *Louisville News*. The suit provided a test case for challenging the constitutionality of Louisville's residential segregation law, which prohibited the sale of homes to blacks on white blocks and vice versa. (A test case is one in which litigants plan to challenge a law they believe is unconstitutional.) The two men challenged the ordinance as a violation of the Fourteenth Amendment. The city had passed the ordinance to ensure racial harmony, keep the public peace, maintain racial purity, and avoid the deterioration of white-owned neighborhoods.

The U.S. Supreme Court unanimously invalidated the ordinance, writing: "The Fourteenth Amendment and these statutes enacted in furtherance of its purpose operate to qualify and entitle a colored man to acquire property without state legislation discriminating against him solely because of color." The Court recognized the problem of racial hostility but said the answer was not to deprive citizens of their constitutional rights. The Court also rejected the argument that the law was necessary to prevent the deterioration of white-owned property, noting that "property may be acquired by undesirable white neighbors or put to disagreeable though lawful uses with like results."

CRIMINAL JUSTICE

In what decision later viewed as a miscarriage of justice did the White Court **refuse to overrule a death-penalty conviction in Georgia**?

The U.S. Supreme Court ruled 7–2 in *Frank v. Mangum* (1915) that Leo Frank was not entitled to federal habeas corpus relief from his death-penalty conviction in Fulton County, Georgia.

Frank, the Jewish owner of the National Pencil Factory in Atlanta, had been charged with the murder of 13-year-old Mary Phagan, one of Frank's employees. Anti-Semitism contributed to a very hostile atmosphere at Frank's trial. Frank and his lawyer were not even present when the guilty verdict was read before a packed courtroom surrounded by a mob of people.

The Georgia Supreme Court affirmed Frank's conviction, finding that there was

no constitutional error in Frank not being present during the rendering of the ver-

CourtSpeak: *Frank v. Mangum* Death-Penalty Conviction Case (1915)

Justice Mahlon Pitney (majority): "The Georgia courts, in the present case, proceeded upon the theory that Frank would have been entitled to this relief had his charges been true, and they refused a new trial only because they found his charges untrue save in a few minor particulars not amounting to more than irregularities, and not prejudicial to the accused. There was here no denial of due process."

Justice Oliver Wendell Holmes (dissenting): "We do not think it impracticable in any part of this country to have trials free from outside control. But to maintain this immunity it may be necessary that the supremacy of the law and of the Federal Constitution should be vindicated in a case like this. It may be that on a hearing a different complexion would be given to the judge's alleged request and expression of fear. But supposing the alleged facts to be true, we are of opinion that if they were before the supreme court, it sanctioned a situation upon which the courts of the United States should act; and if, for any reason, they were not before the supreme court, it is our duty to act upon them now, and to declare lynch law as little valid when practiced by a regularly drawn jury as when administered by one elected by a mob intent on death."

dict. Frank and his lawyers then sought relief in the federal courts through a habeas corpus action. The majority of the Court, in an opinion by Justice Mahlon Pitney, rejected Frank's claims, reasoning that Frank was not denied due process of law because his conviction was reviewed by the Georgia Supreme Court. The state appellate process ensured that Frank's trial was not dominated by mob rule, Justice Pitney wrote.

Who **dissented in the *Frank* case** and what was their position?

Justices Oliver Wendell Holmes and Charles Evans Hughes dissented, with Holmes writing an opinion. Holmes believed that Frank's lawyers had raised allegations at least sufficient to require a federal court hearing to determine whether the trial was indeed dominated by a mob. "Mob law does not become due process of law by securing the assent of a terrorized jury," he warned.

Why was the Court's *Frank* decision considered such a miscarriage of justice?

The Frank case was considered a miscarriage of justice because there was substantial evidence that Leo Frank did not murder Mary Phagan. Anti-Semitism contributed to

181

the way the trial was conducted. Evidence surfaced later that several of the jurors uttered anti-Semitic remarks. Furthermore, the prosecution's star witness, African American janitor Jim Conley, was a troubled individual with a criminal record. Frank was convicted largely on Conley's testimony. Conley testified that Phagan had gone upstairs to Frank's office. The janitor then testified he heard a loud scream and saw Frank trembling with a rope in his hand and Phagan's dead body on the ground. Conley said he and Frank carried the girl's body to the basement where they deposited it. Many believe that Conley may have acted alone in the death of Phagan. After the U.S. Supreme Court denied Frank's relief, Conley's own attorney, William M. Smith, announced that he thought Conley was the likely culprit.

What was **Leo Frank's fate**?

Near the end of his term, popular Georgia governor John Slaton commuted Frank's sentence to life imprisonment. This decision was met with great uproar and the state militia had to be called to protect the governor and his family. Frank was moved from a prison in Atlanta to the more secure Milledgeville Prison Farm. However, twenty-five people overpowered guards at the prison farm and captured Frank. They took him down to Marietta, Georgia, and lynched him. No charges were ever filed against any of the suspected lynchers.

What **surprising turn of events occurred in the 1980s** with respect to the *Frank* case?

An elderly man named Alonzo Mann came forward in 1982, saying he worked at the pencil factory as a 13-year-old boy. Mann said he saw Conley drag Phagan's body in the factory. Mann said he never said anything because Conley had threatened he would kill him if he said anything. Based partly on this new information, the Georgia Board of Pardons granted Frank a posthumous pardon in 1986, more than seventy years after the alleged crime and lynching.

In what famous decision did the U.S. Supreme Court **exclude evidence obtained without a warrant**?

The White Court unanimously ruled in *Weeks v. United States* (1914) that federal law enforcement officials violated the Fourth Amendment when they searched the home of Fremont Weeks without a warrant, seized hundreds of his personal documents, and refused to return them. The Court determined that Weeks's conviction for running an illegal gambling operation had to be overturned because of the federal marshal's Fourth Amendment violations. Justice Rufus Day wrote that "if letters and private documents can thus be seized and held and used in evidence against a citizen ... the protection of the Fourth Amendment ... is of no value." This ruling established the so-

CourtSpeak: *Weeks v. United States* **Fourth Amendment Case (1914)**

Justice William Rufus Day (unanimous): "The tendency of those who execute the criminal laws of the country to obtain conviction by means of unlawful seizures and enforced confessions, the latter often obtained after subjecting accused persons to unwarranted practices destructive of rights secured by the Federal Constitution, should find no sanction in the judgments of the courts, which are charged at all times with the support of the Constitution, and to which the people of all conditions have a right to appeal for the maintenance of such fundamental rights....

"The efforts of the courts and their officials to bring the guilty to punishment, praiseworthy as they are, are not to be aided by the sacrifice of those great principles established by years of endeavor and suffering which have resulted in their embodiment in the fundamental law of the land.... To sanction such proceedings would be to affirm by judicial decision a manifest neglect, if not an open defiance, of the prohibitions of the Constitution, intended for the protection of the people against such unauthorized action."

called exclusionary rule, which said that evidence seized by federal officials in violation of the Fourth Amendment had to be excluded and could not be used in evidence against the defendant.

In what two decisions did the U.S. Supreme Court **reverse the convictions of Samuel Gompers**?

The White Court twice reversed the criminal contempt convictions of Samuel Gompers, the first president of the American Federation of Labor (AFL) in *Gompers v. Buck's Stove & Range Company* (1911) and *Gompers v. United States* (1914). Gompers declared a boycott of the Buck's Stove & Range Company and published in his *American Federationist* newspaper unflattering things about the firm. For example, the newspaper listed the company on its "Unfair" and "We Don't Patronize" lists.

Buck's Stove responded by filing a lawsuit, alleging that Gompers and two other leaders of the AFL conspired to harm its business. A reviewing court granted an injunction, preventing Gompers from continuing these activities. The company then filed contempt proceedings, alleging that Gompers had violated the court's order by continuing the labor protest activities. The court held Gompers in contempt and sentenced him to twelve months in prison.

The U.S. Supreme Court reversed Gompers's conviction, reasoning that the contempt charges were criminal not civil and, thus, should have been initiated by the

183

The White Court twice reversed the criminal convictions of American Federation of Labor (AFL) president Samuel Gompers. *Getty Images.*

court, not the company. According to Justice Joseph Lamar, "This was a proceeding in equity for civil contempt, where the only remedial relief possible was a fine." The Court dismissed the contempt conviction, saying that the Supreme Court of the District of Columbia had the right to institute criminal contempt proceedings if it wished.

The day after the U.S. Supreme Court decision, the district court formed a committee to determine whether the court should pursue criminal contempt charges. The court instituted such contempt charges and Gompers was again found guilty. This suit went to the U.S. Supreme Court and the Court in *Gompers v. U.S.* once again ruled in favor of Gompers, this time because the contempt charges were not filed within the statute of limitations. Justice Oliver Wendell Holmes wrote: "The power to punish for contempt must have some limit in time, and in defining that limit we should have regard to what has been the policy of the law from the foundation of the government. By analogy, if not by enactment, the limit is three years."

What **famous politician represented Samuel Gompers** before the U.S. Supreme Court?

Distinguished New York jurist Alton B. Parker argued for Gompers in both U.S. Supreme Court cases. Parker resigned from the bench to run for president in 1904. He won the Democratic Party nomination but lost the election to his Republican opponent, incumbent president Theodore Roosevelt. After his political defeat, Parker practiced law.

A group of child employees at a Georgia cotton mill. Child labor and workday laws were the subjects of White Court rulings. *Lewis W. Hine/Hulton Archive/Getty Images.*

LABOR

In what decision did the White Court **strike down a federal child labor law**?

The White Court struck down a 1916 federal child labor law 5–4 in *Hammer v. Dagenhart* (1918). Roland Dagenhart's two minor sons, Reuben and John, worked with their father at a cotton mill in North Carolina. The state of North Carolina had a child labor law prohibiting children under twelve from working, but the new federal law prohibited children up to sixteen from working. Dagenhart's two children were between the ages of twelve and sixteen, so their employ complied with state law but violated federal law.

A bare majority of the Court reasoned that the federal law exceeded Congress's commerce powers and invaded the rights of the state under the Tenth Amendment. "Thus, the act in a two-fold sense is repugnant to the Constitution," wrote Justice William Rufus Day. "It not only transcends the authority delegated to Congress over commerce but also exerts a power as to purely local matter to which the federal authority does not extend."

Four justices dissented in an opinion written by Justice Oliver Wendell Holmes, who criticized the majority for its narrow conception of Congress's powers under the Commerce Clause and for "intrud[ing] its judgment upon questions of policy or morals."

In what decision did the Court uphold a **ten-hour work day for mill and factory workers**?

The White Court ruled 5–3 (Justice Louis D. Brandeis did not participate) in *Bunting v. Oregon* (1917) that an Oregon law limiting workers in mills, factories, and manufacturing establishments to a ten-hour work day was constitutional. Franklin Bunting, a foreman at the Lake View Flouring Mill, was charged with violating the law by employing a Mr. Hammersly for thirteen hours in one day. The law allowed for workers to work an extra three hours, but provided that the extra three hours must be paid as overtime, that is, time-and-a-half. Bunting did not pay the worker overtime and, thus, the charges were filed.

Future U.S. Supreme Court justice Felix Frankfurter defended the law before the high court, arguing that it was necessary to protect the health and safety of the workers. The Court refused to overrule the legislative judgment that the law furthered these health and safety interests. The Court also rejected an argument that the law discriminated against mills, factories, and manufacturing establishments. Chief Justice White, Justice Oliver Wendell Holmes, and Justice Willis Van Devanter dissented without issuing an opinion.

In what decision did the White Court outlaw the **secondary boycott**?

A divided White Court ruled 6–3 in *Duplex Printing Press Co. v. Deering* (1921) that members of the International Machinist Union could be enjoined from engaging in a sec-

A child laborer at a spinning loom. The U.S. Supreme Court ruled in *Hammer v. Dagenhart* in 1918 that federal law exceeded Congress's commerce powers; the Court ruled that state labor laws trumped federal labor laws. *Lewis W. Hine/Hulton Archive/Getty Images.*

ondary boycott as opposed to a primary boycott. In a secondary boycott, protestors attempt to prohibit customers and other businesses from dealing with the target of the primary boycott by threatening to boycott those businesses as well. It is often defined as the attempt to influence the actions of the primary business by exerting pressure on other businesses. The question before the Court was whether certain provisions in the Clayton Act, an antitrust law, exempted labor disputes from being enjoined by the courts.

The issue arose in the *Duplex Printing* case because the labor union, the International Association of Machinists, in addition to boycotting Duplex Printing's base in Battle Creek, Michigan, instituted a broad-based boycott of the printing company's products across the country.

The majority ruled in favor of Duplex Printing, reasoning that the Clayton Act did not sanction secondary boycotts that impeded the general flow of commerce outside of a particular employer-employee dispute. "Congress had in mind particular industrial controversies, not a general class war," the Court wrote.

Which justices **dissented in *Duplex Printing*?**

Justices Louis Brandeis, Oliver Wendell Holmes, and John Hessin Clarke dissented in an opinion written by Brandeis. They contended that provisions in the Clayton Act provided that secondary boycotts could not be prohibited or enjoined by courts. Bran-

187

deis wrote that the "Clayton Act substituted the opinion of Congress as to the propriety of the purpose for that of differing judges; and thereby it declared that the relations between employers of labor and workingmen were competitive relations, that organized competition was not harmful and that it justified injuries necessarily inflicted in its course."

What was the **famous *Standard Oil* case**?

One of the White Court's most famous decisions came from *Standard Oil of New Jersey v. United States* (1911). The case involved the prosecution of Standard Oil Company and its various entities and several individuals, including founder John D. Rockefeller, for monopolizing the petroleum industry. The defendants were prosecuted under the 1890 Sherman Antitrust Act, which provided in part: "Every contract, combination in the form of trust or otherwise, or conspiracy, in restraint of trade or commerce among the several states or with foreign nations, is hereby declared to be illegal." Section 2 of the law prohibited any person from monopolizing or attempting to monopolize "any part of the trade or commerce among the several states." A lower court of four circuit judges ruled that Standard Oil should be dissolved. The U.S. Supreme Court affirmed that decision in its 1911 ruling.

What **famous rule did the Court adopt in the *Standard Oil* case**?

Chief Justice White established the so-called "rule of reason" that should guide courts when they are asked to determine whether there has been an antitrust, unreasonable

Cars enter and exit a Standard Oil filling station in 1915. Standard Oil was the defendant in a 1911 Supreme Court case in which the Court affirmed a lower court ruling that said that Standard Oil was monopolizing the petroleum industry. *Hulton Archive/Getty Images.*

restraint of trade allegation. This rule enables the courts to apply a rule of reasonableness to determine whether certain corporate actions were unreasonable enough to constitute a violation of the antitrust law. Supreme Court scholar Bernard Schwartz wrote in his *A History of the Supreme Court* (1993) that the rule of reason was "the principal legal legacy of White's Court tenure."

Why did **Justice Harlan disagree with the "rule of reason"** in his partial dissenting opinion?

Justice John Marshall Harlan issued an opinion that was part concurring and part dissenting. He concurred with the result that Standard Oil violated the Sherman Antitrust Act and should be dissolved. However, he dissented from much of the Court's reasoning and the adoption of the "rule of reason." To Justice Harlan, the law meant what it said when it outlawed any restraint of trade. He did not believe that the judiciary should have the power to add the word "unreasonable" to the statute.

What was **unusual, by current norms, of the arguments before the Court in the *Standard Oil* case?**

The argument was extremely long in the *Standard Oil* case. The first time it was argued for three days in March 1910. The Court then held reargument for four days **189**

CourtSpeak: *Standard Oil* Monopoly Case

Chief Justice Edward White (majority): "If the criterion by which it is to be determined in all cases whether every contract, combination, etc., is a restraint of trade within the intendment of the law, is the direct or indirect effect of the acts involved, then of course the rule of reason becomes the guide, and the construction which we have given the statute, instead of being refuted by the cases relied upon, is by those cases demonstrated to be correct. This is true, because the construction which we have deduced from the history of the act and the analysis of its text is simply that in every case where it is claimed that an act or acts are in violation of the statute, the rule of reason, in the light of the principles of law and the public policy which the act embodies, must be applied. From this it follows, since that rule and the result of the test as to direct or indirect, in their ultimate aspect, come to one and the same thing, that the difference between the two is therefore only that which obtains between things which do not differ at all."

Justice John Marshall Harlan (dissenting): "It thus appears that fifteen years ago, when the purpose of Congress in passing the anti-trust act was fresh in the minds of courts, lawyers, statesmen, and the general public, this court expressly declined to indulge in judicial legislation, by inserting in the act the word 'unreasonable' or any other word of like import....

"When Congress prohibited every contract, combination, or monopoly, in restraint of commerce, it prescribed simple, definite rule that all could understand, and which could be easily applied by everyone wishing to obey the law, and not to conduct their business in violation of law. But, now it is to be feared, we are to have, in cases without number, the constantly recurring inquiry—difficult to solve by proof—whether the particular contract, combination, or trust involved in each case is or is not an 'unreasonable' or 'undue' restraint of trade."

in January 1911. Today, the U.S. Supreme Court gives each side thirty minutes in oral argument.

In what decision did the White Court uphold the power of the federal government to **regulate rates of travel among railways**?

The White Court ruled 7–2 in *Houston, East & West Texas Railway Company v. United States* and *Texas & Pacific Railway Company v. United States* (1914)—collectively called the Shreveport Rate cases—that Congress and the Interstate Commerce Commission (ICC; created by congressional legislation) could regulate intrastate rates to prevent harm to interstate travel. The issue arose because the two railway companies

> ## CourtSpeak: Shreveport Rate Cases (1914)
>
> Justice Charles Evans Hughes (majority): "We find no reason to doubt that Congress is entitled to keep the highways of interstate communication open to interstate traffic upon fair and equal terms. That an unjust discrimination in the rates of a common carrier, by which one person or locality is unduly favored as against another under substantially similar conditions of traffic, constitutes an evil, is undeniable; and where this evil consists in the action of an interstate carrier in unreasonably discriminating against interstate traffic over its line, the authority of Congress to prevent it is equally clear. It is immaterial, so far as the protecting power of Congress is concerned, that the discrimination arises from intrastate rates as compared with interstate rates. The use of the instrument of interstate commerce in a discriminatory manner so as to inflict injury upon that commerce, or some part thereof, furnishes abundant ground for Federal intervention."

were charging far lower rates for travel between Texas cities than they were for travel between Texas and another state, even though the intrastate distance was far greater than the interstate distance. For example, the rate for travel from Dallas to Marshall, Texas (about 150 miles), was 36.8 cents per mile, while the rate for travel from Shreveport, Louisiana, to Marshall (about 45 miles) was 56 cents per mile.

The ICC believed this constituted an "undue preference and advantage" to the Texas cities and harmed interstate commerce. The railways contended that the ICC was overreaching its bounds and exceeded Congress's Commerce Clause powers.

The Court sided with the United States in an opinion written by Justice Charles Evans Hughes, who wrote that "interstate trade was not left to be destroyed or impeded by the rivalries of local government." He noted that the ICC was dealing with intrastate travel that was negatively impacting interstate commerce and, thus, the ICC could regulate it. Justices Horace Lurton and Mahlon Pitney dissented without writing an opinion.

In what decision did the Court uphold the **military draft law**?

The White Court unanimously ruled in six cases, collectively called the Selective Draft Law Cases, that the Selective Service Act of 1917 was constitutional. Six individuals—Joseph Arver, Alfred Grahl, Otto Wangerin, Walter Wangerin, Louis Kramer, and Meyer Graubard—challenged their convictions for failing to register for the draft. They argued that the law conflicted with the Constitution's power to call state militias to duty, violated the religion clauses of the First Amendment, and constituted involuntary servitude in violation of the Thirteenth Amendment.

191

Chief Justice White reasoned in *Arver v. United States* (1918) and the other five cases that the history of the country showed the need for congressional power to raise an army, noting that one of the main reasons for the adoption of the Constitution in 1787 was that the previous Articles of Confederation lacked the power to raise an army. The Court rejected all of the defendants' constitutional challenges, reasoning that the clear language of the Constitution granted Congress the power to create a national army and nothing in the Militia Clause limited that right. The Court brushed aside the First Amendment argument, writing that "its unsoundness is too apparent to require us to do more." The Court also summarily rejected the Thirteenth Amendment argument, noting that military service was "the performance of his supreme and noble duty."

In what decision did the White Court rule that Congress could set limitations for the **ratification of constitutional amendments**?

The White Court unanimously ruled in *Dillon v. Gloss* (1921) that Congress had the power to set time limits for ratification of a constitutional amendment by the states. The issue arose when defendant J. J. Dillon challenged his conviction for violating the National Prohibition Act by arguing that the Eighteenth Amendment, which gave Congress the power to pass the Prohibition Act, had not been ratified at the time of his alleged offense and arrest. The Court determined that Congress could set a time period for ratification of a constitutional amendment. With respect to defendant Dillon, it ruled his conviction valid because the Eighteenth Amendment was consummated on January 16, 1919, and Dillon was arrested a day later on January 17, 1919. "His alleged offense and his arrest were on the following day; so his claim that those provisions had not gone into effect at the time is not well-grounded," White concluded.

What ruling established that **a state can choose its own capital city**?

The White Court ruled 7–2 in *Coyle v. Smith* that the state of Oklahoma could move its capital from Guthrie to Oklahoma City despite a provision enacted by Congress when it admitted Oklahoma into the Union in 1906. The U.S. congressional act that made Oklahoma a state contained a provision that provided that Guthrie should be the capital until at least 1913. However, the state of Oklahoma passed a law in 1910, providing for the change of the capital site to Oklahoma City. The U.S. Supreme Court, in an opinion written by Justice Horace Lurton, ruled that the U.S. Congress could not limit a state's ability to change capital cities. "The power to locate its own seat of government, and to determine when and how it shall be changed from one place to another and to appropriate its own public funds for that purpose, are essentially and peculiarly state powers," he wrote.

CourtSpeak: *Coyle v. Smith* State Capital Case (1910)

Justice Horace Lurton (majority): "To this we may add that the constitutional equality of the states is essential to the harmonious operation of the scheme upon which the Republic was organized. When that equality disappears, we may remain a free people, but the Union will not be the Union of the Constitution."

In what decision involving **a treaty and migratory birds** was the supremacy of treaties over state powers established?

The White Court ruled 7–2 in *Missouri v. Holland* (1920) that the Migratory Bird Treaty Act of 1918 was constitutional and did not invade the state of Missouri's control over birds within its borders. The law arose out of a treaty between the United States and Great Britain over protecting certain migratory birds. The state of Missouri sued a federal game warden to prevent enforcement of the law in Missouri. The state contended that it had sovereign control over birds within its state and that the federal law invaded its sovereignty.

Writing for the Court, Justice Oliver Wendell Holmes determined that the federal law was constitutional to protect a "national interest"—the migratory birds. "But for the treaty and the statute there soon might be no birds for any powers to deal with," he wrote. "We see nothing in the Constitution that compels the Government to sit by while a food supply is cut off and the protectors of our forests and our crops are destroyed." Holmes pointed out that the state did not possess or own the birds, who flew across state and national borders.

In what decision did the White Court uphold a federal law limiting the **shipment of alcohol across state lines**?

The White Court ruled 7–2 in *Clark Distilling Co. v. Western Maryland R. Co.* (1917) that a federal law providing that interstate shipments of liquor could be regulated by state law did not violate the Due Process Clause of the Constitution. The case concerned two railway companies that were transporting liquors from Maryland to West Virginia allegedly in violation of West Virginia law. The distilling company contended that the federal law was unconstitutional in part because it subjected the transportation of liquor to varying state laws. This lack of uniformity, according to the distilling company, doomed the federal legislation. The White Court disagreed, reasoning that there was no requirement in the Constitution that all state legislation dealing with subjects that may travel in interstate commerce be uniform. Congress had the power to pass this law affecting the transportation of liquors, and the federal law did not have to mandate that all state laws on the subject be uniform.

FIRST AMENDMENT

In what famous First Amendment decision did Justice Oliver Wendell Holmes create the **"clear and present danger test"**?

Justice Holmes created the clear and present danger test in *Schenck v. United States* (1919), a case in which two members of the Socialist Party—Charles Schenck and Elizabeth Baer—were convicted of violating the Espionage Act of 1917. Schenck and Baer, members of the party's executive committee, conspired to distribute 15,000 leaflets urging people to resist the draft and avoid service in World War I.

Holmes asked whether the publication would create a "clear and present danger" to the U.S. war effort, the draft, and military recruiting. He noted that many things that may be said in peacetime cannot be said in times of war, concluding that the leaflets constituted a conspiracy to harm the country's war effort.

What was Justice Holmes's famous phrase from this case that involves **fire in a theatre**?

Justice Holmes used the following analogy as an example of a type of speech that was not protected by the First Amendment: "The most stringent protection of free speech would not protect a man in falsely shouting fire in a theatre and causing a panic."

In what famous case were **five Russians convicted of violating the Sedition Act**?

The White Court ruled 7–2 in *Abrams v. United States* (1919) that several Russian immigrants could be convicted for violating the Sedition Act of 1918 for distributing pamphlets criticizing the American government and President Woodrow Wilson's decision to send American troops into Russia. The anarchists distributed two pamphlets, entitled "Revolutionists Unite for Action" and "The Hypocrisy of the United

U.S. Supreme Court justice Oliver Wendell Holmes (above) created the "clear and present danger" test to determine whether or not certain words could be protected under the First Amendment. *Time & Life Pictures/Getty Images.*

States and Her Allies," denounced the president, and urged "Workers of the World! Awake! Rise! Put down your enemy and mine!" They were sentenced to twenty years in prison by a federal trial judge.

The Court majority, in an opinion written by John Clarke, affirmed the anarchists' convictions. He reasoned that "the manifest purpose" of the publications was to "create an attempt to defeat the war plans of the government of the United States." Clarke wrote that "the plain purpose of their propaganda was to excite, at the supreme crisis of the war, disaffection, sedition, riots and, as they hoped, revolution."

Which two justices **dissented in the Russian Sedition Act case**?

Justices Oliver Wendell Holmes and Louis Brandeis dissented in an opinion written by Holmes. Holmes wrote that "surreptitious publishing of a silly leaflet" did not create a "clear and present danger" to the American government. He wrote that the defendants "had as much a right to publish [their leaflets] as the Government has to publish the Constitution of the United States now vainly invoked by them." In his opinion,

195

Holmes made his impassioned defense of free speech as important to the marketplace of ideas: "the best test of truth is the power of the thought to get itself accepted in the competition of the market, and that truth is the only ground upon which their wishes safely can be carried out. That at any rate is the theory of our Consitution."

Who were the Five Russians convicted in the *Abrams* case and what happened to them?

The five Russian defendants were Jacob Abrams, Hyman Lachowsky, Samuel Lipman, Jacob Schwartz, and Mollie Steimer. Schwartz died the night before the defendants' trial, probably from beatings administered by guards. The other four defendants served time in federal prison until President Warren G. Harding commuted their sentences in October 1921. As part of the commutation agreement, the four defendants were shipped to Russia. Lipman, a professor in Moscow, was murdered in the Great Purges of Russian dictator Joseph Stalin in the 1930s. Lachowsky likely died in Minski in 1941 when Adolf Hitler and the German Nazis conquered the city. Steimer and Abrams were exiled from Russia and eventually wound up in Mexico City. Abrams died in 1953 and Steimer lived until 1980.

According to the U.S. Supreme Court, which **presidential candidate violated the Espionage Act of 1917**?

The White Court ruled unanimously in *Debs v. United States* (1919) that Socialist Eugene Debs, who ran for president multiple times, violated the Espionage Act when he gave speeches in Canton, Ohio, and St. Louis, Missouri, that opposed the United States' war effort. Writing for the Court, Justice Oliver Wendell Holmes upheld a jury instruction that told the jurors they could not find Debs guilty based on his speech "unless the words used had as their natural tendency and reasonably probable effect to obstruct the recruiting service, and unless the defendant had the specific intent to do so in his mind." This opinion conflicts with modern-day First Amendment jurisprudence, as many politicians and others condemn U.S. military action abroad in harsher language than that employed by Eugene Debs.

THE TAFT COURT (1921–30)

How many and **which justices served on the Taft Court**?

Thirteen justices served on the Taft Court including: Chief Justice William Howard Taft and Justices Joseph McKenna, Oliver Wendell Holmes, William R. Day, Willis Van Devanter, Mahlon Pitney, James McReynolds, Louis D. Brandeis, John H. Clarke, George Sutherland, Pierce Butler, Edward Sanford, and Harlan Fiske Stone.

What **offices did Taft hold before becoming chief justice**?

Taft held many public service offices during his illustrious career, including the presidency of the United States from 1909 to 1913. He began his career as a journalist and then a lawyer. He worked as a prosecutor for Hamilton County, Ohio, before becoming a superior court judge in 1887. He then served for one year as solicitor general of the United States and judge on the U.S. Court of Appeals for the Sixth Circuit. He also held the following positions: governor of the Philippines, U.S. secretary of war, and joint chairman of the National War Labor Board.

Why was it **not surprising that Taft became a judge**?

Chief Justice Taft's grandfather and father both served as judges. His grandfather, Peter Rawson Taft, served as a probate judge, while his father, Alphonso Taft, served as an Ohio Superior Court judge.

What was **unusual about Taft's confirmation** as chief justice?

The U.S. Senate approved Taft's confirmation the same day he was nominated by President Warren G. Harding on June 30, 1921. In part, this was considered a tribute to a former president, but confirmations also took place much more quickly than they do today.

U.S. Supreme Court chief justice William Howard Taft. *Ernest Walter Histed/Hulton Archive/Getty Images.*

When was **Taft first offered a position as justice** on the U.S. Supreme Court?

President Theodore Roosevelt offered an appointment to Taft in October 1902 after the retirement of Justice George Shiras, while Taft was serving as governor of the Philippines. Roosevelt also offered a Supreme Court appointment to Taft in March 1906 following the retirement of Justice Henry Billings Brown. Taft declined both times, presumably because of his political ambitions.

Why was Taft considered a **great judicial administrator**?

There are many reasons why historians and scholars consider Taft, who was a relatively ineffective president, a great judicial administrator, if not a great chief justice. Taft modernized and improved the U.S. Supreme Court in many ways during his tenure as chief justice. Justice Sandra Day O'Connor wrote in her book *The Majesty of the Law* (2003) that there is "another great Chief Justice … who perhaps deserves almost as much as credit as [John] Marshall for the Court's modern-day role but who does not often get the recognition: William Howard Taft."

Among his many accomplishments, Taft successfully lobbied Congress for eighteen new judgeships, receiving twenty-four; he spearheaded the movement for a conference of senior federal judges that was the predecessor to the present-day Judicial Conference of the United States; he lobbied for the Judiciary Act of 1925, which gave the Court greater flexibility in shaping its own docket; and he successfully petitioned Congress for the creation of a new location for the U.S. Supreme Court, a building that was built in 1935 and that houses the present-day Court.

Taft also lobbied for the creation of uniform federal rules of civil procedure, which—like the U.S. Supreme Court building—was realized after his death. In 1934, Congress passed the Rules Enabling Act, which gave the U.S. Supreme Court the authority to promulgate uniform rules for lower federal trial courts.

Still others praise Taft for his ability to get his fellow justices to agree on matters. More than 80 percent of the opinions during Taft's reign were unanimous, an astonishingly high rate.

RACIAL DISCRIMINATION

What did the Taft Court rule with regard to a **state law that mandated a white primary**?

The Taft Court unanimously invalidated a Texas law that prohibited blacks from voting in party primary elections in *Nixon v. Herndon* (1927). The statute provided that "in no event shall a negro be eligible to participate in a Democratic party primary election

199

held in the State of Texas." L. A. Nixon, an African American living in El Paso, contended that the statute violated his constitutional rights under the Fourteenth and Fifteenth Amendments. Justice Oliver Wendell Holmes wrote the Court's opinion, finding a clear violation of the Fourteenth Amendment Equal Protection Clause. He wrote that it "seems to us hard to imagine a more direct and obvious infringement of the Fourteenth [Amendment]." Holmes noted that the amendment had been passed "with a special intent to protect the blacks from discrimination against them."

Texas did not become a bastion of equality for black voters after the decision. The state then allowed the Democratic Party's executive committee to determine voter qualifications, which they did by race. Although the Hughes Court invalidated that practice in *Nixon v. Condon* (1932), the state still did not stop its racial discrimination. The Stone Court finally ruled in *Smith v. Allwright* (1944) that white-only primaries were unconstitutional whether initiated by state or party officials.

Who was **L. A. Nixon**?

Dr. Lawrence Aaron Nixon was an African American physician who lived from 1883 to 1966. He was a founding member of the El Paso chapter of the National Association for the Advancement of Colored People (NAACP) who remained a resident of El Paso for the bulk of his life.

Which attorney for L. A. Nixon **shares his last name with a famous annual award for African Americans**?

One of the NAACP attorneys who represented Nixon was Arthur B. Spingarn, who along with his brother Joel, a Columbia University president, bears the name of the honored Spingarn Medal, an annual award given to an African American of great distinction and accomplishment. The Spingarn brothers were white Americans but were dedicated to advocating for justice for blacks much of their lives. Winners of the prestigious Spingarn Medal include baseball player Jackie Robinson, civil rights leaders Dr. Martin Luther King Jr. and Jesse Jackson, musician Duke Ellington, comedian Bill Cosby, and talk show host Oprah Winfrey.

Why did the Taft Court **refuse to invalidate a racially restrictive covenant**?

The Taft Court refused to invalidate a racially restrictive covenant in *Corrigan v. Buckley* (1926) because it argued that such agreements between private parties were beyond the reach of the government. The Court reasoned that the prohibitions against racial discrimination found in the Fourteenth Amendment required state action or government participation. Racially restrictive covenants, according to the Court, involved just the actions of private persons, not government officials. Thus, it was beyond the control of the Constitution. This view prevailed in the U.S. Supreme Court until the 1948 decision *Shelley v. Kraemer* in which the Vinson Court ruled that judicial enforcement of racially restrictive covenants constituted state action and violated the Fourteenth Amendment's Equal Protection Clause.

Who were the parties in *Corrigan v. Buckley*?

John J. Buckley was a white homeowner in Washington, D.C., who sued fellow resident Irene Hand Corrigan, because Corrigan sought to sell her property to an African American woman named Helen Curtis and her husband, Dr. Arthur Curtis. In 1921, thirty white persons, including Buckley and Corrigan, had executed a covenant that said that for twenty-one years their houses could not be sold to "any person of the negro race or blood." The next year, Corrigan sought to sell her property to Curtis and Buckley sued to enforce the covenant.

CRIMINAL JUSTICE AND PROCEDURE

In what decision did the Taft Court **invalidate death sentences** because of a mob-like atmosphere during a trial?

The Taft Court ruled 7–2 in *Moore v. Dempsey* (1923) that five African American men had the right to a new hearing in federal court on whether their constitutional rights were violated as a result of a sham trial in state court. The underlying incident arose in 1919 in Phillips County, Arkansas, after a white sheriff's deputy fired upon a group of black cotton farmers who were meeting to discuss ways to organize and better their economic position. After the white sheriff's deputy was killed, an outraged white community formed a mob and killed more than two hundred blacks. Law enforcement arrested twelve black men, including Frank Moore, and charged them with murder.

In the proceeding, the men were tried without the benefit of adequate counsel in 45 minutes. Their lawyer did not call any witnesses on their behalf and an all-white jury convicted them after only five minutes of deliberation. After losing in state court and the lower federal courts, the defendants—with backing from the National Association for the Advancement of Colored People (NAACP)—appealed to the U.S. Supreme Court. The high court sent the case back to the federal district court with instructions to allow the men to present their constitutional claims. Justice Oliver Wendell Holmes wrote:

> But if the case is that the whole proceeding is a mask—that counsel, jury, and judge were swept to the fatal end by an irresistible wave of public passion, and that the State Courts failed to correct the wrong, neither perfection in the machinery for correction nor the possibility that the trial court and counsel

201

saw no other way can prevent this Court from securing to the petitioners their constitutional rights.

Justices James McReynolds and George Sutherland dissented, finding that the Supreme Court should not overrule the judgment of state courts. "The delays incident to enforcement of our criminal laws have become a national scandal and give serious alarm to those who observe," McReynolds wrote.

In what famous decision did the Taft Court narrowly find **no Fourth Amendment problem with wiretapping**?

The Taft Court narrowly ruled 5–4 in *Olmstead v. United States* (1928) that wiretapping by federal prohibition officials did not violate the Fourth Amendment because listening to telephone conversations was not a search within the meaning of the Fourth Amendment. After listening to wiretaps for more than five months, government officials uncovered a large criminal enterprise, led by Roy Olmstead, involving the distribution of liquors. The government enlisted a telephone wiring expert to wiretap numerous telephone lines into the homes and offices of several individuals, including Olmstead.

Olmstead and others contended that the wiretaps constituted an illegal search and seizure, as they were done without a warrant and probable cause. However, Chief Justice Taft, in his majority opinion, found that the use of wiretaps did not constitute a search. He narrowly focused on the Fourth Amendment as protecting person's tangible items from government inspection: "Here we have testimony only of voluntary conversations secretly overhead."

He explained: "There was no searching. There was no seizure. The evidence was secured by the use of the sense of hearing and that only. There was no entry of the houses or offices of the defendants." Taft believed that expanding the Fourth Amendment to protect telephone conversations would constitute an "enlarged and unusual meaning to the Fourth Amendment."

What justice issued a famous dissent **questioning the majority's narrow interpretation of the Fourth Amendment**?

Justice Louis Brandeis issued the most comprehensive dissenting opinion, though Justices Oliver Wendell Holmes, Pierce Butler, and Harlan Fiske Stone also wrote dissenting opinions.

Brandeis recognized that individual privacy can be invaded in different ways through technological advancements. In a moment of prescience, he wrote: "Ways may some day be developed by which the government, without removing papers from secret drawers, can reproduce them in court, and by which it will be enabled to expose to a jury the most intimate occurrences of the home." He explained that invading privacy by listening to telephone conversations was as great, if not greater, than opening

> ## CourtSpeak: *Olmstead v. United States* Wiretapping Case (1928)
>
> Justice Louis Brandeis (dissenting): "The makers of our Constitution undertook to secure conditions favorable to the pursuit of happiness.... They sought to protect Americans in their beliefs, their thoughts, their emotions and their sensations. They conferred, as against the government, the right to be let alone—the most comprehensive of rights and the right most valued by civilized men. To protect that right, every unjustifiable intrusion by the government, whatever the means employed, must be deemed a violation of the Fourth Amendment."

an individual's mail. He also questioned the government's culpability in sanctioning what he termed the unlawful wiretapping. He warned that "the government itself would become a lawbreaker."

Did the U.S. Supreme Court ever **overrule *Olmstead*?**

Yes, the Warren Court overruled *Olmstead* in *Katz v. United States* (1967), finding that wiretapping constituted a search within the meaning of the Fourth Amendment. In *Katz,* the Court wrote that the underpinnings of *Olmstead* had been "eroded" and "can no longer be regarded as controlling."

In what prohibition case did the Taft Court **refuse to find a double jeopardy violation?**

The Taft Court unanimously ruled in *United States v. Lanza* (1922) that bootlegger Vito Lanza could be prosecuted for violation of the National Prohibition Act (called the Volstead Act) even though he had also been prosecuted for violating a similar Washington state law. Lanza had argued that a subsequent federal prosecution amounted to a double jeopardy violation under the Fifth Amendment. The Taft Court disagreed, writing that an "act denounced as a crime by both national and state sovereignties is an offense against the peace and dignity of both and may be punished by each." The Court reasoned that if Congress wanted to bar such subsequent federal prosecutions, it could do so by statute.

In which case did the Taft Court create the **automobile exception to the Fourth Amendment?**

The Taft Court ruled in *Carroll v. United States* (1925) that police officers did not need a search warrant to search the automobile of suspected bootlegger John Carroll for violation of the National Prohibition Act. Writing for the Court, Chief Justice Taft reasoned that a less stringent rule applies for searches of automobiles than homes because auto-

Policemen destroy barrels of illegal rum during Prohibition. The U.S. Supreme Court ruled in *Carroll v. United States* that the search without a warrant of a suspected bootlegger's car was legal because evidence could be destroyed more easily in an automobile due to its mobile nature. *Hulton Archive/Getty Images.*

> ### CourtSpeak: *Carroll v. United States*
> ### Fourth Amendment Automobile Exception Case (1925)
>
> Chief Justice William Howard Taft (majority): "The intent of Congress to make a distinction between the necessity for a search warrant in the searching of private dwellings and in that of automobiles and other road vehicles in the enforcement of the Prohibition Act is thus clearly established by the legislative history of the Stanley Amendment. Is such a distinction consistent with the Fourth Amendment? We think that it is, the Fourth Amendment does not denounce all searches or seizures, but only such as are unreasonable."
>
> Justice James McReynolds (dissenting): "The damnable character of the 'bootlegger's' business should not close our eyes to the mischief which will surely follow any attempt to destroy it by unwarranted methods."

mobiles are mobile and evidence can be easily moved and destroyed. The Fourth Amendment generally requires that searches cannot be conducted without a warrant supported by probable cause. However, given the mobility of automobiles, the Court found that searches of vehicles need no warrant—they need only be supported by probable cause.

The majority then determined that there was probable cause to stop the automobile of John Carroll, noting that it was known that Carroll and his brother were suspected bootleggers. The evidence also showed that the area between the Michigan cities of Detroit and Grand Rapids was known to carry a lot of illegal liquor trafficking. Finally, a prohibition officer testified that Carroll and others had previously agreed to supply liquor to him although they did not follow through with the plan. "In light of these authorities, and what is shown by this record, it is clear the officers here had justification for the search and seizure," the Court wrote.

Justices James McReynolds and George Sutherland dissented in an opinion authored by McReynolds. He wrote that the search of Carroll's vehicle was founded on "mere suspicion—ill-founded as I think." McReynolds questioned the finding of probable cause, asking: "Has it come about that merely because a man once agreed to deliver whisky, but did not, he may be arrested whenever thereafter he ventures to drive an automobile on the road to Detroit!"

Federal juries generally must consist of twelve members
according to what Taft Court decision?

The Taft Court ruled in *Patton v. New York* (1930) that a criminal defendant can waive his or her right to a jury of twelve members when one of the jurors involved in the case becomes sick and is unable to continue. However, the Court reiterated in strong language that a jury should be composed of twelve members absent highly unusual circumstances: "A constitutional jury means twelve men as though that number had been specifically named; and it follows that, when reduced to eleven, it ceases to be such a jury quite as effectively as though the number had been reduced to a single person."

In what case did the Taft Court uphold the **sterilization of a woman**?

The Taft Court upheld the sterilization of an eighteen-year-old woman named Carrie Buck in the decision *Buck v. Bell* (1927). Virginia had passed a law in 1924 that provided that "mental defectives" could be sterilized for the betterment of society. Buck, who was allegedly raped, had a low IQ and a mother who was also institutionalized at the State Colony for Epileptics and Feeble-Minded. The colony petitioned to perform a salpingectomy (removal of at least one of the fallopian tubes) on Buck, which would make her sterile.

The Court ruled 8–1 in favor of the colony officials in an opinion written by Justice Oliver Wendell Holmes. "Three generations of imbeciles are enough," he wrote, adding that the law was justified because it helped society control offspring likely to commit crimes or be dependent upon others.

Justice Pierce Butler was the Court's lone dissenter but he did not write an opinion explaining his opposition.

What did the Taft Court rule with respect to **municipal prohibition courts**?

The Taft Court unanimously ruled in *Tumey v. Ohio* (1927) that a process that allowed a city mayor to try and convict individuals for unlawful possession of liquor and then take a percentage of the fees imposed on the defendants violated due process. The mayor of North College Hill, Ohio, tried and convicted defendants in a "prohibition court" without a jury. The mayor also attempted to receive a small fee from the fines imposed upon the defendants. Ed Tumey, who was convicted under the law, contended that this system of law violated his due-process rights in part because the mayor had a direct financial interest in his conviction.

CourtSpeak: *Tumey v. Ohio* Municipal Prohibition Court Case (1927)

Chief Justice William Howard Taft (unanimous): "There are doubtless mayors who would not allow such a consideration as $12 costs in each case to affect their judgment in it, but the requirement of due process of law in judicial procedure is not satisfied by the argument that men of the highest honor and the greatest self-sacrifice could carry it on without danger of injustice. Every procedure which would offer a possible temptation to the average man as a judge to forget the burden of proof required to convict the defendant, or which might lead him not to hold the balance nice, clear and true between the state and the accused denies the latter due process of law."

The Taft Court agreed in an opinion written by the chief justice. Taft noted that in England there was "the greatest sensitiveness over the existence of any pecuniary interest however small or infinitesimal in the justices of the peace." He also reasoned that the practice simply was not fair to a defendant in that the system was not set up for "the careful and judicial consideration of his guilt or innocence."

In what landmark decision did the Taft Court uphold the **zoning power of cities**?

The Taft Court upheld the zoning power of local officials in *Village of Euclid v. Amber Realty Co.* (1926) by a 6–3 vote. The Village of Euclid, Ohio, located outside Cleveland, passed a comprehensive zoning law that restricted the types of dwellings that could be built in different areas of the cities. Some areas were deemed residential, while others were deemed industrial. The law further provided for different use, height, and area districts.

Amber Realty Co. owned 68 acres of land in the village. The company sued city officials because the zoning law prevented the development of industrial business on some of their land. The net effect of this, according to Amber, was that it could not sell its land for nearly as much money. The company contended that the zoning law violated its due-process and equal-protection rights.

The U.S. Supreme Court rejected the constitutional challenges, writing that the zoning law was a constitutional exercise of the government's police powers to provide for the public welfare. The law reflected a "rational relation to the health and safety of the community," wrote Justice George Sutherland for the majority. The zoning laws would help the development of residential areas free from "the disturbing noises incident to increased traffic and business."

Three justices—Willis Van Devanter, James McReynolds, and Pierce Butler—dissented without writing an opinion.

What **famous attorney represented the Village of Euclid**?

James Metzenbaum represented the Village of Euclid before the U.S. Supreme Court. He wrote a prominent treatise on zoning law entitled *The Law of Zoning* (1930). His cousin was Howard M. Metzenbaum who served for twenty years as a U.S. senator from Ohio.

In what decision did the Taft Court **favor a restaurant over its ex-employees in a picketing dispute**?

In *Truax v. Corrigan* (1921), the Taft Court struck down an Arizona law that prohibited courts from issuing injunctions to prohibit picketing of businesses arising out of labor disputes. Former cooks and waiters of the English Kitchen, a restaurant in Bisbee, Arizona, picketed the store and implored would-be patrons not to enter the restaurant. As a result of the picketing campaign, the business suffered a large loss in revenue, making $12,000 instead of its normal rate of more than $50,000.

The restaurant owner sought an injunction from a court in order to prohibit the picketing campaign. However, an Arizona state law provided that "no restraining order or injunction shall be granted by any court of this state … in any case between an employer and employees … or growing out of a dispute concerning terms and conditions of employment."

The restaurant owner contended that the statute violated the Due Process and Equal Protection clauses of the Fourteenth Amendment. He argued that the law violated due process because it prohibited a court from protecting the property and value of the business, an important property right. He also argued that the law violated equal protection because it prohibited injunctions against picketing by employees or ex-employees and not picketing by other individuals, such as competing restaurant owners.

The Court ruled 5–4 that the statute violated both due-process and equal-protection principles. Focusing on the concerted campaign, which included picketing and allegedly libelous statements about restaurant management, the Court ruled that the statute did deprive the owner of the restaurant of his property. "To give operations to a statute whereby serious losses inflicted by such unlawful means are in effect made remediless, is, we think, to disregard fundamental rights of liberty and property and to deprive the person suffering the loss of due process of law," Chief Justice Taft wrote for the majority.

Taft also reasoned that the law violated equal protection, because it singled out for protection a particular form of picketing. He determined that the effect of the Arizona law was to allow "direct invasion of the ordinary business and property rights of a person" by ex-employees only. "If this is not a denial of the equal protection of the laws, then it is hard to conceive what would be," he wrote.

What was the position of the **dissenting judges in the *Truax* Case**?

Four justices dissented in three separate opinions. Justice Oliver Wendell Holmes wrote that the Court had misapplied the Fourteenth Amendment by preventing a state from experimenting with the particular problems caused by labor disputes. "If, as many intelligent people believe, there is more danger in labor cases than elsewhere I can fell no doubt of the power of the Legislature to deny it in such cases," he wrote.

Justice Mahlon Pitney questioned the majority's conclusions, reasoning that the Arizona law was not arbitrary or irrational. He said the statute was a constitutional "measure of police regulation," entitled to a presumption of constitutionality. He questioned the majority's equal-protection reasoning, accusing it of "transform[ing] the provision of the Fourteenth Amendment from a guaranty of the 'protection of equal laws' into an insistence upon laws complete, perfect, symmetrical."

Justice Louis Brandeis's dissenting opinion focused on the history of labor disputes and the regulation of peaceful picketing. The court noted that historically, court injunctions issued against picketers "endangered the personal liberty of wage earners" and employers seeking to enjoin such picketing were "seeking sovereign power" under "the guise of protecting property rights."

EMPLOYMENT

In what decision did the Taft Court **invalidate a minimum wage law**?

The Court struck down a Washington, D.C., minimum wage law for women and children in *Adkins v. Children's Hospital of the District of Columbia* (1923) by a 5–3 vote (Justice Brandeis did not participate in the case). The majority, in an opinion written by Justice George Sutherland, ruled that the law violated the liberty of contract rights of employer and employee. Sutherland reasoned that "freedom of contract is … the general rule and restraint the exception." According to the majority, the minimum wage law imposes upon all employers, including "those whose bargaining power may be as weak as that of the employee." The majority was far more concerned with the freedom of contract rights of employers than with any hardships possibly endured by workers with little bargaining power. Sutherland also relied on the recently enacted Nineteenth Amendment, which gave women the right to vote, as evidence that women did not need the special protection of this minimum-wage legislation.

Chief Justice William Howard Taft, Justice Oliver Wendell Holmes, and Justice Edward Sanford dissented, with Taft and Holmes writing opinions. Taft recognized that most of the time employees do not have equal bargaining power with their employers. He contended that the Court failed to rely on the Court's 1908 decision in *Muller v. Oregon* (1908) in which the Fuller Court upheld a law that limited the hours of women workers. Holmes questioned the majority's broad notion of liberty of contract, pointing

George Sutherland (above) wrote on behalf of the majority of the U.S. Supreme Court in *Adkins v. Children's Hospital of the District of Columbia* (1923) that a Washington, D.C., minimum wage law for women and children violated the liberty of contract rights of employer and employee. *Library of Congress.*

out that many laws dealing with usury, statutes of frauds, Sunday laws, and others infringed on liberty of contract.

What **future U.S. Supreme Court justice** argued before the Court **in favor of the minimum wage law**?

Felix Frankfurter, who served on the U.S. Supreme Court from 1939 to 1962, argued in favor of the minimum wage law in the *Adkins* case.

In what case did the Taft Court **strike down a state law creating an arbitration court for employer disputes**?

The Taft Court unanimously struck down the Kansas Industrial Relations Act of 1920 in *Chas. Wolf Packing Co. v. Court of Industrial Relations of State of Kansas* (1923). The law created an arbitration court that regulated the wages, hours, and other matters of employment for businesses involved in food, clothing, and fuel. The court had the power to restrict strikes and lockouts by employers. Chief Justice Taft reasoned that this broad law imposed "drastic regulation" on business and restricted the liberty of contract rights of both employers and employees: "These qualifications do not change the essence of the act. It curtails the right of the employer on the one hand, and of the employee on the other, to contract about his affairs." The state sought to justify the law because the businesses affected public interest, but the chief justice warned that such an argument was an example of "running the public interest argument into the ground."

CourtSpeak: *Adkins v. Children's Hospital of the District of Columbia* Minimum Wage Case (1923)

Justice George Sutherland (majority): "That the right to contract about one's affairs is a part of the liberty of the individual protected by this clause is settled by the decisions of this court and is no longer open to question. Within this liberty to contract are contracts of employment of labor. In making such contracts, generally speaking, the parties have an equal right to obtain from each other the best terms they can as the result of private bargaining."

Chief Justice William Howard Taft (dissenting): "Legislatures in limiting freedom of contract between employee and employer by a minimum wage proceed on the assumption that employees, in the class receiving least pay, are not upon a full level of equality of choice with their employer and in their necessitous circumstances are prone to accept pretty much anything that is offered. They are peculiarly subject to the overreaching of the harsh and petty employer. The evils of the sweating system and of the long hours and low wages which are characteristic of it are well known."

Justice Oliver Wendell Holmes (dissenting): "It will need more than the Nineteenth Amendment to convince me that there are no differences between men and women, or that legislation cannot take those differences into account."

In what decision did the Taft Court **invalidate a federal child labor tax law**?

The Taft Court ruled 8–1 in *Bailey v. Drexel Furniture Co.* (1923) that the federal Child Labor Tax Law, which imposed a 10 percent penalty tax on businesses that employed children, invaded the powers of the state in violation of the Tenth Amendment. Drexel Furniture, a North Carolina furniture store, was cited for violating the law because it employed a 14-year-old boy. The government argued that it had broad taxation powers under the Constitution, but the Court responded: "To give such magic to the word 'tax' would be to break down all constitutional limitations of the power of Congress and completely wipe out the sovereignty of the states."

CONGRESSIONAL AND EXECUTIVE POWER

In what case did the Taft Court **strike down a law that regulated congressional candidate spending**?

The Taft Court ruled in *Newberry v. United States* (1921) that Congress did not have the constitutional authority to regulate spending in congressional primary elections.

211

The Court's decision invalidated the convictions of Truman Newberry and sixteen others under the federal Corrupt Practices Act, which limited the contributions and expenditures of congressional candidates for House and Senate seats.

The government argued that the Corrupt Practices Act was justified by Section 4, Article I, of the Constitution, which provides: "The times, places and manner of holding elections for Senators and Representatives shall be prescribed in each state by the Legislature thereof." The Court concluded that this congressional grant of power to control elections did not apply to party primaries or conventions. The Court reasoned that congressional control over primaries "would interfere with purely domestic affairs of the state and infringe upon liberties reserved to the people." The Court's decision caused Congress to pass a new law regulating elections called the Federal Corrupt Practices Act of 1925.

Who was Newberry in *Newberry v. United States*?

Truman H. Newberry was the lead defendant in the *Newberry v. United States* case. He had served as President Theodore Roosevelt's secretary of the Navy. He later defeated automobile manufacturer Henry Ford for a U.S. Senate seat in Michigan. Newberry spent more than $100,000 in his campaign, which led to his conviction under the Federal Corrupt Practices Act, a conviction reversed by the U.S. Supreme Court in 1921. Newberry finished out his term as senator but did not seek a second term.

In what decision did the Taft Court give **broad powers to the executive branch to fire its own employees**?

The Taft Court ruled 6–3 in *Myers v. United States* (1926) that the president had the constitutional authority to remove a federal official he had appointed without the advice and consent of the Senate. The case involved Frank S. Myers, a postmaster from Portland, Oregon, whom President Woodrow Wilson had appointed in July 1917 and removed in February 1920. The president summarily removed Myers without seeking congressional approval after an investigation by postal inspectors found evidence of fraudulent activity. Myers argued that he was protected by an 1876 federal law called the Tenure of Office Act, which provided that several classes of postmaster generals (high-ranking positions in the postal system) could be removed by the president with the advice and consent of the Senate. Myers claimed that since the president unilaterally removed him without senatorial consent, he should receive his salary. The government countered that since the executive branch has the power to appoint such officials, it should also have the power to remove them. By the time the case reached the U.S. Supreme Court, Myers had died but his estate pressed forward with the case.

Writing for the majority, Chief Justice William Howard Taft reasoned that the executive branch had broad authority to control the jobs of executive branch employees. He determined that the Tenure of Office Act, which required senatorial "advice

CourtSpeak: *Myers v. United States* Executive Branch Jobs Case (1926)

Chief Justice William Howard Taft (majority): "The power of removal is incident to the power of appointment, not to the power of advising and consenting to appointment, and when the grant of the executive power is enforced by the express mandate to take care that the laws be faithfully executed, it emphasizes the necessity for including within the executive power as conferred the exclusive power of removal."

Justice James McReynolds (dissenting): "A certain repugnance must attend the suggestion that the President may ignore any provision of an act of Congress under which he has proceeded. He should promote and not subvert orderly government. The serious evils which followed the practice of dismissing civil officers as caprice or interest dictated, long permitted under congressional enactments, are known to all. It brought the public service to a low estate and caused insistent demand for reform.... The long struggle for civil service reform and the legislation designed to insure some security of official tenure ought not to be forgotten. Again and again Congress has enacted statutes prescribing restrictions on removals, and by approving them many Presidents have affirmed its power therein."

Justice Louis Brandeis (dissenting): "The doctrine of the separation of powers was adopted by the convention of 1787 not to promote efficiency but to preclude the exercise of arbitrary power.... Checks and balances were established in order that this should be 'a government of laws and not of men.'"

Justice Oliver Wendell Holmes (dissenting): "We have to deal with an office that owes its existence to Congress and that Congress may abolish tomorrow. Its duration and the pay attached to it while it lasts depend on Congress alone. Congress alone confers on the President the power to appoint to it and at any time may transfer the power to other hands. With such power over its own creation, I have no more trouble in believing that Congress has power to prescribe a term of life for it free from any interference than I have in accepting the undoubted power of Congress to decree its end."

and consent," infringed on the authority of the executive branch and violated separation of powers principles. "The history of the clause by which the Senate was given a check upon the President's power of appointment makes it clear that it was not prompted by any desire to limit removals," he wrote.

Justices James McReynolds, Louis Brandeis, and Oliver Wendell Holmes all wrote dissenting opinions, with McReynolds writing the longest of the three. McReynolds attacked many of the chief justices' arguments. He emphasized that there were many congressional statutes limiting the removal of federal employees.

DUE PROCESS RIGHTS OF PARENTS

In what decision did the Taft Court protect the **right of parents to choose their children's schooling**?

The Taft Court unanimously ruled in *Pierce v. Society of the Sisters of the Holy Names of Jesus and Mary* (1925) that an Oregon law mandating parents send their children to public schools violates the parents' due-process rights. In 1922, the state passed a law requiring parents to send their children aged 8 to 16 to public school. The law, supported by the Ku Klux Klan, was fueled in part because of discrimination against Catholicism and aliens. Two private schools—a Catholic school and a military school—challenged the law as a violation of due process.

Writing for the Court, Justice James McReynolds agreed with the schools that the Oregon law was unconstitutional and "unreasonably interferes with the liberty of parents and guardians to direct the upbringing and education of children under their control." The Court said that a state could require children to attend school but could not mandate that those schools had to be public.

In what decision did the Taft Court **prohibit states from outlawing the teaching of foreign languages**?

The Taft Court ruled 7–2 in *Meyer v. Nebraska* (1923) that the state of Nebraska could not outlaw the teaching of foreign languages. The state had passed a law prohibiting any school—public or private—from teaching any language other than English to students who had not yet finished the eighth grade. Robert Meyer, a teacher at Zion Parochial School, was charged with violating the law for teaching German to student Raymond Panpart. Justice James McReynolds wrote that this law violated the Due Process Clause, noting that "mere knowledge of the German language cannot reasonably be regarded as harmful." Justices Oliver Wendell Holmes and George Sutherland dissented without writing an opinion.

FIRST AMENDMENT

In what decision did the Taft Court rule that the First Amendment **Free Speech and Press clauses extended to the states**?

The Taft Court ruled in *Gitlow v. New York* (1925) that the First Amendment freedoms of speech and press applied to the states via the Fourteenth Amendment's Due Process Clause. The Due Process Clause provides that no state shall infringe on "life, liberty or property without due process of law." The Supreme Court in *Gitlow* determined that

> ## CourtSpeak: *Pierce v. Society of the Sisters of the Holy Names of Jesus and Mary* School Choice Case (1925)
>
> Justice James McReynolds (unanimous): "The fundamental theory of liberty upon which all governments in this Union repose excludes any general power of the state to standardize its children by forcing them to accept instruction from public teachers only. The child is not the mere creature of the state; those who nurture him and direct his destiny have the right, coupled with the high duty, to recognize and prepare him for additional obligations."

the term "liberty" in the Due Process Clause includes the freedom of speech and press found in the First Amendment.

Who was **Benjamin Gitlow** and how did the Court rule in his case?

Benjamin Gitlow was a member of the Left Wing Section of the Socialist Party and the business manager of the party's newspaper, the *Revolutionary Age*. Gitlow believed that mass industrial revolts were necessary to overthrow the capitalistic government of the United States. New York officials charged Gitlow with violating a state criminal anarchy law that prohibited advocating the overthrow of the American government.

The Taft Court affirmed Gitlow's conviction and determined the anarchy statute did not violate the First Amendment. The Court determined that such advocacy was not protected by the First Amendment, that the amendment "does not protect disturbances to the public peace or the attempt to subvert the government." The Court reasoned that writings, such as those found in Gitlow's *Revolutionary Age* and *Left Wing Manifesto*, are by their very nature a "danger to the public peace and to the security of the State." Justice Edward Sanford wrote for the majority: "The State cannot reasonably be required to measure the danger from every such utterance in the nice balance of a jeweler's scale. A single revolutionary spark may kindle a fire that, smoldering for a time, may burst into a sweeping and destructive conflagration."

Which two justices **dissented in the *Gitlow*** decision?

Justices Oliver Wendell Holmes and Louis Brandeis, sometimes called the "Fathers of the First Amendment," dissented. Holmes argued that the Court should have applied his "clear and present danger" test that he had advocated in his *Schenck v. United States* (1919) and *Abrams v. United States* (1919) opinions. Holmes wrote that Gitlow's writings did not induce an immediate uprising or cause a revolution: "There was no present danger of an attempt to overthrow the government by force on the part of the admittedly small minority who shared the defendant's views."

215

Holmes explained: "It is said that this manifesto was more than a theory, that it was an incitement. Every idea is an incitement.... The only difference between the expression of an opinion and an incitement in the narrower sense is the speaker's enthusiasm for the result. Eloquence may set fire to reason. But whatever may be thought of the redundant discourse before us it had no chance of starting a present conflagration."

In what famous decision did the Taft Court uphold **California's criminal syndicalism law**?

The Taft Court unanimously rejected a First Amendment challenge to California's criminal syndicalism law in *Whitney v. California* (1927). Criminal syndicalism laws were passed to keep dissident political groups from disrupting industry and inciting political rebellion. The laws targeted communists, socialists, and other similar dissident groups. Charlotte Anita Whitney was convicted of violating the law as a result of a speech she gave in Oakland, California, on behalf of the Communist Labor Party of California, which supported the International Workers of the World. The California law prohibited persons from organizing, assisting, and assembling together "to advocate, teach, aid and abet criminal syndicalism." Whitney was arrested during the height of the "Red Scare" when government officials were concerned of a Communist uprising similar to the Bolshevik Revolution in Russia led by Vladimir Lenin.

The majority affirmed Whitney's conviction and upheld the statute, finding that it did not violate First Amendment freedoms. Writing for the majority, Justice Edward Sanford concluded that the law is not "an unreasonable or arbitrary exercise of the police power of the State; unwarrantably infringing upon any right of free speech, assembly or association, or that those persons are protected from punishment by the due-process clause who abuse such rights by joining and furthering an organization thus menacing the peace and welfare of the State."

The decision is better known for the concurring opinion of Justice Louis Brandeis, which was joined by Justice Oliver Wendell Holmes. Brandeis's concurrence, which reads more like a dissent, became a blueprint for the justification of free speech. He wrote that even advocacy of illegal conduct could not justify restricting speech unless the speech incites immediate lawless action, a test that the U.S. Supreme Court would eventually adopt in the 1969 decision *Brandenburg v. Ohio*. However, Brandeis concurred with the majority because "there was other testimony which tended to establish the existence of a conspiracy, on the part of members of the International Workers of the World, to commit present serious crimes, and likewise to show that such a conspiracy would be furthered by the activity of the society of which Miss Whitney was a member."

U.S. Supreme Court justice Louis Brandeis believed strongly in the First Amendment. He endorsed the First Amendment principle of countering harmful speech with positive speech, "not enforced silence." *George Grantham Bain Collection/Library of Congress.*

Which **foundational First Amendment principle** did Brandeis's opinion articulate?

One of the fundamental principles of First Amendment jurisprudence is that the government should respond to harmful speech by countering it with positive speech. In other words, the government should not silence negative speech but rather express a better alternative and show why the negative speech is wrong. This is called the counter-speech doctrine.

Brandeis provided the justification for the counter-speech doctrine: "If there be time to expose through discussion the falsehood and fallacies, to aver the evil by the processes of education, the remedy to be applied is more speech, not enforced silence."

Which Supreme Court **justice was related to Charlotte Anita Whitney**?

Charlotte Anita Whitney was a niece of former U.S. Supreme Court justice Stephen J. Field.

After the verdict, **what happened to Charlotte Anita Whitney**?

California governor Clement Calhoun Young pardoned Whitney in June 1927. Named national party chairman of the Communist Party in 1936, she unsuccessfully ran for a U.S. Senate seat in 1950. She died in San Francisco in 1955.

THE HUGHES COURT (1930–41)

How many and **which justices served on the Hughes Court**?

Seventeen justices served on the Hughes Court, which lasted from 1930 to 1941. These included: Chief Justice Charles Evans Hughes and Justices Edward Sanford, Oliver Wendell Holmes, Willis Van Devanter, James C. McReynolds, Louis D. Brandeis, George Sutherland, Pierce Butler, Edward T. Sanford, Harlan Fiske Stone, Owen J. Roberts, Benjamin N. Cardozo, Hugo Black, Stanley F. Reed, Felix Frankfurter, William O. Douglas, and Frank Murphy.

What **offices did Charles Evans Hughes hold before becoming chief justice**?

Charles Evans Hughes held several distinguished positions, including special counsel for the New York State Investigative Committee, governor of New York (1906–10), associate justice on the Supreme Court (1910–16), and U.S. secretary of state (1921–25). He also served as a member of the Permanent Court of International Justice for two years before being nominated as chief justice by President Herbert Hoover.

Why did Hughes **resign from the Court as an associate justice** in 1916?

Hughes resigned from the Court in 1916 to fulfill his political ambitions in becoming president of the United States. He secured the Republican Party's nomination for president but lost to Democratic Party nominee Woodrow Wilson in the general election.

Why did **Hughes's nomination for chief justice raise red flags** to some?

After resigning from the Court as an associate justice in 1916 and failing to capture the presidency, Hughes returned to work as a corporate lawyer on Wall Street. Some mem-

U.S. Supreme Court justice Charles Evans Hughes. *Hulton Archive/Getty Images.*

bers of Congress, such as U.S. senator George W. Norris of Nebraska, believed that Hughes was too tied to powerful financial and political friends to serve as an impartial chief justice. Others, such as U.S. senator Carter Glass of Virginia, criticized Hughes for leaving the Court as an associate justice to pursue the presidency. Glass said: "I believe this whole country felt a shock, as it was grievously distressed, when Mr. Justice Hughes resigned his place on the Supreme Court bench to be a candidate for President." Despite the opposition, the Senate confirmed Hughes by a vote of 52–26.

How did Hughes's position as chief justice **affect his son's job**?

Hughes's son, Charles E. Hughes Jr., resigned his position as solicitor general of the United States when his father was nominated for the position of chief justice. The younger Hughes stepped down because it would create a conflict of interest, as the solicitor general regularly argues cases before the U.S. Supreme Court.

Why is it said there were **two Hughes courts**?

Supreme Court historians often describe the Hughes Court in two terms, the first from 1931 to 1936 and the second from 1937 to 1941. The first Hughes Court, led by the conservative bloc of the so-called Four Horsemen (Justices Pierce Butler, Willis Van Devanter, George Sutherland, and James McReynolds) invalidated much of the "New Deal" economic legislation supported by President Franklin D. Roosevelt. These justices believed that the federal government was overreaching in its attempt to invoke its Commerce Clause powers over local matters. This changed in 1937 when Chief Justice Hughes and Justice Owen Roberts voted against the Four Horsemen to uphold a state minimum wage law in *West Coast Hotel Co. v. Parrish* and to uphold the National Labor Relations Act in *National Labor Relations Board v. Jones & Laughlin Steel Corp.* From the so-called Constitutional Revolution of 1937 forward, the Supreme Court reviewed economic regulations under a lower level of scrutiny (rational basis) than it did for regulations that impacted individual constitutional rights, such as freedom of speech or equal protection. Prior to 1937, the Court was more concerned with property and economic rights than with individual liberties. After 1937, the Court began a pattern of showing great deference in economic matters and applying greater scrutiny to restrictions that impacted individual liberties, such as freedom of speech.

Which **justice on the Hughes Court was nominated after the Senate rejected** President Herbert Hoover's first choice?

In 1930, President Herbert Hoover nominated John J. Parker of North Carolina to the U.S. Supreme Court. For the first time in 36 years, the Senate rejected a Supreme Court nominee by voting down Parker 41–39. Parker faced heavy opposition from the National Association for the Advancement of Colored People (NAACP) for statements he made about blacks and from the American Federation of Labor for upholding "yellow dog" labor contracts. (Yellow dog contracts are those in which an employee and employer agree that as a condition of employment, the employee agrees not to join a labor union). Hoover then nominated Owen Roberts, who was confirmed without opposition by voice vote.

Why did President Herbert Hoover **initially balk at the nomination of Benjamin Cardozo**?

At first, President Hoover did not want to nominate well-known New York judge Benjamin Cardozo for reasons based on religion and geography. First, he believed that the Supreme Court did not need another Jewish justice, as Justice Louis Brandeis already served on the Court. Second, Hoover believed that there should not be a third justice from the state of New York, as Chief Justice Charles Evans Hughes and Justice Harlan Fiske Stone were already from that state. Hoover eventually relented, in part because Justice Stone offered his resignation if the president nominated Cardozo.

Why did Justice **Hugo Black's nomination create controversy**?

The nomination of Justice Hugo Black caused controversy when rumors surfaced that Black once had been a member of the Ku Klux Klan. Black had resigned his Klan membership before he ran for the U.S. Senate in his home state of Alabama. He never rejoined the organization and, in fact, consistently voted on behalf of the downtrodden, including many minorities, during his long tenure on the U.S. Supreme Court. Others opposed Black because while still serving as a U.S. senator from Alabama, he voted on legislation affecting the U.S. Supreme Court (including the issue of salaries for the justices) during the time his nomination as a U.S. Supreme Court justice was being considered by his fellow senators.

What was unusual about Justice Black's **swearing-in as a justice**?

In open Supreme Court proceedings, two prominent individuals—Albert Levitt, a former federal judge and former assistant to the U.S. attorney general, and Boston attorney Patrick Henry Kelly—expressed their opposition to Justice Black the very day he took office. They opposed Black by filing motions contending that then-Senator Black, while waiting to be approved as a Supreme Court justice, had voted on raising the salaries of the justices, thereby making him ineligible to serve on the Court. Justice Black opted to take his oath of office in private, rather than have a public swearing-in ceremony.

CRIMINAL JUSTICE

What did the Hughes Court decide in the **Scottsboro Boys cases**?

The Hughes Court twice invalidated the death-penalty convictions of several of the Scottsboro Boys, nine African American youths who were wrongfully charged and later convicted of raping two white women on a train traveling from Tennessee to Alabama. The youths were immediately arraigned and tried without adequate legal counsel after only six days. The defendants were not provided with an attorney until the morning of trial. Nearly all of the defendants were convicted immediately and another had a hung jury after most the jurors held out for the death penalty when the prosecution had only sought a term of life imprisonment.

The Hughes Court ruled in *Powell v. Alabama* (1932) that the conviction of several of the Scottsboro Boys, including Ozie Powell, was invalid because they had been deprived of due process. The Court ruled 7–2 that the defendants' due-process rights were invalidated because the court failed to provide them with the meaningful assistance of counsel in their own defense. Defendants facing capital crimes have a constitutional right to an attorney, the majority reasoned.

A poster advertising a meeting held on April 14, 1931, to protest the death penalty of Haywood Patterson, one of the Scottsboro Boys. *Hulton Archive/Getty Images.*

After their first convictions were invalidated, the state filed rape charges against most of the defendants again. Clarence Norris, one of the Scottsboro Boys, challenged his second conviction on appeal because the state had failed to allow blacks to serve on juries. The evidence established that in Jackson County, Alabama, no black had ever served on any grand or petit (trial) jury. "That testimony in itself made out a prima facie case of the denial of the equal protection which the Constitution guarantees," Chief Justice Charles Evans Hughes wrote for the Court in *Norris v. Alabama* (1937). The Court ruled 8–0 in favor of Norris. (Justice James C. McReynolds did not participate in the case.)

223

Who were the **nine Scottsboro Boys**?

The nine Scottsboro Boys were Olen Montgomery, Clarence Norris, Haywood Patterson, Ozie Powell, Willie Roberson, Charley Weems, Eugene Williams, Andy Wright, and Roy Wright.

What happened to the **Scottsboro Boys after the trial**?

The Scottsboro Boys went to prison where they were all eventually released. Andy Wright stayed in prison the longest—until 1950. Roy Wright, the youngest Scottsboro Boy, shot his wife and then killed himself. But other Scottsboro defendants managed to overcome the hardships and unfairness to lead productive lives. Clarence Norris, who later cowrote a book entitled *The Last of the Scottsboro Boys,* lived until the age of 76. He finally received a pardon from Alabama governor George Wallace in 1976.

In what case did the Hughes Court first **invalidate coerced confessions**?

The Hughes Court ruled unanimously in *Brown v. Mississippi* (1936) that the murder convictions of three African American men had to be reversed due to the nature of

A group of supporters greet two of the freed Scottsboro Boys, Olen Montgomery (wearing overalls) and Eugene Williams (in suspenders), on July 26, 1937. *AP Images.*

their confessions. Law enforcement officials in Kemper County, Mississippi, dragged one defendant, Yank Ellington, out of his bed and hung him from a tree twice before releasing him. They seized him a couple days later, drove him to Alabama, and beat a confession out of him. A deputy sheriff arrested two other defendants, Ed Brown and Henry Shields, and whipped them with leather straps until they confessed to participating in the murder.

The Hughes Court ruled that these coerced confessions could not withstand constitutional scrutiny, as the defendants only confessed for fear of being beaten to death. "The rack and torture chamber may not be substituted for the witness stand," Hughes wrote. "The state may not permit an accused to be hurried to conviction under mob domination—where the whole proceeding is but a mask—without supplying corrective process." The Court concluded that such coerced confessions were "a clear denial of due process."

Who was the **young prosecuting attorney who obtained a conviction** of the three men in a Mississippi state trial court?

The prosecuting attorney was John C. Stennis, who later served in the U.S. Senate from 1947 to 1989. During the civil rights movement of the 1950s and 1960s, Stennis was a staunch opponent of integration.

In what Florida case did the Hughes Court **invalidate coerced confessions for a second time**?

The Hughes Court unanimously reversed the death-penalty convictions of several African American men in Broward County, Florida, in *Chambers v. Florida* (1940). Law enforcement officials, upset over the robbery and murder of an elderly white man, began a pattern of rounding up and questioning over a period of hours, the African American men in the county. Four men, after a week of repeatedly denying the crime, finally confessed after hours and hours of all-night questioning.

Writing for the Court, Justice Hugo Black wrote: "To permit human lives to be forfeited upon confessions thus obtained would make of the constitutional requirement of due process of law a meaningless symbol."

In what case did the Hughes Court invalidate a **confession obtained by the Texas Rangers**?

The Hughes Court unanimously ruled in *White v. Texas* (1940) that the rape conviction of an illiterate, African American man cannot stand because of the circumstances of his confession. The evidence showed that several Texas Rangers took the man out to the woods and beat him until he confessed. One Texas Ranger testified that he could not even remember how many times he had taken the man out of jail into the woods for these interrogations. Justice Hugo Black wrote that such practice did not comport with the

> ## CourtSpeak: *Johnson v. Zerbst* Right to Counsel Case (1938)
>
> Justice Hugo Black (majority): "The Sixth Amendment stands as a constant admonition that if the constitutional safeguards it provides be lost, justice will not still be done. It embodies a realistic recognition of the obvious truth that the average defendant does not have the professional legal skill to protect himself when brought before a tribunal with power to take his life or liberty, wherein the prosecution is presented by experienced and learned counsel. That which is simple, orderly, and necessary to the lawyer—to the untrained layman—may appear intricate, complex, and mysterious."

Constitution: "Due process of law, preserved for all by our Constitution, commands that no such practice as that disclosed by this record shall send any accused to his death."

What happened to the **defendant in *White v. Texas*?**

After the U.S. Supreme Court invalidated his conviction, prosecutors tried Mr. White at a second trial. During the retrial, the husband of the woman White allegedly raped shot and killed Mr. White. A jury acquitted the husband of any crime.

When did the Hughes Court rule that **federal, non-capital criminal defendants have the right to counsel?**

The Hughes Court ruled 6–2 (Justice Benjamin Cardozo did not participate) in *Johnson v. Zerbst* (1938) that federal criminal defendants have a Sixth Amendment right to the assistance of counsel. The case involved John A. Johnson, who was convicted for passing off counterfeit $20 bills. He was tried and sentenced in federal court in South Carolina to four years without the benefit of an attorney. In a habeas corpus (a later, collateral challenge to an original conviction) proceeding, Johnson (with the benefit of counsel) argued that his conviction should be set aside because he was not afforded an attorney.

Writing for the Court, Justice Hugo Black agreed that the "Sixth Amendment withholds from federal courts, in all criminal proceedings, the power and authority to deprive an accused of his life or liberty unless he has or waives the assistance of counsel." The Court emphasized the importance of counsel and that even intelligent lay persons do not sufficiently know the law to be able to defend themselves adequately. Black also ruled that Johnson did not knowingly waive his right to an attorney.

What attorney in *Johnson v. Zerbst* later **became a famous judge?**

Elbert P. Tuttle served as John Johnson's attorney before the U.S. Supreme Court in *Johnson v. Zerbst* (1938). He served as a federal appeals court judge for the U.S. Court

227

of Appeals for the Fifth Circuit in 1954, where he presided over many important desegregation cases. He continued to serve as a federal appeals court judge on the U.S. Court of Appeals for the Eleventh Circuit until his nineties. (The Fifth Circuit was divided into two circuits in the early 1980s). The building housing the Eleventh Circuit is now known as the Elbert P. Tuttle Court of Appeals Building.

In what decision did the Court **refuse to extend the right against double jeopardy to the states**?

The U.S. Supreme Court unanimously ruled in *Palko v. Connecticut* (1938) that the state of Connecticut could retry defendant Frank Palko for first-degree murder even though a jury already had convicted him of second-degree murder. The law provided that the state could appeal adverse verdicts in criminal cases just as the defendants could "with the permission of the presiding judge."

U.S. Supreme Court justice Benjamin Cardozo. *Underwood and Underwood/Time & Life Pictures/Getty Images.*

Palko had been charged with shooting and killing a police officer who pursued him for stealing a radio from a music store. In his first trial, the jury found him guilty of second-degree murder and he was sentenced to life imprisonment. The state tried Palko again for first-degree murder. The second jury found him guilty of first-degree murder and the trial court sentenced him to death.

Federal prosecutors could not have retried Palko because of the Fifth Amendment's Double Jeopardy Clause, which provides that "No person shall be subject for the same offence to be twice put in jeopardy of life or limb." Palko's attorneys argued that state officials should be subject to the same limitations via the Fourteenth Amendment Due Process Clause. In other words, they argued that the Fourteenth Amendment extended the Fifth Amendment double-jeopardy protection to the states.

The Court rejected Palko's argument in an opinion written by Justice Benjamin Cardozo, who noted that "there is no such general rule" for extending the protections found in the federal bill of rights to the states. Only those freedoms which were "the very essence of a scheme of ordered liberty" were extended to the state by the Fourteenth Amendment. Cardozo reasoned that the protection against double jeopardy, unlike freedom of speech protected in the First Amendment, was not so "fundamental" to liberty. "The state is not attempting to wear the accused out by a multitude of cases with accumulated trials," he wrote. "It asks no more than this, that the case against him shall go on until there shall be a trial free from the corrosion of substantial legal error."

The U.S. Supreme Court eventually overruled the *Palko* decision in *Benton v. Maryland* (1969).

What happened to **Frank Palko**?

After Palko's "double jeopardy" argument was rejected by the U.S. Supreme Court, the state proceeded with his execution. He died in an electric chair in 1937 at Connecticut State Prison.

RACE AND EQUAL PROTECTION

In what Hughes Court case did the **NAACP win its first major desegregation case in education**?

The Hughes Court ruled 7–2 in *Missouri Ex Rel. Gaines v. Canada* (1938) that the state of Missouri violated the equal-protection rights of Lloyd Gaines, who had applied to enter law school at the all-white University of Missouri. The state had argued that it complied with the constitutional requirement of equal protection by offering to pay Gaines to attend a law school for blacks in a nearby state. The state of Missouri at that time did not have a school for blacks that offered law classes. Gaines, who had obtained his undergraduate degree from the all-black Lincoln University, now sought admission to law school.

Chief Justice Hughes, writing for the Court, determined that the state of Missouri could not evade its legal responsibilities by saying it would eventually offer law schools at the all-black Lincoln University. He wrote that "it cannot be said that a mere declaration of purpose, still unfulfilled, is enough." Hughes also reasoned that Missouri could not rely on paying Gaines's tuition at an out-of-state school: "It is an obligation the burden of which cannot be cast by one State upon another." Legal scholars consider *Gaines* to be the first major victory of the National Association for the Advancement of Colored People (NAACP) in its fight to integrate schools.

What **famous attorney represented Lloyd Gaines**?

Charles Hamilton Houston, the special counsel for the NAACP in the late 1930s, argued the case for Lloyd Gaines before the U.S. Supreme Court. Houston attended Harvard Law School, where he became the first black editor of the *Harvard Law Review*. He served as a mentor to future U.S. Supreme Court justice Thurgood Marshall.

What happened to Lloyd Gaines after the trial?

Lloyd Gaines mysteriously disappeared after the U.S. Supreme Court ruling and before the NAACP could challenge Missouri in the lower courts after its victory before the Supreme Court. The website of the Gaines/Oldham Black Cultural Center at the University of Missouri (http://web.missouri.edu/~bccenter/history.php) provides the following information: "Gaines was last seen at his fraternity house in Chicago. One evening around March 19, 1939, he told the housekeeper that he was going to buy some stamps and he was never seen or heard from again." Some believe Gaines was murdered; others believe he accepted money to leave the state and never returned.

In what decision did the Hughes Court strike down a **state voter registration law as discriminatory**?

In *Lane v. Wilson* (1939), the Hughes Court struck down an Oklahoma law that required those who previously were not registered voters to register under a two-week window or forfeit their voting rights. The Court noted that Oklahoma's previous grandfather law provided that those citizens whose grandfathers were eligible to vote could vote themselves, and all others could not. Obviously, this had the effect of disenfranchising African American voters. The Supreme Court had invalidated this system in *Guinn v. United States* (1915). In response, Oklahoma passed a new law that provided that those previously not eligible must register within this two-week period.

The Court, in an opinion written by Justice Felix Frankfurter, viewed this law as violative of the Fifteenth Amendment by a 6–2 vote. (Justice William O. Douglas did not participate.) "We believe that the opportunity thus given negro voters to free themselves from the effects of discrimination to which they should never have been subjected was too cabined and confined," Frankfurter wrote.

In what decision did the Hughes Court **uphold a poll tax**?

The Hughes Court unanimously upheld Georgia's $1 poll tax in *Breedlove v. Suttles* (1937). Nolen R. Breedlove, a 28-year-old white male, challenged the poll tax as a violation of equal protection because it did not provide a poll tax on those older than sixty. The Court rejected that notion and determined the poll tax constitutional. "The payment of poll taxes as a prerequisite to voting is a familiar and reasonable regulation long enforced in many states and for more than a century in Georgia," Justice Pierce Butler wrote for the Court.

A constitutional amendment to prohibit poll taxes was introduced into Congress in 1939. Eventually, Congress passed the Twenty-Fourth Amendment in 1962 and the states ratified it in 1964. The amendment prohibited poll taxes, which were often used by Southern voters in a discriminatory fashion against would-be African American voters.

How did the Hughes Court address **Texas's primary system, which limited African Americans from voting**?

The Hughes Court issued two decisions relating to the Texas Democratic Party and its practice of restricting African Americans from voting. In *Nixon v. Condon* (1927), the Hughes Court invalidated a Texas law that allowed political parties' executive committees to prohibit African Americans from voting in party primaries. The Court narrowly ruled 5–4 that the executive committees were state actors sufficient to trigger the Fourteenth Amendment equal-protection guarantees. "Delegates of the state's power have discharged their official functions in such a way as to discriminate invidiously between white citizens and black," Justice Benjamin Cardozo wrote for the Court.

However, Cardozo wrote that if a private political party discriminated on its own without state authorization, the question might be resolved differently. Texas officials then repealed its primary election law and power to determine voter qualifications resided in the state party conventions. The Democratic Party then determined at its conventions to allow only whites to vote. R. R. Grovey, an African American from Houston, challenged this new system as unconstitutional. However, the U.S. Supreme Court unanimously ruled in *Grovey v. Townsend* (1935) that this new system was not unconstitutional because the discrimination was done by a private political party at its convention, not by state officials. "We are not prepared to hold that in Texas the state convention of a party has become a mere instrumentality or agency for expressing the voice or will of the state," Justice Owen Roberts wrote.

The Stone Court would later overrule *Grovey v. Townsend* in *Smith v. Allwright* (1944).

What **famous footnote** caused major changes in constitutional law?

Justice Harlan Fiske Stone wrote a footnote in his opinion for the Court in *United States v. Carolene Products Co.* that has become known as the famous "Footnote Four." The case concerned the constitutionality of the Filled Milk Act of 1923, which prohibits the shipment in interstate commerce of skimmed milk made up of any fat or oil other than skimmed milk. The Court ruled 6–1 in favor of the constitutionality of the law.

The case is not considered important except for the footnote, which provided that there should be different degrees of judicial scrutiny for different types of laws. Laws that impact economic matters should be reviewed under the deferential rational basis test, which provides that a law is constitutional if Congress had a reasonable, or rational, basis for passing the law. However, other types of law that impact fundamental individual freedoms, such as the freedom of speech or the right to vote, must pass a higher degree of judicial review known as strict scrutiny.

COMMERCE AND LABOR

How did the Hughes Court change its position with respect to the **constitutionality of minimum wage laws**?

The Hughes Court upheld a New York minimum wage law in *Morehead v. New York Ex. Rel. Tipaldo* (1936) but struck down a similar Washington state law in *West Coast Hotel Co. v. Parrish* (1937). The case involved Joseph Tipaldo, a Brooklyn laundry

CourtSpeak: *Schecter Poultry Corp. v. United States* "Sick Chicken" Case (1935)

Chief Justice Charles Evans Hughes (majority): "Extraordinary conditions do not create or enlarge constitutional power. The Constitution established a national government with powers deemed to be adequate, as they have proved to be both in war and peace, but these powers of the national government are limited by the constitutional grants. Those who act under these grants are not at liberty to transcend the imposed limits because they believe that more or different power is necessary."

Justice Benjamin Cardozo (concurring): "If that conception shall prevail, anything that Congress may do within the limits of the Commerce Clause for the betterment of business may be done by the President upon the recommendation of a trade association by calling it a code. This is delegation run riot."

owner arrested for violating the minimum wage law. Justice Pierce Butler wrote for a 5–4 majority that "the right to make contracts about one's affairs is a part of the liberty protected by the due process clause." The majority relied on the Taft Court's 1923 decision *Adkins v. Children's Hospital,* which upheld a similar District of Columbia minimum wage law for women. Butler reasoned that women were not forced to take the laundry job: "In making contracts of employment, generally speaking, the parties have equal right to obtain from each other the best terms they can by private bargaining."

Justice Harlan Fiske Stone wrote for the four dissenters, claiming that the majority opinion ignored economic realities facing many workers: "We have had opportunity to learn that a wage is not always the resultant of free bargaining between employers and employees."

The U.S. Supreme Court overruled *Morehead* the next year in its *Parrish* decision. In that case, hotel chambermaid Elsie Parrish alleged that the hotel paid her less than minimum wage. Chief Justice Charles Evans Hughes wrote for a five-member majority that the state minimum wage law did not violate the employer's due-process rights. He reasoned that legislatures could enact many laws designed to protect workers from harmful conditions. Chief Justice Hughes cited the 1908 decision *Holden v. Hardy,* which upheld a Utah law limiting the daily employment of mine workers to eight hours a day. "In dealing with the relation of employer and employed, the Legislature has necessarily a wide field of discretion in order that there may be suitable protection of health and safety, and that peace and good order may be promoted through regulations designed to insure wholesome conditions of work and freedom from oppression," he wrote.

233

Which **justice changed his vote** from one minimum wage case to the other?

Justice Owen Roberts switched his vote from striking down a minimum wage law in *Morehead* to upholding such a law in *Parrish*. It was said that Roberts's change of mind was the "switch in time that saved nine"—a reference to President Franklin D. Roosevelt's sharp criticism of the Court and his proposal in 1937 to "pack" the Court with additional justices. In reality, Roberts had indicated his support for the minimum wage law in a Court conference in December 1936 before President Roosevelt's court-packing plan was announced.

Associate Justice Owen J. Roberts walks down a street near the U.S. Supreme Court Building. Roberts voted against a minimum wage law in *Morehead v. New York Ex. Rel. Tipaldo* (1936) but voted for it a year later in *West Coast Hotel Co. v. Parrish. John Phillips/Time & Life Pictures/Getty Images.*

What was the **"sick chicken" case** and how did it affect the National Industrial Recovery Act?

The Hughes Court unanimously (9–0) ruled that the National Industrial Recovery Act (NIRA) was unconstitutional in *Schecter Poultry Corp. v. United States* (1935). The NIRA empowered business groups to draw up fair codes of competition in various industries that set wages and established work hours. The codes would have to be approved by the president. One such code dealt with the poultry trade in New York City. The four Schecter brothers—Joe, Martin, Aaron, and Alex—ran a Brooklyn-based wholesale poultry business that sold chickens and poultry to retail shops in the city. The Schecter brothers violated the code by paying lower wages and by selling diseased chickens (hence, the "sick chicken" name) at reduced prices. The government charged the Schecter brothers with violating the federal law. The brothers contended that the law was unconstitutional because it gave too much power to the president in overseeing the various business codes and because the Schecter business did not affect interstate commerce and, thus, Congress exceeded its Commerce Clause powers in regulating an intracommerce business.

The Hughes Court ruled that the NIRA was unconstitutional for several reasons. First, it said that the NIRA gave too much power to the president. "We think

---

CourtSpeak: *United States v. Butler*
Agricultural Production Case (1936)

Justice Owen Roberts (majority): "It does not help to declare that local conditions throughout the nation have created a situation of national concern; for this is but to say that whenever there is a widespread similarity of local conditions, Congress may ignore constitutional limitations upon its own powers and usurp those reserved to the states."

Justice Harlan Fiske Stone (dissenting): "The power of courts to declare a statute unconstitutional is subject to two guiding principles of decision which ought never to be absent from judicial consciousness. One is that courts are concerned only with the power to enact statutes, not with their wisdom. The other is that while unconstitutional exercise of power by the executive and legislative branches of the government is subject to judicial restraint, the only check upon our own exercise of power is our own sense of self-restraint. For the removal of unwise laws from the statute books appeal lies, not to the courts, but to the ballot and to the processes of democratic government."

---

that the code-making authority thus conferred is an unconstitutional delegation of legislative power," Chief Justice Hughes wrote. Second, the Court ruled that the Schecter business did not affect interstate commerce and thus the law reached too far: "Where the effect of intrastate transactions upon interstate commerce is merely indirect, such transactions remain within the domain of state power," Hughes wrote.

In what decision did the Hughes Court **invalidate the Agricultural Adjustment Act of 1933?**

The U.S. Supreme Court struck down the Agricultural Adjustment Act of 1933 by a 6–3 vote in *United States v. Butler* (1936). The law sought to revitalize the economy by controlling the amount and price of farm products, as farmers produced too much supply and received too little money for their products. The law gave financial incentives for farmers to produce less and imposed "processing taxes" on companies that turned farm products into consumer goods, like meatpacking plants. The Court majority determined that Congress had broad powers to tax and spend under Article I, Section 8, of the Constitution but that this law invaded the province of the states. "The act invades the reserved rights of the states," wrote Justice Owen Roberts. "It is a statutory plan to regulate and control agricultural production, a matter beyond the powers delegated to the federal government."

235

New Deal Legislation Invalidated by the U.S. Supreme Court

President Franklin D. Roosevelt submitted his infamous court-packing plan in 1937 because he opposed many decisions of the U.S. Supreme Court. It had struck down much of the New Deal economic relief legislation. Here are some of the decisions that invalidated federal legislation designed to spur the economy:

Federal Law	Invalidated by …
Agricultural Adjustment Act of 1933	*U.S. v. Butler* (1936)
Agricultural Adjustment Act of 1933 (later amendments)	*Rickert Rice Mills v. Fountenot* (1936)
Economy Act of 1933 (one clause)	*Lynch v. U.S.* (1934)
National Industrial Recovery Act (addressing the "Live Poultry Code" passed pursuant to Section 3 of the NIRA)	*Schecter Poultry Co. v. U.S.* (1935)
National Industrial Recovery Act (addressing a provision passed pursuant to Section 1 of the NIRA)	*Panama Refining Co. v. Ryan* (1935)
Home Owners Loan Act of 1933 (1934 amendment)	*Hopkins Savings Assn. v. Cleary* (1935)
Railroad Retirement Act	*Railroad Retirement Board v. Alton R. Co.* (1935)
Bituminous Coal Conservation Act	*Carter v. Carter Coal Co.* (1936)
Frazier-Lemke Act of 1934 (bankruptcy law related to farmers)	*Louisville Bank v. Radford* (1935)

In what famous decision did the Court **uphold the National Labor Relations Act**?

The Hughes Court ruled that the National Labor Relations Act (NLRA) was constitutional in its 1937 decision *National Labor Relations Board v. Jones & Laughlin Steel Corp.* The decision involved the nation's fourth largest steel producer, Jones & Laughlin, which had plants in Pennsylvania.

Federal officials charged that the company violated the NLRA by firing workers who had organized fellow workers into a union. The NLRA prohibited such activity as an unfair labor practice. Attorneys for the steel producer contended that the NLRA amounted to an unconstitutional expansion of congressional power. They contended that the law invaded the reserved powers of the individual states.

The Court ruled that act constitutional by a 5–4 vote, determining that the actions at the plant affected interstate commerce. "The steel industry is one of the great basic industries affecting interstate commerce at every point," Chief Justice Charles Evans Hughes wrote. "When industries organize themselves on a national scale, making their relating to interstate commerce the dominant factor in their activities, how can it be maintained that their industrial labor relations constitute a forbidden field into which Congress may not enter when it is necessary to protect interstate commerce from the paralyzing consequences of industrial war."

In his dissenting opinion, Justice James C. McReynolds wrote, "Whatever effect any cause or discontent may ultimately have upon commerce is far too indirect to justify congressional regulation. Almost anything—marriage, birth, death—may in some fashion affect commerce."

In what decisions did the Hughes Court **uphold portions of the Social Security Act**?

One of the centerpiece pieces of legislation during the New Deal period was the Social Security Act of 1935. President Franklin D. Roosevelt and many members of Congress believed the measure would assist the unemployed and the elderly during the crippling times caused by the Great Depression. The Hughes Court upheld provisions of the Social Security Act in two 1937 decisions decided on the same day: *Steward Machine Co. v. Davis* and *Helvering v. Davis*. In *Steward,* the Court ruled that Congress had the power to require employers with eight or more employees to pay an excise tax that would fund unemployment compensation. In *Helvering,* the Court ruled that Congress had the power to tax employers and employees for "Federal Old-Age Benefits." The Hughes Court determined that the national crisis caused by the Great Depression fueled the need for Congress to spend money to benefit the general welfare. The Court ruled that Congress had the power to pass this legislation under Article I, Section 8, of the Constitution, which gives Congress broad spending powers to aid the "general welfare."

In what decision did the Hughes Court uphold a state law **fixing milk prices**?

The Hughes Court ruled 5–4 in *Nebbia v. People of State of New York* (1934) that a New York law regulating milk prices did not violate the Due Process Clause. Leo Nebbia, a Rochester grocery store owner, challenged a state law that required him to charge nine cents for a quart of milk. Nebbia was charged with violating the law by selling the material cheaper in his store, as he had sold two quarts of milk and a loaf of bread for 18 cents. The Court, in an opinion written by Justice Owen Roberts, determined that the measure was not arbitrary or unreasonable. "The Constitution does not guarantee the unrestricted privilege to engage in a business or to conduct it as one pleases," Roberts wrote. "So far as the requirement of due process is concerned, and in the absence of other constitutional restriction, a state is free to adopt whatever economic policy may reasonably be deemed to promote public welfare, and to enforce that policy by legislation adopted to its purpose."

The Four Horsemen—Pierce Butler, Willis Van Devanter, George Sutherland, and James McReynolds—dissented in an opinion written by McReynolds. These justices believed that the legislature had exceeded its constitutional authority in fixing prices for private businesses. "This is not regulation, but management control, dictation—it amounts to the deprivation of the fundamental right which one has to conduct his own affairs honestly and along customary lines," he wrote.

PRESIDENTIAL POWER

How did the Hughes Court limit the power of a president to remove certain federal officials?

The Hughes Court unanimously ruled in *Humphrey's Executor v. United States* (1935) that President Franklin D. Roosevelt violated separation of powers principles in removing William E. Humphrey as commissioner of the Federal Trade Commission. Roosevelt had removed Humphrey, believing he was too conservative and hostile to Roosevelt's New Deal initiatives. Humphrey sued in U.S. Claims Court, contending that Roosevelt violated a provision of the Federal Trade Commission Act, which provided that commissioners were to serve for a fixed term and could be removed only for "inefficiency, neglect of duty, or malfeasance in office." The president contended that such a law infringed on his executive branch powers.

The court determined that Congress could constitutionally set the limitations for removal in the statute for such an office. "The authority of Congress, in creating quasi-legislative or quasi-judicial agencies, to require them to act in discharge of their duties independently of executive control cannot well be doubted," Justice George Sutherland wrote. "The sound application of a principle that makes one master in his own house precludes him from imposing his control in the house of another who is master there."

The case remains an important precedent for limiting the power of the executive branch and articulating the separation of powers principles in American government.

FIRST AMENDMENT

In what famous decision did the Hughes Court **protect freedom of the press** and prevent prior restraints on expression?

The Hughes Court ruled 5–4 in *Near v. Minnesota* (1931) that a state law allowing the closing of newspapers as public nuisances for publishing scandalous material violated the First Amendment and amounted to "the essence of censorship." The case concerned the *Saturday Press,* a publication owned by Jay Near, which printed several articles alleging that city officials turned a blind eye to crimes committed by Jewish gangsters. Much of the material in the articles was anti-Semitic, such as the following statement:

> There have been too many men in this city and especially those in official life, who HAVE been taking orders and suggestions from JEW GANGSTERS, therefore we HAVE Jew Gangsters, practically ruling Minneapolis.

Hennepin County officials objected to the articles and sought to close down the newspaper pursuant to the law that allowed newspapers to be declared public nuisances if they were "malicious, scandalous and defamatory." Near contended that the statute violated his First Amendment free-press rights. The state courts disagreed but he appealed all the way to the U.S. Supreme Court.

Chief Justice Charles Evans Hughes, writing for the majority, explained that the First Amendment severely limited the ability of government officials to limit publication of newspapers. The proper remedy, if any, was for the government officials to sue the publisher for libel; it was not to silence the publication and prevent it from publishing at all. Hughes noted that any charge of official corruption creates a scandal and would allow the closing of many publications. "The fact that the liberty of the press may be abused by miscreant purveyors of scandal does not make any less necessary the immunity of the press from previous restraint in dealing with official misconduct," Hughes wrote. "Subsequent punishment for such abuses as may exist is the appropriate remedy, consistent with constitutional privilege."

Did the U.S. Supreme Court say **all prior restraints on publications were unconstitutional**?

No, the Court said that the government "might prevent actual obstruction to its recruiting service or the publication of the sailing dates of transports or the number and location of troops." In other words, there could be instances where national security would allow the government to prevent publication of military secrets.

In what famous decision did the Hughes Court strike down a **"red flag" law**?

The Hughes Court struck down a California law that prohibited the display of red flags as opposition to the U.S. government in *Stromberg v. California* (1931). Yetta Stromberg, a 19-year-old member of the Young Communist League, was arrested and convicted of violating the red-flag law for displaying such a flag at a summer camp where she taught history. The California "Red Flag" Law stated: "Any person who displays a red flag, banner or badge or any flag, badge, banner, or device of any color or form whatever in any public place or in any meeting place or public assembly, or from or on any house, building or window as a sign, symbol or emblem of opposition to organized government or as an invitation or stumulus to anarchistic action or as an aid to propaganda that is of a seditious character is guilty of a felony."

The Hughes Court reversed her conviction by a 7–2 vote, reasoning that the statute would sweep within its prohibition "peaceful and orderly opposition to government by legal means and within constitutional limitations." Such a broad prohibition, the Court wrote, was "repugnant to the guaranty of liberty contained in the Fourteenth Amendment."

The case is important because it establishes the principle that the First Amendment protects more than just verbal or written expression. It also involves certain forms of expressive conduct, such as the display of the red flag or the wearing of certain clothes.

In what case did the Hughes Court **protect the freedom of assembly of a communist**?

The U.S. Supreme Court ruled unanimously 8–0 (Justice Harlan Fiske Stone did not participate) in *De Jonge v. Oregon* (1937) that "peaceable assembly for lawful discussion cannot be made a crime." The case involved Oregon-based communist Dirk De Jonge, who was sentenced to seven years for participating in a Communist Party meeting. There was no evidence of any violence or rebellion at the meeting, only lawful political discussions. The Court concluded that the "holding of meetings for peaceable political action cannot be subscribed." The case is also important because for the first time the U.S. Supreme Court made clear that the First Amendment freedom of assembly is extended to the states via the Fourteenth Amendment's Due Process Clause.

In what decision did the Hughes Court **invalidate the criminal conviction of an African American communist on First Amendment grounds**?

The Hughes Court ruled 5–4 in *Herndon v. Lowry* (1937) that African American communist activist Angelo Herndon's conviction could not stand based on First Amendment concerns. Georgia law enforcement officials had charged Herndon under a state

> ## CourtSpeak: *De Jonge v. Oregon* Freedom of Assembly Case (1937)
>
> Chief Justice Charles Evans Hughes (unanimous): "The greater the importance of safeguarding the community from incitements to the overthrow of our institutions by force and violence, the more imperative is the need to preserve inviolate the constitutional rights of free speech, free press and free assembly in order to maintain the opportunity for free political discussion, to the end that government may be responsive to the will of the people and that changes, if desired, may be obtained by peaceful means. Therein lies the security of the Republic, the very foundation of constitutional government."

law that prohibited attempting to incite an insurrection. The officials charged Herndon after learning that he had traveled from Kentucky and held three meetings in which he tried to recruit individuals to the Communist Party. The U.S. Supreme Court reversed Herndon's conviction in part because there was "no evidence … by speech or written word, at meetings or elsewhere, any doctrine or action implying such forcible subversion." The Court concluded that Herndon's meetings did not meet the definition of attempting to incite an insurrection. In his majority opinion, Justice Owen Roberts explained that Herndon's "membership in the Communist Party and his solicitation of a few members wholly fails to establish an attempt to incite others to insurrection." Roberts concluded that the statute itself was too vague to withstand constitutional scrutiny, writing that it "amounts merely to a dragnet which may enmesh any one who agitates for a change of government."

Which dissenting justice **emphasized Herndon's race**?

Justice Willis Van Devanter focused on Herndon's race in his dissenting opinion, writing: "Herndon is a negro and a member of the Communist Party of the U.S.A., which is a section of the Communist International." At a later point in his opinion, Van Devanter wrote: "It should not be overlooked that Herndon was a Negro member and organizer in the Communist Party."

What Hughes Court decision laid the foundation for the **public forum doctrine**?

In *Hague v. Committee for Industrial Organization* (1939), the Hughes Court invalidated a Jersey City, New Jersey, ordinance that allowed the director of public safety to deny permits for the use of city halls for public meetings. Jersey City officials also prohibited labor organizations from distributing printed material on the public streets, while allowing other groups to distribute printed material without interference. The Court majority determined that this violated the labor group's constitutional rights.   241

The conviction of African American communist activist Angelo Herndon (holding child) was overturned by the Hughes Court in 1937. The Court ruled that Herndon's efforts to recruit a few members to the Communist Party did not constitute an attempt to incite an insurrection. *Alfred Eisenstaedt/Time & Life Pictures/ Getty Images.*

In his plurality opinion, Justice Owen Roberts wrote that public streets and parks were places that by tradition should be open to the public to exercise their constitutional rights to assembly, petition, and speech. This statement formed the historical basis for the so-called public forum doctrine in First Amendment law that gives increased free-expression protection in certain public places.

In what decision did the Hughes Court uphold a **flag-salute law**?

The Hughes Court ruled 8–1 in *Minersville School District v. Gobitis* (1940) that a Pennsylvania flag-salute law was constitutional. The law required public school students to stand and recite the Pledge of Allegiance. A family of Jehovah's Witnesses in Minersville, Pennsylvania, contended that the law infringed on their freedom of religion. Twelve-year-old Lillian Gobitas and her ten-year-old brother William were expelled from school for refusing to salute the flag. (The correct spelling of their name was Gobitas; a court clerk misspelled it as "Gobitis" and it stayed that way in the official records).

The U.S. Supreme Court disagreed with the family, finding that the flag-salute was a constitutional patriotic exercise not designed to infringe on religious beliefs. "National unity is the basis of national security," wrote Justice Felix Frankfurter for the majority. "The ultimate foundation of a free society is the binding tie of cohesive sentiment." For their part, the Gobitas children never returned to public school after the decision.

> ### CourtSpeak: *Hague v. Committee for Industrial Organization* Public Forum Doctrine Case (1939)
>
> Justice Owen Roberts (plurality): "Wherever the title of streets and parks may rest, they have immemoriably been held in trust for the use of the public and, time out of mind, have been used for purposes of assembly, communicating thoughts between citizens, and discussing public questions. Such use of the streets and public places has, from ancient times, been a part of the privileges, immunities, rights, and liberties of citizens. The privilege of a citizen of the United States to use the streets and parks for communication of views on national questions may be regulated in the interest of all; it is not absolute, but relative, and must be exercised in subordination to the general comfort and convenience, and in consonance with peace and good order; but it must not, in the guise of regulation, be abridged or denied."

Who was the Court's **lone dissenter in the *Gobitis* decision**?

Justice Harlan Fiske Stone filed the Court's lone dissent in *Gobitis*. He believed that the law infringed on the Jehovah's Witnesses' free-exercise of religion rights. Stone wrote: "Even if we believe that such compulsions [as saluting the flag] will contribute to national unity, there are other ways to teach loyalty and patriotism which are the sources of national unity, than by compelling the pupil to affirm that which he does not believe and by ... commanding a form of affirmance which violates his religious convictions." Stone's view would eventually prevail when he became chief justice, as the Stone Court struck down a West Virginia flag-salute law by a vote of 6–3 in *West Virginia Board of Education v. Barnette*.

What decision reversed the conviction of a **phonograph-playing Jehovah's Witness**?

The Hughes Court ruled unanimously (9–0) in *Cantwell v. Connecticut* that Jesse Cantwell did not commit breach of the peace when he walked door-to-door in a Catholic neighborhood soliciting for Jehovah's Witnesses. Cantwell, his brother Russell, and his father Newton walked down Cassius Street in New Haven, Connecticut, and asked the residents if they would listen to one of their records. These records attacked official religions, including Catholicism. City officials cited the three men for failing to obtain a permit to solicit door-to-door and for breach of the peace.

The Court unanimously ruled that the city law requiring solicitors to obtain a permit violated the First Amendment. The Court focused on the fact that the secre-

243

tary of the welfare council would determine the merits of the solicitation and religious causes before making the permit decision. To the Court, this was unacceptable: "But to condition the solicitation of aid for the perpetuation of religious views or systems upon a license, the grant of which rests in the exercise of a determination by state authority as to what is a religious cause, is to lay a forbidden burden upon the exercise of liberty protected by the Constitution." The court then addressed Jesse Cantwell's conviction for breach of the peace, finding that his conduct did not merit official sanction.

In what decision did the Hughes Court unanimously strike down a **city licensing law applied to Jehovah's Witnesses**?

The Hughes Court unanimously ruled 8–0 (Justice Benjamin N. Cardozo did not participate) in *Lovell v. City of Griffin* (1938) that a Georgia city law prohibiting individuals from distributing materials without a license from the city manager violated the First Amendment. Griffin, Georgia, officials fined Alma Lovell, a Jehovah's Witness, $50 for distributing without a permit a religious magazine called the *Golden Age*. Griffin refused to apply for a permit, saying such an attempt would have been "an act of disobedience to His commandment."

Chief Justice Charles Evans Hughes reasoned that such a law amounted to unconstitutional censorship. He compared it to the licensing laws in England in the sixteenth and seventeenth centuries, where printers had to obtain a license before printing materials. Hughes wrote: "The liberty of the press is not confined to newspapers and periodicals. It necessarily embraces pamphlets and leaflets. These indeed have been historic weapons in the defense of liberty, as the pamphlets of Thomas Paine and others in our own history abundantly attest. The press in its historic connotation comprehends every sort of publication which affords a vehicle of information and opinion."

Children help their parents display Jehovah's Witnesses posters. In *Lovell v. City of Griffin* (1938), the U.S. Supreme Court ruled unanimously that a Georgia city law prohibiting individuals from distributing materials without a license from the city manager violated the First Amendment. Chief Justice Charles Evans Hughes believed such a law amounted to unconstitutional censorship. *Hulton Archive/Getty Images.*

In what other Jehovah's Witness case did the Hughes Court uphold a **state statute requiring a license for parades or marches**?

In *Cox v. New Hampshire* (1941), the U.S. Supreme Court upheld the convictions of five Jehovah's Witnesses who violated a New Hampshire law that required marchers to apply for a permit. More than sixty individuals marched down the city streets with signs reading: "Religion is a Snare and a Racket" without applying for a permit. The individuals challenged the statute on First Amendment grounds, saying it interfered with their free-assembly and free-exercise of religion rights.

The Hughes Court unanimously disagreed, ruling that the state law was constitutional. The Court reasoned that the law on its face merely regulated the time, place, and manner of parades and marches, as opposed to a regulation that discriminated against certain groups based on content. The Court noted that there was "no evidence" that the law had been applied in a discriminatory fashion.

In what context did the Hughes Court rule that **newspapers are not entitled to special exemptions from generally applicable laws**?

The Hughes Court ruled 5–4 in *Associated Press v. NLRB* that the First Amendment rights of the Associated Press (AP) were not violated when a court ordered the media company to rehire an editorial employee allegedly terminated for his membership in a labor organization. The National Labor Relations Board (NLRB) contended that the AP had violated a provision in the National Labor Relations Act that gave employees the right to organize, form, and join labor organizations of their choosing. As one of their defenses, the AP contended that the NLRB violated the free-press rights of the newspaper. The AP argued that it must have an unfettered right to determine who its editors will be.

The Court disagreed with AP. Justice Owen J. Roberts, writing for the majority, said: "The publisher of a newspaper has no special immunity from the application of general laws. He has no special privilege to invade the rights and liberties of others. He must answer for libel. He may be punished for contempt of court. He is subject to the anti-trust laws." The majority reasoned that a newspaper can discharge an employee for poor performance but not for joining a labor union.

In what decision did the Hughes Court **strike down a tax on newspapers**?

The Hughes Court unanimously invalidated a Louisiana tax on newspapers with large circulations (more than 20,000 per week) in *Grosjean v. American Press Co.* (1936). In an opinion written by Justice George Sutherland, the Court noted that the tax applied only to the thirteen largest newspapers, twelve of which were opposed to the administration of the state's governor, Huey Long. "The form in which the tax is imposed is in itself suspicious," Sutherland wrote. "It is measured alone by the extent of the circulation of the publication in which the advertisements are carried, with the plain purpose of penalizing the publishers and curtailing the circulation of a selected group of publishers." Sutherland compared the Louisiana law to policies of the British government, which were used to silence newspapers hostile to the government's policies in colonial times.

THE STONE COURT (1941–46)

How many and **which justices served on the Stone Court**?

Eleven justices served on the Stone Court, including Chief Justice Harlan Fiske Stone and Justices Owen J. Roberts, Hugo Black, Stanley F. Reed, Felix Frankfurter, William O. Douglas, Frank Murphy, James Byrnes, Robert Jackson, Wiley Rutledge, and Harold Burton.

What was **unusual about Harlan Fiske Stone's elevation to chief justice**?

Stone, a Republican, was nominated for chief justice by Democratic president Franklin D. Roosevelt. Stone's appointment became only the second time in history that a president had nominated a chief justice from an opposing party. Previously, Republican president William Howard Taft had elevated Democrat Edward D. White to chief justice in 1910.

What was Chief Justice Stone's **professional experience**?

After graduating from Columbia Law School, Stone took a position teaching at his alma mater. He taught there until 1923, the last thirteen years as law school dean. While teaching at Columbia, Stone also practiced law at the firm Sullivan & Cromwell. In 1924, President Calvin Coolidge tabbed Stone to serve as U.S. attorney general. A year later, Coolidge nominated Stone to the Supreme Court, where he served as an associate justice for seventeen years until his tenure as chief justice began.

How did **Stone die**?

On April 12, 1946, Stone stumbled and faltered while reading one of his dissents from the bench. Justice Hugo Black, sensing something was wrong with the chief justice, grabbed the gavel and announced that the Court would take a break. Black and Justice

U.S. Supreme Court chief justice Harlan Fiske Stone. *National Photo Company Collection/Library of Congress.*

Stanley F. Reed assisted Stone to his chambers and someone called an ambulance. However, Stone died later that evening of a cerebral hemorrhage.

COMMERCE CLAUSE

What **dispute involving a wheat farmer** led to a major U.S. Supreme Court case over Congress's Commerce Clause powers?

Wickard v. Filburn (1942) stands for the principle that Congress has very broad power to regulate commerce—even commerce that would appear to not meet any definition of interstate commerce.

Roscoe Filburn, a farmer who raised chicken and cattle, planted 12 more acres of wheat than he was supposed to under the Agricultural Adjustment Act of 1938. The federal law was designed to control the volume of wheat in commerce to ensure there were no surpluses or shortages that would lead to abnormally high or low wheat prices. Government officials fined Filburn because he produced 239 more bushels than he was allotted under the law. Filburn challenged the fine, contending that Congress exceeded its powers under the Commerce Clause in punishing him for wheat that he did not even sell in interstate commerce. Filburn argued that the Commerce Clause did not give Congress the power to regulate local, intrastate acts that have only an indirect effect on commerce. He sued several federal officials, including Claude R. Wickard, the U.S. secretary of agriculture from 1940 to 1945.

The Supreme Court unanimously ruled 8–0 against Filburn. The Court reasoned that while Filburn's own wheat production may have been trivial, his production when added with the production of other small wheat farmers was "far from trivial." The Court noted that those who produce their own wheat do affect interstate commerce by, at the very least, removing many potential customers for wheat: "Home-grown wheat in this sense competes with wheat in commerce." The Court also noted that Congress was in a far better position to pass laws dealing with the wheat industry which "has been a problem industry for some years."

In what case did the Stone Court rule on the **constitutional right to travel**?

In *Edwards v. California*, the Stone Court unanimously struck down a California law, called an "Okie law," that prohibited anyone in California from transporting into the state an indigent person. The term "okie" originally referred to individuals from Oklahoma, but was later used pejoratively to describe poorer people from other states coming to settle in California. State officials charged Mr. Edwards with violating the law after he traveled to Texas and brought back his indigent brother-in-law, Frank Duncan. The Stone Court ruled that this law violated the Commerce Clause by unreasonably intruding upon interstate commerce. "The burden upon interstate commerce is intended and

Farmers work with bundles of wheat straw in 1939. A wheat farmer's challenge of a fine he received resulted in *Wickard v. Filburn* (1942), which led to a U.S. Supreme Court ruling giving Congress very broad power to regulate commerce. *Margaret Bourke-White/Time & Life Pictures/Getty Images.*

immediate; it is the plain and sole function of the statute," Justice James Byrnes wrote for the Court. "Moreover, the indigent non-residents who are the real victims of the statute are deprived of the opportunity to exert political pressure upon the California legislature in order to obtain a change in policy. We think this statute must fail under any known test of the validity of State interference with interstate commerce."

Four justices—William O. Douglas, Hugo Black, Frank Murphy, and Robert Jackson—concurred with the result but believed the case should not be decided on Commerce Clause grounds. They believed the law violated individual rights under the Fourteenth Amendment. Justice Jackson wrote that "the migrations of a human being … do not fit easily into my notions as to what is commerce."

What case involving **German saboteurs** established the power of the president to order **captured spies tried by military tribunals**?

In *Ex Parte Quirin* (1942), the Stone Court unanimously ruled 8–0 (Justice Frank Murphy did not participate in the case) that the president could establish a military tribunal to try the eight German saboteurs. The Court did hold, however, that the saboteurs had a right to appeal to the U.S. Supreme Court. The saboteurs argued that they could not be tried by a military tribunal but instead must be tried in the normal judicial system with the constitutional guarantees of a grand jury and trial by jury.

> ## CourtSpeak: *Wickard v. Filburn* Interstate Commerce Case (1942)
>
> Justice Robert Jackson (unanimous): "It is said, however, that this Act, forcing some farmers into the market to buy what they could provide for themselves, is an unfair promotion of the markets and prices of specializing wheat growers.... The conflicts of economic interest between the regulated and those who advantage by it are wisely left under our system to resolution by the Congress under its more flexible and responsible legislative process. Such conflicts rarely lend themselves to judicial determination. And with the wisdom, workability, or fairness, of the plan of regulation we have nothing to do."

What was **unusual about the *Quirin* case**?

The case was unusual for many reasons. The case involved enemy spies on a German submarine who embarked upon Long Island. They clothed themselves in civilian garb but were detected by a member of the U.S. Coast Guard. In addition to the interesting set of facts, *Quirin* was unusual due to the timing of the Supreme Court meeting and decision. President Franklin D. Roosevelt had created a special military commission to try the defendants in July 1942. During the trial, seven of the eight saboteurs petitioned the Court for the chance to file a habeas corpus claim, contesting their confinements as illegal. The U.S. Supreme Court met by special session on July 29, 1942, and two days later rejected the petitioners' claims in a short per curiam opinion. The Court indicated that it would file a lengthier opinion explaining its legal position. The Court's opinion was released in October 1942. In the meantime, six of the eight saboteurs had been executed a week after the Court's initial decision in July.

How did the Court in *Quirin* rule against **positions taken by both the government and the saboteurs**?

The Court ruled against the government in a limited but important sense because it ruled that the saboteurs did have a right to judicial review in the U.S. Supreme Court. The Court wrote that "there is certainly nothing in the Proclamation [by President Roosevelt] to preclude access to the courts for determining its applicability to the particular case." However, the Court clearly ruled against the saboteurs and for the government by upholding the right of the president to create the Military Commission and charge the saboteurs with "unlawful belligerency."

In what decision did the U.S. Supreme Court unanimously uphold **exclusion and curfew orders imposed on Japanese citizens** during wartime?

The U.S. Supreme Court unanimously upheld the exclusion and curfew of Japanese Americans in *Hirabayashi v. United States* (1943). The case involved the prosecution of Gordon Hirabayashi, an American-born University of Washington senior who was of Japanese descent. Hirabayashi was charged with failing to report to a military evacuation center and for failing to adhere to a curfew that required Japanese residents to remain in their homes at 8:00 PM.

Chief Justice Harlan Fiske Stone wrote for the Court that the orders, which classified citizens on the basis of race, were constitutional under the extraordinary circumstances that faced the United States after Japan's attack on Pearl Harbor on December 7, 1941: "Whatever views we may entertain regarding the loyalty to this county of the citizens of Japanese ancestry, we cannot reject as unfounded the judgment of the military authorities and of Congress that there were disloyal members of that population, whose number and strength could not be precisely and quickly ascertained." Hirabayashi had argued that it was unconstitutional for the military commander to impose special conditions just on citizens of Japanese descent. However, Stone wrote that the fact that the United States "was threatened by Japan rather than another enemy power set these citizens apart from others who have no particular associations with Japan."

The decision was unanimous, though three justices authored concurring opinions—Justices William O. Douglas, Frank Murphy, and Wiley Rutledge. Murphy's opinion at times reads more like a dissent. He wrote that "distinctions based on color and ancestry are utterly inconsistent with our traditions and ideals." However, Murphy still voted in favor of the government because of what he termed the "critical military situation which prevailed on the Pacific Coast area in the spring of 1942."

Soldiers line up near the American flag at a Japanese American internment camp in California during World War II. The U.S. Supreme Court unanimously upheld the exclusion and curfew of Japanese Americans in *Hirabayashi v. United States* (1943). *Hulton Archive/Getty Images.*

In which related decision did a divided U.S. Supreme Court uphold the internment of Japanese Americans?

The U.S. Supreme Court again upheld the internment of Japanese Americans in the 1944 decision *Korematsu v. United States.* However, unlike the unanimous decision in *Hirabayashi,* three justices dissented in *Korematsu.* Fred Korematsu had worked at a defense plant in the United States. When the internment orders came, he moved, changed his name, and even had plastic surgery. However, he was charged and convicted with violating the military orders. He was interned in Topaz, Utah. Justice Hugo Black wrote the Court's majority decision, reasoning that the military authorities' judgment must be viewed with the perspective that "the need for action was great and the time was short." Black determined that the military actions were not unreasonable given the grave threat from Japan and the reasonable belief that there were some Japanese Americans who would be loyal to Japan.

Which justices dissented in the *Korematsu* case?

Justices Owen J. Roberts, Frank Murphy, and Robert Jackson dissented. Justice Roberts had served on a commission examining the Pearl Harbor incident. From that experience, he knew there was little, if any, evidence of Japanese sabotage on the West Coast. Roberts wrote that the "indisputable facts exhibit a clear violation of Constitutional rights." Murphy, who had questioned the exclusion and curfew orders in

253

Hirabayashi, blasted the Court's decision as "fall[ing] into the ugly abyss of racism." Jackson noted that the majority had "validated the principle of racial discrimination in criminal procedure and of transplanting American citizens."

What did the Stone Court rule with respect to whether the **Sixth Amendment right to assistance of counsel could be extended to the states**?

The Sixth Amendment requires the assistance of counsel for criminal defendants charged with federal crimes. A key question was whether this requirement was extended to the states via the Fourteenth Amendment's Due Process Clause. The Stone Court answered this question in its 1942 decision *Betts v. Brady*. Smith Betts, a Maryland farmhand, was charged with robbery in Carroll County, Maryland. Betts asked the trial judge for an attorney. The trial judge denied the request, stating that indigents could receive court-appointed attorneys only for cases of murder and rape. Betts sued, contending that he had a constitutional right to an attorney.

The U.S. Supreme Court ruled 6–3 that the Constitution did not require Betts to be provided with an attorney. Justice Owen J. Roberts reasoned that the history of state practices revealed that "in the great majority of the states, it has been the consid-

CourtSpeak: *Betts v. Brady (1942)* Right to Counsel Case

Justice Hugo Black (dissenting): "A practice cannot be reconciled with 'common and fundamental ideas of fairness and right,' which subjects innocent men to increased dangers of conviction merely because of their poverty. Whether a man is innocent cannot be determined from a trial in which, as here, denial of counsel has made it impossible to conclude, with any satisfactory degree of certainty, that the defendant's case was adequately presented."

ered judgment of the people, their representatives and their courts that appointment of counsel is not a fundamental right, essential to a fair trial." Roberts wrote that due process did not require all state criminal defendants to be afforded an attorney.

Three justices dissented—Hugo Black, William O. Douglas, and Frank Murphy. Black wrote that the right to counsel was "fundamental" and necessary to satisfy the dictates of due process. Black's view would eventually command a majority of the Court, as *Betts* would be overruled more than twenty years later in *Gideon v. Wainwright* (1963).

How did the Stone Court rule with respect to **criminal sterilization laws**?

The Stone Court unanimously struck down Oklahoma's criminal sterilization law in *Skinner v. Oklahoma* (1942). The law allowed state officials to order the sterilization of certain habitual criminals. Officials sought to apply the law to Jack Skinner, who had been convicted three different times for stealing. When he was nineteen, officials charged him with stealing chickens. Later, he committed armed robbery twice. After his third conviction, state officials ordered Skinner to submit to a vasectomy. The law, however, provided an exemption for crimes of embezzlement and political crimes. The Court ruled that the law violated equal protection because it subjected repeat-larceny offenders to sterilization while exempting those who committed more white-collar crimes. "We are dealing here with legislation which involves one of the basic civil rights of man," Justice William O. Douglas wrote. "Marriage and procreation are fundamental to the very existence and survival of the race. The power to sterilize, if exercised, may have subtle, far-reaching and devastating effects."

In a concurring opinion, Chief Justice Harlan Fiske Stone said that the case should be decided on due process, rather than equal-protection, grounds. He reasoned that the law violated due process because Skinner was not afforded a valid hearing process in which Skinner could show he was not a habitual criminal who would pass these traits to his children. Justice Robert Jackson also authored a concurring opinion, noting that the state does not have unlimited power to "conduct biological experiments at the expense of the dignity and personality and natural powers of a minority—even those who have been guilty of what the majority define as crimes."

FIRST AMENDMENT

In what decision did the Stone Court create the **fighting words exception** to the First Amendment?

The Stone Court determined in *Chaplinsky v. New Hampshire* (1942) that so-called "fighting words"—words that by their very nature inflict injury and cause retaliation—are not protected by the First Amendment . The case involved a former priest named Walter Chaplinsky, who denounced official religion as a "racket" and called a public marshal a "damned fascist" and a "racketeer." The marshal arrested Chaplinsky and charged him with violating a statute that prohibited calling persons annoying or derisive names in public. The U.S. Supreme Court rejected Chaplinsky's First Amendment defense, reasoning that the statute applied only to prohibiting "fighting words."

Justice Frank Murphy wrote for the unanimous Court:

There are certain well-defined and narrowly limited classes of speech, the prevention of which has never been thought to raise any Constitutional problem. These include the lewd and obscene, the profane, the libelous, and the insulting or fighting words—those which by their very utterance inflict injury or tend to incite an immediate breach of the peace. It has been well-observed that such utterances are no essential part of any exposition of ideas, and are of such slight social value as a step to truth that any benefit that may be derived from them is clearly outweighed by the social interest in order and morality.

The U.S. Supreme Court in later years limited—but never overruled—the *Chaplinsky* decision. The fighting words doctrine still remains a part of First Amendment jurisprudence.

In what First Amendment decision did the **U.S. Supreme Court overrule itself only three years later**?

The U.S. Supreme Court overruled a 1940 decision in 1943 by striking down a flag-salute law that required public school children to salute the flag. In *Minersville School District v. Gobitis* (1940), the Court had ruled 8–1 in favor of a Pennsylvania flag-salute law. Justice Harlan Fiske Stone (he was not yet chief justice) was the lone dissenter. A mere three years later, the Court ruled 6–3 in *West Virginia Board of Education v. Barnette* that a similar West Virginia flag-salute law was unconstitutional.

The law required public school students to salute the flag. If students refused to salute the flag, school officials declared them insubordinate and could expel them. State law also imposed criminal penalties on parents whose children were declared insubordinate. Thus, if the students did not salute the flag, they could be expelled and their parents could be jailed.

A group of Jehovah's Witnesses challenged the law on First Amendment grounds. They argued that the forced flag salute infringed on their free-exercise of religion and

Children recite the Pledge of Allegiance. In *West Virginia Board of Education v. Barnette* (1943), the U.S. Supreme Court overruled its own ruling three years earlier in which it favored a Pennsylvania mandatory flag salute law. When a group of Jehovah's Witnesses challenged the law on First Amendment grounds, the Court agreed, reasoning that the government could not coerce people into forced patriotism. *Hulton Archive/Getty Images.*

free-speech rights. The U.S. Supreme Court agreed, holding that the government could not coerce people into forced patriotism. In oft-quoted language, Justice Robert Jackson wrote:

> If there is any fixed star in our constitutional constellation, it is that no official, high or petty, can prescribe what shall be orthodox in politics, nationalism, religion, or other matters of opinion or force citizens to confess by word or act their faith therein.

What was **ironic about the date** of the Court's decision in the *Barnette* case?

The U.S. Supreme Court issued its decision in *Barnette* on June 14, 1943—Flag Day.

Why did the U.S. Supreme Court **overrule itself**?

The *Gobitis* decision unfortunately caused a wave of violence against Jehovah's Witnesses in various parts of the country. In the book *To the Flag: The History of the Pledge of Allegiance,* author Richard J. Ellis writes: "The persistent pattern of expulsions, arbitrary arrests, and violent intimidation led to a rethinking among the

257

Supreme Court Justices of the wisdom of the *Gobitis* decision." Ellis also relates that thousands of Jehovah's Witnesses had been expelled from school.

Which **justices changed their votes in the two flag-salute cases**?

Justices Hugo Black, William O. Douglas, and Frank Murphy changed their votes from *Gobitis* to *Barnette*. The three had voted to uphold the flag salute in *Gobitis* but voted to strike down such a law in *Barnette*. The three justices had signaled their displeasure with *Gobitis* in a dissenting opinion in another Jehovah's Witness case, *Jones v. Opelika* (1942). The three justices wrote: "Since we joined in the opinion in the *Gobitis* case, we think this is an appropriate occasion to state that we now believe that it was also wrongly decided."

In what decision did the Court declare that the **First Amendment did not protect advertising**?

The U.S. Supreme Court ruled in *Valentine v. Chrestensen* (1942) that the First Amendment does not protect advertising. Entrepreneur F. J. Chrestensen owned a naval submarine that he was exhibiting for tourists for a fee in a New York City harbor. City officials prohibited Chrestensen from distributing handbills advertising tours for his submarine because they said city law prohibiting commercial advertising. The enterprising Chrestensen then printed double-sided handbills. On one side was the commercial advertising but the other side contained a statement of protest over the city's policies with respect to advertising. Chrestensen claimed that city officials could not cite him for violation of the law because his handbills contained political speech in addition to advertising.

The Court wrote that "the Constitution imposes no such restraint on government as respects purely commercial advertising." The Court also explained that Chrestensen could not evade the city law by adding political speech to his handbills: "It is enough for the present purpose that the stipulated facts justify the conclusion that the affixing of the protest against official conduct to the advertising circular was with the intent, and for the purpose, of evading the prohibition of the ordinance. If that evasion were successful, every merchant who desires to broadcast advertising leaflets in the streets need only append a civic appeal, or a moral platitude, to achieve immunity from the law's command."

The U.S. Supreme Court later overruled the *Chrestensen* decision in the mid-1970s.

Did the Stone Court allow a **religious exemption to child labor laws for Jehovah's Witnesses**?

No, the Stone Court ruled in *Prince v. Massachusetts* (1944) that Sarah Prince could be punished for allowing her niece to distribute religious pamphlets for sale on the

CourtSpeak: *Murdock v. Pennsylvania* Religious Rights Case (1943)

Justice William O. Douglas (majority): "The taxes imposed by this ordinance can hardly help but be as severe and telling in their impact on the freedom of the press and religion as the 'taxes on knowledge' at which the First Amendment was partly aimed. They may indeed operate even more subtly. Itinerant evangelists moving throughout a state or from state to state would feel immediately the cumulative effect of such ordinances as they become fashionable. The way of the religious dissenter has long been hard. But if the formula of this type of ordinance is approved, a new device for the suppression of religious minorities will have been found. This method of disseminating religious beliefs can be crushed and closed out by the sheer weight of the toll or tribute which is exacted town by town, village by village. The spread of religious ideas through personal visitations by the literature ministry of numerous religious groups would be stopped."

public streets. Massachusetts law prohibited boys under 12 and girls under 18 from selling periodicals in public places. Prince, who was guardian of her 9-year-old niece Betty Simmons, argued she had a religious freedom right to allow Betty to sell religious pamphlets. The state countered that it had a strong interest in protecting children from harm. The Court ruled 5–4 against Prince, writing that "the state has a wide range of power for limiting parental freedom and authority in things affecting the child's welfare." The Court focused on the "crippling effects of child employment" in reaching its decision.

Four justices dissented, including Frank Murphy, who believed that the state law unreasonably impacted religious freedom. "The sidewalk, no less than the cathedral or the evangelist's tent, is a proper place, under the Constitution, for the orderly worship of God."

How did the Stone Court deal with **licensing laws that imposed fees on those who distributed religious materials**?

The Stone Court examined several cases that dealt with city licensing laws that were challenged by Jehovah's Witnesses. In three consolidated cases from Alabama, Arkansas, and Arizona, the U.S. Supreme Court ruled 5–4 in *Jones v. City of Opelika* (1942) that cities could impose licensing fees on religious groups that sold materials for money on public streets. "When proponents of religious or social theories use the ordinary commercial methods of sales of articles to raise propaganda funds, it is a natural and proper exercise of the power of the state to charge reasonable fees for the privilege of canvassing," Justice Stanley Reed wrote for the majority.

259

U.S. Supreme Court justice Wiley Rutledge. *Marie Hansen/Time & Life Pictures/Getty Images.*

The Stone Court changed course in a series of seven consolidated cases in *Murdock v. Pennsylvania* (1943). The lead case involved a Jeannette, Pennsylvania, ordinance that imposed a $7-a-week licensing fee for solicitors. A group of Jehovah's Witnesses who went door-to-door distributing religious books (for which they requested donations) challenged the law on First Amendment grounds. The U.S. Supreme Court ruled 5–4 that the law violated the free-exercise-of-religion rights of the Jehovah's Witnesses. "The constitutional rights of those spreading their religious beliefs through the spoken and printed word are not to be gauged by standards governing retailers or wholesalers of books," Justice William O. Douglas wrote for the majority. "The right to use the press for expressing one's views is not to be measured by the protection afforded commercial handbills."

What caused the Court to **shift course in the licensing fees on Jehovah's Witnesses**?

In 1942, the Stone Court upheld a licensing fee as applied to the Jehovah's Witnesses, while the next year the Court ruled 5–4 that such laws were unconstitutional. This change was caused by the replacement of Justice James Byrnes with Wiley Rutledge. Byrnes had voted in favor of the licensing laws, while Rutledge voted that they infringed on the religious liberty rights of the Witnesses.

Did the Stone Court uphold a state law that made it a **crime to urge people not to salute the flag**?

No, the Stone Court ruled in *Taylor v. Mississippi* (1943) that the state of Mississippi could not imprison people who urged others not to support the U.S. government and salute the flag. The case involved three Jehovah's Witnesses—R. E. Taylor, Betty Benoit, and a man named Cummings—who allegedly urged others not to salute the American flag. The state law in question provided that those who engaged in conduct that "reasonably tends to create an attitude of stubborn refusal to salute, honor or

Jehovah's Witnesses Decisions by the Stone Court

Chaplinsky v. New Hampshire (1942): The U.S. Supreme Court establishes the "fighting words" exception to the First Amendment in a case involving Walter Chaplinsky, a Jehovah's Witness who allegedly cursed a New Hampshire city official.

Jones v. Opelika (1942): The U.S. Supreme Court upholds a city law that imposes a licensing fee on all those, including Jehovah's Witnesses, who sell books or pamphlets.

West Virginia Board of Education v. Barnette (1943): The U.S. Supreme Court rules that public school officials cannot force Jehovah's Witnesses and other students into saluting the flag and reciting the Pledge of Allegiance.

Martin v. Struthers (1943): The U.S. Supreme Court strikes down an Ohio city law that prohibited Jehovah's Witnesses and others from going door-to-door to convey their religious beliefs.

Jamison v. Texas (1943): The U.S. Supreme Court reverses the conviction of a Jehovah's Witness woman charged with distributing handbills on a Dallas street.

Largent v. Texas (1943): The U.S. Supreme Court unanimously strikes down a Paris, Texas, law that gave the mayor unbridled discretion to determine whether or not to issue a permit for distributing materials. The mayor denied such permits to Jehovah's Witnesses.

Taylor v. Mississippi (1943): The U.S. Supreme Court strikes down the conviction of several Jehovah's Witnesses for urging others to refuse to salute the flag and recite the Pledge of Allegiance.

respect the flag or government of the United States … shall be guilty of a felony" and could be imprisoned for up to ten years.

Taylor allegedly told several women, whose sons were killed in World War II, that they should oppose the war effort. Benoit allegedly distributed a religious pamphlet that counseled against saluting the flag and Cummings allegedly distributed a book, called *The Children,* that contained a passage against flag salutes. All three were convicted in Mississippi state courts.

The Supreme Court unanimously reversed the convictions. It reasoned that if a state cannot force individuals to salute the flag, then it also cannot punish individuals for encouraging others not to salute the flag: "If the state cannot constrain one to violate his conscientious religious conviction by saluting the national emblem, then cer-

261

tainly it cannot punish him for imparting his views on the subject to his fellows and exhorting them to accept those views."

Did the Stone Court reverse a criminal conviction for **discrimination in the grand jury selection process**?

Yes, the Stone Court unanimously reversed a rape conviction in *Hill v. Texas* (1942) when it found that in Dallas County, Texas, no black had been called to serve on the grand jury for sixteen years. Henry Allen Hill, a black male defendant, was convicted to die for the rape of a woman in 1940. On appeal, he alleged that this conviction was tainted by the county's racially discriminatory process, which did not allow blacks to serve on the grand jury.

For years, the county commissioners had, in the words of the Court, "consciously omitted to place the name of any negro on the jury list." This smacked of racial discrimination and required a reversal of the conviction. The Court emphasized that the state could re-try the defendant for the rape "by the procedure which conforms to constitutional requirements."

What was the subject matter of the decision that **Justice Stone announced when he fell ill**?

Chief Justice Harlan Fiske Stone became fatally ill on the bench while reading from his dissent in *Girouard v. United States* (1946), an immigration case. The decision concerned whether Canadian James Louis Girouard could become a U.S. citizen when he stated that he would not bear arms for the United States for religious reasons. Girouard said he would be loyal to the country but that his religion (Seventh Day Adventist) prevented him from combat duty. The Court majority reasoned that Girouard could become a citizen, writing: "Refusal to bear arms is not necessarily a sign of disloyalty or a lack of attachment to our country."

Chief Justice Stone, along with two other justices, dissented. He reasoned that the 1931 U.S. Supreme Court decisions of *U.S. v. Schwimmer, U.S. v. Macintosh,* and *U.S. v. Bland* controlled. In those opinions, the Court denied citizenship to individuals who would not bear arms in defense of the United States.

How did the Stone Court address **Texas's white primary system**?

The Stone Court unanimously ruled in *Smith v. Allwright* (1944) that the Democratic Party of Texas violated the Fifteenth Amendment with its resolution allowing only whites to vote in its primary. Party and state officials argued that the primary system was run by party, not state, officials and, therefore, was not a form of governmental (or state) action that triggered constitutional review. The officials relied on the Hughes Court's decision in *Grovey v. Townsend* (1935) in which the Court ruled that the white primary

U.S. Supreme Court justice Harold Burton was the lone dissenter in *Morgan v. Virginia* (1946), which struck down a Virginia law requiring that bus passengers be segregated. *George Skadding/Time & Life Pictures/Getty Images.*

was a form of private discrimination not subject to the Constitution. The Stone Court overruled the *Grovey* decision, finding that the primary system was a form of state action because it was an integral part of the election process. "Primary elections are conducted by the party under state statutory authority," the Court wrote.

Once it found state action, the Court had little difficulty in concluding that the Texas white-only primary violated the Fifteenth Amendment right to vote. The Court had noted earlier in its opinion: "Under our Constitution the great privilege of the ballot may not be denied a man by the State because of his color." 263

On what grounds did the Stone Court invalidate a Virginia law requiring **segregation of bus passengers**?

In *Morgan v. Virginia* (1946), the Stone Court struck down a Virginia segregation law because it violated the Commerce Clause. The state law required separation of white and black passengers on buses traveling on the roads, including interstates. This posed a problem because other states and the District of Columbia did not require segregation of passengers. This meant that passengers might have to move several times during a single trip to ensure compliance with different state laws. According to the majority of the Supreme Court, this amounted to interference with interstate commerce. Justice Stanley Reed wrote for the majority that "the enforcement of the requirements for reseating would be disturbing." He concluded that "seating arrangements for the different races in interstate motor travel require a single, uniform rule to promote and protect national travel."

Justice Harold Burton was the Court's lone dissenter. He reasoned that the states were free to adopt their own laws regarding seating in the absence of a federal law on the subject. He wrote: "The inaction of Congress is an important indication that, in the opinion of Congress, this issue is better met without nationally uniform affirmative regulation than with it."

THE VINSON COURT (1946–53)

How many and **which justices served on the Vinson Court**?

Eleven justices served on the Vinson Court, including Chief Justice Fred Vinson and Justices Hugo Black, Stanley F. Reed, Felix Frankfurter, William O. Douglas, Frank Murphy, Robert Jackson, Wiley B. Rutledge, Harold H. Burton, Tom C. Clark, and Sherman Minton.

What was the **professional background of Fred Vinson**?

Fred Vinson had a distinguished career of public service. He served several terms in the U.S. House of Representatives from his home state of Kentucky. He served as a judge on the U.S. Court of Appeals for the District of Columbia for five years from 1938 to 1943. He then held several positions under Presidents Franklin D. Roosevelt and Harry S. Truman, including director of the Office of Economic Stabilization, director of the Office of War Mobilization and Reconversion, and secretary of the treasury. President Truman nominated him as chief justice of the U.S. Supreme Court on June 6, 1946.

In what opinion did the Vinson Court **limit executive branch authority to seize the nation's steel mills**?

The Vinson Court ruled 6-3 in *Youngstown Sheet & Tube Co. v. Sawyer* (1952) that President Harry S. Truman exceeded his constitutional authority in empowering Secretary of Commerce Charles Sawyer to seize private steel mills. The president did not follow the procedures outlined in the Labor Management Relations Act, known as the Taft-Hartley Act. Truman believed this would take too much time. Instead, the president took the unusual action because the United Steel Workers of America were on the verge of a strike that could cripple the nation's steel production during a time when the United States was involved in a major conflict with Korea. Truman believed the impending strike could negatively impact national security.

U.S. Supreme Court chief justice Fred Vinson. *Hulton Archive/Getty Images.*

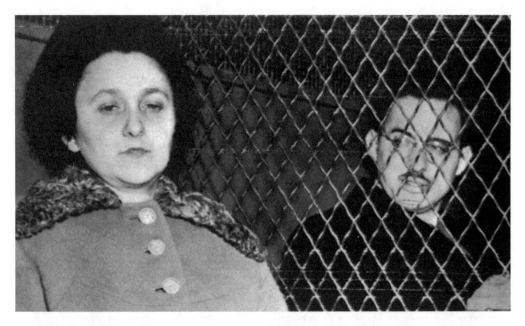

Ethel and Julius Rosenberg. The Vinson Court refused to stay the execution of the husband-and-wife spies who were sentenced to death after they were convicted of passing on atomic secrets to the Soviets. *Getty Images.*

His executive order stated in part: "A work stoppage would immediately jeopardize and imperil our national defense and the defense of those joined with us in resisting aggression, and would add to the continuing danger of our soldiers, sailors, and airmen engaged in combat in the field."

The steel companies contended in court that only Congress, not the president, could take such action over private companies. They argued that the president had violated fundamental separation of powers principles by taking Congress's law-making powers for himself.

The majority of the U.S. Supreme Court agreed with the steel mills and rebuffed the president's arguments. "The President's power, if any, to issue the order must stem either from an act of Congress or from the Constitution itself," wrote Justice Hugo Black. "There is no statute that expressly authorizes the President to take possession of property as he did here. Nor is there any act of Congress to which our attention has been directed from which such a power can fairly be implied."

In what **famous capital case involving alleged spies** did the Vinson Court deny relief?

The Vinson Court refused to stay the execution of Julius and Ethel Rosenberg in *Rosenberg v. United States* (1953) by a 6–3 vote. The Rosenbergs allegedly violated the Espionage Act of 1917 by providing military secrets, including some related to the

267

CourtSpeak: *Youngstown Sheet & Tube Co. v. Sawyer* Presidential Authority Case (1952)

Justice Hugo Black (majority): "The Founders of this Nation entrusted the lawmaking power to the Congress alone in both good and bad times. It would do no good to recall the historical events, the fears of power and the hopes for freedom that lay behind their choice. Such a review would but confirm our holding that this seizure order cannot stand."

Justice Felix Frankfurter (concurring): "To find authority so explicitly withheld is not merely to disregard in a particular instance the clear will of Congress. It is to disrespect the whole legislative process and the constitutional division of authority between President and Congress."

Justice William O. Douglas (concurring): "If we sanctioned the present exercise of power by the President, we would be expanding Article II of the Constitution and rewriting it to suit the political conveniences of the present emergency."

Justice Robert Jackson (concurring): "When the President takes measures incompatible with the expressed or implied will of Congress, his power is at its lowest ebb, for then he can rely only upon his own constitutional powers minus any constitutional powers of Congress over the matter."

Justice Harold Burton (concurring): "The controlling fact here is that Congress, within its constitutionally delegated power, has prescribed for the President specific procedures, exclusive of seizure, for his use in meeting the present type of emergency. Congress has reserved to itself the right to determine where and when to authorize the seizure of property in meeting such an emergency. Under these circumstances, the President's order of April 8 invaded the jurisdiction of Congress. It violated the essence of the principle of the separation of governmental powers."

Justice Tom C. Clark (concurring): "I cannot sustain the seizure in question because ... Congress had prescribed methods to be followed by the President in meeting the emergency at hand."

Chief Justice Fred Vinson (dissenting): "Those who suggest that this is a case involving extraordinary powers should be mindful that these are extraordinary times. A world not yet recovered from the devastation of World War II has been forced to face the threat of another and more terrifying global conflict."

atomic bomb, to the Soviet Union. Justice William O. Douglas had granted a stay of execution but the full Court reversed Douglas's ruling two days later. The Rosenbergs were executed on the day of the decision. The case is still considered controversial because some believe the Rosenbergs were not guilty of a capital crime.

Did the Vinson Court invalidate **confessions obtained by extreme duress**?

Yes, the Vinson Court ruled in *Watts v. Indiana* (1949) that a confession obtained through duress can violate the Due Process Clause. Indiana police charged Robert Watts, a 17-year-old African American, with murder and attempted rape. The police interrogated him for hours at a time for six days. On many days, police would question Watts for eight straight hours. He finally relented and confessed to the crime. His attorney argued that the subsequent conviction should be invalidated because the police officers violated Watts's due-process rights. The Vinson Court agreed 6–3. "Protracted, systematic, and uncontrolled subjection of an accused to interrogation by the police for the purpose of eliciting disclosures or confessions is subversive of the accusatorial system," Justice Felix Frankfurter wrote. "It is the inquisitorial system without its safeguards." Justice William O. Douglas was even blunter in his concurring opinion: "The man was held until he broke…. The procedure breeds coerced confessions. It is the root of the evil."

What type of police conduct did the Vinson Court say **"shocks the conscience?"**

The Vinson Court unanimously ruled in *Rochin v. California* (1952) that police officers violated the Due Process Clause when they forcibly entered the home of a man suspected of selling narcotics. The police then opened the bedroom door of Antonio Richard Rochin and noticed that he had swallowed something. The officers suspected that he had swallowed narcotics. They seized Rochin, took him to a hospital, and pumped his stomach. The stomach showed that Rochin had swallowed some narcotics. Writing for the Court, Justice Felix Frankfurter said such conduct by the police "shocks the conscience." He explained:

> Illegally breaking into the privacy of the petitioner, the struggle to open his mouth and remove what was there, the forcible extraction of his stomach's contents—this course of proceedings by agents of government to obtain evidence is bound to offend even hardened sensibilities. They are methods too close to the rack and the screw to permit of constitutional differentiation.

Did the Vinson Court rule that the **right against self-incrimination protected state court defendants**?

No, the Vinson Court ruled in *Adamson v. California* (1947) that the Fifth Amendment's privilege against self-incrimination was not extended to the states via the Fourteenth Amendment's Due Process Clause. Dewey Adamson was charged with first-degree murder. At his trial, pursuant to California law, the prosecutor pointed out to the jury that Adamson had refused to testify in his own defense. Adamson contended on appeal that his conviction should be invalidated because the prosecution violated his privilege against self-incrimination by asking the jury to consider the fact that he did not testify in his own defense. The majority rejected Adamson's arguments, reasoning that "the Due Process Clause does not protect, by virtue of its mere existence the accused's freedom from giving testimony by compulsion in state trials that is secured to him against federal interference by the Fifth Amendment." The majority relied on precedent for the principle that the Fourteenth Amendment "does not draw all the rights of the federal Bill of Rights under its protection."

The U.S. Supreme Court reversed the Adamson decision and applied the Fifth Amendment Clause against self-incrimination to the states in *Griffin v. California* (1965).

Which justice argued for **total incorporation of the federal Bill of Rights**?

Justice Hugo Black argued that the Fourteenth Amendment incorporated all of the protections found in the Bill of Rights to the states. Black believed that the Thirty-Ninth Congress, when it passed the Fourteenth Amendment, meant for it to incorporate all of the provisions of the Bill of Rights to the states. He explained:

> My study of the historical events that culminated in the Fourteenth Amendment, and the expressions of those who sponsored and favored, as well as those who opposed its submission and passage, persuades me that one of the chief objects that the provisions of the Amendment's first section, separately, and as a whole, were intended to accomplish was to make the Bill of Rights, applicable to the states. With full knowledge of the import of the Barron decision, the framers and backers of the Fourteenth Amendment proclaimed its purpose to be to overturn the constitutional rule that case had announced. This historical purpose has never received full consideration or exposition in any opinion of this Court interpreting the Amendment.

What did the Vinson Court rule with respect to the **exclusionary rule in state courts**?

The Vinson Court ruled in *Wolf v. Colorado* (1949) that the exclusionary rule was not constitutionally required in state court proceedings. The exclusionary rule had applied in federal court proceedings since *Weeks v. United States* (1914). However, Justice Felix Frankfurter reasoned that the rule was not mandated for states in part because thirty states did not require adherence to the exclusionary rule. "We cannot brush aside the experience of States which deem the incidence of such conduct by the police too slight to call for a deterrent remedy not by way of disciplinary measures but by overriding the relevant rules of evidence," he wrote.

In his concurring opinion, Justice Hugo Black referred to the exclusionary rule as a "judicially created rule of evidence." Justice Frank Murphy wrote a dissenting opinion, arguing that the exclusionary rule was the only effective deterrent to unlawful police conduct: "The conclusion is inescapable that but one remedy exists to deter violations of the search and seizure clause. That is the rule which excludes illegally obtained evidence. Only by exclusion can we impress upon the zealous prosecutor that violation of the Constitution will do him no good."

The Warren Court overruled *Wolf v. Colorado* in *Mapp v. Ohio* (1961).

Did the Vinson Court address the issue of **segregation in public schools**?

Yes, the Vinson Court decided several cases involving segregation at schools of higher education. The Court ruled in *Sipuel v. Board of Regents of the University of Oklahoma* (1948) that the state must admit African American Ada Lois Sipuel to the state's law school or create a substantially equal educational opportunity for blacks. "The State must provide it for her in conformity with the equal protection clause of the Fourteenth Amendment and provide it as soon as it does for applicants of any other group," the Court wrote in a per curiam opinion decided only four days after oral argument.

Two years later, the Court decided two cases on the same day—June 5, 1950— involving African American graduate students at all-white institutions.

In *Sweatt v. Painter* (1950), the Vinson Court ruled that Texas must admit African American student Herman Sweatt into the University of Texas Law School. The state had contended that it did not have to admit Sweatt, because he could attend a newly created school for blacks. However, this new school had far fewer resources and would provide a lower degree of education than the University of Texas Law School. The Vinson Court ruled that Texas failed to provide substantially equal schools under the separate but equal doctrine. The Court concluded that "the Equal Protection Clause of the Fourteenth Amendment requires that petitioner be admitted to the University of Texas Law School."

In *McLaurin v. Oklahoma State Regents for Higher Education,* the Court ruled that the University of Oklahoma also violated the Equal Protection Clause in its treatment of George W. McLaurin, an African American who was pursing his doctorate in education. The university had admitted McLaurin because there was no comparable school for black students, but they had imposed special conditions on him. He had to sit in a designated area of the classroom separated by a railing with a sign "Reserved for Colored." He had to eat at a certain table in the cafeteria apart from white students. He also had to use a specific place in the school library. "We conclude that the conditions under which this appellant [McLaurin] is required to receive his education deprive him of his personal and present right to the equal protection of the laws," the Court wrote.

Famed civil rights attorney and future U.S. Supreme Court justice Thurgood Marshall successfully argued on behalf of his clients in both *Sipuel v. Board of Regents of the University of Oklahoma* and *Sweatt v. Painter* (1950).

How did the Vinson Court rule with respect to **restrictive covenants**?

The Vinson Court ruled in the companion cases of *Shelley v. Kraemer* and *McGhee v. Sipes* 6–0 (Justices Stanley Reed, Wiley Rutledge, and Robert Jackson did not participate) that the judicial enforcing of racially discriminatory restrictive covenants violated the Equal Protection Clause of the Fourteenth Amendment.

Shelley v. Kraemer began when a Mr. Fitzgerald sold his house to J. D. Shelley, an African American. Louis Kraemer, a white neighbor, brought suit to void the sale of the home to Shelley. Kraemer cited a restrictive covenant signed in 1911 by thirty of the thirty-nine surrounding homeowners that prohibited the sale of homes to anyone who was not Caucasian. In a related case, Benjamin Sipes and his attorney, civil rights lawyer Thurgood Marshall, sought to enforce a similar restrictive covenant against African American Orsel McGhee in Detroit, Michigan. Kraemer and McGhee both asserted that the restrictive covenants violated their Fourteenth Amendment Equal Protection rights. The white homeowners countered that the covenants did not violate the Constitution in part because it was private, not state, action. State courts in Missouri and Michigan had ruled that the restrictive covenants were enforceable and that the Kraemers and McGhees had to move. They both appealed to the U.S. Supreme Court.

The Court agreed that the restrictive covenant itself was a form of private discrimination beyond the reach of the Fourteenth Amendment's Equal Protection Clause. However, the Court also ruled that the enforcement of a restrictive covenant by a court amounted to state action. "State action, as that phrase is understood for the purposes of the Fourteenth Amendment, refers to exertions of state power in all forms," Chief Justice Fred Vinson wrote for the Court. "We hold that in granting judicial enforcement of the restrictive agreements in these cases, the States have denied petitioners the equal protection of the laws and that, therefore, the action of the state courts cannot stand."

Do **enemy aliens have a right to seek relief** in U.S. federal courts?

No, the Vinson Court ruled in *Johnson v. Eisentrager* (1950) that twenty-one German nationals who allegedly continued military action against the United States in China after Germany had surrendered in World War II did not have a right to seek access to U.S. federal courts. These enemy aliens were tried and convicted by a military commission. They sought to challenge their confinement in U.S. federal courts. The Court rejected their claim by a narrow 5–4 vote. Justice Robert Jackson, who wrote the Court's majority opinion, noted that the aliens' offense, their capture, their trial, and their punishment were all beyond the territorial jurisdiction of any court of the United States. He wrote that if these enemy aliens could obtain access to U.S. courts, then they could assert other protections in the Bill of Rights:

> Such a construction would mean that during military occupation irreconcilable enemy elements, guerrilla fighters, and "were-wolves" could require the American Judiciary to assure them freedoms of speech, press, and assembly as in the First Amendment, right to bear arms as in the Second, security against "unreasonable" search and seizures as in the Fourth, as well as rights to jury trial as in the Fifth and Sixth Amendments.

FIRST AMENDMENT

In what decision did the Vinson Court uphold a **federal law designed to charge members of the Communist Party with crimes**?

The Vinson Court upheld the Smith Act of 1940 in *Dennis v. United States* (1951). The Alien Registration Act of 1940, called the Smith Act after its chief sponsor, U.S. representative Howard W. Smith of Virginia, prohibited individuals from advocating the physical overthrow of the United States. One provision of the law provided: "Whoever organizes or helps or attempts to organize any society, group, or assembly of persons who teach, advocate, or encourage the overthrow or destruction of any such government by force or violence … shall be … imprisoned not more than 20 years."

Eugene Dennis and eleven other members of the American Communist Party were convicted of violating the Smith Act. They challenged their convictions on First Amendment grounds. The Court upheld the convictions, writing: "Overthrow of the Government by force and violence is certainly a substantial enough interest for the Government to limit speech." The Supreme Court modified the "clear and present danger" test advocated by former justices Oliver Wendell Holmes and Louis Brandeis in the 1920s. Instead, the Court majority adopted the test advocated by federal appeals court judge Learned Hand. The test provided: "In each case courts must ask whether the gravity of the evil, discounted by its improbability, justifies such invasion of free speech as is necessary to avoid the danger."

273

Which **two justices dissented in the** *Dennis* **case?**

Justices Hugo Black and William O. Douglas, the two greatest defenders of First Amendment freedoms on the Vinson Court, dissented. They believed that the majority had watered down the clear-and-present-danger test. Black concluded: "Public opinion being what it now is, few will protest the conviction of these Communist petitioners. There is hope, however, that in calmer times, when present pressures, passions and fears subside, this or some later Court will restore the First Amendment liberties to the high preferred place where they belong in a free society." Douglas echoed similar sentiments in his opinion: "Yet free speech is the rule, not the exception. The restraint to be constitutional must be based on more than fear, on more than passionate opposition against the speech, on more than a revolted dislike for its contents. There must be some immediate injury to society that is likely if speech is allowed."

American Communist Eugene Dennis leaves prison in 1955. Dennis had been convicted of violating the Smith Act of 1940, which prohibited individuals from advocating the physical overthrow of the U.S. government. The U.S. Supreme Court upheld the Smith Act in *Dennis v. United States* (1951), resulting in Dennis's imprisonment. *Robert W. Kelley/Time & Life*

In what decision did the Vinson Court uphold a **group libel law**?

The Vinson Court upheld a group libel law in its 5–4 decision in *Beauharnais v. Illinois* (1952). State officials charged white supremacist Joseph Beauharnais with violating a law that prohibited any publication that "portrays depravity, criminality, unchastity, or lack of virtue of a class of citizens, of any race, color, creed or religion" or that "exposes the citizens of any race, color, creed or religion to contempt, derision, or obloquy."

CourtSpeak: *Beauharnais v. Illinois* Group Libel Case (1952)

Justice Hugo Black (dissenting): "Today's case degrades First Amendment freedoms to the 'rational basis' level. It is now a certainty that the new 'due process' coverall offers far less protection to liberty than would adherence to our former cases compelling states to abide by the unequivocal First Amendment command that its defined freedoms shall not be abridged.

"The Court's holding here and the constitutional doctrine behind it leave the rights of assembly, petition, speech and press almost completely at the mercy of state legislative, executive, and judicial agencies."

Beauharnais, president of the White Circle League, distributed literature that advocated for separation of the races, warned against "mongrelization" by the "Negro" race, and included other hateful comments. He appealed his conviction in the lower courts all the way to the U.S. Supreme Court. Justice Felix Frankfurter wrote that the state of Illinois had a strong interest in passing laws to prohibit racial unrest. He noted that "Illinois has been the scene of exacerbated tension between races, often flaring into violence and destruction." He reasoned that the state could reasonably pass a law that would "curb false or malicious defamation of racial and religious groups, made in public places and by means calculated to have a powerful emotional impact on those to whom it was presented."

What did the Vinson Court rule with respect to the **regulation of sound trucks**?

The Vinson Court ruled in *Kovacs v. Cooper* (1949) that the city of Trenton, New Jersey, could prohibit the use of sound amplifiers or loudspeakers on vehicles. The challenge to the ordinance occurred after a city police officer found a sound truck that was broadcasting music. The owner of the truck, Charles Kovacs, was found guilty of violating the ordinance. He contended that the ordinance violated his First Amendment free-expression rights. The U.S. Supreme Court disagreed, reasoning that city officials could restrict such devices. "There is no restriction upon the communication of ideas or discussion of the issues by the human voice, by newspapers, by pamphlets, by dodgers," the Court wrote. "We think that the need for reasonable protection in the homes or business houses from the distracting noises of vehicles equipped with such sound amplifying devices justifies the ordinance."

However, the Vinson Court ruled that city officials may not pick and choose which persons can use loudspeakers. In *Saia v. New York* (1948), the Court invalidated a Lockport, New York, ordinance that required individuals to obtain a permit before being able to use a loudspeaker on public streets. The ordinance gave the mayor unbridled discretion to determine which individuals could have a permit. The mayor denied a request by a Jehovah's Witness minister. "When a city allows an official to ban them in his uncontrolled discretion, it sanctions a device for suppression of free communication of ideas," the Court wrote.

In what case did the U.S. Supreme Court **invalidate a breach-of-the-peace conviction** on First Amendment grounds?

The U.S. Supreme Court struck down a breach-of-the-peace conviction by a 5–4 vote in *Terminiello v. City of Chicago* (1949). Police charged Arthur Terminiello with breach of the peace after he delivered a speech in an auditorium denouncing several political and racial groups. Terminiello's speech apparently led to many disturbances in the crowd. A trial court convicted him because he had stirred the public to anger and invited disputes. The Court majority reversed his conviction in an opinion written by Justice William O. Douglas, who wrote that "a function of free speech under our system is to invite dispute." He explained: "Speech is often provocative and challenging. It may strike at prejudices and preconceptions and have profound unsettling effects as it presses for acceptance of an idea."

In what famous decision did the Vinson Court **define the meaning of the Establishment Clause**?

The Vinson Court ruled that the First Amendment's Establishment Clause—"Congress shall make no law respecting an establishment of religion"—applied to the

CourtSpeak: *Zorach v. Clauson* Religious Education Case (1952)

Justice William O. Douglas (majority): "Moreover, apart from that claim of coercion, we do not see how New York by this type of 'released time' program has made a law respecting an establishment of religion within the meaning of the First Amendment.... There cannot be the slightest doubt that the First Amendment reflects the philosophy that Church and State should be separated. And so far as interference with the 'free exercise' of religion and an 'establishment' of religion are concerned, the separation must be complete and unequivocal. The First Amendment within the scope of its coverage permits no exception; the prohibition is absolute. The First Amendment, however, does not say that in every and all respects there shall be a separation of Church and State.... That is the common sense of the matter. Otherwise the state and religion would be aliens to each other—hostile, suspicious, and even unfriendly. Churches could not be required to pay even property taxes. Municipalities would not be permitted to render police or fire protection to religious groups. Policemen who helped parishioners into their places of worship would violate the Constitution. Prayers in our legislative halls; the appeals to the Almighty in the messages of the Chief Executive; the proclamations making Thanksgiving Day a holiday; 'so help me God' in our courtroom oaths—these and all other references to the Almighty that run through our laws, our public rituals, our ceremonies would be flouting the First Amendment. A fastidious atheist or agnostic could even object to the supplication with which the Court opens each session: 'God save the United States and this Honorable Court.'"

states in *Everson v. Board of Education* (1947). The case concerned a New Jersey law that allowed school districts to reimburse parents for the costs of bus transportation to and from schools. The town of Ewing applied this law to allow reimbursements for all parents, including those whose children attended private religious schools. Arch Everson sued, contending that the practice of paying monies to parents whose children attended private religious schools violated the Establishment Clause.

The Court determined that the Establishment Clause meant to ensure that there was a "wall of separation" between church and state. However, a narrow majority of the Court determined that the wall did not prevent the town from paying the bus transportation costs of all its students, from both public and private schools. Justice Black explained: "We must be careful, in protecting the citizens of New Jersey against state-established churches, to be sure that we do not inadvertently prohibit New Jersey from extending its general State law benefits to all its citizens without regard to their religious belief." He concluded: "The First Amendment has erected a wall between church and state. That wall must be kept high and impregnable. We could not approve the slightest breach. New Jersey has not breached it here."

William O. Douglas was the longest-serving U.S. Supreme Court justice, wearing his robe from 1939 to 1975. *Hulton Archive/Getty Images.*

What did the Vinson Court say about **released-time plans that allow religious education for public school students**?

The Vinson Court issued decisions concerning release-time plans in two cases—*McCollum v. Board of Education* (1948) and *Zorach v. Clauson* (1952)—with contrasting results. Release-time plans allow students in public schools to receive religious instruction during the school day. In *McCollum,* schools in Champaign County, Illinois, allowed paid religious instructors to come to the public schools to provide religious instruction to students thirty minutes every week. Students whose parents signed a permission slip could attend the classes. A parent sued, contending that the practice violated the Establishment Clause. "Pupils compelled by law to go to school for secular education are released in part from their legal duty upon the condition that they attend the religious classes," wrote Justice Hugo Black for the majority. "This is beyond all question a utilization of the tax-established and tax-supported public school system to aid religious groups to spread their faith."

However, the Court reached a different result in *Zorach v. Clauson,* which reviewed a New York Board of Education policy that allowed public school students to travel during the school day to receive religious instruction. The U.S. Supreme Court ruled this practice acceptable, focusing on the fact that the students in *Zorach* were not receiving religious instruction on school grounds, as in *McCollum.* "In the *McCollum* case the classrooms were used for religious instruction and the force of the public school was used to promote that instruction," Justice William O. Douglas wrote for the majority. "Here, as we have said, the public schools do no more than accommodate their schedules to a program of outside religious instruction."

THE WARREN COURT (1953–69)

How many and **which justices served on the Warren Court**?

Seventeen justices served on the Warren Court: Chief Justice Earl Warren and Justices Hugo Black, William O. Douglas, Felix Frankfurter, Stanley F. Reed, John Marshall Harlan, Robert Jackson, Harold Burton, Tom C. Clark, Sherman Minton, William Brennan, Charles Whittaker, Potter Stewart, Byron White, Arthur Goldberg, Abe Fortas, and Thurgood Marshall.

Which **two justices served on the Supreme Court both before and after Earl Warren's tenure** as chief justice?

The two justices were Hugo Black, who served from 1937 to 1971, and William O. Douglas, who served from 1939 to 1975.

What **prior experience did Earl Warren have** before assuming the position of chief justice?

Earl Warren served in public office from 1919 until his resignation from the U.S. Supreme Court in 1969. From 1919 to 1920, he served as deputy city attorney for Oakland, California. From 1920 to 1925, he served as district attorney for Alameda County. From 1939 to 1943, he served as California attorney general. From 1943 to 1953, he served as governor of California. In 1948, Warren was unsuccessful Republican presidential candidate Thomas E. Dewey's vice presidential running mate. In 1952, Warren sought the Republican nomination for president but later withdrew and supported General Dwight D. Eisenhower. Eisenhower returned the favor the next year by nominating Warren as chief justice.

U.S. Supreme Court chief justice Earl Warren. *Fabian Bachrach/Time & Life Pictures/Getty Images.*

> ## CourtSpeak: Thoughts on Earl Warren
>
> **R**onald Rotunda (writer): "Not all Chief Justices were really influential enough to have a slice of history named after them. Earl Warren does deserve the title. There really was a Warren Court. And its influence has lasted beyond the time that Warren graced the office of Chief Justice."
>
> Justice William Brennan: "He was always the Chief, the Super Chief."

What was the **historical irony** of the Warren Court being the **great liberal court**?

Earl Warren was not considered a great liberal during his tenure as California governor. For instance, he supported the internment of thousands of Japanese American citizens during World War II. Nearly 120,000 persons of Japanese ancestry were removed from the West Coast of the United States and placed in "War Relocation Camps." Warren publicly stated his support for the relocation: "If the Japs are released, no one will be able to tell a saboteur from any other Jap." Warren later acknowledged his regret for this, writing in his memoirs: "I have since deeply regretted the removal order and my own testimony advocating it, because it was not in keeping with our American concept of freedom and the rights of citizens."

Which **justice resigned** from the Warren Court **because of his son**?

Justice Tom C. Clark resigned from the Court in 1967 when President Lyndon B. Johnson named Clark's son, Ramsey, U.S. attorney general. Clark wanted to avoid any conflict of interest since his son would be presenting cases regularly before the Court.

Which member of the Warren Court played **professional football**?

Justice Byron White played professional football with the Pittsburgh Pirates (now Steelers) and the Detroit Lions. He led the National Football League in rushing in his rookie year of 1938 with the Pirates. White earned All-American honors as a running back for the University of Colorado, where he earned the nickname "Whizzer."

What was the **Warren Commission**?

The Warren Commission was a group formed by then-President Lyndon B. Johnson to investigate the November 22, 1963, assassination of President John F. Kennedy. Johnson tapped Chief Justice Warren to head the commission. The committee included U.S. representative Gerald R. Ford of Michigan, who would later serve as U.S. president from 1974 to 1977. The Commission concluded that assassin Lee Harvey Oswald was not part of a massive conspiracy but acted alone. The Warren Commission report has been heavily criticized by historians, scholars, and others.

RACIAL DISCRIMINATION

What was *Brown v. Board of Education*?

Brown v. Board of Education was one of the most important U.S. Supreme Court decisions. On May 17, 1954, the Court's opinion invalidated segregated public schools as violative of the Equal Protection Clause. The decision was a consolidation of challenges to segregated public schools in the states of Kansas, Delaware, South Carolina, and Virginia. The other cases were *Briggs v. Elliott* (South Carolina), *Davis v. County School Board of Prince Edward County* (Virginia), and *Gebhart v. Belton* (Delaware). A group of African Americans, represented by the National Association for the Advancement of Colored People (NAACP), mounted a challenge to the segregated school systems. They not only alleged that the schools their children attended were inferior to schools attended by white children, but they also alleged that separate schools based on race was unconstitutional on its face.

The Court ruled that segregated public schools were "inherently unequal." The Court wrote: "We conclude that, in the field of public education, the doctrine of 'separate but equal' has no place. Separate educational facilities are inherently unequal. Therefore, we hold that the plaintiffs and others similarly situated for whom the actions have been brought are, by reason of the segregation complained of, deprived of the equal protection of the laws guaranteed by the Fourteenth Amendment."

What was **Footnote 11** in the *Brown* case and why has it received so much attention?

Footnote 11 in the Brown decision cited numerous social science studies that showed how segregation harmed black children and imposed on them feelings of inferiority. The first work cited was that of social scientist Kenneth B. Clark, well known for his studies involving the effects of segregation. Clark tested African American students in Philadelphia, Boston, and other cities by showing them white and black dolls. A large percentage of students preferred the white dolls. Critics charged that the Court relied too much on imprecise social science studies rather than on more concrete constitutional law principles.

What **decision did *Brown v. Board of Education* overrule**?

The Court overruled its 1896 decision *Plessy v. Ferguson,* which had established the separate-but-equal doctrine. The Court ruled that the separate-but-equal doctrine had "no place" in public education. The *Brown* decision led to the invalidation of a whole host of segregation laws across the country.

How was **Earl Warren crucial to the *Brown* decision**?

Brown v. Board of Education originally came before the U.S. Supreme Court for argument in 1952. The justices were divided on the question and ordered reargument.

Then, in September 1953, Chief Justice Fred Vinson died. Earl Warren assumed the mantle of chief justice and he persuaded his colleagues that the importance of their decision required a unanimous voice from the Court. Warren wrote a short, 10-page opinion for both lawyer and layperson to understand. Historians say that without Warren's leadership, the Supreme Court may not have been able to speak with such a single voice. Justice Felix Frankfurter allegedly told two law clerks upon hearing of the death of Chief Justice Vinson: "This is the first indication that I have ever had that there is a God." Frankfurter did not feel that Vinson was up to the challenge intellectually of serving upon the U.S. Supreme Court. The two also did not get along personally. The feelings were so bitter between the two men that Frankfurter would not even attend Vinson's funeral.

Linda Brown (front) sits in her classroom in Topeka, Kansas. Her father, Oliver Brown, agreed to allow his family to be represented by the local NAACP in its fight against segregated schools. This led to *Brown v. Board of Education*. *Carl Iwasaki/Time & Life Pictures/Getty Images.*

Who was "Brown" in *Brown v. Board of Education*?

Linda Brown was an elementary school student in Topeka, Kansas. Her father, Oliver Brown, agreed to be one of the families represented by the local NAACP in its fight against segregated schools. The Browns were one of thirteen families involved in the lawsuit.

Was there a **second *Brown* decision**?

Yes, in its first *Brown* decision in 1954, the U.S. Supreme Court had ruled that segregated public schools were unconstitutional. However, the Court deferred ruling on a remedy, or solution, to fix the problem of segregated schools across the country. In

283

Brown v. Board of Education II (1955), the Court instructed trial court judges to monitor cases before them to ensure that public schools were integrated "with all deliberate speed." In some jurisdictions, local school authorities focused more on the adjective "deliberate" than the noun "speed." This resulted in a situation where public schools were not integrated in some Southern states until the 1970s.

What attorney in the *Brown* case **later became a member of the Warren Court**?

Thurgood Marshall, the director of the NAACP's Legal Defense and Education Fund, argued before the U.S. Supreme Court in *Brown v. Board of Education* along with several other noted African American attorneys, such as Robert Carter and Spottswood Robinson III. It was one of 29 decisions that Marshall won before the U.S. Supreme Court. In 1967, President Lyndon B. Johnson made history by elevating Marshall to the U.S. Supreme Court, making him the first African American to serve on the high court.

What **law clerk memo about the *Brown* case** would cause much controversy in later years?

In 1952–53, future U.S. Supreme Court chief justice William Rehnquist served as a law clerk for Justice Robert Jackson. Law clerks often write memos to "their" justice about the cases before the Court. One such memo written by Rehnquist stated that the *Brown* cases asked the Court to "read its own sociological views into the Constitution." It concluded: "I think *Plessy v. Ferguson* was right and should be re-affirmed." This memo surfaced during Rehnquist's confirmation hearings to the U.S. Supreme Court in 1971. Rehnquist explained that he wrote the memo merely as a draft of Justice Jackson's initial views on the case. Several legal scholars on the *Brown* case dispute that assertion.

What did the Court say about a **county that closed its schools rather than desegregate**?

In response to the *Brown* decision, county officials in Prince Edward County, Virginia, closed its public schools rather than desegregate its school system. The county provided tuition grants and tax credits to whites-only private schools. The U.S. Supreme Court ruled in *Griffin v. County School Board of Prince Edward County* (1964) that the actions of county officials violated the Equal Protection Clause. Justice Hugo Black wrote for the Court: "There has been entirely too much deliberation and not enough speed in enforcing the constitutional rights which we held in *Brown v. Board of Education, supra,* had been denied Prince Edward County Negro children."

How did the Warren Court respond to **arguments that a state governor was not bound to obey its decision** in *Brown v. Board of Education*?

The Warren Court unanimously held in *Cooper v. Aaron* (1958) that state governors and legislators are bound under the Constitution—and its Supremacy Clause—to obey deci-

NAACP Legal Defense and Education Fund director Thurgood Marshall, who gained national acclaim when he argued before the U.S. Supreme Court in *Brown v. Board of Education* in 1954. In 1967, Marshall became the first African American Supreme Court justice. *Hank Walker/Time & Life Pictures/Getty Images.*

Minnijean Brown (center) and several other classmates, part of the so-called Little Rock Nine, are blocked by the Arkansas National Guard on September 4, 1957, on orders from Arkansas governor Orval Faubus. The governor was defying a federal order by seeking to keep African Americans from integrating with white students. *Francis Miller/Time & Life Pictures/Getty Images.*

sions by the U.S. Supreme Court. Quoting *Marbury v. Madison,* the Court wrote that "it is emphatically the province and duty of the judicial department to say what the law is."

Arkansas governor Orval Faubus had ordered the Arkansas National Guard to prevent the integration of nine African American students into Little Rock's Central High School in 1957—a defiance of a federal court order. This led to President Dwight D. Eisenhower sending in federal troops to ensure the protection of the students and the integration of the school.

The U.S. Supreme Court emphasized: "No state legislator or judicial officer can war against the Constitution without violating his undertaking to support it."

Did the Warren Court issue **other desegregation decisions outside of the school context**?

Yes, the Warren issued numerous desegregation decisions not involving schools. Some of these included:

Turner v. City of Memphis (1962): Restaurants and restrooms in the Memphis airport must be integrated.

Bailey v. Patterson (1962): No state, including in this case Mississippi, could pass a law mandating racial segregation of interstate and intrastate transportation facilities and carriers.

Watson v. City of Memphis (1963): Memphis could not delay in integrating its public parks.

Evans v. Newton (1966): A public park in Georgia had to be integrated even though the land for the park had been willed by someone who specified that the land was to be used by whites only.

Lee v. Washington (1968): The U.S. Supreme Court struck down an Alabama law requiring segregation of races in prisons.

What did the Warren Court rule with respect to **interracial marriages**?

The Warren Court unanimously ruled in the 1967 decision *Loving v. Virginia* that a Virginia law banning interracial marriages violated the "central meaning" of the Fourteenth Amendment. At the time of the decision, sixteen states had laws barring such marriages. The Virginia law banned interracial marriages and said that those in violation could be imprisoned from one to five years. The Supreme Court reasoned that racial classifications are subject to the highest degree of scrutiny under the Equal Protection Clause. The state argued that the law did not violate the Equal Protection Clause because whites and blacks in interracial marriages were punished equally. The state relied on the Supreme Court's 1883 decision *Pace v. Alabama,* which had upheld an Alabama law that imposed greater penalties on those who committed adultery with a person of another race. The Court in *Loving* rejected this precedent, reasoning that the purpose of the Equal Protection Clause was "to eliminate all official state sources of invidious racial discrimination in the States."

Who were the **plaintiffs in *Loving v. Virginia***?

The plaintiffs in the historic *Loving v. Virginia* case were Richard Loving, a white man, and Mildred Jeter, a black woman. The two lived in Virginia but married in the District of Columbia, which did not have an antimiscegenation law. However, Virginia authorities charged the two with violating state law when they returned to Virginia to live. The Lovings pleaded guilty and were sentenced to one year in jail. The trial judge suspended the sentence for a period of twenty-five years if the couple agreed to move out of state and not return together for that period of time. In imposing his sentence, the trial judge wrote: "Almighty God created the races white, black, yellow, malay and red, and he placed them on separate continents. And but for the interference with his arrangement there would be no cause for such marriages. The fact that he separated the races shows that he did not intend for the races to mix." The Lovings later challenged the constitutionality of this law, leading to the Supreme Court decision bearing Richard's last name.

How did the Warren Court uphold the **Civil Rights Act of 1964**?

The Warren Court ruled that Congress had the power to pass the Civil Rights Act of 1964 based on its broad powers under the Commerce Clause in two cases: *Heart of Atlanta Motel v. United States* and *Katzenbach v. McClung.* The owner of the Heart of Atlanta motel contended that he had the right to refuse to rent rooms to black patrons.

He argued that Congress exceeded its constitutional powers by regulating private businesses. The U.S. Supreme Court noted that there was "overwhelming evidence that discrimination by hotels and motels impedes interstate travel." The motel owner argued that Congress simply did not have the power to correct what it considered a moral wrong. The motel owner argued that Congress was overstepping and exceeding its constitutional authority in regulating private businesses. The Supreme Court said that did not matter because discrimination in public accommodations harmed interstate commerce: "In framing Title II of this Act Congress was also dealing with what it considered a moral problem. But that fact does not detract from the overwhelming evidence of the disruptive effect that racial discrimination has had on commercial intercourse."

The second case, *Katzenbach v. McClung,* involved Ollie's Barbecue, a privately owned restaurant in Birmingham, Alabama, that limited blacks to take-out service while providing seating to whites in the restaurant's dining area. The Court reasoned that Congress had a rational basis for concluding that "refusals of service to Negroes have imposed burdens both upon the interstate flow of food and upon the movement of products generally."

What did the Warren Court rule with respect to the **Thirteenth Amendment and private racial discrimination**?

The Warren Court ruled in *Jones v. Alfred H. Mayer Co.* (1968) that Congress had the power under the Thirteenth Amendment to pass laws prohibiting racial discrimination in the private sector. Joseph Lee Jones sued after a real estate company refused to sell him land in the Paddock Woods community of St. Louis, Missouri.

Jones sued, alleging violation of federal law 42 U.S.C. section 1982, which provides: "All citizens of the United States shall have the same right, in every State and

> ## CourtSpeak: *South Carolina v. Katzenbach* Voting Rights Case (1966)
>
> Chief Justice Earl Warren (unanimous): "After enduring nearly a century of widespread resistance to the Fifteenth Amendment, Congress has marshaled an array of potent weapons against the evil, with authority in the Attorney General to employ them effectively. Many of the areas directly affected by this development have indicated their willingness to abide by any restraints legitimately imposed upon them. We here hold that the portions of the Voting Rights Act properly before us are a valid means for carrying out the commands of the Fifteenth Amendment. Hopefully, millions of non-white Americans will now be able to participate for the first time on an equal basis in the government under which they live. We may finally look forward to the day when truly 'the right of citizens of the United States to vote shall not be denied or abridged by the United States or by any State on account of race, color, or previous condition of servitude.'"

Territory, as is enjoyed by white citizens thereof to inherit, purchase, lease, sell, hold, and convey real and personal property."

The lower courts ruled against Jones, finding that the federal law in question did not apply to acts of purely private racial discrimination. The U.S. Supreme Court disagreed 7–2. First, Congress reasoned that the text of the law applied to all acts of racial discrimination dealing with the selling of property—both public and private.

Then, the Court reached the larger constitutional question of whether Congress had the authority under the Thirteenth Amendment to regulate acts of private racial discrimination. The Court ruled that Congress had such power. "Surely Congress has the power under the Thirteenth Amendment rationally to determine what are the badges and the incidents of slavery, and the authority to translate that determination into effective legislation," the Court wrote.

In what decision did the Warren Court uphold the **Voting Rights Act of 1965**?

The Warren Court unanimously upheld the constitutionality of the Voting Rights Act in *South Carolina v. Katzenbach* (1966). The Act suspended the use of literacy tests, which were designed to keep African Americans from voting. The Act also provided for the placement of federal examiners to ensure that states did not engage in voting discrimination. Several states gave alternative tests to illiterate whites to ensure their right to vote. South Carolina—supported by Alabama, Georgia, Louisiana, Mississippi, and Virginia—had challenged the constitutionality of various provisions of the Voting Rights Act. The Court, in an opinion written by Chief Justice Earl Warren, found that Congress had the power under Section 2 of the Fifteenth Amendment, which protects the right to vote, to pass laws prohibiting voting discrimination.

CourtSpeak: *Reynolds v. Sims* (1964)
Legislative District Boundaries Case

Chief Justice Earl Warren (majority): "Since the achieving of fair and effective representation for all citizens is concededly the basic aim of legislative apportionment, we conclude that the Equal Protection Clause guarantees the opportunity for equal participation by all voters in the election of state legislators. Diluting the weight of votes because of place of residence impairs basic constitutional rights under the Fourteenth Amendment just as much as invidious discriminations based upon factors such as race or economic status. Our constitutional system amply provides for the protection of minorities by means other than giving them majority control of state legislatures. And the democratic ideals of equality and majority rule, which have served this Nation so well in the past, are hardly of any less significance for the present and the future."

What was **unusual about the *South Carolina v. Katzenbach* decision**?

The case was unusual because it is one of the relatively few cases in which the U.S. Supreme Court exercises original jurisdiction. This means that the U.S. Supreme Court was the only court to hear the case—there were no lower court decisions. The Supreme Court had original jurisdiction under Article III, Section 2, of the Constitution because the case involved a controversy between a state suing a citizen of another state, in this case the attorney general of the United States.

Why is *Baker v. Carr* considered one of the most important decisions of the Warren Court?

Baker v. Carr allowed litigants to sue state officials in federal courts to reapportion or reorganize legislative districts to reflect a fairer balance of power between urban and rural areas. The case arose in Tennessee because state officials had refused to redraw legislative district boundaries, giving rural voters a much greater proportional share of voting power. The state argued that it did not have the authority to consider this political question. However, the Court ruled 6–2 that it had such authority: "We conclude that the complaint's allegations of a denial of equal protection present a justiciable constitutional cause of action upon which appellants are entitled to a trial and a decision." He concluded that "the right asserted is within the reach of judicial protection under the Fourteenth Amendment." Chief Justice Earl Warren later called the decision "the most vital" of any during his tenure. He wrote in his memoirs: "The reason I am of the opinion that *Baker v. Carr* is so important is because I believe so devoutly that, to paraphrase Abraham Lincoln's famous epigram, ours is a government of all the people, by all the people, and for all the people." The decision directly led to a series of reapportionment cases, such as *Reynolds v. Sims* (1964).

Where does the principle **"one person, one vote"** come from in Supreme Court decisions?

Justice William O. Douglas used this phrase in his opinion for the Court in *Gray v. Sanders* (1963). He wrote: "The conception of political equality from the Declaration of Independence, to Lincoln's Gettysburg Address, to the Fifteenth, Seventeenth, and Nineteenth Amendments can mean only one thing—one person, one vote." The phrase arose in a series of cases in the early 1960s that dealt with the imbalance of voting power between rural and urban areas of various states.

CRIMINAL PROCEDURE AND CONSTITUTIONAL RIGHTS

How was the Warren Court instrumental in advancing the **freedoms in the Bill of Rights**?

Most notably, the Warren Court ruled in a series of cases that many of the freedoms in the Bill of Rights were extended to the states through the Due Process Clause of the Fourteenth Amendment. The text of the Bill of Rights begins with the words "Congress shall make no law." This means that the Bill of Rights only applies to protections from the federal government. However, over the course of the twentieth century, most freedoms found in the Bill of Rights have been extended to the states through the Due Process Clause. The Warren Court was known for extending many of the criminal procedure rights. These cases included:

Mapp v. Ohio (1961): Fourth Amendment exclusionary rule

Robinson v. California (1962): Eighth Amendment ban on cruel and unusual punishment

Gideon v. Wainwright (1963): Sixth Amendment right to counsel

Malloy v. Hogan (1964): Fifth Amendment right against self-incrimination

Pointer v. Texas (1965): Sixth Amendment right to confront witnesses

Parker v. Gladden (1966): Sixth Amendment right to an impartial jury

Klopfer v. North Carolina (1967): Sixth Amendment right to a speedy trial

Washington v. Texas (1967): Sixth Amendment right to compulsory process

Duncan v. Louisiana (1968): Sixth Amendment right to a jury trial in criminal cases

Benton v. Maryland (1969): Fifth Amendment right to be free from double jeopardy

What was the case that established that the **ban on Cruel and Unusual Punishment Clause of the Eighth Amendment applied to the states**?

In *Robinson v. California* (1962), the Warren Court invalidated a California law that made it a crime for a person to be "addicted to narcotics." Police officers charged

Lawrence Roberts for violating the law after noticing scar tissue and scabs on his arms, apparently caused by excessive needle use. The Court held that "a state law which imprisons a person thus afflicted as a criminal, even though he has never touched any narcotic drug within the State or been guilty of any irregular behavior there, inflicts a cruel and unusual punishment in violation of the Fourteenth Amendment."

What case involving a **wartime deserter** led to a landmark standard under the Eighth Amendment?

The Warren Court ruled in *Trop v. Dulles* (1958) that a statute authorizing a wartime deserter to be expatriated (forfeit one's U.S. citizenship) was excessive punishment under the Eighth Amendment. Albert Trop, a private in the U.S. army, escaped from a stockade in Casablanca where he had been held for a disciplinary violation. Upon his capture, the army court-martialed Trop for desertion, sentencing him to three years of hard labor and a dishonorable discharge. Several years later, Trop applied for a U.S. passport. Officials denied his request, citing a provision of the Nationality Act of 1940 that provided that wartime deserters were no longer U.S citizens. Chief Justice Earl Warren wrote that the statute violated the Cruel and Unusual Punishment Clause of the Eighth Amendment. "The Amendment must draw its meaning from the evolving standards of decency that mark the progress of a maturing society," the Court wrote. The "evolving standards of decency" has become the modern-day Supreme Court's guidepost in capital punishment cases.

What did the Warren Court say with respect to **"Miranda rights"**?

The U.S. Supreme Court ruled in four consolidated cases—*Miranda v. Arizona, Vignera v. New York, Westover v. United States,* and *California v. Stewart*—that law enforcement officials could not use statements obtained from a police interrogation "unless it demonstrates the use of procedural safeguards effective to secure the privilege against self-incrimination." The Court held that police violate the Fifth Amendment if they do not inform a suspect prior to questioning that he or she has: (1) a right to remain silent; (2) that any statement he or she makes can be used against them in a court of law; (3) that he or she has the right to have an attorney present during questioning; and (4) that if he or she cannot afford an attorney, one will be provided to them. If law enforcement officials fail to provide these procedural safeguards, the Court said that evidence obtained during such interrogations cannot be used against the suspect.

Who was **Miranda**?

Ernesto A. Miranda was a criminal defendant convicted of rape who challenged his conviction in a Supreme Court case that bears his name. Miranda was arrested on suspicion of robbery. During a two-hour interrogation at a Phoenix police station, Miranda not only confessed to the robbery, but also to sexually assaulting and raping a woman eleven days earlier. The police officers never informed Miranda that he had a right to have a lawyer present during questioning. A jury convicted Miranda of kidnapping and rape and sentenced him to twenty to thirty years for each offense. Miranda's lawyers argued that their client's Fifth Amendment right against self-incrimination was violated by the coercive interrogation. In *Miranda v. Arizona* (1966), the U.S. Supreme Court agreed.

What happened to Miranda after the Supreme Court decision?

Prosecutors retried Miranda without evidence obtained from his confession. The prosecution presented the testimony of Miranda's common-law wife, who claimed that during a prison visit, Miranda confessed to her that he had raped the victim. A jury convicted him again on charges of kidnapping and rape in 1966. Miranda was paroled in 1972. However, in 1976, Miranda was stabbed to death in a bar fight.

What did the Warren Court decree on the **exclusionary rule**?

The Warren Court ruled 6–3 in *Mapp v. Ohio* (1961) that the Fourth Amendment–based exclusionary rule—which holds that evidence illegally seized by law enforcement officials must be excluded from trial—applies to the states through the Fourteenth Amendment Due Process Clause. In 1949, the Court had ruled in *Wolf v. Colorado* that "in a prosecution in a State court for a State crime the Fourteenth Amendment does not forbid the admission of evidence obtained by an unreasonable search and seizure." The Court overruled that aspect of its *Wolf* decision twelve years later in *Mapp*.

Justice Tom C. Clark, a former prosecutor, wrote: "We hold that all evidence obtained by searches and seizures in violation of the Constitution is, by that same authority, inadmissible in a state court."

Who was the **defendant in *Mapp v. Ohio*** and what other events brought her in the public eye?

The case of *Mapp v. Ohio* began when at least seven Cleveland police officers searched for gambling paraphernalia in the home of Dollree Mapp. Instead, the officers found pornographic books, which they labeled obscene. Mapp was found not guilty of gambling charges but was convicted on the obscenity charges. The case eventually reached the U.S. Supreme Court, which reversed her conviction because the police officers failed to produce a search warrant before rummaging through Mapp's home.

Mapp was known in boxing circles. She was the ex-wife of former top-ranked light-heavyweight and heavyweight boxer Jimmy Bivins. Then, in 1956, Mapp filed a $750,000 lawsuit against world light-heavyweight champion Archie Moore. She claimed that Moore broke a promise to marry her and physically assaulted her. Mapp moved to Queens, New York. In 1970, police officers seized $250,000 in drugs and stolen property. Mapp was convicted and sentenced to a prison term of twenty years to life. Mapp claimed the charges were a vendetta against her after her famous case. In 1981, Governor Hugh Carey commuted Mapp's sentence. She had served more than nine years in a women's prison in New Bedford, New York.

How did the Warren Court expand the right to counsel in criminal cases?

The Warren Court expanded the right to counsel by ruling that criminal defendants charged with felonies in state courts do have a fundamental right to an attorney even if they cannot afford an attorney. The Sixth Amendment provides that "in all criminal prosecutions, the accused shall enjoy the right ... to have the Assistance of Counsel for his defence." In *Johnson v. Zerbst* (1938), the U.S. Supreme Court ruled that indigent criminal defendants charged with crimes in federal court have the right to counsel. However, the Sixth Amendment applied only to the federal government, meaning that only those charged with federal crimes were entitled to legal representation. The legal question was whether the Sixth Amendment right to counsel should be extended to the states through the Fourteenth Amendment's Due Process Clause, which provides that states shall not deprive individuals of "life, liberty or property without due process of law." In 1942, the U.S. Supreme Court answered no in *Betts v. Brady,* writing that the "appointment of counsel is not a fundamental right, essential to a fair trial." This meant that criminal defendants not charged with capital (death penalty) crimes did not have a constitutional right to the appointment of counsel. The Warren Court changed all this in its 1963 decision *Gideon v. Wainwright.*

What did the Court rule in *Gideon v. Wainwright*?

The story of *Gideon v. Wainwright* began when prosecutors in Florida charged Clarence Earl Gideon with breaking into the Bay Harbor Poolroom in Panama City,

Florida. Gideon was not a man likely to change the legal system. He had spent time in prison for four different felonies. Gideon asked the state court judge to appoint him counsel, saying: "The United States Supreme Court says I am entitled to be represented by Counsel." The trial judge denied his request. Gideon appealed all the way to the U.S. Supreme Court. The Supreme Court accepted his case and appointed Washington D.C. attorney Abe Fortas to argue the case for Gideon before the high court. (Fortas later became a justice on the U.S. Supreme Court). The Supreme Court overruled *Betts v. Brady* and determined that state criminal defendants charged with felonies have a constitutional right to the assistance of counsel.

Writing for the Court, Justice Hugo Black stated that "in our adversary system of criminal justice, any person hauled into court, who is too poor to hire a lawyer, cannot be assured a fair trial unless counsel is provided to him." The Court reversed Gideon's conviction. This meant that the state would have to appoint Gideon counsel if it sought to prosecute him again.

Washington, D.C., attorney Abe Fortas (above) was appointed the attorney for Clarence Earl Gideon, who had failed in earlier attempts to have counsel appointed to him. In *Gideon v. Wainwright,* the U.S. Supreme Court reversed Gideon's conviction and ruled he had the right to counsel if the prosecution sought to retry him. Fortas later became a Supreme Court justice. *Al Fenn/Time & Life Pictures/Getty*

What happened to Clarence Earl Gideon after the Supreme Court's decision?

The Supreme Court's decision meant that Gideon would be retried again, this time with the benefit of counsel. Attorney Abe Fortas told Gideon that he would be better off with local (Florida) counsel. He recommended that Gideon write the American Civil Liberties Union (ACLU) of Florida, asking for the assistance of counsel. The ACLU sent two lawyers to meet with Gideon. However, much to their (and the court's) surprise, Gideon did not want to be represented by these lawyers. Local Panama City attorney Fred Turner was appointed to represent Gideon. Turner effectively cross-examined one of the state's chief witnesses during the second trial. The jury voted "not guilty" and Gideon was freed after serving two years in prison. He died in 1972.

Author Anthony Lewis, in his book *Gideon's Trumpet,* discussed the importance of the *Gideon* case: "[It] is in part a testament to a single human being. Against all the odds of inertia and ignorance and fear of state power, Clarence Earl Gideon insisted that he had a right to a lawyer and kept on insisting all the way to the Supreme Court of the United States. His triumph there shows that the poorest and least powerful of men—a convict with not even a friend to visit him in prison—can take his cause to the highest court in the land and bring about a fundamental change in the law."

What did the Warren Court rule about **guilty pleas**?

The Warren Court determined in *Boykin v. Alabama* (1969) that trial judges must ensure that criminal defendants understand and agree to the waiver of their constitutional rights when they plead guilty to criminal offenses. The case involved a twenty-seven-year-old African American defendant Edward Boykin, Jr., who pled guilty to five counts of robbery. The trial judge accepted Boykin's plea without inquiring whether he understood the consequences of such action. A jury sentenced Boykin to death. The U.S. Supreme Court wrote that "it was error ... for the trial judge to accept petitioner's [Boykin's] guilty plea without an affirmative showing that it was intelligent and voluntary."

What did the Warren Court do with respect to **jailhouse lawyers**?

The Warren Court ruled in *Johnson v. Avery* (1969) that the state of Tennessee could not bar inmates from assisting other inmates in legal matters unless it provided some avenue of legal assistance to inmates. The case involved William Joe Johnson, an inmate sentenced to life in prison for rape. Johnson alleged that prison officials denied him privileges accorded other inmates because he served as a jailhouse lawyer, assisting other inmates with their legal claims. The Court concluded that "unless and until the State provides some reasonable alternative to assist inmates in the preparation of their petitions for post-conviction relief," the state could not ban inmates from serving as jailhouse lawyers.

CourtSpeak: *Johnson v. Avery* Jailhouse Lawyer Case (1969)

Justice William O. Douglas (concurring): "Where government fails to provide the prison with the legal counsel it demands, the prison generates its own. In a community where illiteracy and mental deficiency is notoriously high, it is not enough to ask the prisoner to be his own lawyer. Without the assistance of fellow prisoners, some meritorious claims would never see the light of a courtroom. In cases where that assistance succeeds, it speaks for itself. And even in cases where it fails, it may provide a necessary medium of expression."

What did the Warren Court rule in the **case of Sam Sheppard**?

Dr. Sam Sheppard was convicted in state court of murdering his pregnant wife in their suburban home near Cleveland, Ohio. He later sought federal habeas corpus review of his conviction, alleging that his Sixth Amendment rights to an impartial jury and fair trial were violated because the trial judge failed to take any measures to prevent prejudicial publicity that affected the trial. The U.S. Supreme Court reversed Sheppard's conviction in *Sheppard v. Maxwell* (1966), writing that "bedlam reigned at the courthouse during the trial and newsmen took over practically the entire courtroom, hounding most of the participants in the trial, especially Sheppard." The Court also noted that the jurors were bombarded by the press, having their names and photographs published. The Court said that trial judges should consider sequestering a jury to protect it from massive pretrial coverage of a high profile case.

What happened to **Sheppard after the Court's decision**?

Prosecutors retried Sheppard after he was ordered released from custody by the U.S. Supreme Court. His trial began in October 1966. In November 1966, a jury found Dr. Sheppard not guilty. He died in April 1970.

What famous **television show and movie were inspired by the Sheppard case**?

In September 1963, the television show *The Fugitive* first aired on ABC. It dealt with the ordeal of Dr. Richard Kimble, played by actor David Janssen, who was unlawfully convicted of murder. The show was inspired by the Sheppard case. In 1993, the hit movie *The Fugitive,* starring Harrison Ford and Tommy Lee Jones, was released.

What Warren Court decision became the **leading search-and-seizure precedent dealing with privacy rights**?

The U.S. Supreme Court established in *Katz v. United States* (1967) that the Fourth Amendment privacy protections applied to "people, not places." The case involved the wiretapping of a public phone booth to record the gambling phone calls of defendant

297

Charles Katz. The Federal Bureau of Investigation (FBI) wiretapped the phone without obtaining a warrant. Katz contended that he had a right to privacy in his telephone calls. He alleged that government officials violated the Fourth Amendment because they did not seek a warrant backed by probable cause but had illegally wiretapped the phone. The government argued to the Court that Katz had no Fourth Amendment rights in the phone calls because he made such calls from a public phone. The Court agreed with Katz, finding that the government should have obtained a warrant based on probable cause from a magistrate before eavesdropping on the phone calls.

What **Fourth Amendment standard** emerged from the Court's *Katz* decision?

The prevailing standard that still dominates the Supreme Court's current Fourth Amendment jurisprudence came from Justice John Marshall Harlan's concurring opinion in *Katz*. Harlan wrote that the important question was whether a person had a "reasonable expectation of privacy." He explained that this was a two-part test: "first that a person have exhibited an actual (subjective) expectation of privacy and, second, that the expectation be one that society is prepared to recognize as 'reasonable.'"

How did the Warren Court increase the **power of the police in street-level encounters**?

The Warren Court strengthened the authority of the police by upholding the practice of "stop and frisk" in its 1968 decision *Terry v. Ohio*. The Court noted that the Fourth

Actor David Janssen in a scene from TV's *The Fugitive.* The television series was inspired by the Sam Sheppard case, in which the U.S. Supreme Court ruled that the defendant was wrongfully convicted of the murder of his wife because of the failure to secure an impartial jury. *Hulton Archive/Getty Images.*

Amendment does not prohibit all searches and seizures but only "unreasonable searches and seizures." The Court reasoned that if a police officer reasonably believes that individuals pose a safety risk to the officer or to the general public, the officer may "conduct a carefully limited search of the outer clothing of such persons in an attempt to discover weapons which might be used to assault him."

What single justice objected to the *Terry v. Ohio* decision?

Justice William O. Douglas filed the lone dissent in *Terry v. Ohio*. Douglas believed that the police should not be able to search and seize a person unless they had probable cause. He explained:

> To give the police greater power than a magistrate is to take a long step down the totalitarian path. Perhaps such a step is desirable to cope with modern forms of lawlessness. But if it is taken, it should be the deliberate choice of the people through a constitutional amendment. Until the Fourth Amendment, which is closely allied with the Fifth, is rewritten, the person and the effects of the individual are beyond the reach of all government agencies until there are reasonable grounds to believe (probable cause) that a criminal venture has been launched or about to be launched.

How did the Warren Court deal with alleged claims of discrimination in jury selection?

The Warren Court ruled in *Hernandez v. Texas* (1954) that a Latino defendant was entitled to a new trial because prosecutors had engaged in a systemic pattern of exclusion against Mexican Americans for jury service. The defendant presented evidence that no Mexican American had served on a jury for the past twenty-five years. The Warren Court reasoned that this type of pattern smacked of discrimination. It explained:

To say that this decision revives the rejected contention that the Fourteenth Amendment requires proportional representation of all the component ethnic groups of the community on every jury ignores the facts. The petitioner did not seek proportional representation, nor did he claim a right to have persons of Mexican descent sit on the particular juries which he faced. His only claim is the right to be indicted and tried by juries from which all members of his class are not systematically excluded—juries selected from among all qualified persons regardless of national origin or descent. To this much, he is entitled by the Constitution.

The Court also addressed the issue of discrimination in jury selection in *Swain v. Alabama* (1965). The Court reiterated the principle that a defendant could establish an Equal Protection Clause violation by presenting proof that prosecutors struck, or dismissed, jurors on the basis of race in case after case. However, the defendant could not establish a constitutional violation only by showing that prosecutors struck jurors on the basis of race in his particular case. According to the Court, the African American defendant in *Swain* had failed to establish a clear pattern in "case after case" of discriminatory jury strikes. The Court explained: "Undoubtedly the selection of prospective jurors was somewhat haphazard and little effort was made to ensure that all groups in the community were fully represented. But an imperfect system is not equivalent to purposeful discrimination based on race."

In *Swain,* the Court also rejected the idea that a defendant could establish a constitutional violation if a prosecutor exercised his peremptory challenges (challenges to jurors for virtually any reason) on prospective jurors based on race. The Burger Court overruled this aspect of the Swain case in *Batson v. Kentucky* (1986), holding that prosecutors may not exercise peremptory challenges in a racially discriminatory manner.

What did the Warren Court rule with respect to the **constitutional rights of juvenile suspects**?

The Warren Court extended many constitutional protections to juvenile defendants in its 1967 decision *In Re Gault*. The Court ruled that juvenile defendants possess procedural due-process rights (such as notice of hearings), the right to be informed of the privilege against self-incrimination, the right to counsel, and the right to cross-examine witnesses. "Whatever may be their precise impact, neither the Fourteenth Amendment nor the Bill of Rights is for adults alone," the Court wrote.

What happened in the *Gault* juvenile case?

Law enforcement officials in Arizona arrested 15-year-old Gerald Gault for allegedly making a lewd phone call to a woman in his neighborhood. Officers arrested Gault without informing his parents. A juvenile court judge held a hearing the next day and no transcript was made of the hearing. At a later hearing, the woman who claimed she received the lewd phone call did not testify. Gault was convicted solely on the basis of the testimony of a police officer who claimed that Gault had confessed to him. A juvenile court judge committed Gault as a delinquent, sentencing him to an industrial school until he turned twenty-one.

Gault's parents filed a lawsuit, contending that their son's constitutional rights had been violated. The U.S. Supreme Court voted 8–1 in favor of the Gaults. The Court wrote: "The essential difference between Gerald's case, and a normal criminal case is that safeguards available to adults were discarded in Gerald's case."

How did the Warren Court rule in **criminal and constitutional cases involving communists**?

Communism was a major world threat in the eyes of the United States and its allies. The Warren Court existed during the time of the Cold War between the United States and the Soviet Union. Thus, it is not surprising that the Court had the opportunity to rule in many cases involving communists or laws that impacted suspected communists. Some of these included:

Yates v. United States (1957): The U.S. Supreme Court reversed the conviction of fourteen Communist Party leaders under the Smith Act. The Court reasoned that the jury instructions failed to distinguish between the teaching of abstract doctrine and the organized planning for the overthrow of the U.S. government.

Barenblatt v. United States (1959): The U.S. Supreme Court ruled that the government did not violate the First Amendment rights of an individual who was forced to testify about his relationship to the Communist Party before the House Committee on Un-American Activities.

Communist Party v. Subversive Activities Control Board (1961): The U.S. Supreme Court upheld the registration requirements of the McCarran Act, a

> ## CourtSpeak: *In Re Gault* Juvenile Rights Case (1967)
>
> Justice Abe Fortas (majority): "It would be extraordinary if our Constitution did not require the procedural regularity and the exercise of case implied in the phrase 'due process.' Under our Constitution, the condition of being a boy does not justify a kangaroo court."

1950 law designed to compel the Communist Party to register and provide information about its organization.

Scales v. United States (1961): The U.S. Supreme Court upheld the conviction of an active member of the Communist Party. The Court reasoned that the membership clauses of the Smith Act did not violate the First Amendment because the statute applied to individuals who were actively seeking the overthrow of the U.S. government.

Albertson v. Subversive Activities Control Board (1965): The U.S. Supreme Court ruled that orders of the Subversive Activities Control Board, created to monitor the Communist Party, requiring members of the Communist Party to register violated the members' Fifth Amendment rights against self-incrimination.

Elfbrandt v. Russell (1966): The U.S. Supreme Court invalidated a loyalty oath program for Arizona state employees that made it a violation to be a member of the Communist Party.

U.S. v. Robel (1967): The U.S. Supreme Court struck down a provision of the Subversive Activities Control Act that prohibits any person who is a member of the Communist Party from working at a defense facility. "The statute quite literally establishes guilt by association alone, without any need to establish that an individual's association poses the threat feared by the Government in proscribing it," the Court explained.

Keyishian v. Board of Regents (1967): The U.S. Supreme Court struck down New York regulations that barred the employment of "subversive" teachers and professors in the state. The state had applied the regulations to bar employment of those who were or had been members of the Communist Party. The Court ruled that the regulations were too vague and infringed on academic freedom.

PRIVACY

In what decision did the Warren Court recognize a **general right to privacy**?

The Warren Court recognized a constitutional right to privacy in its 1965 decision *Griswold v. Connecticut.* The case involved a nineteenth-century state law that pro-

U.S. Supreme Court justice Arthur J. Goldberg. *Bob Gomel/Time & Life Pictures/Getty Images.*

hibited the use of birth control devices and criminalized counseling or providing contraceptives. Estelle Griswold, the executive director of the Planned Parenthood League of Connecticut, and Dr. C. Lee Burton, the clinic's medical director, were fined $100 each for violating the law. They contended that the law invaded people's constitutional right to privacy.

Where did the Warren Court find this general **right to privacy in the Bill of Rights**?

Justice William O. Douglas, who wrote the Court's majority opinion, determined that the right to privacy was found in several provisions of the Bill of Rights, including the First, Third, Fourth, Fifth, and Ninth Amendments. He contended that these provisions had penumbras, or zones, around them that encompassed this general right to privacy. He wrote that the case "concerns a relationship lying within the zone of privacy created by several fundamental constitutional guarantees."

Justice Arthur Goldberg wrote a concurring opinion in which he based the right to privacy on the Ninth Amendment, which provides: "The enumeration in the Constitution, of certain rights, shall not be construed to deny or disparage others retained by the people." To Goldberg, the language of the Ninth Amendment meant that there are "additional fundamental rights" that exist along with those rights specifically listed in the first eight amendments.

Justice John Marshall Harlan wrote a concurring opinion in which he determined that the Connecticut law violated the Fourteenth Amendment.

Which two Warren Court **justices dissented in *Griswold v. Connecticut,*** finding no constitutional right to privacy?

Justices Hugo Black and Potter Stewart dissented in *Griswold v. Connecticut.* They both agreed that the law was unwise but thought that the majority had overstepped its judicial authority in creating a new constitutional right not found explicitly in the text of the Bill of Rights. Justice Stewart, for instance, called the Connecticut law "uncom-

> ## CourtSpeak: *Griswold v. Connecticut* Right to Privacy Case (1965)
>
> Justice Arthur Goldberg (concurring): "In sum, the Ninth Amendment simply lends strong support to the view that the 'liberty' protected by the Fifth and Fourteenth Amendments from infringements by the Federal Government or the States is not restricted to rights specifically mentioned in the first eight amendments....
>
> "In sum, I believe that the right to privacy in the marital relation is fundamental and basic—a personal right 'retained by the people' within the meaning of the Ninth Amendment."

monly silly." However, he wrote that "to say that the Ninth Amendment has anything to do with this case is to turn somersaults into history."

Why is *Griswold v. Connecticut* considered such an important decision?

Griswold v. Connecticut is an important decision for several reasons. First, the Court established a general constitutional right to privacy when the word "privacy" never appears in the Bill of Rights. The decision established the principle that there are implied rights within the Bill of Rights. Second, it is one of the only Supreme Court decisions to interpret the Ninth Amendment and its notion of "unenumerated rights." Finally, *Griswold v. Connecticut* is important to understand for supporters and opponents alike because it was the key precedent for the Burger Court to later hold, in *Roe v. Wade* (1973), that the right of privacy included a woman's right to choose whether or not to have an abortion.

FREEDOM OF EXPRESSION

How did the Warren Court **protect press freedoms**?

The Warren Court protected press freedom by constitutionalizing libel law. In its landmark decision *New York Times Co. v. Sullivan* (1964), the Court ruled that public officials could not recover damages for libel unless they showed by clear and convincing evidence that the press acted with actual malice—knowing falsity or reckless disregard as to the truth or falsity of statements. The case ensured that the press would not be liable for all factual errors, only those that were committed with actual malice.

What was the **alleged defamation in *New York Times v. Sullivan*?**

The case involved a March 1960 editorial advertisement published in the *New York Times* called "Heed Their Rising Voices." The ad referred to violations of civil rights in the South; it contained several errors. For example, the ad said that police in Montgomery, Alabama, padlocked a dining hall at Alabama State College. The ad also said that Dr. Martin Luther King Jr. had been arrested seven times. These were not true, as the police did not padlock the dining hall and King had only been arrested four times. Montgomery police commissioner L. B. Sullivan sued for libel in Alabama state court. A jury awarded him $500,000 in damages.

Why did the Court **reverse the state court libel ruling**?

The U.S. Supreme Court reasoned that the central purpose of the First Amendment was to ensure citizens the right to freely criticize government officials. The Court considered the *Times* case "against the background of a profound national commitment to the principle that debate on public issues should be uninhibited, robust, and wide-open, and that it may well include vehement, caustic, and sometimes unpleasantly sharp attacks on government and public officials." The Court also reasoned that sometimes the press would veer away from reporting on important matters if it could be punished for every mistake: "That erroneous statement is inevitable in free debate, and that it must be protected if the freedoms of expression are to have the breathing space that they need to survive."

Which justices would have gone even farther than the majority in protecting the press in *Times v. Sullivan*?

Justices Hugo Black, William O. Douglas, and Arthur Goldberg would have given the press even more freedom under the First Amendment than the majority gave in *New York Times Co. v. Sullivan*. Justice Black wrote a concurring opinion that was joined by Douglas. Black expressed the view that the newspaper had "an absolute, unconditional constitutional right to publish in the *Times* advertisement their criticisms of the Montgomery agencies and officials." Black explained that the First Amendment flatly prohibited such libel suits: "In my opinion the Federal Constitution has dealt with this deadly danger to the press in the only way possible without leaving the free press open to destruction—by granting the press an absolute immunity for criticism of the way public officials do their public duty." Justice Goldberg also wrote a concurring opinion (which Douglas also joined) that expressed a view similar to Black: "In my view, the First and Fourteenth Amendments to the Constitution afford to the citizen and to the press an absolute, unconditional privilege to criticize official conduct despite the harm which may flow from excesses and abuses."

Why was the case so important for the **civil rights movement**?

The case was important for the civil rights movement because the Court's decision allowed the press to report on civil rights abuses without fear of being sued for every error. In his concurring opinion, Justice Hugo Black noted that there were eleven libel

> ## CourtSpeak: *New York Times Co. v. Sullivan* Freedom of the Press Case (1964)
>
> Justice William Brennan (majority): "A rule compelling the critic of official conduct to guarantee the truth of all his factual assertions—and to do so on pain of libel judgments virtually unlimited in amount—leads to a comparable self-censorship....
>
> "The constitutional guarantees require, we think, a federal rule that prohibits a public official from recovering damages for a defamatory falsehood relating to his official conduct unless he proves that the statement was made with actual malice—that is, with knowledge that it was false or with reckless disregard of whether it was false or not."

suits against the *New York Times* and five libel suits against CBS for reporting on similar civil rights abuses. Black wrote: "Moreover, this technique for harassing and punishing a free press—now that it has been shown to be possible—is by no means limited to cases with racial overtones; it can be used in other fields where public feelings may make local as well as out-of-state newspapers easy prey for libel verdict seekers."

How did the Warren Court **extend the ruling of *Times v. Sullivan*?**

The Warren Court expanded the libel law decision in *Times v. Sullivan* in the companion cases of *Curtis Publishing Co. v. Butts* and *Associated Press v. Walker* (1967). In these decisions, the Court ruled that public figures, in addition to public officials like L. B. Sullivan in the *Times* case, must prove actual malice in a defamation case. In his concurring opinion, Chief Justice Earl Warren wrote that "differentiation between 'public figures' and 'public officials' and adoption of separate standards of proof for each have no basis in law, logic, or First Amendment policy." This ruling makes it harder for celebrities and other people in the public eye to sue for libel.

The same year the Court extended the *Times v. Sullivan* rule to an invasion of privacy action in *Time, Inc. v. Hill*. The case involved a *Life* magazine article about the play *The Desperate Hours*. The play dramatized a family of four that showed great heroism while being held hostage by three convicts. The magazine article reported that the play was based on an ordeal suffered by James Hill and his family.

However, in the *Hill* incident, the perpetrators did not harm the Hill family. In the play, the convicts beat both the father and son and the daughter suffered a "verbal sexual insult." The Hills sued under a New York civil rights law protecting the right of privacy. Though the *Time v. Hill* case involved a New York statute, the case is cited for the proposition that plaintiffs suing for false-light invasion of privacy about matters of

307

public importance must meet the actual malice standard required in defamation cases involving public officials.

What decisions regarding the **freedom of association** also arose out of the civil rights movement?

In two decisions, the Warren Court protected the right of the National Association for the Advancement of Colored People (NAACP) to freely associate without governmental interference. In *NAACP v. Alabama* (1958), the Court ruled that the state of Alabama could not compel the NAACP to release its membership list. The Court wrote that "privacy in group association may in many circumstances be indispensable to preservation of freedom of association, particularly where a group espouses dissident beliefs." In *NAACP v. Button* (1963), the Court struck down a Virginia law that prohibited organizations from seeking out people to file lawsuits. The state had attempted to use the law to prohibit the NAACP from finding persons to be plaintiffs in racial discrimination suits. The Court wrote that the NAACP's litigation tactics were "modes of expression and association protected by the First Amendment." The *Button* case ensured the survival of public interest law firms, which often seek clients to advance certain causes through litigation.

What Warren Court decisions involved **freedom of assembly or petition during the civil rights movement**?

The Warren Court decided many cases that protected the First Amendment rights of those participating in the civil rights movement. The First Amendment provided the constitutional tool by which aggrieved individuals were able to assemble together to protest injustices and petition the government to change such unjust laws. These decisions included:

Garner v. Louisiana (1961): The U.S. Supreme Court reverses the breach-of-peace convictions of several African American students who had engaged in "sit-ins" at restaurants that would serve only white customers.

Edwards v. South Carolina (1963): The U.S. Supreme Court reverses the breach-of-the-peace convictions of 187 African American students who marched on the South Carolina statehouse in Columbia to protest segregation. The students were arrested even though they only sang religious and patriotic songs. The Court wrote that "the Fourteenth Amendment does not permit a state to make criminal the peaceful expression of unpopular views."

Shuttlesworth v. City of Birmingham (1965): The U.S. Supreme Court reversed the conviction of civil rights activist Fred Shuttlesworth, who did nothing more than stand on a public sidewalk with several other individuals outside a department store in Birmingham.

Cox v. Louisiana (1965): The U.S. Supreme Court reversed the conviction of a civil rights protester who was punished for leading a group of two thousand persons who picketed across the street from a courthouse to protest the illegal arrest of twenty-three students.

Adderley v. Florida (1966): The U.S. Supreme Court upholds the trespass convictions of thirty-two college students who demonstrated outside a county jail to protest the arrest of some of their classmates.

Shuttlesworth v. City of Birmingham (1969): The U.S. Supreme Court reverses another conviction of Shuttlesworth for violation of a Birmingham law that made it a crime to participate in a parade or march on city streets without first obtaining a permit.

Gregory v. City of Chicago (1969): The U.S. Supreme Court reverses the disorderly conduct conviction of activist/comedian Dick Gregory, who led a procession down city streets while advocating for school desegregation.

What civil rights activist was a **successful challenger in two separate cases**?

The Rev. Fred Shuttlesworth prevailed in two U.S. Supreme Court cases in 1965 and 1969. Both cases dealt with Birmingham, Alabama, city ordinances that police applied in order to limit Shuttlesworth's protest activities. Shuttlesworth challenged segregation even in the face of a house bombing, numerous arrests, and other threats. He still campaigns for racial justice as a minister in Cincinnati, Ohio.

Which civil rights activist successfully challenged a **state legislature that sought to expel him for his critical speech**?

Julian Bond, a longtime official in the National Association for the Advancement of Colored People (NAACP), successfully challenged the Georgia state legislature, which sought to exclude him from the state congress because of his critical comments of U.S. involvement in Vietnam. In June 1965, Bond was elected to the Georgia House of Representatives. However, Bond's congressional colleagues voted 184–12 to exclude him from taking his seat. They opposed Bond because of statements such as: "I think it is sort of hypocritical for us to maintain that we are fighting for liberty in other places and we are not guaranteeing liberty to citizens inside the continental United States."

Bond's case reached the U.S. Supreme Court, which ruled in his favor. "The manifest function of the First Amendment in a representative government requires that legislators be given the widest latitude to express their views on issue of policy," Chief Justice Earl Warren wrote in *Bond v. Floyd* (1966). "Just as erroneous statements must be protected to give freedom of expression the breathing space it needs to survive, so statements criticizing public policy and the implementation of it must be similarly protected."

How did the Warren Court deal with **incitement**?

The Warren Court ruled in its 1969 decision *Brandenburg v. Ohio* that the First Amendment protects even the advocacy of illegal conduct unless that advocacy incites imminent lawless action and is likely to bring about such illegal conduct. The case involved Ku Klux Klan leader Clarence Brandenburg, who spoke at a Klan rally on a farm in Hamilton County, Ohio. He said: "We're not a revengent organization, but if our President, our Congress, our Supreme Court, continues to suppress the white, Caucasian race, it's possible that there might have to be some revengeance." Officials charged Brandenburg with violating a state criminal syndicalism law. The U.S. Supreme Court reversed Brandenburg's conviction, finding that the Ohio law violated the First Amendment.

What test did the Warren Court create to evaluate restrictions on conduct that has expressive and non-expressive elements?

The Warren Court created such a test in its 1968 decision *United States v. O'Brien*. The case involved the prosecution of David Paul O'Brien for burning his draft card on the steps of a Boston courthouse. A federal law prohibited the knowing mutilation of draft cards. O'Brien countered that he had a First Amendment right to express his political beliefs and opposition to the Vietnam War. The Court established the following test, later called the O'Brien test:

> Whatever imprecision inheres in these terms, we think it clear that a government regulation is sufficiently justified if it is within the constitutional power of the Government; if it furthers an important or substantial governmental interest; if the governmental interest is unrelated to the suppression of free expression; and if the incidental restriction on alleged First Amendment freedoms is no greater than is essential to the furtherance of that interest.

The Court applied this test to determine that O'Brien's conviction did not violate his First Amendment rights. "The governmental interest and the scope of the 1965 Amendment are limited to preventing harm to the smooth and efficient functioning of the Selective Service System," the Court wrote.

A group of men burn their draft cards in 1968 to protest U.S. involvement in the Vietnam War. The Supreme Court ruled in *United States v. O'Brien* (1968) that the conviction of a man for burning his draft card did not violate his free speech rights. *Hulton Archive/Getty Images.*

What did the Warren Court rule with respect to **burning the American flag**?

The Warren Court did not rule specifically on whether the physical act of burning the flag was a form of free expression under the First Amendment. The Court did reverse the conviction of Sidney Street for burning an American flag in New York. Street burned his flag after learning that civil rights activist James Meredith had been shot in Mississippi. Street allegedly said while burning the flag: "We don't need no damn flag" and "If they let that happen to Meredith, we don't need no damn flag." Authorities charged Street under a state law that criminalized defying or "casting contempt" upon the flag by words.

In *Street v. New York* (1969), the U.S. Supreme Court reversed the conviction, finding that the law violated the First Amendment "because it permitted him to be punished merely for speaking defiant or contemptuous words about the American flag." The Court added that "it is firmly settled that under our Constitution the public expression of ideas may not be prohibited merely because the ideas are themselves offensive to some of their hearers."

How did Chief Justice **Warren rule in the flag-burning case**?

Chief Justice Earl Warren dissented in *Street v. New York*. Warren believed that the record in the case established that Street was tried for his physical act of burning the

311

French actress Jeanne Moreau appeared in the film *Les Amants* (The Lovers), the source of the Supreme Court trial *Jacobellis v. Ohio. Hulton Archive/Getty Images.*

flag, not for his words casting disrespect upon the flag. Warren also wrote that the physical act of burning the flag is not protected by the First Amendment: "I believe that the States and the Federal Government do have the power to protect the flag from acts of desecration and disgrace."

What did the Warren Court rule with respect to **"true threats"**?

The U.S. Supreme Court ruled in *Watts v. United States* (1969) that true threats are not entitled to First Amendment protection. However, the Court reversed the conviction of Robert Watts because it found that his statements amounted to mere "political hyperbole." Watts was prosecuted because he allegedly said at a protest: "I am not going. If they ever make me carry a rifle the first man I want to get in my sights is L.B.J. They are not going to make me kill my black brothers." For this statement, Watts was charged and convicted of threatening the president of the United States (who, at the time, was Lyndon B. Johnson). The Court agreed with Watts that his statement was "a kind of very crude offensive method of stating political opposition to the President."

How did the Warren Court deal with **obscenity and the First Amendment**?

The Warren Court ruled in *Roth v. United States* (1957) that obscenity was a category of expression not entitled to First Amendment protection. Writing for the majority, Justice William Brennan reasoned that "obscenity is not within the area of constitutionally protected speech or press." He noted that for years, many states had passed laws outlawing obscene material. However, the difficult task was fashioning a test that judges could use to distinguish unprotected obscenity from sexual expression deserving of protection. In *Roth,* Brennan fashioned the following test: "whether to the average person, applying contemporary community standards, the dominant theme of the material taken as a whole appeals to prurient interest." In later cases, the Warren Court modified its test for obscenity to include three parts: (1) whether the dominant theme of the material appeals to the prurient interest; (2) whether the material is patently offensive; and (3) whether the material is utterly without redeeming social value.

Which justice wrote that **he couldn't define obscenity but "I know it when I see it"**?

Justice Potter Stewart wrote in a concurring opinion in *Jacobellis v. Ohio* (1964): "I shall not today attempt further to define the kinds of material I understand to be embraced within that shorthand description; and perhaps I could never succeed in intelligibly doing so. But I know it when I see it, and the motion picture involved in this case is not that." The movie in question was a French drama film entitled *Les Amants* (meaning *The Lovers*), featuring French actress Jeanne Moreau. The phrase became one of the most well-known and oft-cited phrases in modern Supreme Court history. Stewart

U.S. Supreme Court justice Potter Stewart, in his famous concurring opinion in *Jacobellis v. Ohio,* said he could not define obscenity but "I know it when I see it." *Ed Clark/Time & Life Pictures/Getty Images.*

later regretted that his phrase became so popular, saying: "I think that's going to be on my tombstone."

In what decision did the Warren Court protect the movie *Lady Chatterley's Lover*?

The Warren Court ruled in *Kingsley International Pictures Corp. v. Regents of the University of New York* (1959) that New York state officials violated the First Amendment by refusing to grant a license for the distribution of the movie *Lady Chatterley's Lover.* The state argued that the film could be prohibited because it dealt with and even supported the immoral theme of adultery. The Supreme Court rejected the state's justification:

> What New York has done, therefore, is to prevent the exhibition of a motion picture because that picture advocates an idea—that adultery under certain circumstances may be proper behavior. Yet the First Amendment's basic guarantee is of freedom to advocate ideas. The State, quite simply, has thus struck at the very heart of constitutionally protected liberty.

In what decision did the Court rule against a **state motion picture censorship law** for failing to provide prompt judicial review?

The Warren Court invalidated a Maryland motion picture censorship law in *Freedman v. Maryland* (1965). The law required motion picture distributors to submit their movies for approval before they could be released. If the board rejected the film, then the dis-

313

Justice William Brennan (unanimous): "By dispensing with any requirement of knowledge of the contents of the book on the part of the seller, the ordinance tends to impose a severe limitation on the public's access to constitutionally protected matter. For if the bookseller is criminally liable without knowledge of the contents, and the ordinance fulfills its purpose, he will tend to restrict the books he sells to those he has inspected; and thus the State will have imposed a restriction upon the distribution of constitutionally protected as well as obscene literature.... 'Every bookseller would be placed under an obligation to make himself aware of the contents of every book in his shop. It would be altogether unreasonable to demand so near an approach to omniscience.' And the bookseller's burden would become the public's burden, for by restricting him the public's access to reading matter would be restricted. If the contents of bookshops and periodical stands were restricted to material of which their proprietors had made an inspection, they might be depleted indeed."

tributor bore the costs of a time-consuming appeal. There was no guarantee that the Court would issue a decision in a timely manner. The Warren Court believed this state motion picture law constituted an invalid prior restraint on expression. The Court established certain procedural safeguards that had to be followed, including that the government censor bears the burden of proof that the film is not protected by the First Amendment and that the licensing scheme must assure a "prompt final judicial decision."

What decision **prohibited imposing strict liability on booksellers for the contents of books**?

The Warren Court ruled in *Smith v. California* that the First Amendment prohibits imposing criminal liability on booksellers unless they actually know that the material is obscene. The Court ruled that it was unreasonable to require booksellers to know the contents of every book that they sell.

How did the Warren Court justify **limiting the First Amendment rights of broadcasters**?

The Warren Court ruled in *Red Lion Broadcasting Co. v. FCC* (1969) that the First Amendment rights of broadcasters should be limited because of the scarcity of broadcast frequencies. This is known as the scarcity rationale. The idea is that if the government does not license and control broadcast frequencies, then the public will be bombarded by different, competing frequencies that will interfere with each other signals.

CourtSpeak: *Tinker v. Des Moines Independent Community School District* First Amendment Rights Case (1969)

Justice Abe Fortas (majority): "First Amendment rights, applied in light of the special characteristics of the school environment, are available to teachers and students. It can hardly be argued that either students or teachers shed their constitutional rights to freedom of speech or expression at the schoolhouse gate....

"In our system, state-operated schools may not be enclaves of totalitarianism. School officials do not possess absolute authority over their students. Students in school as well as out of school are 'persons' under our Constitution. They are possessed of fundamental rights which the State must respect, just as they themselves must respect their obligations to the State. In our system, students may not be regarded as closed-circuit recipients of only that which the State chooses to communicate. They may not be confined to the expression of those sentiments that are officially approved. In the absence of a specific showing of constitutionally valid reasons to regulate their speech, students are entitled to freedom of expression of their views."

Justice Hugo Black (dissenting): "The Court's holding in this case ushers in what I deem to be an entirely new era in which the power to control pupils by the elected 'officials of state supported public schools' in the United States is in ultimate effect transferred to the Supreme Court.... And I repeat that if the time has come when pupils of state-supported schools, kindergartens, grammar schools, or high schools, can defy and flout orders of school officials to keep their minds on their own schoolwork, it is the beginning of a new revolutionary era of permissiveness in this country fostered by the judiciary."

"Without government control, the medium would be of little use because of the cacophony of competing voices, none of which could be clearly and predictably heard," the Court wrote. "It would be strange if the First Amendment, aimed at protecting and furthering communications, prevented the Government from making radio communication possible by requiring licenses to broadcast and by limiting the number of licenses so as not to overcrowd the spectrum."

How did the Warren Court **expand public employee First Amendment rights**?

The Warren Court ruled in its 1968 decision *Pickering v. Board of Education* that school district officials in Will County, Illinois, violated the First Amendment rights of public school teacher Marvin Pickering when they fired him for writing a letter to a local newspaper criticizing the school district's allocation of finances. The Court ruled that "a teacher's exercise of his right to speak on issues of public importance may not furnish the basis for his dismissal from public employment." The Court created the *Pickering* test which provides that public employees' right to speak on matters of public concern must be weighed against a public employer's efficiency interests.

What did the Warren Court do for **students' First Amendment rights?**

The Warren Court protected public school students' First Amendment rights in its 1969 decision *Tinker v. Des Moines Independent Community School District.* The Court ruled that Des Moines, Iowa, public school officials violated the free-expression rights of several students when they suspended them for wearing black armbands to protest U.S. involvement in the Vietnam War. School officials singled out black armbands as forbidden symbols, allowing students to wear other symbols such as iron crosses. The Court ruled 7–2 that the students' act of wearing the black armbands was a form of symbolic speech "akin" to pure speech. The case also established the *Tinker* standard, which provides that school officials cannot censor student expression unless they can reasonably forecast that it will create a substantial disruption of school activities or invade the rights of others.

FREEDOM OF RELIGION

What did the Warren Court say about **government-sponsored prayer in public schools**?

The Warren Court ruled that teacher-led prayer in public schools violated the Establishment Clause of the First Amendment, which is designed to ensure a degree of separation between church and state. The Court first reached this conclusion in its 1962 decision *Engel v. Vitale.* The court dealt with a New York Board of Regents prayer that read: "Almighty God, we acknowledge our dependence upon Thee, and we beg Thy blessings upon us, our parents, our teachers, and our Country."

"The New York laws officially prescribing the Regents' prayer are inconsistent both with the purposes of the Establishment Clause and with the Establishment Clause itself," Justice Hugo Black wrote for the Court majority. "It is neither sacrilegious nor antireligious to say that each separate government in this country should stay out of the business of writing or sanctioning official prayers and leave that purely religious function to the people themselves and to those the people choose to look to for religious guidance."

The Court reached a similar ruling in the companion cases *School District of Abington Township v. Schempp* and *Murray v. Curlett* (1963). These cases came from the states of Pennsylvania and Maryland respectively. The Pennsylvania law required the reading of ten Bible verses a day. The Maryland law required the reading of a sec-

> ## CourtSpeak: *Abington Township v. Schempp*
> ## Prayer in Schools Case (1963)
>
> Justice Tom C. Clark (majority): "We cannot accept that the concept of neutrality, which does not permit a State to require a religious exercise even with the consent of the majority of those affected, collides with the majority's right to free exercise of religion. While the Free Exercise Clause clearly prohibits the use of state action to deny the rights of free exercise to anyone, it has never meant that a majority could use the machinery of the State to practice its beliefs."

tion from the Bible or the Lord's Prayer. The school district defendants argued that the prayer exercises advanced the secular purposes of promoting morality, contradicting a "materialistic trend" in society and teaching literature. The Court invalidated both state laws, describing them as "religious exercises ... in violation of the command of the First Amendment that the Government maintain strict neutrality, neither aiding nor opposing religion."

Did the Supreme Court say the **Bible could not be discussed in public schools**?

No, the Court did not rule that the Bible was banned from public schools. Popular opposition to the Supreme Court grew after the school prayer decisions, as some alleged that the Court had "kicked God out of the public schools." However, a close reading of the Court's *Abington Township* decision reveals the opposite. Justice Tom C. Clark explained:

> It might well be said that one's education is not complete without a study of comparative religion or the history of religion and its relationship to the advancement of civilization. It certainly may be said that the Bible is worthy of study for its literary and historic qualities. Nothing we have said here indicates that such study of the Bible or of religion, when presented objectively as part of a secular program of education, may not be effected consistently with the First Amendment.

Who was the Warren Court's **only justice to dissent in the school prayer decisions**?

Justice Potter Stewart was the lone dissenter in both *Engel v. Vitale* and *Abington School District v. Schempp.* He explained his view in *Engel:* "With all respect, I think the Court has misapplied a great constitutional principle. I cannot see how an 'official religion' is established by letting those who want to say a prayer say it. On the contrary, I think that to deny the wish of these school children to join in reciting this prayer is to deny them the opportunity of sharing in the spiritual heritage of our Nation."

317

How did the Warren Court protect the **free exercise of individuals' religion rights**?

In *Sherbert v. Verner* (1963), the Warren Court ruled 7–2 in favor of Seventh Day Adventist Adele Sherbert, who was denied unemployment compensation by South Carolina officials for refusing to work on her Sabbath day of Saturday. The state courts rejected Sherbert's free-exercise claims, finding that she could still practice her religious faith. The U.S. Supreme Court reversed, writing that the state rulings infringed her religious liberty rights and that the state could not justify such an infringement by a compelling state interest. "Significantly, South Carolina expressly saves the Sunday worshipper from having to make the kind of choice which we here hold infringes the Sabbatarian's religious liberty," the Court explained. The state had argued that the denial of benefits was justified because the state had a compelling interest in preventing fraudulent claims. The U.S. Supreme Court ruled that the state had failed to carry its burden of showing a danger of such claims.

What did the Warren Court say about **Sunday closing laws**?

The Warren Court upheld the constitutionality of Sunday closing laws or Sunday blue laws in a pair of 1961 decisions: *McGowan v. Maryland* and *Braunfeld v. Brown.* In *McGowan,* the Court determined that such a law did not violate the Establishment Clause of the First Amendment by preferring the Christian Sabbath day of Sunday. Instead, the Court reasoned that the closing laws had a valid, secular purpose—to provide a day of rest for everyone in the community. In *Braunfeld,* the Court ruled that a closing law did not violate the free-exercise rights of Orthodox Jews who shut their businesses down on their Sabbath day of Saturday and then were forced to shut down Sundays as well. Chief Justice Earl Warren wrote that the closing law "does not make unlawful any religious practices" and "simply regulates a secular activity."

What did the Warren Court rule about the **evolution/creationism controversy**?

The Warren Court struck down an Arkansas law that forbade the teaching of evolution in public schools. The Court wrote in *Epperson v. Arkansas* (1968) that the law violated the Establishment Clause because it was passed for religious reasons. "The State's undoubted right to prescribe the curriculum for its public schools does not carry with it the right to prohibit, on pain of criminal penalty, the teaching of a scientific theory or doctrine where that prohibition is based upon reasons that violate the First Amendment," Justice Abe Fortas wrote for the Court.

What did the Warren Court rule with respect to the **power of eminent domain**?

The Warren Court gave a relatively broad interpretation of the power of eminent domain in *Berman v. Parker* (1954). The case involved a challenge to the District of Columbia Redevelopment Act of 1945. Under this law, Congress gave D.C. officials the

CourtSpeak: *Berman v. Parker* Power of Eminent Domain Case (1954)

Justice William O. Douglas (unanimous): "We do not sit to determine whether a particular housing project is or is not desirable. The concept of the public welfare is broad and inclusive. The values it represents are spiritual as well as physical, aesthetic as well as monetary. It is within the power of the legislature to determine that the community should be beautiful as well as healthy, spacious as well as clean, well-balanced as well as carefully patrolled. In the present case, the Congress and its authorized agencies have made determinations that take into account a wide variety of values. It is not for us to reappraise them. If those who govern the District of Columbia decide that the Nation's Capital should be beautiful as well as sanitary, there is nothing in the Fifth Amendment that stands in the way....

"Here one of the means chosen is the use of private enterprise for redevelopment of the area. Appellants argue that this makes the project a taking from one businessman for the benefit of another businessman. But the means of executing the project are for Congress and Congress alone to determine, once the public purpose has been established.... We cannot say that public ownership is the sole method of promoting the public purposes of community redevelopment projects."

power to condemn land and sell it to private developers under the auspices of urban renewal. The owners of a department store in an area subject to condemnation contended that the government violated their Fifth Amendment rights to their property by taking their land. The Warren Court determined that there was no Fifth Amendment violation, ruling that "it is within the power of the legislature to determine that the community should be beautiful as well as healthy." The challengers contended that the legislature cannot take land from one private landowner and give it to another private landowner. However, the Court determined that as long as the transfer served a "public purpose," there was no constitutional violation.

What was Chief Justice **Warren's last opinion for the Court**?

Chief Justice Earl Warren's last opinion for the Court was *Powell v. McCormack,* delivered June 16, 1969. The case concerned the constitutionality of the U.S. House of Representatives' action in expelling controversial African American New York congressman Adam Clayton Powell. Warren wrote that Congress did not have the constitutional power to exclude Powell from Congress when he had been elected by his constituents and met the qualifications for congressional membership mentioned in Article I, Section 2, of the Constitution. Warren explained: "A fundamental principle of our representative democracy is, in [Alexander] Hamilton's words, 'that the people should choose whom they please to govern them.'"

THE BURGER COURT (1969–86)

Which **justices served on the Burger Court**?

Thirteen justices served on the Burger Court, from 1969 to 1986: Chief Justice Warren Burger and Justices Hugo Black, William Douglas, John Marshall Harlan, Byron White, Potter Stewart, William Brennan, Thurgood Marshall, Harry Blackmun, Lewis Powell, William Rehnquist, John Paul Stevens, and Sandra Day O'Connor.

What was unique about **changes on the Burger Court**?

The Burger Court is the only collection of justices in Supreme Court history (not including the new-in-2005 Roberts Court) in which changes on the bench resulted *only* from the retirement of a justice. Every other Court from the Marshall Court to the Rehnquist Court had justices who died while still serving on the bench.

What **technological advances** occurred during the Burger Court era?

During the Burger Court era, the Court saw many technological advances. When Burger became chief justice, the Court had only one photocopying machine and the justices still used carbon paper to circulate their opinions to each other. Burger changed that by obtaining more copiers, leading to the justices providing each other with photocopies of their draft opinions. In 1981, Burger Court justices also obtained their first personal computers.

What were some of the **administrative programs** that were developed during the Burger Court era?

Warren Burger was known to spend many hours fulfilling his duties as the chief of the federal judiciary. Under his watch, the Institute for Court Management (1970), the

U.S. Supreme Court chief justice Warren Burger. *Robert S. Oakes/Library of Congress.*

National Institute for State Courts (1971), and the National Institute for Correction (1974) were established. In 1973, Burger founded the Supreme Court Fellows program, which allows talented individuals to work for the Court, the Federal Judicial Center, and the Administrative Office of the Courts for one year.

What was the **prior legal experience for Warren Burger** before ascending to the U.S. Supreme Court?

After graduating from night law school at St. Paul College of Law (now William Mitchell College of Law) in 1931, Burger entered private practice. He worked at a law firm in St. Paul for more than twenty years, from 1931 to 1953. In 1953, he entered public service as an assistant U.S. attorney general in charge of the Claims Division. In 1956, he was nominated to the U.S. Court of Appeals for the District of Columbia, often considered the "second" highest court in America behind the U.S. Supreme Court. In 1969, he replaced the retiring Earl Warren and became the nation's fifteenth chief justice of the U.S. Supreme Court.

Upon **retirement** from the Court, what did Warren Burger do?

After retirement, Burger continued his work as chairman of the Commission on Bicentennial of the Constitution. Appointed by President Ronald Reagan in July 1985, Burger served in that role until 1992. He died in 1995 at the age of 87.

Which **Burger Court justice faced an investigation** that could have led to impeachment?

Justice William O. Douglas faced heavy criticism, including a heated attack from House minority leader Gerald R. Ford, who later became vice president and president of the United States. Ford accused Douglas of endorsing revolution in the justice's book *Points of Rebellion*. Ford, a U.S. representative from Michigan, also criticized Douglas for serving as the president and a director of the Parvin Foundation, an institution named after casino businessman Albert Parvin that provided financial aid study in the United States for students from other countries. Ford sponsored a resolution in the House in April 1970 calling for Douglas's impeachment, contending that the Parvin Foundation had ties to the gambling world. The House judiciary committee set up a subcommittee to investigate the allegations against Douglas. The subcommittee filed a report that rejected the charges and vindicated Douglas.

H. Earl McBride published a book in 1971 entitled *Impeach Justice Douglas: Volume I: Subversion*. The author argued that Douglas supported "subversion, criminality and obscenity" in his opinions. Douglas survived these attacks and remained on the Court until his retirement in 1975, serving a record thirty-six years on the Court. The irony is that Douglas retired while Ford was president and Ford got to name his replacement—Justice John Paul Stevens.

The *Roe v. Wade* trial of 1973, which allowed women the right to terminate a pregnancy, has long been the source of controversy. These demonstrators in 1989 made their opinions clear when *Webster v. Reproductive Health Services* threatened to overturn *Roe v. Wade*. *Cynthia Johnson/Time & Life Pictures/Getty Images.*

What **book exposed some of the inner workings** of the early Burger Court?

Watergate reporter Bob Woodward and Scott Armstrong, a senior investigator for the Senate Watergate Committee, published a book entitled *The Brethren: Inside the Supreme Court* (1979) that examined the inner workings of the Burger Court from 1969 to 1976. The authors obtained some of their information from interviews with former Supreme Court law clerks and court personnel. The book painted an unflattering portrait of Chief Justice Burger, depicting him as pompous, ineffective, and manipulative. It charged him with withholding his initial vote in a case in order to make sure he was in the majority and could assign the majority opinion. It also quotes him as saying he would never hire a female law clerk and for saying to a fellow justice: "We are the Supreme Court and we can do what we want." The book reveals that other justices had a low opinion of the quality of Burger's opinions and his intellect.

COURT DECISIONS

What did the Court decide in *Roe v. Wade?*

The Burger Court ruled 7–2 in *Roe v. Wade* (1973) that the "Fourteenth Amendment's concept of personal liberty … is broad enough to encompass a woman's decision

> ## CourtSpeak: *Roe v. Wade* and *Doe v. Bolton* Abortion Cases (1973)
>
> Justice Byron White (dissenting in both cases): "I find nothing in the language or history of the Constitution to support the Court's judgment. The Court simply fashions and announces a new constitutional right for pregnant mothers and, with scarcely any reason or authority for its action, invests that right with sufficient substance to override most existing state abortion statutes. The upshot is that the people and the legislatures of the fifty states are constitutionally disentitled to weigh the relative importance of the continued existence and development of the fetus, on the one hand, against a spectrum of possible impacts on the mother, on the other hand. As an exercise of raw judicial power, the Court perhaps has authority to do what it does today; but in my view its judgment is an improvident and extravagant exercise of the power of judicial review that the Constitution extends to this Court."

whether or not to terminate her pregnancy." The Fourteenth Amendment's Due Process Clause generally protects individuals' rights to "life, liberty and property" from state interference. According to the Court, the meaning of "liberty" in the Due Process Clause includes a woman's personal, qualified right to have an abortion. The Court did not rule that women have an unfettered, or free, constitutional right to decide whether to have an abortion. Rather, Justice Harry Blackmun's opinion balanced a woman's interest in personal privacy against the state's interest in protecting future life. Blackmun's opinion divided the pregnancy term into three periods, or trimesters. During the first trimester, women have an unqualified right to have an abortion. During the second trimester, the state can regulate abortions "in ways that are reasonably related to maternal health." During the last trimester—when the fetus becomes viable or able to live outside the mother's womb—the state can regulate and even prohibit abortions. The Court also determined that a fetus was not a person within the meaning of the Fourteenth Amendment.

The Court's decision invalidated a Texas law that criminalized abortions except when the abortion was necessary to save the life of the mother.

Who wrote the Court's opinion in *Roe v. Wade?*

Harry Blackmun, who formerly served as counsel to the prestigious Mayo Clinic, wrote the Court's decision in *Roe v. Wade*. Blackmun received countless letters over the years, both praising and criticizing him for his part in the Court's historic opinion. At a news conference held upon his retirement, Blackmun reflected on the decision: "I think it was right in 1973, and I think it was right today. It's a step that had to be taken as we go down the road toward the full emancipation of women."

Norma McCorvey, a.k.a. Jane Roe of *Roe v. Wade*.
Cynthia Johnson/Time & Life Pictures/Getty Images.

Which **two justices dissented in** *Roe v. Wade?*

The two dissenting justices were Byron White and William Rehnquist. White criticized the majority for an "improvident and extravagant exercise of the power of judicial review." Rehnquist wrote that he had "difficulty in concluding, as the Court does, that the right of privacy is involved in this case."

Who were **"Roe" and "Wade"** in *Roe v. Wade?*

"Jane Roe" was Norma Jane McCorvey, an unmarried carnival worker in Dallas, Texas, who believed that she could not afford to raise another child. She was only twenty-one years old when she filed her lawsuit. She was pregnant for the third time. She later wrote a book entitled *I Am Roe: My Life, Roe v. Wade, and Freedom of Choice* in which she described her role in the lawsuit. Ironically, in the late 1990s, Roe switched sides and became a vocal critic of abortion. She started a pro-life ministry called Roe No More, located in Dallas.

Henry Wade was the district attorney for Dallas County, Texas. Roe named him as the lead defendant because he was the public official responsible for enforcing the abortion statute. Wade held the district attorney job for more than thirty-five years. He had achieved acclaim in 1963 and 1964 for successfully prosecuting Jack Ruby, the man convicted of killing Lee Harvey Oswald, the accused assassin of President John F. Kennedy. Wade died in 2001 at the age of eighty-six.

What was the Court's **other abortion case** decided the same day as *Roe v. Wade?*

The Court's other abortion decision decided on January 22, 1973, was *Doe v. Bolton*. The decision involved a constitutional challenge to Georgia's abortion statute. Georgia's statute prohibited abortions unless the pregnancy would endanger the health of the mother, would lead to a damaged fetus, or resulted from a rape. The Court's decision in *Roe* established that the Georgia statute was also unconstitutional. But, the Georgia statute also had several procedural requirements for abortions that the Court addressed in a separate opinion. These requirements included limiting abortions to residents of Georgia, requiring abortions to be done in licensed hospitals, and requiring advance approval by an abortion committee of three members of the hospital staff. The Court invalidated these procedural requirements as unduly restricting a woman's

right to obtain an abortion.

How did the Burger Court expand the reach of **federal antidiscrimination law**?

The Burger Court expanded the reach of Title VII of the Civil Rights Act of 1964—which prohibits employment discrimination on the basis of race, color, religion, sex, or national origin—by holding that the law applies to not only policies that on their face hurt certain groups, but also to policies neutral on their face that adversely impact certain groups. For example, an employer policy that says the employer will only hire white workers is discriminatory on its face. It is an example of disparate treatment, explicitly treating people differently based on race.

Henry Wade, the district attorney for Dallas County, Texas, and the lead defendant in *Roe v. Wade. Shelly Katz/Time & Life Pictures/Getty Images.*

On the other hand, an employer policy that says the employer will only hire workers who obtain a certain score on a test may disparately impact a certain group of people. This is an example of disparate impact discrimination.

Title VII clearly prohibits employers from intentionally discriminating against workers based on race. This is called disparate treatment discrimination. The key question facing the Supreme Court in *Griggs v. Duke Power Co.* (1971) was whether a facially neutral employer policy that applied across the board to all employees could be prohibited because it adversely impacted African American employees.

Duke Power Co., which previously had only hired African Americans for its lowest labor division, changed its employment policies after the passage of Title VII. Thereafter, Duke Power required employees to have a high school diploma or pass two intelligence tests before they could transfer to other divisions outside of labor in the company. Thirteen African American employees sued, claiming that Duke Power violated Title VII because its testing requirements created an adverse impact on them and the tests were not related to job performance.

In *Griggs,* the U.S. Supreme Court ruled 8–0 (Justice William Brennan did not participate in the case) that Duke Power violated Title VII by implementing test requirements that were not related to job performance.

Chief Justice Warren Burger wrote for the Court: "The Act [Title VII] proscribes not only overt discrimination but also practices that are fair in form, but discriminatory in operation. The touchstone is business necessity. If an employment practice which operates to exclude Negroes cannot be shown to be related to job performance, the practice is prohibited."

327

The Court noted that many white employees without a high school diploma had performed quite well in the job. The Court further noted that "neither the high school diploma completion requirement nor the general intelligence test is shown to bear a demonstrable relationship to successful performance of the jobs for which it was used." Employers bear the burden of proving that such requirements "have a manifest relationship to the employment in question."

The *Griggs* decision is significant because it stood for the proposition that Title VII prohibited disparate impact discrimination, that policies neutral on their face could still be unlawful if they negatively impacted certain groups of people.

Did the *Griggs* decision speak to **affirmative action or preferences for certain groups**?

The *Griggs* decision did not deal with affirmative action but certain passages in Chief Justice Warren Burger's decision have long been cited by those who disfavor affirmative action policies. Consider the following language from *Griggs:*

- "In short, the Act does not command that any person be hired simply because he was formerly the subject of discrimination, or because he is a member of a minority group. Discriminatory preference for any group, minority or majority, is precisely and only what Congress has proscribed."

- "Congress has not commanded that the less qualified be preferred over the better qualified simply because of minority origins. Far from disparaging job qualifications as such, Congress has made such qualifications the controlling factor, so that race, religion, nationality, and sex become irrelevant."

How did the Court explain what an **employment discrimination plaintiff must prove to establish a violation of Title VII**?

The Burger Court established a general three-part, burden-shifting test for employees and employers in Title VII disputes in *McDonnell Douglas Corp. v. Green* (1973). The three stages are (1) prima facie case; (2) legitimate nondiscriminatory reason; and (3) pretext.

First, an employee suing under Title VII must establish a prima facie, or basic, case of discrimination. The Court explained that in a failure-to-hire case based on race, the applicant must show: (i) that he or she belongs to a racial minority; (ii) that he or she applied for and was qualified for the position; (iii) that despite his or her qualifications, the employee was not hired; and (iv) that after rejecting the plaintiff, the employer kept seeking applications from other employees outside of the plaintiff's protected class.

If the employee or applicant establishes a prima facie case of race discrimination, the employer must articulate a legitimate, nondiscriminatory reason for rejecting the applicant. If the employer does present such a legitimate, nondiscriminatory reason for its action, then the burden shifts back to the employee to establish that the employer's supposed legitimate nondiscriminatory reason was pretextual or false.

This three-stage process is still referred to in American employment jurisprudence as the McDonnell Douglas test.

What happened in the *McDonnell Douglas* case?

Percy Green, an African American, worked for McDonnell Douglas for twelve years as a mechanic and laboratory technician. In 1964, he was laid off as part of a general reduction in force. Green, a civil rights activist, contended that the company's layoff policy was racially discriminatory. Green and other members of the Congress on Racial Equality (CORE) engaged in a "stall-in" by stalling their cars on the main roads leading to the entrance of the McDonnell Douglas plant. Another civil rights group of which Green was a leading member participated in a "lock-in" in which members padlocked the doors of McDonnell Douglas, thereby preventing employees from leaving. Shortly after these protest activities, Green applied for a mechanics position. He was not rehired. Green sued McDonnell Douglas, contending that the company refused to rehire him because of his race and participation in civil rights activities.

A federal court rejected his claim, finding that the company refused to rehire him for illegal demonstrations rather than legitimate civil rights activity. An appeals court reversed the decision, claiming that Green should have been afforded the opportunity to rebut the company's stated reason for rejecting him.

The U.S. Supreme Court unanimously ruled that Green should have been given "a fair opportunity to show that petitioner's [McDonnell Douglas] stated reason" for rejecting him was pretextual or false. The Court said that McDonnell Douglas could refuse to rehire a former employee who was engaged in disruptive acts, "but only if this criterion is applied alike to members of all races." The Court explained: "In short, on the retrial respondent [Green] must be given a full and fair opportunity to demonstrate by competent evidence that the presumptively valid reasons for his rejection were in fact a coverup for a racially discriminatory decision."

Did the Burger Court rule that **Title VII protected all races**?

Yes, the Burger Court ruled in *McDonald v. Santa Fe Trail Transportation Company* (1976) that the terms of Title VII "are not limited to discrimination against members of any particular race." The case involved claims by two white employees of a transportation company who were terminated for stealing cans of antifreeze. The white employees claimed discrimination because a black employee who also took the cans of antifreeze was not fired. The white employees claimed that its employer treated them worse because of their race. "While Santa Fe may decide that participation in a theft of cargo may render an employee unqualified for employment, this criterion must be

Demonstators march in New York City in protest of the U.S. Supreme Court's decision in *Regents of University of California v. Bakke* (1978). *AP Images.*

applied, alike to members of all races," the Court wrote.

In what case did the Burger Court first consider the **constitutionality of affirmative action**?

The Burger Court considered the constitutionality of an affirmative action program in *Regents of University of California v. Bakke* (1978). The case concerned the admissions policy at the medical school of the University of California at Davis. The UC Davis medical school had a policy that reserved sixteen of its one hundred seats for minority applicants. Allan Bakke, a white male rejected by the school in 1973 and 1974, sued the school, claiming that the school violated his rights under Title VI of the Civil Rights Act of 1964 and the Equal Protection Clause of the Fourteenth Amendment. Bakke's grade point average and MCAT scores were significantly higher than many minority candidates. The U.S. Supreme Court ruled 5–4 that the school's policy amounted to a quota. The Court determined that the school could not carry its burden of proving that Bakke would have been denied entrance without its "unlawful special admissions program."

Did the Court rule that an educational institution could not consider **race in its admissions policy**?

No, the U.S. Supreme Court also ruled 5–4 that a university has a compelling interest in achieving a diverse class and that race can be an important factor in reaching that goal. Justice Lewis Powell wrote that diversity "clearly is a constitutionally permissible

> ## *Regents of University of California v. Bakke* Affirmative Action Case (1978)
>
> Justice Lewis Powell (concurring): "The guarantee of equal protection cannot mean one thing when applied to one individual and something else when applied to a person of another color. If both are not accorded the same protection, it is not equal.... Preferring members of any one group for no reason other than race or ethnic origin is discrimination for its own sake. This the Constitution forbids."
>
> Harry Blackmun (dissenting): "I suspect it would be impossible to arrange an affirmative-action program in a racially neutral way and have it successful. To ask that this be so is to demand the impossible. In order to get beyond racism, we must first take account of race. There is no other way. And in order to treat some persons equally, we must treat them differently. We cannot—we dare not—let the Equal Protection Clause perpetuate racial supremacy."

goal for an institution of higher learning." He explained that a university constitutionally can institute an admissions policy where "race or ethnic background is simply one element in the selection process."

What was the **vote breakdown in the *Bakke* case**?

The U.S. Supreme Court ruled 5–4 that the UC Davis medical school policy was unconstitutional under the Equal Protection Clause and that Allen Bakke should be admitted. The U.S. Supreme Court also ruled 5–4 that race is a factor that can be considered in university admission programs. Justice Lewis Powell was the key swing vote on both major issues. Justices William Brennan, Byron White, Thurgood Marshall, and Harry Blackmun voted against Bakke and believed that race should be a factor in university admissions. Chief Justice Warren Burger, John Paul Stevens, Potter Stewart, and William Rehnquist voted for Bakke and argued that the Court should not consider the larger issue of whether race should be considered in university admissions.

What happened to **Allen Bakke**?

After prevailing in the U.S. Supreme Court, UC Davis admitted Bakke to its medical school. He graduated from the medical school in 1982. He then practiced as an anesthesiologist in Minnesota.

What did the Burger Court rule with respect to **busing in the desegregation of schools**?

Several of the Burger Court decisions dealt with how far and by what methods a school system must go in order to achieve desegregation of its public schools. In *Swann v.*

Allen Bakke (center) attends his first day at the Medical School of the University of California at Davis on September 25, 1978. The U.S. Supreme Court ruled in his favor in a reverse discrimination case after his application to medical school was rejected because he was white. *Walt Zeboski/AP Images.*

Charlotte-Mecklenburg Board of Education (1971), the Burger Court unanimously ruled that public school systems could use busing as a means of achieving the desegregation of public schools. "We find no basis for holding that the local school authorities may not be required to employ bus transportation as one tool of school desegregation," the Court wrote. "Desegregation plans cannot be limited to the walk-in school."

Some southern school districts contended that children should simply attend their neighborhood schools. However, the Court recognized that given the realities of segregated housing patterns, remaining in those schools might never lead to any real desegregation of the schools. Burger wrote in *Swann:*

> All things being equal, with no history of discrimination, it might well be desirable to assign pupils to schools nearest their homes. But all things are not equal in a system that has been deliberately constructed and maintained to enforce racial segregation. The remedy for such segregation may be administratively awkward, inconvenient, and even bizarre in some situations and may impose burdens on some; but all awkwardness and inconvenience cannot be avoided in the interim period when remedial adjustments are being made to eliminate the dual school systems.

In *Swann,* the Burger Court said that school authorities and district court judges should make sure that school constructions and closings do not operate in a way that reestablishes a dual school system. The goal in the school desegregation cases was for school systems to achieve unitary status.

The Court in *Swann* also noted that schools do not have to achieve the precise ratio of students by race found in the school system district wide. However, the Court said that it was within the equitable powers of district court judges to rely on "mathematical ratios."

Burger cautioned in his opinion that remedies must not exceed the court's equitable powers and that such remedial powers could be exercised "only on the basis of a constitutional violation."

To many school desegregation advocates, the *Swann* decision represented the high point of the Court's desegregation cases. The Court cut back on some of these rulings in later decisions, such as *Milliken v. Bradley* (1974) and *Pasadena Board of Education v. Spangler* (1976).

How did *Milliken v. Bradley* change the Court's direction on school desegregation?

The *Swann* case involved the desegregation of one school district in Charlotte, North Carolina. In the *Milliken* case, a federal district court overseeing the case had approved of plans to desegregate the Detroit school system by imposing a multidistrict remedy. The plan would call for many suburban students to be moved to Detroit city schools and vice versa. The federal district court had implemented a plan that would affect several school districts that had not participated in *de jure* (segregation by statute or law) segregationist practices. Supporters of the plan argued that it was necessary to involve the suburban districts to achieve real desegregation to counter the effects of "white flight," a phenomenon where many whites moved from larger cities to surrounding suburbs.

The U.S. Supreme Court ruled 5–4 in *Milliken v. Bradley* that the desegregation plan was invalid because it imposed burdens on school districts that were operating as unitary school systems and engaging in no racial segregation. Burger wrote that "without an interdistrict violation and interdistrict effect, there is no constitutional wrong calling for an interdistrict remedy." The ruling meant that many children in the suburbs did not have to be bused to the Detroit city schools and vice versa.

Did the Burger Court hold that **education was a fundamental right**?

No, the Burger Court ruled 5–4 in *San Antonio Independent School District v. Rodriguez* (1973) that there is no fundamental right of education in the Constitution. As such, the Court ruled that Texas's system of funding public schools by property taxes within individual districts was constitutional as long as it was rationally related to a legitimate state interest.

Demetrio Rodriguez had filed a class-action lawsuit challenging the Texas public school financing system on equal protection grounds. He argued that the system led to better education for students in wealthier districts and worse education for students in poorer districts.

In his majority opinion, Justice Lewis Powell wrote that "it is not the province of this Court to create substantive constitutional rights in the name of guaranteeing equal protection of the laws." The Court concluded that the Texas plan of funding school districts with local property taxes was rationally related to a legitimate state purpose. Four justices dissented, including Justice Thurgood Marshall, who wrote: "The majority's holding can only be seen as a retreat from our historic commitment to equality of educational opportunity and as unsupportable acquiescence in a system which deprives children in their earliest years of the chance to reach their full potential as citizens."

How did the Court rule with respect to **illegal aliens and public school education**?

The Burger Court ruled 5–4 in *Plyler v. Doe* (1982) that Texas must provide a free public education to "undocumented school-age children" (illegal aliens). Justice William Brennan, writing for the majority, reasoned that the Equal Protection Clause prohibits excluding such children from the public schools. The Equal Protection Clause provides that no state shall "deny to any person within its jurisdiction the equal protection of the laws." Brennan reasoned that "any person within its jurisdiction" included illegal aliens living in the state. He wrote that "denial of education to some isolated group of children poses an affront to one of the goals of the Equal Protection Clause: the abolition of governmental barriers preventing unreasonable obstacles to advancement on the basis of individual achievement."

Chief Justice Burger authored a stinging dissent, accusing the majority of legislating from the bench. He explained: "The Constitution does not constitute us as 'Platonic Guardians' nor does it vest in this Court the authority to strike down laws because they do not meet our standards of desirable social policy. We trespass on the assigned function of the political branches under our structure of limited and separated powers when we assume a policymaking role as the Court does today."

How did the Burger Court decide whether the IRS could deny **tax-exempt status for schools and universities that discriminate on the basis of race**?

The Burger Court ruled 8–1 in *Bob Jones University v. United States* (1983) that the Internal Revenue Service (IRS) policy denying tax-exempt status to schools and universities that discriminate on the basis of race was constitutional. In 1970, the IRS modified its regulations to deny tax-exempt status. Two schools—a college and a private Christian elementary and high school—filed separate lawsuits challenging the IRS policy. Bob Jones University, a South Carolina corporation that operated schooling from kindergarten through college and graduate school, forbade students from interracial dating and marriage. The university provided that those who married interracially, dated interracially, or encouraged others to do so would be expelled. Goldsboro Christian School generally admitted only Caucasian students. These schools contended that they met the regulatory definition of a tax-exempt organization. They also argued that they had a First Amendment free-exercise right to their religious beliefs that interracial associations were a sin.

The Supreme Court, in an opinion authored by Chief Justice Warren Burger, rejected the schools' position. The Court determined that the IRS regulations included the fundamental principle that institutions seeking tax-exempt status must act according to "established public policy." The Court cited the nation's commitment to eradicating racial discrimination as public policy of the highest order. The Court majority also reasoned that the IRS had the power to issue a new interpretation of its regulations. Finally, the Court also rejected both schools' First Amendment free-exercise of religion challenge. Burger wrote that the government's fundamental interest in eradicating racial discrimination "substantially outweighs whatever burden denial of tax benefits placed" on the schools in question.

Who was the **lone dissenter** in the *Bob Jones University* decision?

Justice William Rehnquist was the sole dissenter in this case, justifying his nickname "the Lone Ranger," which he earned for his solo dissenting opinions. Rehnquist agreed that the nation had a fundamental interest in opposing racial discrimination. However, he believed that any change in the IRS code denying tax-exempt status to these schools must come from Congress.

How did the Burger Court rule with respect to **gender discrimination**?

The Burger Court decided many gender discrimination cases. In *Reed v. Reed* (1971), the Court issued the first Supreme Court decision ever striking down a state law for discriminating against women. The case concerned an Idaho law that gave preference

The Burger Court poses with President Ronald Reagan. Seated are (left to right) Thurgood Marshall, William Brennan, Warren Burger, Reagan, Byron White, and Harry Blackmun. Standing are (left to right) John Paul Stevens, Lewis Powell, William Rehnquist, and Sandra Day O'Connor. *Diana Walker/Time & Life Pictures/Getty*

to males in the administration of estates. The unanimous Court, in an opinion written by Chief Justice Burger, reasoned that gender-based classifications must be reasonable and not arbitrary. "By providing dissimilar treatment for men and women who are thus similarly situated, the challenged section violates the Equal Protection Clause," he wrote. In *Frontiero v. Richardson* (1973), the Court struck down a federal law that assumed female wives of military servicemen were dependents but refused to assume that husbands of female servicewomen were dependents. The Court treated this distinction as a paternalistic assumption rooted in gender discrimination. Justice William Brennan wrote in his plurality opinion: "With these considerations in mind, we can only conclude that classifications based upon sex, like classifications based upon race, alienage, or national origin, are inherently suspect, and must therefore be subjected to strict judicial scrutiny."

The Court did not strike down all laws in which there were allegations of gender discrimination. In *Rostker v. Goldberg* (1981), the Court upheld a law that excluded women from the military draft. "The Constitution requires that Congress treat similarly situated persons similarly, not that it engage in gestures of superficial equality," the Court wrote.

What standard of review did the Burger Court eventually adopt for gender-based classifications?

In the *Reed* case (1971), the Court applied the rational basis standard of review, while in *Frontiero* (1973), the Court applied strict scrutiny, the highest form of judicial review. The Burger Court eventually adopted a mid-level form of review between rational basis and strict scrutiny. This mid-level form of review was called intermediate scrutiny. The Court adopted this standard in its 1976 decision *Craig v. Boren* and its 1982 decision *Mississippi University for Women v. Hogan. Craig v. Boren* involved an Oklahoma law that allowed the sale of 3.2% (alcohol) beer to women 18 years of age and older but to men 21 years of age and older. The Court invalidated this gender-based distinction. In *Mississippi University for Women v. Hogan,* the Court struck down a nursing school's rejection of male applicant Joe Hogan.

In what decision did the Court uphold a state sodomy law?

The Court ruled 5–4 in *Bowers v. Hardwick* (1986) that Georgia's antisodomy law was constitutional. Michael Hardwick, a gay man, had challenged the constitutionality of the law after police arrested him for violating the law. Though the prosecutor declined to press forward with the charges, Hardwick—with help from the American Civil Liberties Union—pursued a federal lawsuit against the law. The Court rejected Hardwick's challenges, ruling that there was no fundamental right to engage in homosexual sodomy. Justice Byron White wrote in his majority opinion that the law was subject only to a rational basis challenge and the law furthered the state's interests in upholding morality. He rejected the notion that because the law punishes sex acts between consenting adults in the privacy of homes, the law was invalid. He explained: "Plainly enough, otherwise illegal conduct is not always immunized whenever it occurs in the home. Victimless crimes, such as the possession and use of illegal drugs, do not escape the law when they are committed at home." In his concurring opinion, Chief Justice Burger wrote: "To hold that the act of homosexual sodomy is somehow protected as a fundamental right would be to cast aside millennia of moral teaching."

The Rehnquist Court later overruled *Bowers v. Hardick* in *Lawrence v. Texas* (2003).

CRIMINAL LAW AND PROCEDURE

How did the Burger Court rule on the **constitutionality of the death penalty**?

The Burger Court first ruled 5–4 in *Furman v. Georgia* (1972) that capital punishment was unconstitutional. The five justices in the majority joined in a one-paragraph, per curiam opinion. (A per curiam opinion is an opinion not signed by a particular justice but one that speaks for multiple justices.) All nine justices wrote separately, making the decision one of the longest in Supreme Court history. The *Furman* decision effectively ended capital punishment in America for more than four years.

The one-paragraph per curiam opinion stated: "The Court holds that the imposition and carrying out of the death penalty in these cases constitute cruel and unusual punishment in violation of the Eighth and Fourteenth Amendments." Justices William Douglas, William Brennan, and Thurgood Marshall broadly attacked the death penalty. Justice Douglas wrote that the states' death penalty laws were "pregnant with discrimination." Justices Brennan and Marshall reasoned that capital punishment inherently constituted cruel and unusual punishment. Brennan wrote that the death penalty was "condemned as fatally offensive to human dignity," while Marshall said it was "morally unacceptable."

Justices Potter Stewart and Byron White wrote narrower opinions, focusing on the fact that the state laws in question did not provide sufficient guidance to jurors in capital sentencing to determine who should live and who should die. Stewart captured this sentiment in oft-quoted language: "These death sentences are cruel and unusual in the same way that being struck by lightning is cruel and unusual."

Four justices dissented, including Chief Justice Warren Burger, who noted the long history of capital punishment: "In the 181 years since the enactment of the Eighth Amendment, not a single decision of this Court has cast the slightest shadow of a doubt on the constitutionality of capital punishment." Justice Harry Blackmun, who in 1994 reversed his position on the issue, emphasized that the imposition of the death penalty was a legislative, not a judicial, decision. According to Blackmun, state legislators—not federal judges—should decide whether a state has the ultimate pun-

CourtSpeak: *Furman v. Georgia* Death Penalty Case (1972)

Justice William Douglas (concurring): "These discretionary statutes are unconstitutional in their operation. They are pregnant with discrimination and discrimination is an ingredient not compatible with the idea of equal protection of the laws that is implicit in the ban on 'cruel and unusual' punishments."

Justice William Brennan (concurring): "Death is truly an awesome punishment. The calculated killing of a human being by the State involves, by its very nature, a denial of the executed person's humanity."

Justice Potter Stewart (concurring): "These death sentences are cruel and unusual in the same way that being struck by lightning is cruel and unusual."

Justice Byron White (concurring): "The death penalty is exacted with great infrequency even for the most atrocious crimes ... there is no meaningful basis for distinguishing the few cases in which it is imposed from the many cases in which it is not."

Justice Thurgood Marshall (concurring): "The death penalty is an excessive and unnecessary punishment that violates the Eighth Amendment.... It is morally unacceptable to the people of the United States at this time in their history."

Chief Justice Warren Burger (dissenting): "In the 181 years since the enactment of the Eighth Amendment, not a single decision of this Court has cast the slightest shadow of a doubt on the constitutionality of capital punishment. In rejecting Eighth Amendment attacks on particular modes of execution, the Court has more than once implicitly denied that capital punishment is impermissibly 'cruel' in the constitutional sense."

Justice Harry Blackmun (dissenting): "Athough personally I may rejoice at the Court's result, I find it difficult to accept or to justify as a matter of history, of law, or of constitutional pronouncement. I fear the Court has overstepped. It has sought and has achieved an end."

Justice Lewis Powell (dissenting): "In terms of the constitutional role of this Court, the impact of the majority's ruling is all the greater because the decision encroaches upon an area squarely within the historic prerogative of the legislative branch—both state and federal—to protect the citizenry through the designation of penalties for prohibitable conduct. It is the very sort of judgment that the legislative branch is competent to make and for which the judiciary is ill-equipped."

Justice William Rehnquist (dissenting): "The task of judging constitutional cases imposed by Art. III cannot for this reason be avoided, but it must surely be approached with the deepest humility and genuine deference to legislative judgement. Today's decision to invalidate capital punishment is ... significantly lacking in those attributes."

ishment. Justice Lewis Powell noted how the Court's dissent broke with long-standing precedent: "Today's departure from established precedent invalidates a staggering number of state and federal laws. The capital punishment laws of no less than 39 States and the District of Columbia are nullified." Justice William Rehnquist wrote in his dissent that the Supreme Court should exercise restraint and show deference to state legislators in this contentious area. He wrote that the majority decision "expand[ed] judicial authority beyond the limits contemplated by the Framers."

When did the Supreme Court rule the **death penalty constitutional** again?

The *Furman* decision caused many states to pass new death penalty statutes that would provide more guidance to jurors on whether a defendant should be sentenced to death. Georgia's new statute required jurors to focus on aggravating and mitigating factors associated with the capital crime. In 1976, the U.S.

In 1977, Gary Gilmore became the first person to be executed since the U.S. Supreme Court had ruled in 1972 in *Furman v. Georgia* that Georgia's death penalty had violated the Eighth Amendment. *Hulton Archive/Getty Images.*

Supreme Court ruled 7–2 that this Georgia law was constitutional in *Gregg v. Georgia*. Because it focused on these aggravating and mitigating factors, Justice Potter Stewart wrote: "No longer can a jury wantonly and freakishly impose the death sentence; it is always circumscribed by the legislative guidelines." Stewart wrote that the new statute focused the jury on "the particularized nature of the crime and the particularized characteristics of the individual defendant." Since *Gregg*, the U.S. Supreme Court has never ruled that the death penalty is per se unconstitutional.

Only Justices William Brennan and Thurgood Marshall dissented in *Gregg*. Brennan wrote: "Death is not only an unusually severe punishment, unusual in its pain, in its finality, and in its enormity, but it serves no penal purpose more effectively than a less severe punishment.... The fatal constitutional infirmity in the punishment of death is that it treats members of the human race as nonhumans, as objects to be toyed with and discarded." Marshall agreed in his dissent: "The death penalty, unnecessary to promote the goal of deterrence or to further any legitimate notion of retribution, is an excessive penalty forbidden by the Eighth and Fourteenth Amendments."

What is the **exclusionary rule** and how did the Burger Court limit it?

The exclusionary rule is a principle that holds that evidence seized in violation of the Fourth Amendment, which prohibits unreasonable searches and seizures, cannot be used to convict a defendant. In other words, the exclusionary rule excludes evidence that is illegally obtained. The famous saying attributed to Justice Benjamin N. Cardozo explained the exclusionary rule as "the criminal goes free because the constable has blundered." It was (and is) considered controversial because it sometimes means that a guilty person can go free.

The Burger Court limited the exclusionary rule in its 1984 decision *U.S. v. Leon* by holding that the rule would not apply when a police officer acted in reasonable good faith on the validity of a search warrant. The good faith exception provides that "evidence need not be suppressed when police obtain the evidence through objective good faith reliance on a facially valid warrant that later is found to lack probable cause." Under the Fourth Amendment, the police need probable cause to obtain a search warrant. The good-faith exception means that sometimes even if the search warrant was not backed by probable cause, the exclusionary rule will not apply and the evidence obtained through execution of the search warrant can be used at trial. The Court did not eliminate the exclusionary rule. The *Leon* exception applied to some search warrants that were found lacking in probable cause. The Court noted several exceptions to the good-faith exception, including: (1) where the magistrate issued the warrant based on a deliberately or recklessly false affidavit; (2) where the issuing magistrate failed to act in a neutral and detached manner; (3) where a warrant is based on an affidavit so lacking in evidence of probable cause as to render official belief in its existence entirely unreasonable; and (4) where a warrant is so devoid of information that the executing officers cannot reasonably presume it to be valid.

How did the Burger Court give police more discretion in the use of **confidential informant information**?

The Warren Court had decided a pair of cases, *Aguilar v. Texas* (1964) and *Spinelli v. United States* (1969) that made the warrant requirement tougher for police when they relied on confidential informants. Under the *Aguilar-Spinelli* test, an informant's tip can furnish probable cause for an arrest if the State establishes (1) the basis of the informant's information and (2) the credibility of the informant or the reliability of the informant's information.

The Burger Court changed this in its 1983 decision *Illinois v. Gates* when it abandoned the *Aguilar-Spinelli* test in favor of a more deferential totality of the circumstances test. Under this test, the Court wrote: "The task of the issuing magistrate is simply to make a practical, common-sense decision whether, given all the circumstances set forth in the affidavit before him, including the veracity and basis of knowledge of persons supplying hearsay information, there is a fair probability that contraband or evidence of a crime will be found in a particular place."

Major Death Penalty Decisions of the 1970s

*F*urman v. Georgia (1972): The U.S. Supreme Court rules 5–4 that Georgia's death penalty scheme violates the Eighth Amendment. Three justices in the majority attack the death penalty in general, while Justices Potter Stewart and Lewis Powell focus on the fact that the death penalty law does not give jurors sufficient guidance as to which capital defendants should receive the ultimate punishment. Stewart writes that "these death sentences are cruel and unusual in the same way that being struck by lightning is cruel and unusual." This ruling leads to a halt on all executions in the country until 1977.

Gregg v. Georgia (1976): The Court rules that some death penalty statutes are constitutional because they provide sufficient guidance to the jury in terms of aggravating and mitigating factors. The Court writes that "the concerns expressed in *Furman* that the penalty of death not be imposed in an arbitrary or capricious manner can be met by a carefully drafted statute that ensures that the sentencing authority is given adequate information and guidance."

Roberts v. Louisiana (1976): The Court strikes down a Louisiana statute that required the death penalty for defendants who kill police officers and did not allow those defendants to offer any mitigating factors.

Woodson v. North Carolina (1976): The Court strikes down a North Carolina statute that required the death penalty for all criminal defendants convicted of first-degree murder.

Gilmore v. Utah (1976): The Court rules that Utah inmate Gary Gilmore could waive his rights to appeal his death sentence. Gilmore wanted to be executed but his mother and his attorneys had filed petitions on his behalf. He becomes the first person (in 1977) executed in the United States since the *Furman* decision. His execution becomes memorialized in author Norman Mailer's *The Executioner's Song.*

Coker v. Georgia (1976): The Court rules that a sentence of death for rape is excessive punishment under the Eighth Amendment. The Court writes: "Rape is without doubt deserving of serious punishment; but in terms of moral depravity and of the injury to the person and to the public, it does not compare with murder."

Lockett v. Ohio (1978): The Court invalidates Ohio's death penalty statute because it restricts mitigating evidence during the sentencing phase. The Court writes: "The Eighth and Fourteenth Amendments require that the sentencer, in all but the rarest kind of capital case, not be precluded from considering, as a mitigating factor, any aspect of a defendant's character or record and any of the circumstances of the offense that the defendant proffers as a basis for a sentence less than death."

Major Death Penalty Decisions of the 1980s

Adams v. Texas (1980): The Court invalidates a Texas inmate's death sentence because the trial judge dismissed prospective jurors who said they would be "affected" by the possibility of imposing the death penalty. The Court writes that "a juror may not be challenged for cause based on his views about capital punishment unless those views would prevent or substantially impair the performance of his duties as a juror in accordance with his instructions and his oath."

Edmund v. Florida (1982): The Court rules that a defendant cannot be sentenced to death for participating in a felony that leads to murder if the defendant did not participate in the killing, attempt to kill, or intend for killing to take place.

Eddings v. Oklahoma (1982): The Court vacates the death sentence of an inmate, who was 16 years old at the time of the murder for which he was sentenced, because the trial court refused to allow his attorney to introduce mitigating factors, such as his turbulent family history, beatings by his father, and emotional problems.

California v. Ramos (1983): The Court rules that a California trial judge did not violate the constitutional rights of a criminal defendant by instructing the jury that the governor could commute a defendant's life sentence to a sentence with the possibility of parole.

Barclay v. Florida (1983): The Court rejects the claims of a Florida inmate who alleges his death sentence should be overturned because the trial judge allowed the jury to consider his criminal record as an aggravating factor.

Spaziano v. Florida (1984): The Court rules that a trial judge may sentence a criminal defendant to death even though a jury has recommended a life sentence. The Court writes that "the purpose of the death penalty is not frustrated

How did the Burger Court limit the Warren Court's *Miranda* decision?

The Burger Court never overruled *Miranda,* the famous 1966 Warren Court decision that established that the police must provide suspects with warnings—called Miranda warnings—before interrogating them. Under the Miranda decision, prosecutors cannot use incriminating statements given by criminal defendants when they were not told of their right not to incriminate themselves and right to have an attorney present during questioning. The Court issued the decision partly because of the problem of coerced confessions. However, the Burger Court created exceptions to it in several decisions. In *Harris v.*

New York (1971), the Court ruled that prosecutors can impeach defendants at trial with

by, or inconsistent with, a scheme in which the imposition of the penalty in individual cases is determined by a judge."

Strickland v. Washington (1984): The Court sets the standard for determining when a death sentence can be set aside for ineffective assistance of counsel. The Court writes that "the defendant must show that there is a reasonable probability that, but for counsel's unprofessional errors, the result of the proceeding would have been different."

Caldwell v. Mississippi (1985): The Court sets aside a Mississippi inmate's death sentence when the prosecutor told the jury that an appeals court would review its determination of life or death. The Court writes "it is constitutionally impermissible to rest a death sentence on a determination made by a sentencer who has been led to believe that the responsibility for determining the appropriateness of the defendant's death rests elsewhere."

Ford v. Wainwright (1986): The Court rules that the Eighth Amendment prohibits the execution of insane persons.

Darden v. Wainwright (1986): The Court rules that a prosecutor's improper comments during closing arguments in a death penalty case did not justify vacating the sentence. The Court writes that a sentence should be set aside based on a prosecutor's comments only when the comments "so infected the trial with unfairness as to make the resulting conviction a denial of due process."

Skipper v. South Carolina (1986): The Court sets aside a death sentence when the trial judge excluded as mitigating evidence the testimony of jailers regarding the good behavior of the defendant before his trial.

statements they previously made without receiving their Miranda warnings. The Court ruled that the *Miranda* decision should not be read as sanctioning perjury. In *Quarles v. New York* (1984), the Court created a public-safety exception to *Miranda* when police officers do not have time to deliver Miranda warnings. Then, in *Oregon v. Elstad* (1985), the Court ruled that an initial failure to deliver Miranda warnings does not prevent the use of confessions and admissions made after Miranda warnings have been given.

In what decision did the Burger Court allow individuals to **sue police officers for violations of constitutional rights**?

The Court ruled in *Bivens v. Six Unknown Agents* (1971) that individuals could sue federal government officials for violation of their constitutional rights. Agents of the Federal Bureau of Narcotics invaded the apartment of Webster Bivens and arrested

CourtSpeak: *Batson v. Kentucky*
"Purposeful Discrimination" Case (1986)

Justice Lewis Powell (majority): "The harm from discriminatory jury selection extends beyond that inflicted on the defendant and the excluded juror to touch the entire community. Selection procedures that purposefully exclude black persons from juries undermine public confidence in the fairness of our system of justice."

Justice Thurgood Marshall (concurring): "The decision today will not end the racial discrimination that peremptories inject into the jury-selection process. That goal can be accomplished only by eliminating peremptory challenges entirely."

Justice William Rehnquist (dissenting): "In my view, there is simply nothing 'unequal' about the State's using its peremptory challenges to strike black defendants, so long as such challenges are also used to exclude whites in cases involving white defendants, Hispanics in cases involving Hispanic defendants, Asians in cases involving Asian defendants and so on."

him in the presence of his wife and children. The agents allegedly threatened to arrest other members of the family. Agents searched his home for drugs. They then took him to a Brooklyn, New York, courthouse and subjected him to a strip search. They later released Bivens. He then filed a lawsuit, alleging a violation of his Fourth Amendment rights to be free from unreasonable searches and seizures. The U.S. Supreme Court ruled that Bivens could sue the federal officials for violating his Fourth Amendment rights. In legal terms, the Court ruled that Bivens had an implied private right of action. It is called an implied private right of action because the text of the Fourth Amendment does not say that an individual can sue the government when federal officials unlawfully search his home. The case established the right of individuals to bring "Bivens actions" when federal officials violate their constitutional rights.

In what decision did the U.S. Supreme Court expand the rights of criminal defendants to a **jury process free from discrimination**?

In *Swain v. Alabama* (1965), the Warren Court had ruled that removing jurors on the basis of race could constitute a violation of the Equal Protection Clause of the Fourteenth Amendment. However, the Court ruled that a criminal defendant would have to show a pattern of discriminatory jury strikes in case after case to establish a constitutional violation. This proved a nearly insurmountable hurdle for most defendants.

THE WHITE HOUSE

WASHINGTON

July 22, 1971

EYES ONLY

MEMORANDUM FOR: JOHN EHRLICHMAN

FROM: CHARLES COLSON

SUBJECT: Further on Pentagon Papers

As we discussed earlier this week I met today with Bud Krogh and reviewed with him what he has done to date and what his immediate plans are.

We both agreed that the major task at hand is to pull together all of the information that is available in Justice, Defense, CIA, State and outside. We must determine whether we have a case that can be made public with respect to Ellsberg and any conspiracy with his colleagues.

At the moment I think Bud has a good investigative mechanism (although he thinks he will need the full time services of Jack Caulfield, a matter I would like to discuss with you). Leddy is an excellent man. Hunt can be very useful.

A memo between Nixon officials Charles Colson and John Ehrlichman regarding the Pentagon Papers. In the Pentagon Papers case, the U.S. Supreme Court ruled that the *New York Times* and the *Washington Post* could publish a classified study of U.S. involvement in the Vietnam War. *Cynthia Johnson/Time & Life Pictures/Getty*

The Burger Court broke new ground in *Batson v. Kentucky* (1986) when it ruled that a criminal defendant could establish "purposeful discrimination ... solely on evidence concerning the prosecutor's exercise of peremptory challenges at the defendant's trial." A peremptory challenge means that a litigant can challenge (remove) a juror without providing a reason for the challenge.

The case involved the burglary trial of James Batson, an African American man. The prosecutor used his peremptory challenges to strike all four black persons in the jury pool. Batson's attorneys argued that the prosecutor's selective use of peremptories to strike African Americans violated Batson's constitutional rights under the Sixth and Fourteenth Amendments.

A jury convicted Batson and rejected his constitutional challenges. The Supreme Court of Kentucky affirmed the conviction. On appeal, the U.S. Supreme Court reversed, finding that the trial judge should have made the prosecutor offer a race-neutral explanation for his striking of the four African American jury pool members. The Court established that if a defendant establishes a basic inference or showing of discrimination, the prosecutor must rebut that with a race-neutral explanation for his actions. If the prosecutor articulates a nonracial reason or his or her actions, the defendant must then establish that the prosecutor's reason was pretexual or false.

What test is applied by a court if a criminal defendant asserts a *Batson* claim?

Courts hearing *Batson* claims apply a three-step process: (1) the defendant must make a prima facie (or basic) showing of using peremptory challenges on the basis of race; (2) the prosecutor must offer a race-neutral explanation for her actions; and (3) the trial court must determine if the defendant has established purposeful discrimination. This means that the defendant's attorneys must show that the prosecutor's allegedly race-neutral reasons are pretextual or false.

Did the Burger Court **invalidate state laws providing for less than twelve jurors** in criminal cases?

No, the Burger Court ruled in *Williams v. Florida* (1970) that a Florida law providing for six-member juries in noncapital cases was constitutional. The Court ruled that twelve-person juries were a "historical accident" and "unrelated to the great purposes which gave rise to the jury in the first place." However, in *Ballew v. Georgia* (1978), the Court ruled that five-person juries in criminal cases were unconstitutional. "Statistical studies suggest that the risk of convicting an innocent person rises as the size of the jury diminishes," Justice Harry Blackmun wrote for the majority.

FIRST AMENDMENT

What were the **major First Amendment cases of the Burger Court**?

In *New York Times Co. v. United States* (1971), the Court ruled 6–3 that the government could prohibit the *New York Times* and the *Washington Post* from publishing the Pentagon Papers, a government study about U.S. foreign policy in Vietnam and the Vietnam War.

In *Cohen v. California* (1971), the Court reversed the breach-of-peace conviction of an individual who wore a jacket with the words "F— the Draft" in a courthouse. Justice John Marshall Harlan wrote that "one man's vulgarity is another's lyric."

In *Lemon v. Kurtzman* (1971), the Court established a three-part test to determine whether a government action violates the Establishment Clause, the part of the First Amendment that provides for separation between church and state. The test required that (1) the action must have a secular purpose; (2) its primary effect must neither advance nor inhibit religion; and (3) there must be no excessive government entanglement.

In *Branzburg v. Hayes* (1972), the Court ruled 5–4 that the First Amendment does not give reporters the right to refuse to testify about their confidential sources before a grand jury.

In *Wisconsin v. Yoder* (1972), the Court ruled that Wisconsin cannot require Amish children to attend school beyond the eighth grade on the grounds that doing so would violate the free exercise of religion. The Court held that only "those interests of the highest order and those not otherwise served could overbalance legitimate claims to the free exercise of religion."

In *Miller v. California* (1973), the Court refined its test for determining when expression constitutes obscenity. The Court established the three-part *Miller* test: (1) whether the "average person applying contemporary community standards" would find that the work, taken as a whole, appeals to the prurient interest; (2) whether the work depicts or describes, in a patently offensive way, sexual conduct specifically defined by the applicable state law; and (3) whether the work, taken as a whole, lacks serious literary, artistic, political, or scientific value.

In *Miami Herald Publishing Co. v. Tornillo* (1974), the Court unanimously struck down a Florida "right of reply" statute which required newspapers to give political candidates the right to equal space to respond to political attacks in the newspapers. The Court ruled that such a statute infringed on the newspapers' "exercise of editorial control and judgment."

In *Buckley v. Valeo* (1976), the Court ruled that certain provisions of the Federal Election Campaign Act of 1976, which limited expenditures and contributions to political campaigns, violated the First Amendment. The Court upheld contribution limits but struck down the expenditure limits.

In *Young v. American Mini-Theatres* (1976), the Court upheld by 5–4 a Detroit ordinance that restricted the locale of adult businesses. "Even within the area of protected speech, a difference in content may require a different governmental response," the Court ruled.

In *Virginia State Board of Pharmacy v. Virginia Citizens Consumer Council* (1976), the Court ruled explicitly that commercial speech is a form of speech that deserves a degree of First Amendment protection. The Court invalidated a Virginia law that prohibited the advertisement of prescription drug prices.

In *Nebraska Press Association v. Stuart* (1976), the Court unanimously struck down a judicial order gagging the press, writing that "prior restraints on speech and publication are the most serious and the least tolerable infringement on First Amendment rights."

Hugo Black (concurring): "Both the history and language of the First Amendment support the view that the press must be left to publish news, whatever the source, without censorship, injunctions, or prior restraints. In the First Amendment the Founding Fathers gave the free press the protection it must have to fulfill its essential role in our democracy. The press was to serve the governed, not the governors.… Only a free and unrestrained press can effectively expose deception in government."

William Douglas (concurring): "Secrecy in government is fundamentally anti-democratic, perpetuating bureaucratic errors. Open debate and discussion of public issues are vital to our national health."

William Brennan (concurring): "Only governmental allegation and proof that publication must inevitably, directly, and immediately cause the occurrence of an event kindred to imperiling the safety of a transport already at sea can support even the issuance of an interim restraining order.… Unless and until the Government has clearly made out its case, the First Amendment commands that no injunction may issue."

Potter Stewart (concurring): "I am convinced that the Executive is correct with respect to some of the documents involved. But I cannot say that disclosure of any of them will surely result in direct, immediate, and irreparable damage to our Nation or its people. That being so, there can under the First Amendment be but one judicial resolution of the issues before us."

In *Bates v. State Bar of Arizona* (1977), the Court ruled 5–4 that truthful attorney advertising was a form of commercial speech deserving of First Amendment protection.

In *FCC v. Pacifica* (1978), the Court ruled 5–4 that the Federal Communications Commission (FCC) could fine a radio station for broadcasting comedian George Carlin's "Filthy Words" monologue during daytime hours.

In *Central Hudson Gas & Electric Corporation v. Public Service Commission* (1980), the Court established a four-part test to determine whether restrictions on commercial speech passed First Amendment review. The Central Hudson test provided that: (1) the speech must not be misleading or involve illegal activity; (2) the government must have a substantial interest in its regulation; (3) the regulation must directly advance the asserted government interest; and (4) the government regulation must be narrowly drawn.

In *Richmond Newspapers, Inc. v. Virginia* (1980), the Court ruled that the public, including the press, had a First Amendment right to attend criminal trials. The Court

Byron White (concurring): "I concur in today's judgments, but only because of the concededly extraordinary protection against prior restraints enjoyed by the press under our constitutional system."

Thurgood Marshall (concurring): "It would, however, be utterly inconsistent with the concept of separation of powers for this Court to use its power of contempt to prevent behavior that Congress has specifically declined to prohibit."

Warren Burger (dissenting): "To me it is hardly believable that a newspaper long regarded as a great institution in American life would fail to perform one of the basic and simple duties of every citizen with respect to the discovery or possession of stolen property or secret government documents.... This duty rests on the taxi drivers, Justices and the *New York Times*."

John Marshall Harlan (dissenting): "Pending further hearings in each case conducted under the appropriate ground rules, I would continue the restraints on publication. I cannot believe that the doctrine prohibiting prior restraints reaches to the point of preventing courts from maintaining the status quo long enough to act responsibly in matters of such national importance as those involved here."

Harry Blackmun (dissenting): "The First Amendment, after all, is only one part of an entire Constitution. Article II of the great document vests in the Executive Branch primary power over the conduct of foreign affairs and places in that branch the responsibility for the Nation's safety. Each provision of the Constitution is important, and I cannot subscribe to a doctrine of unlimited absolutism for the First Amendment at the cost of downgrading other provisions."

established that trial judges may close trial proceedings only after finding that such closure is necessary to ensure a fair trial for the defendant.

In *New York v. Ferber* (1982), the Court ruled 5–4 that child pornography was not protected by the First Amendment.

In *Board of Education v. Pico* (1982), the Court ruled that public school officials could not remove books from school library shelves simply because they disliked the ideas found in those books.

In *Connick v. Myers* (1983), the Court ruled a district attorney did not violate the First Amendment rights of an assistant district attorney who was terminated for circulating a questionnaire critical of office policy and practices. The Court ruled that "when close working relationships are essential to fulfilling public responsibilities, a wide degree of deference to the employer's judgment is appropriate."

351

In *Roberts v. United States Jaycees* (1984), the Court unanimously ruled that a Minnesota law requiring the U.S. Junior Chamber of Commerce, or Jaycees, to admit women did not violate the group's First Amendment freedom of association rights. The Court noted that the law "imposes no restrictions on the organization's ability to exclude individuals with ideologies or philosophies different from those of its existing members."

In *Wallace v. Jaffree* (1985), the Court invalidated an Alabama law authorizing a one-minute silent period at the start of each school day "for meditation or voluntary prayer." The Court found that the law was enacted to endorse religion, thus violating the Establishment Clause.

In *City of Renton v. Playtime Theatres, Inc.* (1986), the Court ruled that the city of Renton, Washington, could pass a law limiting the location of adult businesses by relying on a study of such businesses and the harmful secondary effects they caused in nearby Seattle.

In *Bethel School District v. Fraser* (1986), Chief Justice Burger's last opinion, the Court ruled 7–2 that public school officials could discipline a student for giving a vulgar, sexually-themed speech before the student body. The Court ruled that "surely it is a highly appropriate function of public school education to prohibit the use of vulgar and offensive terms in public discourse."

What did the Court rule in the **"Pentagon Papers" case**?

The U.S. Supreme Court ruled 6–3 in *New York Times Co. v. United States* (1971) that the *New York Times* and the *Washington Post* could publish a classified study of U.S. involvement in the Vietnam War. The newspapers contended that allowing the government to halt the publication on matters of urgent public interest would constitute an invalid prior restraint on free expression. The government contended further publication of the study would compromise U.S. intelligence and endanger U.S troops. The six justices in the majority wrote a three-paragraph joint, unsigned opinion that noted that prior restraints are presumptively invalid and that the government failed to carry its burden that such a prior restraint was justified in this case. Three justices dissented, emphasizing that more time was needed to carefully evaluate the thousands of pages in the Pentagon Papers to determine if the government's national security interests were compelling. All nine justices wrote separate opinions.

What exactly were the **Pentagon Papers**?

The Pentagon Papers referred to a seven-thousand-page study commissioned by Secretary of Defense Robert S. McNamara. McNamara ordered a study that traced the history of U.S. involvement in the Vietnam conflict. Only fifteen copies of this classified study existed.

How did the **newspapers acquire a copy of the Pentagon Papers**?

Daniel Ellsberg, one of the authors of the study, made a copy of the Pentagon Papers for Neil Sheehan, a reporter with the *New York Times*. Ellsberg, a former Marine and consultant to the Department of Defense and the State Department, believed that the study needed to be released to expose government dishonesty. Ellsberg had access to the study because he worked at the Rand Corporation, a research institution specializing in national security issues that worked with the federal government. He also gave copies of parts of the story to other newspapers, including the *Washington Post*.

What happened to **Daniel Ellsberg**?

Ellsberg was first indicted on theft of government property charges on June 29, 1971 (the day before the U.S. Supreme Court decision in the *New York Times Co. v. United States* decision). He faced a second indictment in Los Angeles in December 1971 for thirteen counts ranging from conspiracy to espionage to theft of government property. Ellsberg and codefendant Anthony Russo faced a trial beginning in January 1973. The trial lasted eighty-nine days. U.S. District Court judge William Matthew Byrne Jr. dismissed the charges after a series of disclosures, including the revelation that White House operatives had engineered a burglary of Ellsberg's psychiatrist to obtain his file. The FBI had intercepted Ellsberg's phone conversations and, apparently, President Richard Nixon spoke to Judge Byrne about him becoming the new FBI director. The judge determined: "The bizarre events have incurably infected the prosecution of this case … the only remedy available that would assure due process and a fair administration of justice is that this trial be terminated and the defendants' motion for dismissal be granted and the jury discharged." Ellsberg continues in his role as a lecturer, writer, and activist, campaigning against government corruption and nuclear weapons. In 2002, he published a book about the Pentagon Papers entitled *Secrets: A Memoir of Vietnam and the Pentagon Papers*.

What did the Burger Court do with respect to **commercial speech**?

In 1942, the U.S. Supreme Court ruled in *Valentine v. Chrestensen* that the "Constitution imposes no such restraint on government as respects purely commercial advertising." However, the Burger Court overruled this precedent, recognizing that consumers have a First Amendment right to receive information and ideas from commercial advertising. In *Virginia State Board of Pharmacy v. Virginia Citizens Consumer Council* (1976), the Court recognized that "the free flow of commercial information is indispensable" and that consumers' "interest may be as keen, if not keener by far, than his interest in the day's most urgent political debate." The next year, in *Bates v. State Bar of Arizona* (1977), the U.S. Supreme Court ruled that attorneys had a First Amendment right to engage in truthful newspaper advertising.

In its 1980 decision *Central Hudson Gas & Electric Co. v. Public Service Commission,* the Court struck down a ban on utility advertising. More importantly, the Court established the so-called *Central Hudson* test to determine whether restrictions on commercial speech were constitutional. As a threshold prong, the commercial speech must concern lawful activity and not be misleading. The government can regulate false and misleading speech. Then, the government must have a substantial interest in its regulation; regulation must directly advance the government's substantial interest; and the restriction must be narrowly drawn.

What happened in the Court's **first attorney advertising case**?

Two young attorneys, John R. Bates and Van O'Steen, submitted an advertisement for low-cost legal services in the *Arizona Republic*. The Arizona Bar disciplined the two attorneys for violating an attorney discipline rule that provided: "A lawyer shall not publicize himself ... through newspaper or magazine advertisements ... nor shall he authorize or permit others to do so in his behalf."

Bates and O'Steen asked their former constitutional law teacher, William Canby (who as of 2007 served as a judge on the Ninth U.S. Circuit Court of Appeals), to represent them in a constitutional challenge of the attorney disciplinary rule. The attorneys lost in the Arizona state courts, but appealed to the U.S. Supreme Court.

The high Court ruled 5–4 in *Bates v. State Bar of Arizona* that the attorney disciplinary rule prohibiting attorneys from advertising in the newspapers violated the First Amendment. Justice Harry Blackmun wrote that "the disciplinary rule serves to inhibit the free flow of commercial information and to keep the public in ignorance." In his dissenting opinion, Justice Lewis Powell warned that attorney advertising "will effect profound changes in the practice of law, viewed for centuries as a learned profession."

What did the Burger Court rule with respect to **reporters' privilege to withhold confidential sources**?

The Burger Court ruled 5–4 in *Branzburg v. Hayes* (1972) that reporters do not have a First Amendment right to avoid testifying before a grand jury pursuant to a subpoena issued in good faith. The reporters involved in the cases contended that forcing reporters to testify and reveal their confidential sources would burden the reporters' newsgathering efforts. The result, according to the press, would be that sources would be less willing to talk to reporters and the public would receive less information about important events. The government officials countered that the public's compelling interest in combating crime outweighed any speculative harm on the reporters' newsgathering process.

Justice Byron White reasoned that "we see no reason to hold that these reporters, any more than other citizens, should be excused from furnishing information that may help the grand jury in arriving at its initial determination." The majority concluded that reporters were not entitled to any special constitutional-based privilege to avoid their civic duty to testify to grand juries than any other citizens.

Four justices dissented, with Justices Potter Stewart, William Douglas, and William Brennan, each writing separate opinions. Stewart's opinion became the most influential. He said that before a reporter could be forced to testify before the grand jury regarding his or her confidential sources, the government must: (1) "show that there is probable cause to believe that the newsman has information that is clearly relevant to a specific probable violation of law; (2) demonstrate that the information sought cannot be obtained by alternative means less destructive of First Amendment rights; and (3) demonstrate a compelling and overriding interest in the information." Stewart's opinion became the basis for many states to pass so-called reporter shield statutes, providing a degree of protection to reporters.

Why have lower courts struggled with determining the **meaning of the *Branzburg* case**?

Lower courts have read the *Branzburg* case differently because of the concurring opinion written by Justice Lewis Powell. Powell, who provided a fifth vote for the majority, wrote a concurrence that almost reads like a dissenting opinion. He said that if reporter testimony gives "information bearing only a remote and tenuous relationship to the subject of the investigation," the reporter may file a motion to quash the subpoena. He also wrote, unlike Justice Byron White, that "the balance of these vital constitutional and societal interests" must be done on a "case-by-case basis."

Some lower courts have determined that *Branzburg* stands for the principle that there is a First Amendment–based reporters' privilege. They reach this conclusion by saying that the four dissenters plus Justice Powell equals a necessary five votes for the privilege.

Other courts disagree, pointing out that Justice Powell joined White's majority opinion and wrote a concurring (not a dissenting) opinion.

Did the majority rule that there were any **limits on grand jury investigations into a reporter's sources**?

Yes, Justice Byron White said that grand jury investigations conducted in bad faith "would pose wholly different issues for resolution under the First Amendment." He added: "Official harassment of the press undertaken not for purposes of law enforcement but to disrupt a reporter's relationship with his news sources would have no justification."

Who were the **actual reporters** in the *Branzburg* case?

The reporters in the consolidated cases were Paul Branzburg of the *Louisville Courier-Journal;* Paul Pappas, a television reporter from New Bedford, Massachusetts; and Nat Caldwell of the *New York Times*. Branzburg wrote stories, such as "The Hash They

355

Make Isn't to Eat," about two young people from Kentucky growing and selling hash. Pappas filmed the militant group the Black Panthers in a boarded-up store. Caldwell wrote a series of articles about the Black Panthers and other black militant groups.

What did the Court rule with respect to **gag orders on the press**?

The Burger Court ruled in *Nebraska Press Association v. Stuart* (1976) that gag orders on the press represented prior restraints on expression that should be tolerated only under extremely limited circumstances. The case began in a small Nebraska town when Edwin Charles Simants allegedly murdered six members of the Henry Kellie family in Sutherland, Nebraska. The attorneys in the case (both the prosecution and the defense) asked the judge to limit pretrial publicity. Both a county and district judge limited pretrial publicity in the case. The district judge, Hugh Stuart, wrote that "because of the nature of the crimes charged in the complaint that there is a clear and present danger that pre-trial publicity could impinge upon the defendant's right to a fair trial."

The Nebraska Press Association appealed the judge's order limiting pretrial publicity to the U.S. Supreme Court. The Court determined that the trial judge's order violated the press' First Amendment rights. Chief Justice Warren Burger wrote that "prior restraints on speech and publication are the most serious and the least tolerable infringement on First Amendment rights."

In order for a trial judge to issue a prior restraint, the U.S. Supreme Court said that a trial judge must make three determinations: (1) the nature and extent of pretrial news coverage; (2) whether other measures (change of venue, jury sequestration) would lessen the effects of pretrial publicity; and (3) how effective the prior restraint would be to prevent the threatened danger.

What **alternatives** did the Court say that **trial judges must consider** before issuing a **gag order on the press**?

Chief Justice Warren Burger said trial judges should consider the following alternatives: a change of trial venue (location of the trial), postponement of the trial, intensive questioning of prospective jurors, clear and emphatic jury instructions, and sequestration (segregation) of the jurors. Burger also wrote that "trial courts in appropriate cases may limit what the contending lawyers, the police and witnesses may say to anyone."

What happened to **Edwin Charles Simants,** the alleged murderer in the case?

A jury convicted Simants of murder and sentenced him to death in his first trial. However, in a post-conviction proceeding, evidence was revealed that the local sheriff had made inappropriate contact with the jurors who were sequestered in a local hotel. The sheriff allegedly visited and even played cards with the jurors. Thus, Simants's conviction was vacated. Simants was tried a second time. The second jury found Simants not guilty by reason of insanity. Nebraska law provided that the state could bring civil commitment proceedings against inmates found not guilty by reason of insanity. The state did so and Simants has remained institutionalized as a ward of the state at Lincoln Regional Center.

How did the Burger Court deal with **obscenity law**?

The Burger Court formulated a new standard for obscenity cases in *Miller v. California* (1973). Chief Justice Warren Burger's opinion established a new three-part test to guide jurors in obscenity cases. The three-prong test provided that material is obscene if: "(a) the average person, applying contemporary community standards would find that the work, taken as a whole, appeals to the prurient interest; (b) whether the work depicts or describes, in a patently offensive way, sexual conduct specifically defined by the applicable state law; and (c) whether the work, taken as a whole, lacks serious literary, artistic, political, or scientific value."

How did the *Miller* test for obscenity differ from prior Warren Court definitions of obscenity?

The Warren Court test for obscenity, first articulated in *Roth v. United States* (1957), had required that the material in question be "utterly without redeeming social value." The Burger Court rejected that formulation and replaced it with the "lacks serious literary, artistic, political, or scientific value" statement. The *Miller* test also introduced the concept of "contemporary community standards," meaning that jurors could consider what types of materials were generally permitted in their own local community.

357

"It is neither realistic nor constitutionally sound to read the First Amendment as requiring that the people of Maine or Mississippi accept public depiction of conduct found tolerable in Las Vegas, or New York City," Chief Warren Justice Burger wrote.

Who was Miller in *Miller v. California*?

Marvin Miller was the owner of a mail-order business based in California that trafficked in pornography. Miller mailed catalogs that advertised several adult-oriented books, including "Intercourse," "Man-Woman," "Sex Orgies Illustrated," and "An Illustrated History of Pornography." He also advertised a film entitled *Marital Intercourse.* Miller mailed the brochures to families in Newport Beach, California, that did not request them.

Which Supreme Court justice **changed his mind on the obscenity question**?

Justice William Brennan had authored many of the Court's obscenity decisions, including *Roth v. United States* (1957) in which the Court declared that obscenity was not protected by the First Amendment. However, Brennan dissented in *Miller v. California* and its companion case *Paris Adult Theatre v. Slaton* (1973). In his *Paris Slaton* dissent, Brennan said that he had changed his mind on the obscenity question: "I am convinced that the approach initiated 16 years ago in *Roth v. United States* (1957), and culminating in the Court's decision today, cannot bring stability to this area of the law without jeopardizing fundamental First Amendment values, and I have concluded that the time has come to make a significant departure from that approach."

What **famous movie** became the subject of a U.S. Supreme Court **obscenity case**?

The U.S. Supreme Court determined in *Jenkins v. Georgia* (1974) that the film *Carnal Knowledge* was not obscene. The film starred Jack Nicholson, Art Garfunkel, Ann-Margret, Rita Moreno, and Carol Kane. It was considered a Top-Ten movie of the year and even received an Oscar nomination. Justice William Rehnquist wrote that the film could not be considered obscene because it did not depict sexual conduct in a patently offensive way: "We hold that the film could not, as a matter of constitutional law, be found to depict sexual conduct in a patently offensive way, and that it is therefore not outside the protection of the First and Fourteenth Amendments because it is obscene."

Comedian George Carlin, whose "Filthy Words" routine led to the *FCC v. Pacifica Foundation* Supreme Court case, in which the high court ruled that the Federal Communications Commission could prohibit indecent material in the broadcast medium. *Ken Howard/Hulton Archive/Getty Images.*

What **famous comedian's case** formed the basis for an important U.S. Supreme Court case on **indecency**?

Comic George Carlin's "Filthy Words" monologue, in which he elaborates on the seven dirty words that are not to be used on television, led to an important U.S. Supreme Court decision on indecency. Carlin had delivered his 12-minute "Filthy Words" routine to an audience in California. Pacifica Foundation, which owned a radio station in New York, later played Carlin's routine during afternoon hours. A father heard the afternoon broadcast with his young son in their car. The father filed a complaint with the Federal Communications Commission (FCC). The FCC fined Pacifica Foundation, saying the company had violated FCC standards against the broadcast of indecent communications. The U.S. Supreme Court ruled 5–4 in *FCC v. Pacifica Foundation* that in order to protect children, the FCC can prohibit indecent material in the broadcast medium.

How did the Burger Court rule on a **moment of silence law in public schools**?

The Burger Court ruled 6–3 in *Wallace v. Jaffree* (1985) that Alabama's moment of silence law violated the Establishment Clause of the First Amendment, which is designed to ensure separation of church and state. The Alabama legislature had a law that provided students in Alabama with a one-minute period of silence or "meditation." A few years later, the legislature amended the statute to provide the one-minute period for "meditation or voluntary prayer." The sponsor of the new legislation said that the purpose of the law was "an effort to return voluntary prayer" to the public schools. The majority of the U.S. Supreme Court determined that the law violated the Establishment Clause because the clear purpose of the law was religious rather than secular. The law represented an endorsement of religion that was "not consistent with the established principle that the government must pursue a course of complete neutrality toward religion."

Which of the three dissenters in *Wallace v. Jaffree* criticized the Court's entire Establishment Clause jurisprudence since 1947?

Justice William Rehnquist noted that the U.S. Supreme Court in 1947 had quoted for-mer president Thomas Jefferson's phrase "wall of separation between church and

> ## CourtSpeak: *Wallace v. Jaffree*
> ## Separation of Church and State Case (1985)
>
> **Justice John Paul Stevens** (majority): "The legislative intent to return prayer to the public school is, of course, quite different from merely protecting every student's right to engage in voluntary prayer during an appropriate moment of silence during the schoolday."
>
> **Justice Sandra Day O'Connor** (concurring): "A state-sponsored moment of silence in the public schools is different from state-sponsored vocal prayer or Bible reading. First, a moment of silence is not inherently religious. Silence, unlike prayer or Bible reading, need not be associated with a religious exercise. Second, a pupil who participates in a moment of silence need not compromise his or her beliefs.... It is difficult to discern a serious threat to religious liberty from a room of silent, thoughtful schoolchildren."
>
> **Chief Justice Warren Burger** (dissenting): "Some who trouble to read the opinions in these cases will find it ironic—perhaps even bizarre—that on the very day we heard arguments in the cases, the Court's session opened with an invocation for Divine protection."
>
> **Justice William Rehnquist** (dissenting): "It is impossible to build sound constitutional doctrine upon a mistaken understanding of constitutional history, but unfortunately the Establishment Clause has been expressly freighted with Jefferson's misleading metaphor for nearly 40 years."

state" to describe the meaning of the Establishment Clause. Rehnquist said that "the Establishment Clause has been expressly freighted with Jefferson's misleading metaphor for nearly 40 years." Rehnquist cited many examples of religious influences in public life and said that there was "no historical foundation" for the Court's interpretation of the Establishment Clause.

How did the Burger Court decide the famous case dealing with President **Richard Nixon's claims of executive privilege**?

The Burger Court ruled 8–0 in *United States v. Nixon* that President Richard Nixon could not refuse to respond to a subpoena for tape recordings with his aides by claiming executive privilege. Nixon refused to respond to requests for a subpoena made by special prosecutors Archibald Cox and Leon Jaworski. Cox (who was fired) and Jaworski were conducting an investigation into alleged corrupt actions by the administration,

361

including the infamous Watergate scandal. Nixon refused to comply with the subpoena. A federal district court ordered him to respond and produce the tapes. Nixon appealed to the U.S. Supreme Court, arguing that the judiciary did not have jurisdiction because the case was a dispute between officials of the executive branch (the president and the special prosecutor). Nixon also asserted a claim of executive privilege.

The U.S. Supreme Court said the U.S. Supreme Court had jurisdiction and that the president had to comply with the subpoena. Burger wrote that "neither the doctrine of separation of powers, nor the need for confidentiality of high-level communications, without more, can sustain an absolute, unqualified Presidential privilege of immunity from judicial process under all circumstances." Burger noted that Nixon based his claim of executive privilege on "disclosure of confidential communications" rather than "military or diplomatic secrets."

Which **justice did not participate in *United States v. Nixon*** and why?

Justice William Rehnquist recused himself from the case because he had worked as an assistant U.S. attorney general in the Nixon administration.

What **immediate effect of great political import** did the Court's decision have?

The Court issued its unanimous decision in *United States v. Nixon* on July 24, 1974. President Nixon released the tapes, including the so-called "smoking gun" tape that

A television screen shows President Richard Nixon announcing his resignation on August 8, 1974. This occurred after the *United States v. Nixon* ruling by the U.S. Supreme Court forced the president to turn over audiotapes that incriminated him in the Watergate scandal. Nixon had claimed that he had executive privilege and was not required to turn over the tapes. *Pierre Manevy/Hulton Archive/Getty Images.*

revealed Nixon ordering the FBI to quit investigating the Watergate break-in. President Nixon resigned from office on August 9, 1974, rather than face impeachment.

In what case did the **Burger Court strike down the legislative veto**?

The Burger Court ruled that the congressional practice of including legislative vetoes in laws violated the principle of separation of powers in *Immigration and Naturalization Service v. Chadha* (1983). Since 1932, Congress had passed provisions in various laws that allowed one house of Congress—either the House or the Senate—to veto the legislation if either house felt executive administrative agencies were implementing the laws improperly. The U.S. Supreme Court reasoned that the legislature has the power to pass laws but it does not have the power to execute those laws. That task falls to the executive branch and its administrative agencies.

The case involved a legislative veto provision in the Immigration and Nationality Act. That provision enabled Congress to veto deportation decisions by immigration judges and the Immigration and Naturalization Service (INS). The INS had suspended the deportation of Jagdish Chadha, an East Indian born in Kenya. Chadha obtained a student visa to attend college but stayed in the United States after his visa expired. An immigration judge suspended an INS deportation order that applied to Chadha. Congress vetoed the decision of Chadha and several others, believing they had not presented a case of extreme hardship. That set the stage for the Supreme Court decision.

What provisions of the Constitution did Chief Justice Burger rely on to find a **separation of powers problem**?

Chief Justice Warren Burger based his decision in *Immigration and Naturalization Service v. Chadha* on two provisions in Article I, Section 7, of the Constitution. The first was the so-called Presentment Clause, which provides that all legislation passing Congress be presented to the president for his signature. The second part was the "bicameralism" requirement that both houses of Congress pass legislation before it becomes law. Burger explained: "Disagreement with the Attorney General's decision on Chadha's deportation—that is, Congress' decision to deport Chadha—no less than Congress' original choice to delegate to the Attorney General the authority to make that decision, involves determinations of policy that Congress can implement in only one way; bicameral passage followed by presentment to the President." Burger believed that Congress could not unilaterally veto the actions of an executive agency or an executive branch official. Congress can pass laws that go through both houses of Congress and are presented to the president for signature. What Congress could not do was override the determinations of immigration officials through the use of a legislative veto.

What was the **effect of the *Chadha* decision**?

The decision invalidated at least parts of hundreds of federal laws. In his concurrence, Justice Lewis Powell noted: "The breadth of this holding gives one pause. Congress has included the veto in literally hundreds of statutes, dating back to the 1930s." Justice Byron White was even more explicit in his dissenting opinion: "Today the Court not only invalidates 244(c)(2) of the Immigration and Nationality Act, but also sounds the death knell for nearly 200 other statutory provisions in which Congress has reserved a 'legislative veto.' For this reason, the Court's decision is of surpassing importance."

In what **federalism decisions involving the Tenth Amendment** did the Burger Court switch sides?

The Burger Court switched sides in two 5–4 decisions involving the application of provisions of the Fair Labor Standards Act (FLSA) to state employees. The two cases were *National League of Cities v. Usery* (1976) and *Garcia v. San Antonio Metropolitan Transit Authority* (1985). In *Usery,* the Supreme Court ruled 5–4 that a 1974 law extending the minimum wage and maximum hours provisions of the FLSA could not be applied to the states. The Court determined that the application of this federal law to the states infringed on the states' Tenth Amendment rights by violating "traditional aspects of state sovereignty." Many Court observers said that the Usery decision breathed life into the Tenth Amendment.

However, the Court changed course in *Garcia* by ruling that "we perceive nothing in the overtime and minimum-wage requirements of the FLSA ... that is destructive of state sovereignty or violative of any constitutional provision." The Court's change was caused by Justice Harry Blackmun, who switched sides from *Usery* to *Garcia*.

Which **Burger Court decision led to a Constitutional Amendment**?

The Burger Court's decision in *Oregon v. Mitchell* (1970) led to the Twenty-sixth Amendment to the U.S. Constitution, an amendment ratified faster than any in history. In its decision, the Court ruled 5–4 that Congress did not have the power to pass a law lowering the voting age to 18 in state and local elections. Justice Hugo Black explained: "Since Congress has attempted to invade an area preserved to the States by the Constitution without a foundation for enforcing the Civil War Amendments' ban on racial discrimination, I would hold that Congress has exceeded its power to lower the voting age in state and local elections."

The decision caused a public outcry as young men could be sent to fight in the Vietnam War at age 18 but could not vote in state and local elections. This caused the quickest ratification of a constitutional amendment in U.S. history. Section I of the Twenty-sixth Amendment provides: "The right of citizens of the United States, who are eighteen years of age or older, to vote shall not be denied or abridged by the United States or by any State on account of age."

RIGHTS OF STUDENTS

Do **public school students have due-process rights**?

Yes, the Burger Court ruled in *Goss v. Lopez* (1975) that public school students are entitled to a degree of due process. The case involved 10-day suspensions of several students in Columbus, Ohio, for a disturbance in the lunchroom. One of the suspended students, Dwight Lopez, contended that he was not involved in the lunchroom disturbance but was merely an innocent bystander.

Ohio law allowed school officials to suspend students without giving them an opportunity to defend themselves in a hearing. Lopez and other students sued, contending that the school's process in suspending them violated their rights to procedural due process under the Fourteenth Amendment.

The U.S. Supreme Court ruled in favor of Lopez and the other students, finding that a 10-day suspension triggered the protections of the Due Process Clause. The Court concluded that "at a minimum," the students "must be given some kind of notice and afforded some kind of hearing."

Do public school officials need **probable cause before searching a student**?

No, the Burger Court ruled in *New Jersey v. T.L.O.* (1985) that public school officials can conduct searches of students based upon a reasonableness standard rather than probable cause. The case involved a search by an assistant school principal of a fourteen-year-old girl whom a teacher suspected of smoking in the bathroom. An assistant principal searched the student's purse, noticing cigarettes and rolling papers, which are associated with marijuana.

The student argued that the search of her purse violated her Fourth Amendment rights because the official did not have probable cause to search her. The state countered that the Fourth Amendment does not apply to searches conducted by school officials. The Court said neither party was correct. The Court ruled that the Fourth Amendment applied to student searches but that such searches could be justified based on a standard much lower than probable cause. This standard required the initial search to be justified at its inception and reasonable under the circumstances.

This reasonableness standard "will spare teachers and school administrators the necessity of schooling themselves in the niceties of probable cause and permit them to regulate their conduct according to the dictates of reason and common sense." The Court concluded that the official's search was reasonable under the circumstances.

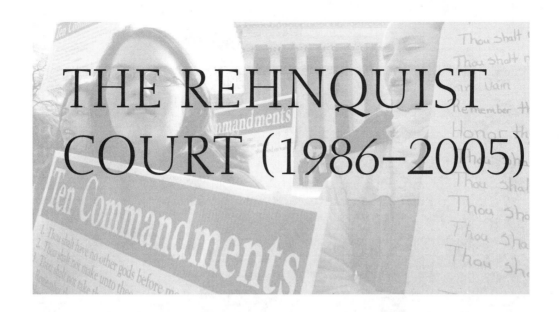

THE REHNQUIST COURT (1986–2005)

How many and **which justices served on the Rehnquist Court**?

Fourteen justices served on the Rehnquist Court, including Chief Justice William Rehnquist and Justices Lewis Powell, William Brennan, Thurgood Marshall, Byron White, Harry Blackmun, John Paul Stevens, Sandra Day O'Connor, Antonin Scalia, Anthony Kennedy, David Souter, Clarence Thomas, Ruth Bader Ginsburg, and Stephen Breyer.

What is **noteworthy about the tenure of the final Rehnquist Court justices**?

From 1994 until 2005, Chief Justice Rehnquist and Justices Stevens, O'Connor, Scalia, Kennedy, Souter, Thomas, Ginsburg, and Breyer served the second-longest tenure of any sitting nine justices in the Court's history. The longest tenure of Supreme Court justices occurred in the years of the Marshall Court from 1812 to 1824, when the members were Chief Justice John Marshall and Justices Bushrod Washington, William Johnson, Thomas Todd, Gabriel Duvall, Joseph Story, and Smith Thompson.

Who was **scheduled to become the fifteenth justice** to serve on the Rehnquist Court?

In July 2005, President George W. Bush nominated John G. Roberts Jr. to replace Justice Sandra Day O'Connor on the Court, following the announcement that she would retire. However, on September 3, Rehnquist died; two days later, President George W. Bush nominated the not-yet-confirmed Roberts to the post of chief justice. He was confirmed and O'Connor briefly served on the Roberts Court until a replacement was nominated and confirmed.

U.S. Supreme Court chief justice William Rehnquist. *Hulton Archive/Getty Images.*

When did William Rehnquist **become chief justice**?

President Ronald Reagan nominated then-Associate Justice Rehnquist to the position of chief justice on June 20, 1986. The Senate confirmed him by a vote of 65–33. In October 2004, Rehnquist underwent surgery for thyroid cancer. Speculation ran rampant that Rehnquist would retire in July 2005. However, Rehnquist issued a statement that month, saying that he planned to continue as chief justice as long as his health enabled him to do so. But he lost his battle with cancer in September 2005.

Clarence Thomas (above) was the subject of very stressful confirmation hearings in 1991 after being nominated to the U.S. Supreme Court by President George H. W. Bush. A subordinate from years earlier claimed Thomas had sexually harassed her, a charge he vehemently denied. *Getty Images.*

Why was his **confirmation vote so contentious**?

Rehnquist's vote was contentious because many Democratic senators believed he was very conservative and would tilt the Court too far to the right. Rehnquist was the most conservative member of the Burger Court. His pattern of filing lone dissents earned him the nickname "the Lone Ranger." Much of the opposition came from allegations surfacing, or more accurately resurfacing, concerning Rehnquist's efforts in Phoenix, Arizona, in which he argued against a public accommodations law. There were also unproven allegations that Rehnquist attempted to prevent blacks from voting in a local election. Also, a memo Rehnquist authored when he was a law clerk for Supreme Court Justice Robert H. Jackson in the 1952–53 term on the *Brown v. Board of Education* school desegregation case raised concerns. In the memo, Rehnquist wrote that the separate but equal doctrine should be upheld. During the Senate confirmation hearings, Rehnquist said that the memo reflected Justice Jackson's views, not his own. Many historians and legal scholars have questioned that assertion.

Which Rehnquist Court justice had the **closest confirmation vote**?

Justice Clarence Thomas survived very contentious confirmation hearings to earn a close 52–48 favorable Senate vote. Thomas's confirmation hearings were marked by testimony from law professor Anita Hill, who claimed that Thomas sexually harassed her when she worked for him at the Equal Employment Opportunity Commission (EEOC). The allegations were controversial, in part, because Hill initiated the charges years after the fact, on the eve of Thomas's confirmation. Thomas vehemently denied the allegations and even referred to the proceedings as a "high-tech lynching." The hearings were televised.

Law professor Anita Hill, whose claims in 1991 that she was sexually harassed years earlier by Supreme Court nominee Clarence Thomas led to televised confirmation hearings. *Jennifer K. Law/AFP/Getty*

How was **Rehnquist viewed as a chief justice**?

Perhaps to the surprise of his critics, Rehnquist was viewed by his colleagues as an excellent chief justice. He was known to be very efficient in his administration and very fair in doling out opinion assignments. Even his ideological opponents on the Court routinely praised him for his abilities and efforts as chief justice. Former Justice Thurgood Marshall, a strong liberal voice on the Court, called Rehnquist "a great Chief Justice." William Brennan, another liberal stalwart, also praised Rehnquist's abilities in the role of chief.

What were some of the **hallmarks of the Rehnquist Court**?

Some scholars have divided the Rehnquist Court into two periods: 1986–1993 and 1994–2005. The first part of the Rehnquist Court was dominated by large turnover. During that time period, Justices Lewis Powell, Byron White, Thurgood Marshall, William Brennan, and Harry Blackmun all left the court. Since Stephen Breyer was appointed in 1994, the Rehnquist Court membership remained unchanged. The Rehnquist Court was generally viewed as a conservative court that emphasized, or even reintroduced, federalism—the relationship between federal and state governments—as a driving constitutional force. The Rehnquist Court was also known for the low number of cases it accepted for review.

Who was the only member of the Rehnquist Court to **never have any prior judicial experience before becoming a member of the Court**?

Ironically, Chief Justice William Rehnquist was the only member of the Court to never have any prior judicial experience before becoming an associate justice. He practiced law in Phoenix, Arizona, from 1953 to 1969 before becoming an assistant U.S. attorney general from 1969 to 1971.

Which two justices were **law school classmates**?

Chief Justice William Rehnquist and Justice Sandra Day O'Connor were classmates at Stanford Law School.

FIRST AMENDMENT

What did the Rehnquist Court rule with respect to the **burning of the American flag as a First Amendment right**?

In two decisions, *Texas v. Johnson* (1989) and *U.S. v. Eichman* (1990), a sharply divided U.S. Supreme Court ruled 5–4 that individuals have a First Amendment right to burn the American flag as a form of political dissent. In *Texas v. Johnson,* the Court overturned a Texas law prohibiting flag desecration. In *Eichman,* the Court invalidated the Flag Protection Act of 1990. The Court majority reasoned that the flag burners were engaging in a form of symbolic speech and expressive conduct even though most would find such expression reprehensible.

Justice William Brennan wrote the majority opinions in both cases. He stated in oft-quoted language in the *Texas v. Johnson* decision: "If there is a bedrock principle underlying the First Amendment, it is that the government may not prohibit the expression of an idea simply because it finds it offensive or disagreeable." In response to the decisions, Congress introduced several amendments to the Constitution to prohibit the burning of the flag. Several times, the amendments passed the House of Representatives, but they failed to garner the necessary two-thirds majority in the Senate. Most recently, in June 2006, a flag protection amendment passed the House but failed in the Senate by a single vote. The amendment needed 67 votes in the Senate (the necessary two-thirds as required by the Constitution) but only received 66.

How did the Rehnquist Court treat **restrictions on commercial speech**?

The U.S. Supreme Court in the Rehnquist era became more protective of commercial speech. Commercial speech is a type of speech that does no more than propose a commercial transaction. For most of the twentieth century, purely commercial advertising received no First Amendment protection. It was not until the mid-1970s that the Burger Court first ruled that commercial speech was entitled to some First Amendment protection. However, commercial speech made far more advances during the Rehnquist era.

In its 1996 decision *44 Liquormart, Inc. v. Rhode Island,* the Court invalidated two Rhode Island laws that prohibited sellers from advertising the price of alcoholic beverages. The state argued that the measures would encourage temperance. The U.S. Supreme Court unanimously invalidated the law, finding it to be more extensive than necessary to serve the state's interests. In his concurring opinion, Justice Clarence Thomas went so far as to say that he did not see "a philosophical or historical basis" for giving commercial speech less First Amendment protection than noncommercial speech.

In more recent decisions, the Court rejected a federal law that banned casino gaming ads in *Greater New Orleans Broadcasting Co. v. United States* (1999), state restrictions on tobacco advertising in *Lorillard Tobacco Co. v. Reilly* (2001), and a federal law that prohibited drug providers from advertising or promoting compounded drugs in *Thompson v. Western States Medical Center* (2002). Even though the Court generally expanded advertisers' First Amendment rights, the Court did not go so far as to elevate commercial speech to the same level of protection as political speech. The Court still applied the *Central Hudson* test to most commercial speech regulations. This test came from the Burger Court's decision in *Central Gas & Electric v. Public Service Commission.*

How did the Rehnquist Court deal with **regulations on Internet pornography**?

The Rehnquist Court was very protective of Internet speech in the face of federal laws designed to protect children from harmful material online. In its 1997 decision *Reno v. ACLU,* the Court invalidated key provisions of the Communications Decency Act that prohibited the online display of indecent and patently offensive material. The Court reasoned that the law would stifle the free-speech rights of adults in its efforts to protect minors. The Court also pointed out that the regulations could prohibit speech that could actually be helpful and informative to older minors. Finally, the Court pointed out that the law was too vague, in part because it did not define what expression was indecent. The case is important because the Court said that speech on the Internet was entitled to the highest degree of First Amendment protection akin to that of the print media.

The Communications Decency Act represented Congress's first attempt at restricting pornography on the Internet. After *Reno v. ACLU,* Congress created a narrower law called the Child Online Protection Act (COPA). This law criminalized the knowing transmission of online material to minors for commercial purposes that is "harmful to minors." In its 2004 decision *ACLU v. Ashcroft,* the U.S. Supreme Court agreed with lower federal courts that the government could not enforce COPA because of First Amendment concerns. The Supreme Court determined 5–4 that there were "a number of plausible, less restrictive alternatives" to COPA, including filtering products, that parents can purchase to filter the Internet.

The Court did uphold one federal law dealing with pornography on the Internet. In *United States v. American Library Association* (2003), the Court upheld by a 6–3 vote the Children's Internet Protection Act, a federal law that required public libraries and schools to filter the Internet in order to receive federal funds for Internet hookups. "Most libraries already exclude pornography from their print collections because they deem it inappropriate for inclusion," Chief Justice William Rehnquist wrote in his plurality opinion. "We do not subject these decisions to heightened scrutiny; it would make little sense to treat libraries' judgments to block online pornography any differently, when these judgments are made for just the same reason."

How did the Rehnquist Court deal with the **First Amendment rights of minor students**?

The Rehnquist Court issued one major decision, *Hazelwood School District v. Kuhlmeier* (1988), that restricted the First Amendment rights of secondary school

Members of the Ku Klux Klan burn crosses in Georgia. The U.S. Supreme Court ruled in *Virginia v. Black* (2003) that a Virginia statute that made it unlawful for crosses to be burned with the intent of intimidating a person or group did not violate the First Amendment. *Getty Images.*

students. The decision gives school officials broad leeway in restricting school-sponsored student speech. Under the so-called *Hazelwood* standard, school officials can restrict any student speech that is school-sponsored if they have a reasonable educational justification for their actions. The decision arose after a high school principal in Missouri objected to two articles produced by a high school newspaper that dealt with teen pregnancy and the impact of divorce upon teens. The principal ordered the stories deleted from the school newspaper, which was produced as part of a journalism class. In response to the decision, several states passed their own laws, called anti-Hazelwood laws, that provide greater protection to student journalists. Nevertheless, *Hazelwood* remains the law of the land for the vast majority of high school students.

Can a state pass a law criminalizing **cross burning**?

Yes, the U.S. Supreme Court ruled in *Virginia v. Black* (2003) that most of a Virginia law dealing with cross burning did not violate the First Amendment. The statute provided: "It shall be unlawful for any person or persons, with the intent of intimidating any person or group of persons, to burn, or cause to be burned, a cross on the property of another, a highway or other public place."

The defendants contended that the Court should follow its 1992 decision in *R.A.V. v. City of St. Paul,* in which the Court unanimously invalidated a city ordinance that   373 banned certain symbolic conduct, including cross burning, when done with the knowledge that such conduct would "arouse anger, alarm or resentment in others on the basis of race, color, creed, religion or gender." The Court ruled that the law was unconstitutional because it discriminated on the basis of content by targeting only a certain type of speech.

The U.S. Supreme Court distinguished the Virginia statute from the ordinance in *R.A.V.*, noting that the Virginia statute did not single out certain types of cross burnings. Rather, the Virginia law bans all cross burning done with the intent to intimidate. "Unlike the statute at issue in *R.A.V.*, the Virginia statute does not single out for opprobrium only that speech directed toward one of the specified disfavored topic," Justice Sandra Day O'Connor wrote for the Court. The Court also noted that cross burnings done with the intent to intimidate were a form of true threats, a category of expression entitled to no First Amendment protection. "The First Amendment permits Virginia to outlaw cross burnings done with the intent to intimidate because burning a cross is a particularly virulent form of intimidation," she wrote. "Instead of prohibiting all intimidating messages, Virginia may choose to regulate this subset of intimidating messages in light of cross burning's long and pernicious history as a signal of impending violence."

The Court did invalidate a part of the statute that said any cross burning is prima facie evidence of the intent to intimidate. The Court noted that there could be some cross burnings done without the intent to intimidate. "The act of burning a cross may mean that a person is engaging in constitutionally proscribable intimidation," O'Connor wrote. "But that same act may mean only that the person is engaged in core political speech."

What were some of the key **First Amendment Freedom of Expression decisions** of the Rehnquist Court?

In *Turner v. Safley* (1987), the Court established a very deferential standard for prison officials when confronted with constitutional claims by inmates. The Court said that prison officials can restrict inmates' First Amendment rights if they have a reasonable penological justification, such as safety concerns.

In *Hustler Magazine v. Falwell* (1988), the Court rejected the intentional infliction of emotional distress filed by Jerry Falwell against *Hustler Magazine* and its publisher, Larry Flynt, for a parody it published. The Court determined that in order for a public figure to recover for intentional infliction for emotional distress, he or she must show that the defendant made false statements of fact with actual malice. The Court reasoned that because the parody could not be interpreted as conveying actual facts about Falwell, it was protected.

In *The Florida Star v. B.J.F.* (1989), the Court held that the First Amendment prohibits the imposition of damages against a newspaper for publishing the name of a rape victim when the press lawfully obtained the material from a government press release.

In *Texas v. Johnson* (1989), the Court ruled 5–4 that a Texas flag desecration statute violated the First Amendment in part because it punished people for their offensive political dissent. The Court ruled that the government could not prohibit expression "simply because it finds it offensive or disagreeable."

In *Sable Communications of Cal. v. FCC* (1989), the Court unanimously struck down a federal law that prohibited indecent, dial-a-porn telephone expression. "Sexual expression which is indecent but not obscene is protected by the First Amendment," the Court wrote.

In *United States v. Eichman* (1990), the Court ruled 5–4 that the Flag Protection Act of 1989 violated the First Amendment.

In *Rutan v. Republican Party of Illinois* (1990), the Court ruled 5–4 that government officials could not transfer, fail to promote, or otherwise adversely affect the jobs of government employees based on their political affiliation. In essence, the Court extended the patronage decisions issued by the Burger Court in *Elrod v. Burns* and *Branti v. Finkel.*

In *Milkovich v. Lorain Journal Co.* (1990), the Court determined that "an additional separate constitutional privilege for 'opinion' is required to ensure the freedom of expression guaranteed by the First Amendment." This decision meant that there was no longer a wholesale exemption from defamation laws for anything classified as opinion.

In *Simon & Schuster v. New York Crime Victims Board* (1991), the Court invalidated a New York "Son of Sam" law that prohibited felons and former felons from recovering monies from any literary works that discussed their past crimes. (The law was created in response to concerns that "Son of Sam" serial killer David Berkowitz might make large financial gains in exchange for his story.) The Court ruled the statute was overbroad because it would apply to such works as *The Confessions of Saint Augustine, The Autobiography of Malcolm X,* and *Civil Disobedience* by Henry David Thoreau.

In *Rust v. Sullivan* (1991), the Court ruled 5–4 in favor of federal regulations that prohibited entities or doctors who receive federal funds from discussing abortion as a family planning option. The majority determined that the regulations did not discriminate against speech based on viewpoint but rather served the government's own interests in funding speech that served its basic purposes.

In *Cohen v. Cowles Media Co.* (1991), the Court ruled 5–4 that the First Amendment did not prohibit a person from suing a newspaper for promissory estoppel (a promise that is enforceable because the person to whom the promise was made reasonably relied on it) when the newspaper failed to abide by a promise of confidentiality to a former source.

In *R.A.V. v. City of St. Paul* (1992), the Court struck down a city "hate-crime" ordinance that criminalized a law that prohibited the placing of symbols on private property for the purpose of arousing anger in others on the basis of race, color, creed, religion, or gender. Justice Antonin Scalia's controversial opinion held that the law was unconstitutional because the city could not selectively choose to bar certain types of fighting words. Other justices agreed the law was unconstitutional because it was too broad, but disagreed heavily with Scalia's reasoning.

In *Burson v. Freeman* (1992), the Court upheld a Tennessee law that prohibited the solicitation of voters and the display of campaign materials within 100 feet of polling places. The Court determined that "an examination of the evolution of election reform, both in this country and abroad, demonstrates the necessity of restricted areas in or around polling places."

In *City of Cincinnati v. Discovery Network* (1993), the Court ruled that a city may not discriminate against newsracks that contain publications composed mainly of advertising. The Court determined that the city's interests in fighting litter applied equally to commercial and noncommercial publications.

In *Madsen v. Women's Health Center, Inc.* (1994), the Court upheld several restrictions on antiabortion protestors outside of health clinics. The Court's decision was its first foray into analyzing the constitutionality of a trial court injunction limiting the free-speech rights of antiabortion protestors.

In *Rosenberger v. Rector & Visitors of the University of Virginia* (1995), the Court ruled 5–4 that a public university engaged in impermissible viewpoint discrimination by refusing to fund student religious publications while funding other student publications.

In *Florida Bar v. Went for It, Inc.* (1995), the Court upheld by a vote of 5–4 a Florida rule prohibiting attorneys from sending solicitation letters to accident victims or their family members within 30 days of such accidents.

In *Hurley v. Irish-American Gay Group of Boston* (1995), the Court unanimously ruled that a veterans group could not be forced to include a gay and lesbian group into its parade. The Court reasoned that parade organization had a First Amendment free-association right to determine what groups and messages they wanted to support.

In *McIntyre v. Ohio Elections Commission* (1995), the Court struck down an Ohio statute that prohibited the distribution of anonymous campaign literature. The Court reasoned the law was too broad because it would punish even truthful, nonmisleading anonymous speech.

In *O'Hare Truck Service v. City of Northlake* (1996), the Court ruled that a city could not retaliate against an independent contractor who did work for the city because he did not support the mayor's political aspirations.

In *44 Liquormart, Inc. v. Rhode Island* (1996), the Court unanimously struck down two Rhode Island laws prohibiting the truthful-price advertising of alcoholic beverages. The Court's decision is viewed by scholars as an important commercial speech decision.

In *Reno v. ACLU* (1997), the Court invalidated two sections of the Communications Decency Act, which prohibited indecent and patently offensive online communications. The Court said that speech on the Internet was entitled to the highest degree of First Amendment protection akin to the print medium.

In *National Endowment for the Arts v. Finley* (1998), the Court ruled 8–1 that the National Endowment for the Arts did not violate the First Amendment by considering "general standards of respect and decency" before determining grants.

In *Arkansas Educational Television Commission v. Forbes* (1998), the Court ruled 6–3 that a public broadcasting station did not violate the First Amendment by exercising editorial discretion to exclude certain marginal political candidates.

In *Greater New Orleans Broadcasting Association v. United States* (1999), the Court unanimously ruled that a federal law prohibiting truthful advertising by privately owned casinos violated the First Amendment.

In *United States v. Playboy Entertainment Group* (2000), the Court ruled 5–4 that a federal law requiring cable operators to fully scramble indecent and sexually oriented programming violated the First Amendment.

In *Hill v. Colorado* (2000), the Court upheld by a 6–3 vote a Colorado statute limiting the speech rights of antiabortion protestors near health clinics.

In *City of Erie v. PAP's A.M.* (2000), the Court upheld a city public indecency law that, in effect, prohibited totally nude performance dancing at adult entertainment establishments.

In *Boy Scouts of America v. Dale* (2000), the Court ruled 5–4 that the Boy Scouts had a free-association right to exclude a gay scoutmaster who did not reflect the organization's values.

In *Bartnicki v. Vopper* (2001), the Court ruled 6–3 that a federal law imposing civil liability on those who use or broadcast the contents of illegally intercepted wire communications violated the First Amendment rights of the press who publish the information.

In *Republican Party of Minnesota v. White* (2002), the Court, by a 5–4 vote, struck down a Minnesota rule prohibiting judicial candidates from announcing their views on disputed legal and political issues.

In *Ashcroft v. Free Speech Coalition* (2002), the Court struck down provisions of a computer child pornography law that punished virtual child pornography that was created without the use and harm of actual children.

In *Virginia v. Black* (2003), the Court upheld the bulk of a Virginia cross burning law from a First Amendment challenge. The Court reasoned that the statute targeted a particular virulent form of intimidation that often constituted a true threat.

In *United States v. American Library Association, Inc.* (2003): The Court upheld 5–4 a federal law requiring public libraries and schools to install filters on computers in order to receive federal funds for Internet hook-ups.

In *McConnell v. Federal Election Commission* (2003), the Court upheld the bulk of the Bipartisan Campaign Reform Act of 2002, which imposed many restrictions on campaign finance.

In *Ashcroft v. ACLU* (2004), the Court ruled that the Child Online Protection Act, Congress's second major regulation directed at content on the Internet, suffered from many of the same defects as its predecessor, the Communications Decency Act. The Court reasoned that there were several less speech-restrictive alternatives available to regulators.

In *Johanns v. Livestock Marketing Association* (2005), the Court ruled that mandatory assessments on beef producers for generic advertising did not violate the First Amendment because the federal government had its own First Amendment right to convey messages of support for the beef industry. This is the so-called government speech defense.

FREEDOM OF RELIGION

How did the Rehnquist Court deal with the issue of **school prayer**?

The Court addressed the issue of school prayer in two decisions. In both decisions, the Court struck the policies down as violations of the Establishment Clause. In the first decision, *Lee v. Weisman* (1992), the Court struck down, 5–4, a middle school graduation prayer in Rhode Island. Even though the prayer was nonsectarian, the Court reasoned that it amounted to psychological coercion on the students attending the ceremony, who were a captive audience. "The undeniable fact is that the school district's supervision and control of a high school graduation ceremony places public pressure, as well as peer pressure, on attending students to stand as a group or, at least, maintain respectful silence during the invocation and benediction," Justice Anthony Kennedy wrote in his majority opinion. "This pressure, though subtle and indirect, can be as real as any overt compulsion."

Then, in *Santa Fe Independent School District v. Doe* (2000), the U.S. Supreme Court invalidated, by a 6–3 vote, a Texas high school's practice of student-sponsored prayers announced over the loudspeakers at high school football games. "In this context the members of the listening audience must perceive the pregame message as a public expression of the views of the majority of the student body delivered with the approval of the school administration," Justice John Paul Stevens wrote in his majority opinion.

CourtSpeak: *Santa Fe Independent School District v. Doe* School Prayer Case (2000)

Justice John Paul Stevens (majority): "This policy likewise does not survive a facial challenge because it impermissibly imposes upon the student body a majoritarian election on the issue of prayer. Through its election scheme, the District has established a governmental electoral mechanism that turns the school into a forum for religious debate. It further empowers the student body majority with the authority to subject students of minority views to constitutionally improper messages.... Such a mechanism established by the District undermines the essential protection of minority viewpoints. Such a system encourages divisiveness along religious lines and threatens the imposition of coercion upon those students not desiring to participate in a religious exercise. Simply by establishing this school-related procedure, which entrusts the inherently nongovernmental subject of religion to a majoritarian vote, a constitutional violation has occurred. No further injury is required for the policy to fail a facial challenge."

Chief Justice William Rehnquist (dissenting): "The Court distorts existing precedent to conclude that the school district's student-message program is invalid on its face under the Establishment Clause. But even more disturbing than its holding is the tone of the Court's opinion; it bristles with hostility to all things religious in public life. Neither the holding nor the tone of the opinion is faithful to the meaning of the Establishment Clause, when it is recalled that George Washington himself, at the request of the very Congress which passed the Bill of Rights, proclaimed a day of 'public thanksgiving and prayer, to be observed by acknowledging with grateful hearts the many and signal favors of Almighty God.'"

Can the **Ten Commandments** be posted on government property?

There remains a sharp dispute over this matter even after two U.S. Supreme Court decisions on this subject by the Rehnquist Court in June 2005. The Burger Court had ruled 5–4 in *Stone v. Graham* that a Kentucky law requiring the posting of the Ten Commandments in public school classrooms violated the Establishment Clause. The ruling focused on the special environment of the school and the impressionable young ages of the viewers (the students). Lower courts continued to divide over the constitutionality of the posting of the Ten Commandments on other government property. On June 27, 2005, the Court issued 5–4 decisions in *Van Orden v. Perry* and *McCreary County, KY. v. ACLU of Kentucky*.

In *Van Orden,* the Court ruled that a Ten Commandments monument on government property did not violate the Establishment Clause. In his plurality opin-

Supporters of the Ten Commandments rally in front of the Supreme Court Building in 2005. The high court ruled in two cases: in one, the justices said that because a Ten Commandments monument was one of many markers and monuments near the Texas capital, it could stay; in the other case, a Ten Commandments plaque was by itself in a courthouse, so it should be removed. *Alex Wong/Getty Images.*

ion, Chief Justice William Rehnquist noted that there were twenty-one historical markers and seventeen monuments surrounding the Texas state capital, that the monument was placed there in 1961, and that even the challenger had walked by the monument for many years before filing a lawsuit. Rehnquist also noted the large number of government buildings in Washington, D.C., that contained religious displays or monuments. "We need only look within our own Courtroom," the chief justice wrote. "Since 1935, Moses has stood, holding two tablets that reveal portions of the Ten Commandments written in Hebrew, among other lawgivers in the south frieze."

In *McCreary,* the Court ruled that Ten Commandment displays in two Kentucky county courthouses did violate the Establishment Clause. Justice David Souter wrote the Court's plurality opinion, finding that the display in the courthouse violated the Establishment Clause. He noted that initially the Ten Commandments plaque was placed by itself in the courthouse: "When the government initiates an effort to place this statement alone in public view, a religious object is unmistakable." The decisions seem to indicate that context, history, and the purpose behind the placing of the Ten Commandments are key factors. A look at the Court's decisions shows that eight justices ruled the same way in each case, with Justice Stephen Breyer providing the key fifth vote in both cases. It may well take more litigation to clarify the constitutionality of such displays.

How did the Rehnquist Court rule on the issue of **teaching evolution in public schools**?

The Rehnquist Court issued only one opinion on the divisive issue of the evolution-creationism debate. In *Edwards v. Aguillard* (1987), the Court struck down a Louisiana law that required public school teachers to give "balanced time" to the teaching of evolution and creationism. Under Louisiana's "Balanced Treatment for Creation-Science and Evolution-Science in Public School Instruction" Act, if a science curriculum included evolution, creationism theory would have to receive nearly equal time. A teacher could not teach just evolution. The state argued that the purpose of the law was to enhance academic freedom. The U.S. Supreme Court disagreed 7–2, writing that the "preeminent purpose of the Louisiana Legislature was clearly to advance the religious viewpoint that a supernatural being created humankind."

The latest dispute in the evolution-creationism debate is the teaching of intelligent design—the theory that life's origins point to a designer or creator. Intelligent design is a modern-day version of creationism. The teaching of intelligent design led to a lawsuit in federal court, which led to a federal trial judge striking down an intelligent design program in a school district in Dover, Pennsylvania. The U.S. Supreme Court has not had the opportunity to weigh in on the issue of intelligent design.

Did the U.S. Supreme Court strike down the **Pledge of Allegiance in public schools**?

No. The Court dismissed a lawsuit, finding that the individual who challenged the Pledge, Michael Newdow, did not have standing because he was not the custodial parent of his child. In addition, the Court did not rule that the inclusion of the words "under God" amounted to a church-state violation.

Newdow had claimed that the Pledge violated the Establishment Clause because the Pledge contains the words "under God." The Pledge was created in 1892 but amended in 1954 with the words "under God" to distinguish our country from the "Godless Communists." Newdow claimed that this language promoted or endorsed religion. The school countered that the Pledge over time had acquired a secular meaning and was primarily a patriotic, not religious, exercise.

The Court did make a ruling in *Elk Grove Unified School District v. Newdow* (2004), which dealt with Newdow's claim that the Pledge of Allegiance was unconstitutional. A divided three-judge panel of the Ninth U.S. Circuit Court of Appeals had ruled that the Pledge was unconstitutional. However, the U.S. Supreme Court reversed, though it did not address the underlying First Amendment issue. Instead, the Court decided that Newdow did not have standing to file the lawsuit because he was not the primary custodial parent of his daughter. Though the Court did not reach the Establishment Clause issue, John Paul Stevens's majority opinion seemed to cast

Maryland kindergartners recite the Pledge of Allegiance. In *Elk Grove Unified School District v. Newdow* (2004), the U.S. Supreme Court reversed a lower court's ruling that the Pledge was unconstitutional. *Mark Wilson/Getty Images.*

doubt on Newdow's argument. For example, Stevens referred to the Pledge as a "patriotic exercise designed to foster national unity" as opposed to a religious ceremony. It also seemed ironic to at least some Court observers that the Court issued the *Newdow* decision on June 14—Flag Day.

What did the Rehnquist Court say with respect to **Bible clubs in public schools**?

The Court ruled in *Westside Community Board of Education v. Mergens* (1990) that an Omaha, Nebraska, public school district violated the Equal Access Act when it prohibited high school student Bridgette Mergens from forming a student Bible club. The school allowed other student clubs, such as a scuba diving club and chess club, to meet at school during noninstructional time. The Court determined that under the 1984 federal Equal Access Act, schools cannot discriminate against student clubs based on their religious or philosophical viewpoints. The school board had argued that it prohibited giving official recognition to the student Bible club because it did not want to violate the Establishment Clause. The U.S. Supreme Court determined that the Equal Access Act did not violate the Establishment Clause. "We think that secondary school students are mature enough and are likely to understand that a school does not endorse or support student speech that it merely permits on a nondiscriminatory basis," the Court wrote.

Did the Rehnquist Court rule on the constitutionality of a **school voucher program**?

Yes, a narrow majority of the U.S. Supreme Court upheld a school voucher program in Cleveland, Ohio, in *Zelman v. Simmons-Harris* (2002). The case involved a program that provided tuition assistance to low-income parents. The vast majority of the participating schools in the program were private religious schools. In fact, a majority of the students in the program attended Catholic schools. A constitutional challenge was filed, contending that the state of Ohio violated the Establishment Clause by funding a program that gave substantial benefits to private religious schools. A federal district judge and a federal appeals court ruled that the voucher program violated the Establishment Clause, reasoning that the primary effect of the program was to benefit religion. However, the U.S. Supreme Court reversed, focusing on private choice and neutrality. Chief Justice William Rehnquist wrote that the program was one of "true private choice." He added: "Program benefits are available to participating families on neutral terms, with no reference to religion. The only preference stated anywhere in the program is a preference for low-income families, who receive greater assistance and are given priority for admission at participating schools."

Did the Rehnquist Court change **Free Exercise Clause jurisprudence**?

Yes, the Rehnquist Court changed Free Exercise Clause jurisprudence with its controversial 1990 decision *Employment Division v. Smith.* The Free Exercise Clause is designed to ensure that people have the right to practice their religious faith free from governmental interference. Traditionally, the U.S. Supreme Court since the time of the Warren Court had held that the government could not infringe upon a person's free exercise rights unless the government met strict scrutiny—showing the government's regulation advancing a compelling governmental interest in the least restrictive way possible. In the 1963 decision *Sherbert v. Verner,* the Court ruled that the state of South Carolina violated the free-exercise rights of Seventh Day Adventist Adele Sherbert by denying her unemployment compensation when she was terminated for refusing to work on Saturday, her Sabbath day. *Sherbert v. Verner* stated the law of the land in the free-exercise area until *Employment Division v. Smith.*

In *Smith,* two Native American drug counselors, Alfred Smith and Galen Black, were terminated from their jobs in Oregon and denied unemployment compensation for using a hallucinogenic drug (peyote) for religious reasons. The state asserted it had a clear interest in preventing illegal drug use. Smith and Black argued that the denial of the unemployment benefits infringed on their free-exercise rights to use peyote for religious reasons. Justice Antonin Scalia wrote that the Court had "never held that an individual's religious beliefs excuse him from compliance with an otherwise valid law prohibiting conduct that the State is free to regulate."

383

Scalia ruled that the government does not violate the Free Exercise Clause when it acts pursuant to a generally applicable law that does not target religion but merely has an incidental effect. The decision lowered the standard of review in many Free Exercise Clause cases. In her concurring opinion, Justice Sandra Day O'Connor opined that Scalia's opinion is "incompatible with our Nation's fundamental commitment to individual religious liberty."

How did **Congress and the Court disagree over the Free Exercise Clause**?

The *Smith* decision caused great uproar in the religious liberty community, who felt the decision would have a dramatic negative impact on free-exercise protections in the country. This led to Congress passing a 1993 law called the Religious Freedom Restoration Act (RFRA), which restored the compelling interest test articulated in the *Sherbert* decision. Under RFRA, the government cannot substantially burden the free exercise of religion rights unless the government advances a compelling governmental interest in the least restrictive means. Congress passed RFRA in direct response to the *Smith* decision. In a sense, RFRA represented a congressional overturning of the Court's decision. This led to another U.S. Supreme Court decision in *City of Boerne v. Flores* (1997), which dealt with a land-zoning dispute involving a church that wanted to expand. City officials denied the church a permit because its planned expansion would take place within the city's historic district.

The city contended that Congress exceeded its constitutional power under Section 5 of the Fourteenth Amendment in passing RFRA and applying it to the states. The Court majority determined that RFRA swept too broadly, particularly because Congress did not have sufficient evidence of discrimination against religious freedoms in the states. In his concurring opinion, Justice John Paul Stevens added that RFRA violated the Establishment Clause by creating a governmental preference for religion. The Court's opinion also reaffirmed the fundamental principle articulated in *Marbury v. Madison* that the Supreme Court has the ultimate power to determine the meaning of the Constitution:

> Our national experience teaches that the Constitution is preserved best when each part of the Government respects both the Constitution and the proper actions and determinations of the other branches. When the Court has interpreted the Constitution, it has acted within the province of the judicial branch, which embraces the duty to say what the law is. When the political branches of the Government act against the background of a judicial interpretation of the Constitution already issued, it must be understood that in later cases and controversies the Court will treat its precedents with the respect due them under settled principles, including stare decisis, and contrary expectations must be disappointed. RFRA was designed to control cases and controversies, such as the one before us; but as the provisions of the federal

statute here invoked are beyond congressional authority, it is this Court's precedent, not RFRA, which must control.

In response to this decision, Congress passed a second law called the Religious Land Use and Institutionalized Persons Act (RLUIPA), which was similar to RFRA but not quite as broad. It applied in land use and prisoner cases but was grounded on Congress's Commerce Clause and Spending Clause powers rather than just Congress's powers under Section 5 of the Fourteenth Amendment. In 2005, the U.S. Supreme Court ruled in *Cutter v. Wilkinson* that RLUIPA did not violate the Establishment Clause but represented a permissible accommodation of prisoners' religious liberty rights. However, other constitutional questions remain as to whether RLUIPA is constitutional. The U.S. Supreme Court likely will have to address this controversy in later cases.

CRIMINAL JUSTICE

How did the Rehnquist Court treat the **exclusionary rule**?

The exclusionary rule provides that evidence seized illegally in violation of the Bill of Rights cannot be used to convict a person of a crime. The exclusionary rule operates as a judicially created remedy designed to safeguard against future violations of Fourth Amendment rights through the rule's general deterrent effect. Justice Benjamin Cardozo famously described it when he was a New York state court judge in 1926 as "the criminal goes free because the constable has blundered."

The Rehnquist Court expanded the reach of the exclusionary rule, continuing a trend that developed during the Burger Court. In *Illinois v. Krull* (1987), the Court ruled that the exclusionary rule did not apply when a law enforcement official relied on a state statute that authorized warrantless searches even though the statute was subsequently declared unconstitutional. "Unless a statute is clearly unconstitutional, an officer cannot be expected to question the judgment of the legislature that passed the law," Justice Harry Blackmun wrote for the Court. "If the statute is subsequently declared unconstitutional, excluding evidence obtained pursuant to it prior to such a judicial declaration will not deter future Fourth Amendment violations by an officer who has simply fulfilled his responsibility to enforce the statute as written." In *Arizona v. Evans* (1995), the Court ruled 6–3 that the exclusionary rule did not prohibit the introduction of evidence seized from a person after an arrest that was based on a computer error. The Court held that evidence seized in violation of the Fourth Amendment as a result of clerical errors of court employees, causing incorrect computer records, fell within the *Leon* good faith exception to exclusionary rule. The Court noted that "the exclusionary rule was historically designed as a means of deterring police misconduct, not mistakes by court employees."

Can the police **search garbage bags in front of a house** without a warrant?

Yes, the U.S. Supreme Court sanctioned this practice in *California v. Greenwood* (1988). The police searched the garbage bags placed in front of an individual's lawn and found evidence that tied him to drug transactions. They used the information gathered from the trash bags to obtain warrants to search the defendant's home. That search produced illegal narcotics. The individual claimed the warrantless search of his garbage bags in front of his home violated his Fourth Amendment rights. The Supreme Court disagreed, writing: "Here, we conclude that respondents exposed their garbage to the public sufficiently to defeat their claim to Fourth Amendment protection. It is common knowledge that plastic garbage bags left on or at the side of a public street are readily accessible to animals, children, scavengers, snoops, and other members of the public."

Is it an unreasonable search when **officers hover in a helicopter 400 feet above a home** and observe illegal activity?

No, the U.S. Supreme Court ruled in *Florida v. Riley* (1989) that a law enforcement officer's naked-eye observation of a partially covered greenhouse at a residence from a helicopter circling 400 feet above did not constitute a "search" within the meaning of the Fourth Amendment. "Any member of the public could legally have been flying over Riley's property in a helicopter at the altitude of 400 feet and could have observed Riley's greenhouse," the Court wrote. "The police officer did no more."

What did the Rehnquist Court say about the use of **thermal imagers**?

In its 2001 decision *Kyllo v. United States,* a sharply divided (5–4) Court ruled that the use of a thermal imager was a search within the meaning of the Fourth Amendment. This means that the government cannot use a thermal imager to scan a home without first obtaining a warrant. In somewhat of a surprise, Justice Antonin Scalia wrote for the majority: "We think that obtaining by sense-enhancing technology any information regarding the interior of the home that could not otherwise have been obtained without physical 'intrusion into a constitutionally protected area,' constitutes a search—at least where (as here) the technology in question is not in general public use."

How did the Rehnquist Court rule on the **constitutionality of roadblocks**?

In its 2000 decision *City of Indianapolis v. Edmonds,* the Court invalidated a city policy of instituting roadblocks to search for drug smugglers. Justice Sandra Day O'Connor wrote in her majority opinion: "We cannot sanction stops justified only by the generalized and ever-present possibility that interrogation and inspection may reveal that any given motorist has committed some crime." The Court distinguished this type of roadblock from the sobriety checkpoints that it has approved in past decisions.

Can government officials **drug-test pregnant women in efforts to reduce crack babies**?

No, the U.S. Supreme Court ruled 6–3 in *Ferguson v. City of Charleston* that the city violated the Fourth Amendment rights of pregnant women by testing them without their consent for drugs. The majority reasoned that the primary purpose of the policy was a law enforcement policy that failed to adequately protect the privacy rights of the women. The city contended that it had a special needs rationale that justified its policy—to protect the health and safety of women and their children. However, the Court ruled against the city, focusing on the fact that "the immediate objective of the searches was to generate evidence for law enforcement purposes."

U.S. Supreme Court justice Antonin Scalia. *Getty Images.*

Must **police officers knock and announce their presence** before entering a suspect's home?

The Court ruled in *Wilson v. Arkansas* (1995) that "in some circumstances an officer's unannounced entry into a home might be unreasonable under the Fourth Amendment." Justice Clarence Thomas examined the state of the common law during the time of the Founders, noting that "the common-law knock and announce principle was woven quickly into the fabric of early American law." The Court did not say that a law enforcement official must knock and announce his or her presence before every search. Rather, the Court said that the failure to knock and announce is a relevant factor in determining whether a search is reasonable. This means that officers may be able to establish special factors showing that it was reasonable to engage in an unannounced entry.

Do social guests enjoy Fourth Amendment protection from police searches?

Yes, the Rehnquist Court ruled in *Minnesota v. Olson* (1990) that an overnight house guest is entitled to a legitimate expectation of privacy in the home he or she is staying. "To hold that an overnight guest has a legitimate expectation of privacy in his host's home room merely recognizes the every day expectations of privacy that we all share," the Court wrote. However, this same reasoning does not extend to persons who are not overnight social guests. In the 1998 decision *Minnesota v. Carter,* the Court ruled that persons in an apartment for two-and-a-half hours packaging cocaine were not entitled to a legitimate expectation of privacy in another's apartment. Given that the persons were in the apartment for only a short time, had no previous connection to the apartment owner, and used the apartment for a commercial transaction, the Court refused to find that they had a legitimate expectation of privacy.

Can school officials drug-test students?

Yes. In a pair of decisions, *Vernonia School District v. Acton* (1995) and *Board of Education v. Earls* (2002), the U.S. Supreme Court approved of the drug testing of students participating in school-sponsored extracurricular activities. The Court in *Vernonia* upheld an Oregon school district's policy of random drug testing for athletes. The majority reasoned that student athletes already have limited expectations of privacy in communal locker rooms. The Court also focused on the privacy of the drug tests.

The Court in *Earls* upheld a Tecumseh, Oklahoma, school district's policy of random drug testing for all students engaged in extracurricular activities. The Court noted that students participating in extracurricular activities often have limited privacy interests similar to athletes. The majority also emphasized that the drug test results were not shared with law enforcement officials.

The Court did not, however, sanction the random drug testing of all students.

What did the Rehnquist Court say about Miranda rights?

In the landmark *Miranda v. Arizona* (1966) decision, the Warren Court ruled inadmissible a confession by a suspect because he had not been given warnings about the constitutional rights he had even under arrest. These came to be known as Miranda rights. Justice William Rehnquist had criticized the *Miranda* decision while a member of the Burger Court. For this reason, many assumed that when Chief Justice Rehn-

> ## CourtSpeak: *Board of Education v. Earls* Student Drug Test Case (2002)
>
> Justice Clarence Thomas (majority): "This Court must consider the nature and immediacy of the government's concerns and the efficacy of the Policy in meeting them. This Court has already articulated in detail the importance of the governmental concern in preventing drug use by schoolchildren. The drug abuse problem among our Nation's youth has hardly abated since *Vernonia* was decided in 1995. In fact, evidence suggests that it has only grown worse. As in *Vernonia,* 'the necessity for the State to act is magnified by the fact that this evil is being visited not just upon individuals at large, but upon children for whom it has undertaken a special responsibility of care and direction.' The health and safety risks identified in *Vernonia* apply with equal force to Tecumseh's children. Indeed, the nationwide drug epidemic makes the war against drugs a pressing concern in every school."

quist announced that he had written the decision in *Dickerson v. U.S.* for the Court in 2000, that the Court would overrule *Miranda.* To the surprise of many, Chief Justice Rehnquist refused to overrule *Miranda,* writing that "Miranda has become embedded in routine police practice to the point where the warnings have become part of our national culture."

Did the Rehnquist Court expand limitations on the use of peremptory challenges?

Yes, the Rehnquist Court—much to the chagrin of Chief Justice Rehnquist himself—extended the limitation on peremptory challenges announced by the Burger Court in *Batson v. Kentucky* (1986). *Batson* held that prosecutors could not use peremptory challenges in a racially discriminatory manner by striking jurors based on their race. The Rehnquist Court extended the *Batson* rule to civil cases in *Edmonson v. Leesville Concrete Co.* (1991). Thaddeus Donald Edmonson, a construction worker, had sued Leesville Concrete Co. for negligence after he suffered injuries on a job site in Louisiana. Edmonson, an African American, alleged that attorneys for the concrete company had dismissed several African American jurors because of their race. "If peremptory challenges based on race were permitted, persons could be required by summons to be put at risk of open and public discrimination as a condition of their participation in the justice system," Justice Anthony Kennedy wrote for the Court. "The injury to excluded jurors would be the direct result of governmental delegation and participation."

The Court also extended the *Batson* rationale in criminal cases. In *Powers v. Ohio* (1990), the Court ruled that prosecutors may not exclude jurors based on race even

389

when the race of the jurors is different from the race of the defendant. *Powers* involved a white defendant who alleged discrimination because the prosecution dismissed several African Americans from the jury. In *Georgia v. McCollum* (1992), the Court ruled that a criminal defendant also could not dismiss jurors based on race. The case involved a white defendant charged with assaulting two African Americans. The defendant sought to limit African Americans on the jury and the prosecution objected. "We hold that the Constitution prohibits a criminal defendant from engaging in purposeful discrimination on the ground of race in the exercise of peremptory challenges," the Court wrote.

Finally, in *J.E.B. v. Alabama Ex. Rel. T.B.* (1994), the Court ruled that prosecutors could use peremptories to strike jurors based on gender. The case involved a paternity action against a male defendant. The Alabama prosecutor used nine of his ten peremptory challenges to remove men from the jury panel. "We recognize that whether the trial is criminal or civil, potential jurors, as well as litigants have an equal protection right to jury selection procedures that are free from state-sponsored group stereotypes rooted in, and reflective of, historical prejudice."

MISCELLANEOUS

What was the position of the Rehnquist Court on the **death penalty**?

The Rehnquist Court did not invalidate the death penalty on its face. In fact, a solid majority of the Court refused to declare that the death penalty was cruel and unusual punishment in violation of the Eighth Amendment. However, the Rehnquist Court overruled a couple of its prior decisions with respect to the execution of mentally retarded inmates and inmates who committed their crimes when they were juveniles. For example, in 1989 the Rehnquist Court ruled in *Penry v. Lynaugh* that the Eighth Amendment did not forbid the execution of a mentally retarded inmate. However, in the 2002 decision *Atkins v. Virginia,* the Court ruled that the execution of a mentally retarded inmate did violate the Eighth Amendment. Likewise, in *Stanford v. Kentucky* (1989), the U.S. Supreme Court ruled 5–4 that it was constitutional for a state to execute an inmate who committed murder when he or she was sixteen years of age. However, in *Roper v. Simmons* (2005), the U.S. Supreme Court effectively overruled its *Stanford* decision by ruling 5–4 that executing a juvenile murderer violates the Eighth Amendment.

The Court's death penalty jurisprudence changed over time and many of the cases showed a deeply divided Court. Some other key death-penalty decisions of the Rehnquist Court include:

McCleskey v. Kemp (1987): The Court ruled that a death penalty defendant cannot invalidate his death penalty based on a broad statistical study showing correlation between race and the death penalty. Rather, the majority rules that the defendant must show "that the decisionmakers in his case acted with discriminatory purpose."

Tison v. Arizona (1987): The Court ruled that the Eighth Amendment does not prohibit the death penalty for a defendant who participates in a felony that leads to a murder.

Thompson v. Oklahoma (1988): The Court ruled that it is unconstitutional for a state to execute a criminal defendant who was fifteen years old when he committed murder.

Penry v. Lynaugh (1989): The Court ruled that the Eighth Amendment does not prohibit the execution of a mentally retarded inmate.

Stanford v. Kentucky (1989): The Court ruled that the Eighth Amendment does not prohibit the execution of a criminal defendant who was sixteen or seventeen when he or she committed murder. This decision was overruled by the Court in its 2005 decision *Roper v. Simmons*.

Coleman v. Thompson (1991): In a controversial ruling, the Court ruled that a federal court could not review a death sentence issued by state courts when the defendant's lawyer in his habeas corpus appeal missed the appeal deadline by one day. The case is controversial because some believe the inmate in question, Roger Coleman, was innocent; later DNA testing, however, apparently showed that he was guilty.

Payne v. Tennessee (1991): The Court ruled that a death-penalty jury can hear evidence from the victim's family during the sentencing phase. This case effectively overruled *Booth v. Maryland* (1987).

Herrera v. California (1993): The Court ruled that "actual innocence" is not a constitutional claim in and of itself in a federal habeas corpus claim. This means that a defendant is not entitled to federal court review of his death sentence unless he or she can show an independent constitutional violation that occurred during the original state court trial proceedings.

Romano v. Oklahoma (1994): The Court ruled that it was not a constitutional violation for a capital jury to hear evidence that the defendant had received a prior death sentence for another murder.

Buchanan v. Angellone (1998): The Court ruled that a capital defendant was not entitled to jury instructions on specific mitigating factors.

Atkins v. Virginia (2002): The Court ruled that a state cannot execute a mentally retarded inmate. This decision overruled the Court's 1989 decision in *Penry v. Lynaugh*.

Ring v. Arizona (2002): The Court ruled that a jury, not a trial judge, should make the factual determinations necessary of the presence of aggravating factors in determining whether a defendant should receive a sentence of life in prison or death. This decision overruled the Court's 1990 decision in *Walton v. Arizona.*

Wiggins v. Smith (2003): The Court ruled that a capital defendant's Sixth Amendment right to counsel was violated when his attorney failed to put forth any evidence of mitigating factors during his sentencing phase.

Roper v. Simmons (2005): The Court ruled that a state cannot execute an inmate who committed his capital crime when he was a juvenile. The Court overruled its 1989 decision in *Stanford v. Kentucky.*

What did the Court decide with respect to **criminal three-strikes laws**?

The U.S. Supreme Court upheld California's Career Criminal Punishment Act (also known as the "three-strikes" law) sentencing law in *Ewing v. California* (2003) and *Lockyer v. Andrade* (2003). Under the California law, if a criminal defendant is convicted of at least three felonies, he or she is subject to the three-strikes law, which carries a penalty of 25 years to life.

The cases involved Gary Ewing, who stole three golf clubs, and Leandro Andrade, who stole $150 worth of videotapes. However, both defendants had multiple criminal convictions in their past, including burglaries, that made them eligible as recidivist (habitual) offenders under the state law. They challenged their sentences and the three-strikes law as a violation of the Eighth Amendment's Cruel and Unusual Punishment Clause.

The Court rejected the argument that the defendants' sentences violated the Eighth Amendment's prohibition against cruel and unusual punishment. "The gross disproportionality principle reserves a constitutional violation for only the extraordinary case," Justice Sandra Day O'Connor wrote for the Court in *Andrade.* In her *Ewing* opinion, Justice O'Connor explained that states have the right to pass laws protecting the public from career criminals: "When the California Legislature enacted the three-strikes law, it made a judgment that protecting the public safety requires incapacitating criminals who have already been convicted of at least one serious or violent crime. Nothing in the Eighth Amendment prohibits California from making that choice." She also cited statistics showing that a disturbing number of inmates committed repeat offenses upon release from incarceration.

Did the Rehnquist Court address constitutional issues related to **sexual predators**?

Yes, the Rehnquist Court addressed many legal issues related to sexual predators. In its 1994 decision *Kansas v. Hendricks,* the Court upheld the constitutionality of Kansas' Sexually Violent Predator Act. This law allowed the state to initiate civil commitment proceedings to those sexual predators who suffer from a mental abnormality or personality disorder that makes them likely to commit other acts of sexual violence. Under this Kansas law, the state sought to commit offender Leroy Hendricks, a career child abuser who admitted he could not control his urges. Hendricks, who had nearly completed a long sentence for sexually offending two youths, contended the law violated his due-process rights and amounted to double jeopardy by punishing him for the same act twice. The Court rejected those constitutional challenges. It reasoned that the civil commitment proceeding did not violate double jeopardy because the statute was a civil, not criminal, law with the primary goal of punishment. "If detention for the purpose of protecting the community from harm necessarily constituted punishment, then all involuntary civil commitments would have to be considered punishment," the Court wrote. "But we have never so held." The Court also noted that Hendricks was placed under the supervision of the state Department of Health and Social and Rehabilitative Services, which was segregated from the general prison population and not manned by employees of the Department of Correction.

Eight years later, the U.S. Supreme Court addressed the very same Kansas law in *Crane v. Kansas* (2002). This case required the Court to address whether a sexual predator could be civilly confined under the state sexual predator law if the state did not prove that the sexual offender had some difficulty controlling his behavior. The Court ruled that the Constitution required the state of Kansas to prove that the sexual offender has "serious difficulty" controlling his behavior before seeking civil commitment proceedings under the sexual predator law. Otherwise, according to the court, the civil law could be used as "a mechanism for retribution or general deterrence." In another case, *Seling v. Young* (2001), the U.S. Supreme Court upheld Washington's Community Protection Act of 1990, another law that provided for the civil confinement of certain sexual predators.

The Court also addressed another type of law, called Megan's Laws, that inform the public where sex offenders live in the community. The Court upheld Alaska's Sex Offender Registration Act in its 2003 decision *Smith v. Doe.* The Alaska law requires former sex offenders to register with the state. The law provides notification to the community about these sex offenders through a publicly accessible database on the Internet. Two former sex offenders, who already served their prison terms before the law was passed, challenged the law on ex post facto and due process grounds.

These former offenders argued the law violated the Ex Post Facto Clause because it imposed additional punishment on them for conduct that occurred before the passage of the law. The state countered that the law did not violate the clause because it was not intended to punish offenders, but to protect and inform the public. The Court sided with the state, finding that the law fundamentally was civil, rather than criminal.

The Court refused to rule in favor of the former offenders even though the information was disseminated on the Internet. "It must be acknowledged that notice of a criminal conviction subjects the offender to public shame, the humiliation increasing in proportion to the extent of the publicity," the Court wrote. "And the geographic reach of the Internet is greater than anything which could have been designed in colonial times. These facts do not render Internet notification punitive. The purpose and the principal effect of notification are to inform the public for its own safety, not to humiliate the offender."

The Court also upheld Connecticut's Megan's Law from constitutional attack in its 2003 decision *Connecticut Department of Public Safety v. Doe.* The Court determined that Connecticut had the right to disseminate information on all sex offenders to the public even if particular sex offenders posed no threat to the community.

U.S. Supreme Court justice Sandra Day O'Connor, the high court's first woman justice. *Mark Wilson/Getty Images.*

Did the Rehnquist Court overrule *Roe v. Wade*?

No, to the consternation of many conservatives, the Burger Court's 1973 opinion in *Roe v. Wade* has never been overruled. It remains arguably the most controversial decision of the past half-century. Even though the Rehnquist Court did not overrule *Roe v. Wade,* it did issue several rulings that have limited it to a certain extent. For example, in the 1989 decision *Webster v. Reproductive Health Services,* the Court upheld a Missouri law that declared that life began at conception and forbade the use of public funds for abortions. In her concurring opinion, Justice Sandra Day O'Connor urged the Court to follow the "undue burden" standard—a regulation impacting abortion law does not violate the Constitution unless it unduly burdens a woman's right to receive an abortion.

In 1992, many believed that the Court would overrule *Roe v. Wade* outright with the additions of David Souter and Clarence Thomas to the Court. These two justices replaced the consistent liberal votes of William Brennan and Thurgood Marshall respectively. However, the Court surprised many observers with its 1992 decision in

Planned Parenthood v. Casey, which upheld many aspects of Pennsylvania law dealing with abortions, including an informed consent requirement and a twenty-four hour waiting period. The Court did invalidate a provision that required a woman to tell her husband before obtaining an abortion. The Court also questioned *Roe v. Wade*'s trimester formulation, which divided a pregnancy into three periods called trimesters. However, in their plurality opinion, Justices Sandra Day O'Connor, David Souter, and Anthony Kennedy refused to flatly overrule *Roe v. Wade*. While they acknowledged that the undue burden standard would replace strict scrutiny as the legal standard, they also reaffirmed the central holding of the landmark case: "The woman's right to terminate her pregnancy before viability is the most central principle of *Roe v. Wade*. It is a rule of law and a component of liberty we cannot renounce."

O'Connor, Kennedy, and Souter were concerned that a decision overturning *Roe v. Wade* would politicize the Court, threaten stare decisis, and lead to questioning of the Court's legitimacy. Justice Antonin Scalia authored a scathing dissent, calling the plurality opinion "outrageous" and comparing it to the *Dred Scott* decision.

The Court continued to issue decisions in the abortion area. In *Stenberg v. Carhart* (2000), the Court, by a narrow 5–4 vote, invalidated a Nebraska law prohibiting partial-birth abortions. The majority noted that the law failed to include a health exception for women who needed partial birth abortions to save their own health. Scalia once again dissented in strong language: "I am optimistic enough to believe that, one day, *Stenberg v. Carhart* will be assigned its rightful place in the history of this Court's jurisprudence beside *Korematsu* and *Dred Scott*."

The abortion controversy is far from over for the Court. In April 2007, the Roberts Court issued a decision in *Gonzales v. Carhart,* narrowly upholding a federal law that prevented certain types of partial-birth abortions.

How did the Rehnquist Court deal with **affirmative action**?

A majority of the Rehnquist Court believed that any racial classifications, even those designed to help historically disadvantaged groups, must satisfy the highest form of judicial review—known as strict scrutiny. However, in a narrow 5–4 decision, the Court approved of the University of Michigan Law School's affirmative action policy in its 2003 decision *Grutter v. Bollinger*. Writing for the Court, Justice Sandra Day O'Connor reasoned that the law school's policy, which sought to achieve a "critical mass" of minority students but not a specific numerical quota, furthered the compelling state interest of achieving a diverse student body. The majority reasoned that the law school's policy allowed for an individualized review of each applicant. At the end of her opinion, O'Connor wrote that there would no longer be a need for such policies 25 years from now: "We expect that 25 years from now, the use of racial preferences will no longer be necessary to further the interest approved today."

However, in the companion case *Gratz v. Bollinger,* the U.S. Supreme Court invalidated an affirmative action policy by the University of Michigan's undergraduate institution. The undergrad policy gave twenty points to many minority candidates. A majority of the justices believed that this policy was closer to the quota policy struck down by the Court in its 1978 *Bakke* decision. The justices said that the policy of adding points automatically failed to give sufficient individualized consideration of prospective students.

Did the Rehnquist Court find there to be a **constitutional right to die**?

No, the majority of the U.S. Supreme Court declined to recognize that the Fourteenth Amendment's Due Process Clause and its protection of life, liberty, and property included a right to die. In *Washington v. Glucksberg* (1997), the Court determined that terminally ill patients did not possess such a constitutional right to physician-assisted suicide. Chief Justice William Rehnquist wrote that there was a "consistent and almost universal tradition" of criminalizing the assisting of suicide. "The States' assisted-suicide bans are not innovations," he wrote. "Rather, they are longstanding expressions of the States' commitment to the protection and preservation of human life."

The Court had dealt with a related issue in *Cruzan v. Director, Missouri Department of Health* (1990). In that decision, the Court determined that a state could refuse to withdraw life support from a person in a vegetative state absent clear and convincing evidence that the patient would have wanted such a course of action. However, the Court said there was a clear difference between the two cases. Chief Justice Rehnquist wrote that there was a large distinction between assisted suicide and the refusal of unwanted medical treatment. He explained: "In *Cruzan* itself, … we certainly gave no indication that the right to refuse unwanted medical treatment could be somehow transmuted into a right to assistance in committing suicide."

Do **detained "enemy combatants"** have constitutional rights and access to the U.S. court system?

Yes, they have some rights with regard access to courts, although the exact nature of their rights has yet to be determined. Most recently, the Roberts Court ruled in *Hamdan v. Rumsfeld* (2006) that certain military commissions created by President George W. Bush were unconstitutional. However, the Court's opinion still did not explain the exact level of constitutional rights for the detainees. It will likely take more decisions from the Roberts Court to settle these divisive issues.

In the War on Terror, which began during the Rehnquist Court, following the September 11, 2001, terrorist attacks, the American government declared hostile individuals fighting U.S. and allied forces in Afghanistan and Iraq as "enemy combatants." This designation carries legal significance because persons classified as "prisoners of

U.S. Supreme Court justice John Paul Stevens in his chambers in 2002. *David Hume Kennerly/Getty Images.*

war" receive the protection of the Geneva Convention. Enemy combatants do not receive the full protection of the Bill of Rights, as do regular criminal defendants. Instead, the U.S. government argued that individuals classified as enemy combatants had virtually no rights at all.

The U.S. Supreme Court disagreed in a pair of decisions—*Hamdi v. Rumsfeld* (2004) and *Rasul v. Bush* (2004).

In *Hamdi v. Rumsfeld,* the Court ruled 6–3 that an American citizen fighting for the Taliban against the United States did have a right to contest the factual basis of his confinement before some sort of neutral decisionmaker. "A state of war is not a blank check when it comes to the rights of the Nation's citizens," wrote Justice Sandra Day O'Connor. She added that "history and common sense teach us that an unchecked system of detention carries the potential to become a means for oppression and abuse of others."

However, the Court did find in the government's favor on the threshold question of whether the executive branch could detain persons identified as "enemy combatants." On this question, Justice O'Connor reasoned that the executive branch had this power because the U.S. Congress authorized it in a resolution called "Authorization for Use of Military Force."

In *Rasul v. Bush,* the Court ruled 6–3 that even noncitizen detainees at Guantanamo Bay have the right to access U.S. courts to challenge their confinement in a federal habeas corpus proceeding. However, the Court did not explain exactly what procedure was due the detainees. Justice John Paul Stevens explained in his opinion that the question before the court was "only whether the federal courts have jurisdiction to determine the legality of the Executive's potentially indefinite detention of individuals who claim to be wholly innocent of wrongdoing."

How did the Rehnquist Court rule in the area of **sexual harassment in employment**?

In its 1993 decision *Harris v. Forklift Systems, Inc.,* the U.S. Supreme Court unanimously ruled that a sexual harassment plaintiff did not have to show evidence of a severe psychological injury in order to recover for sexual harassment. The plaintiff has to show evidence of severe and pervasive harassment that unreasonably interfere with the plaintiff's workplace environment.

In its 1998 decisions *Burlington Industries, Inc. v. Ellerth* and *Faragher v. City of Boca Raton,* the Court clarified when an employee can recover against an employer for sexual harassment. In the case of harassment by a supervisor, the Court said that it depends on whether the employee suffers a tangible employment action (such as a discharge or demotion). If an employee is harassed by a supervisor and suffers a tangible employment action, then the employer is strictly liable. If an employee suffers harassment from a supervisor but does not suffer the loss of any tangible benefits in the workplace, then the employer can present an affirmative defense. This affirmative defense consists of two elements: "(a) that the employer exercised reasonable care to prevent and correct promptly any sexually harassing behavior, and (b) that the plaintiff employee unreasonably failed to take advantage of any preventive or corrective opportunities provided by the employer or to avoid harm otherwise."

In the same year, the Court also ruled in *Oncale v. Sundowner Offshore Services, Inc.,* the Court ruled that Title VII does cover same-sex sexual harassment. The *Oncale* case involved a male employee who alleged that other male employees sexually harassed him.

How did the Rehnquist Court deal with the **Americans with Disabilities Act**?

The Rehnquist Court had a mixed record with respect to the 1990 federal law known as the Americans with Disabilities Act. In some decisions, the Court narrowed the reach of the federal law. For example, in *Toyota Manufacturing v. Williams* (2002), the Court ruled that in order for a worker to prove that her disability was substantially limiting, she must show that her disability affected her daily life activities as opposed to merely making it difficult for her to do her job. The decision involved an auto line worker who had carpal tunnel syndrome.

In other decisions, the Court clarified that in determining whether a worker is substantially limited, the evaluation of the worker must occur with the worker's miti-

Golfer Casey Martin rides a golf cart during a golf tournament in June 2001. The U.S. Supreme Court ruled that the PGA Tour must allow Martin, who has a disabling condition in his left leg, to use a golf cart during competition, in order to comply with the Americans with Disabilities Act. *David Maxwell/Getty Images.*

gating measures, such as high blood pressure medicine or glasses. For example, in *Murphy v. United Parcel Service, Inc.* (1999), the Court determined that a worker with high blood pressure was not disabled within the meaning of the ADA because his medicine controlled his blood pressure problem.

In *U.S. Airways, Inc. v. Barnett* (2002), the Court determined that an employee's request for a reasonable accommodation under the ADA (a more favorable work schedule, more break time, less physically demanding job) must often give way to a fairly applied seniority system. In the case, a worker with a disability requested the employer accommodate him by giving him a less physically demanding job. However, a more senior employee later sought the same job and under traditional rules, the more senior employees get such jobs. The employee with a disability sought to trump the employer's seniority system.

In other situations, the Court has upheld disability discrimination claims filed under the ADA. In *PGA Tour, Inc. v. Martin* (2001), the Court ruled that the PGA Tour must give disabled golfer Casey Martin a golf cart when he participates in PGA tournaments. Martin suffers from a condition in his left leg in which the blood vessels do not function properly. The Court wrote that the PGA Tour's "refusal to consider Martin's personal circumstances in deciding whether to accommodate his disability runs counter to the clear language and purpose of the ADA." The Court added that "allowing Martin to use a golf cart would not fundamentally alter the nature" of the PGA's tournaments.

In *Pennsylvania Boot Camp v. Yeskey* (1998), the U.S. Supreme Court ruled that Title II of the ADA applied to state inmates. The case concerned a prison inmate who was denied admission to a prison boot camp (and thus eligibility for early release) because of his history of hypertension. Justice Antonin Scalia wrote for the Court that "the statute's language unmistakably includes State prisons and prisoners within its coverage."

In *Tennessee v. Lane* (2004), the Court refused to dismiss the disability discrimination suit of a paraplegic who was forced to crawl up several floors of courthouse steps to appear at a criminal court hearing. The Court determined that Congress did not exceed its constitutional authority to eliminate states' immunity from suits (under the Eleventh Amendment) under Title II of the ADA. This decision meant that states have an affirmative obligation to ensure that disabled persons have access to the courts.

Did the Rehnquist Court rule on the constitutionality of **anti-sodomy laws**?

Yes, the Rehnquist Court issued its landmark decision in *Lawrence v. Texas* in 2003, which struck down a Texas anti-sodomy law. The Texas law made it a crime for two persons of the same sex to engage in sodomy. The case occurred when police went to the apartment of John Geddes Lawrence after receiving a report of weapons disturbance. Police found no weapons but did find Lawrence having sex with a man named Tyron Garner. The police charged Lawrence and Garner with violating the anti-sodomy law. The two men contended the law violated their due-process rights by violating their fundamental rights of liberty and privacy.

The law appeared to be against Lawrence and Garner because of the Burger Court precedent in *Bowers v. Hardwick* (1986). In that decision, the U.S. Supreme Court upheld a Georgia sodomy law, finding that there was no fundamental constitutional right for homosexuals to engage in sodomy. Lawrence and Garner asked the U.S. Supreme Court to overturn *Bowers*.

To the surprise of some, the U.S. Supreme Court overruled *Bowers* in its decision. Justice Anthony Kennedy, in his majority opinion, wrote: "Bowers was not correct when it was decided, and it is not correct today. It ought not to remain binding precedent. *Bowers v. Hardwick* should be and now is overruled."

Kennedy reasoned that the State did not have the legal authority to regulate the private conduct of two consenting adults. "The petitioners [Lawrence and Garner] are entitled to respect for their private lives," Kennedy wrote. "The State cannot demean their existence or control their destiny by making their private sexual conduct a crime. Their right to liberty under the Due Process Clause gives them the full right to engage in their conduct without intervention of the government."

In her separate concurring opinion, Justice Sandra Day O'Connor reasoned that the law was unconstitutional because it violated the Equal Protection Clause to single out sodomy acts by persons of the same sex. Justice Antonin Scalia authored one of his patented stinging dissents, accusing the majority of having "taken sides in the culture war." He criticized the majority for questioning the state's moral justification for its homosexual sodomy law. He warned that state laws against bigamy, same-sex marriage, adult incest, prostitution, masturbation, adultery, fornication, bestiality, and obscenity are "called into question" by the majority's decision.

Did the Rehnquist Court in *Lawrence v. Texas* indicate how it would rule on the issue of **same-sex marriage**?

The Court did not decide the issue of same-sex marriage in *Lawrence v. Texas*. However, the Court did state that the *Lawrence* case "does not involve whether the government must give formal recognition to any relationship that homosexual persons seek to enter." This was the closest that the majority came to speaking on the same-sex marriage issue.

How did the Court rule on **male-only military educational institutions**?

The Court struck down a military university's male-only admissions policy as violative of the Equal Protection Clause in *United States v. Virginia* (1996). The case began when a female high school student sought admission to Virginia Military Institute (VMI). VMI denied her admission, prompting the United States to file a lawsuit against the university.

A federal district court rejected the lawsuit, finding that there were substantial educational benefits to single-sex education. However, a federal appeals court reversed. The state then proposed a remedy—the creation of a separate military school for women called the Virginia Women's Institute for Leadership at Mary Baldwin. The state argued that it did not violate the Equal Protection Clause if it afforded a similar educational benefit for women. The state also argued that men and women learned military training differently.

The U.S. Supreme Court sided with the United States and against the state of Virginia by a vote of 7–1. (Justice Clarence Thomas did not participate in the case because his son was a student at VMI at the time.) Justice Ruth Bader Ginsburg wrote that the State of Virginia failed to advance an "exceedingly persuasive justification" to justify its gender-based classification under Equal Protection jurisprudence. Ginsburg also questioned Virginia's proposed remedy of creating a separate school for women. First, she noted that the women's school could not hope to be equal to VMI: "In myriad respects other than military training, VWIL does not qualify as VMI's equal. VWIL's student body, faculty, course offerings, and facilities hardly match VMI's. Nor can the VWIL graduate anticipate the benefits associated with VMI's 157-year history, the school's prestige, and its influential alumni network."

She compared Virginia's proposed solution to the state of Texas's similar response more than 50 years earlier when confronted with the application of an African American to one of its law schools. In *Sweatt v. Painter* (1950), the Court rejected the state's proposal to create a law school for African American students, pointing out that the proposal would fail to achieve any semblance of substantial equality. "In line with *Sweatt,* we rule here that Virginia has not shown substantial equality in the separate educational opportunities the Commonwealth supports at VWIL and VMI," Ginsburg wrote.

How did the Rehnquist Court deal with the issue of **punitive damages**?

The Rehnquist Court reaffirmed the principle that the Due Process Clause imposes some limits on excessive punitive damage awards. In *BMW, Inc. v. Gore* (1996), the Court overturned by a vote of 5–4 a $2 million punitive damage award given by an Alabama jury to a doctor who purchased a BMW automobile with a faulty paint job. The Court focused on the large ratio between the actual (compensatory damages) damages suffered by Ira Gore Jr. and the punitive damage award.

"Elementary notions of fairness enshrined in our constitutional jurisprudence dictate that a person receive fair notice not only of the conduct that will subject him to punishment, but also of the severity of the penalty that a State may impose," the Court wrote.

Justices Antonin Scalia and Clarence Thomas dissented, believing that the issue was one for state courts: "Since the Constitution does not make that concern any of our business, the Court's activities in this area are an unjustified incursion into the province of state governments."

In *State Farm Mutual Automobile Insurance Co. v. Campbell* (2003), the U.S. Supreme Court struck down a $145 million punitive damage award by a vote of 6–3. The case involved an insurance company's representation of its insured in an automobile accident. The insured caused an automobile accident that resulted in a fatality. The insurance company rejected two $50,000 settlement offers from the opposing side and assured its customer that his personal assets were safe from a legal judgment. The insurance company was wrong and a jury imposed $185,000 in damages. The insured then filed a bad-faith action against his insurance company. A jury imposed $1 million in compensatory damages and $145 million in punitive damages. The insurance company appealed all the way to the U.S. Supreme Court, contending that the punitive damage award was so excessive as to violate the Due Process Clause.

"While States possess discretion over the imposition of punitive damages, it is well established that there are procedural and substantive constitutional limitations on these awards," Justice Anthony Kennedy wrote for the majority. "The Due Process Clause of the Fourteenth Amendment prohibits the imposition of grossly excessive or arbitrary punishments on a tortfeasor [defendant].... To the extent an award is grossly excessive, it furthers no legitimate purpose and constitutes an arbitrary deprivation of property."

FEDERALISM

Did the Rehnquist Court strike down **laws that it believed exceeded Congress's power** under the Commerce Clause?

Yes, the Rehnquist Court ruled on several occasions that Congress exceeded its constitutional authority under the Commerce Clause. Generally speaking, the U.S. Supreme Court historically has been reluctant to strike down legislation that has been passed pursuant to Congress's Commerce Clause powers. The Commerce Clause gives Congress broad power to regulate interstate commerce. For example, in the 1942 decision *Wickard v. Filburn,* the Court ruled that Congress had the Commerce Clause power to regulate the amount of wheat consumption produced by a private farmer.

However, in the landmark 1995 decision *United States v. Lopez,* the Court ruled 5–4 that Congress exceeded its Commerce Clause powers in passing the Gun Free School Zones Act of 1990. The case involved high school student Alphonso Lopez Jr., who brought a gun to school. He was arrested, charged, and convicted of violating the federal gun law that made it a crime "knowingly to possess a firearm at a place that the individual knows, or has reasonable cause to believe, is a school zone." Chief Justice William Rehnquist wrote in his majority opinion that the federal gun law "has nothing to do with 'commerce' or any sort of economic enterprise, however broadly one might define those terms." Lopez represented the first time in more than sixty years that the Court had invalidated legislation enacted under Congress's Commerce Clause powers.

The Rehnquist Court reached a similar result in its 2000 decision *U.S. v. Morrison,* a case dealing with the constitutionality of the Violence Against Women Act. The majority of the Court reasoned that Congress once again exceeded its powers under the Commerce Clause because gender-based violence against women was not a commercial or economic activity. The majority reasoned that state governments, not the federal government, should pass legislation dealing with such problems.

How did the Rehnquist Court rule with regard to **civil rights laws and state sovereign immunity**?

The Eleventh Amendment provides: "The Judicial power of the United States shall not be construed to extend to any suit in law or equity, commenced or prosecuted against one of the United States by Citizens of another State, or by Citizens or Subjects of any Foreign State." This Amendment has been interpreted to mean that states often cannot be sued in federal court. This presents a problem when several civil rights/employment discrimination laws specifically provide that states can be sued.

The Rehnquist Court decided numerous cases dealing with this thorny constitutional problem. In *Kimel v. Florida Board of Regents* (2000), the Court ruled that Congress exceeded its constitutional powers under Section 5 of the Fourteenth Amendment when it eliminated states's sovereign immunity. "Congress's failure to uncover any significant pattern of unconstitutional discrimination here confirms that Congress had no reason to believe that broad prophylactic legislation was necessary in this field," Justice Sandra Day O'Connor wrote for the Court. "In light of the indiscriminate scope of the Act's substantive requirements, and the lack of evidence of widespread and unconstitutional age discrimination by the States, we hold that the ADEA [Age Discrimination in Employment Act] is not a valid exercise of Congress's power under section 5 of the Fourteenth Amendment. The ADEA's purported abrogation of the States' sovereign immunity is accordingly invalid." Similarly, in *Board of Trustees of Univ. of Ala. v. Garrett,* the Court ruled that Congress exceeded its authority in abrogating state immunity from suits by individuals under the Americans with Disabilities Act (ADA).

However, the Court changed course in a case involving the Family and Medical Leave Act (FMLA) of 1993. In *Nevada Department of Human Resources v. Hibbs* (2003), the Court held 6–3 that state workers may sue their employers for failure to comply with the 1993 FMLA. The decision departed from the *Kimel* and *Garrett* line of cases that immunized states from employees suing under a series of federal laws.

Chief Justice William Rehnquist distinguished *Garrett* and *Kimel* because those cases involved age- and disability-based distinctions, which the court reviews under a less intense standard. "Here, however, Congress directed its attention to state gender discrimination, which triggers a heightened level of scrutiny," Rehnquist wrote.

Did Congress exceed its powers when it passed a law **banning controlled substances such as marijuana**?

No, the U.S. Supreme Court ruled that Congress did not exceed its constitutionality authority under the Commerce Clause when it passed the Controlled Substances Act (CSA). In the 2005 decision *Gonzalez v. Raich,* the Court addressed the constitutionality of this federal law in the context of a California ballot initiative that decriminalized medical marijuana usage. The majority wrote that "we have no difficulty concluding that Congress had a rational basis for believing that failure to regulate the intrastate manufacture and possession of marijuana would leave a gaping hole in the CSA."

What did the U.S. Supreme Court decide in the **2000 presidential election case**?

In the tightly contested presidential election of 2000, between the Republican nominee, Texas governor George W. Bush, and the Democratic nominee, Vice President Al Gore, the result came down to Florida and its twenty-five electoral votes. Whichever of the two candidates carried the state would win the presidency.

Bush narrowly held the lead in Florida after the initial vote tally. After an automatic machine recount, Bush maintained an even narrower lead. Gore's legal team then filed legal motions, asking for manual recounts of votes in four counties. They alleged there were many voters who intended to vote for Gore but who did not mark the ballot properly. The Bush legal team sought to stop the recount process and have Bush declared the winner.

The Florida Supreme Court had ruled 4–3 that a manual recount should proceed. However, the U.S. Supreme Court reversed by a controversial 5–4 vote in *Bush v. Gore* (2000). The majority reasoned that there were equal protection problems in ensuring fairness in the manual recount process.

"Instead, we are presented with a situation where a state court with the power to assure uniformity has ordered a statewide recount with minimal procedural safeguards," the Court wrote. "When a court orders a statewide remedy, there must be at least some assurance that the rudimentary requirements of equal treatment and fundamental fairness are satisfied."

Three justices in the majority—Chief Justice William Rehnquist, Justice Antonin Scalia, and Justice Clarence Thomas—wrote a concurring opinion explaining that the Florida Supreme Court decision was invalid because Article II of the U.S. Constitution provides that state legislatures, not state supreme courts, have the exclusive power in such election matters.

Several of the dissenting justices bitterly criticized the ruling. Justice John Paul Stevens wrote: "Although we may never know with complete certainty the identity of the winner of this year's Presidential election, the identity of the loser is perfectly clear. It is the Nation's confidence in the judge as an impartial guardian of the rule of law."

Can a **sitting president be subjected to a civil lawsuit**?

Yes, a sitting president can be subjected to such a lawsuit for unofficial acts, according to the U.S. Supreme Court in its 1997 decision *Clinton v. Jones*. In 1982, the Court had ruled in *Nixon v. Fitzgerald* that a president enjoys absolute immunity from damages based on official acts.

The suit in question was a sexual harassment complaint filed by former Arkansas state employee Paula Jones against President Bill Clinton. Jones alleged that Clinton, at the time the governor of Arkansas, propositioned her for sexual favors in a Little

A protestor expresses his opinion of the U.S. Supreme Court's ruling in *Bush v. Gore* in 2000. The high court's decision assured victory for Texas governor George W. Bush over Vice President Al Gore in the 2000 presidential election. *Paul J. Richards/Getty Images.*

Rock hotel room. She filed a sexual harassment claim in federal court. Attorneys for the president argued that he should enjoy immunity from the lawsuit while he occupied the White House and performed his duties as president.

The U.S. Supreme Court determined that Jones's lawsuit could proceed in part because the conduct complained of was not an official act of the president. The conduct occurred before he became president. President Clinton argued that separation of powers principles supported his contention that the lawsuit should be delayed until after he left office. The Court unanimously rejected that argument, writing that "the doctrine of separation of powers does not require federal courts to stay all private actions against the President until he leaves office."

The case proceeded against President Clinton after the Court's decision. He gave a deposition in January 1998 at the Washington, D.C., office of his lawyer, Robert Bennett. In April 1998, a federal district court judge dismissed the lawsuit. Jones appealed this dismissal to the Eighth U.S. Circuit Court of Appeals, which heard arguments in the case in October 1998. Clinton settled with Jones by agreeing to pay her $850,000, though he admitted no wrongdoing.

What was the Court's **controversial eminent domain ruling** in 2005?

The most controversial decision of the Court's 2004–5 term was *Kelo v. City of New London* (2005). The city of New London, Connecticut, instituted its power of eminent domain to take property away from nine landowners to transfer the property to a private corporation as part of an economic development and revitalization plan. The landowners sued, contending that the city violated the Fifth Amendment, which provides in part: "Nor shall private property be taken for public use without just compensation." The landowners contended that the forced transfer of property from themselves to another private owner was not a "public use." The Court majority determined that the city's decision to take the property for the purpose of economic development satisfied the "public use" requirement of the Fifth Amendment."

Justice Sandra Day O'Connor authored a strong dissent. "Under the banner of economic development, all private property is now vulnerable to being taken and transferred to another private owner, so long as it might be upgraded—i.e., given to an owner who will use it in a way that the legislature deems more beneficial to the public—in the process." Justice Clarence Thomas also wrote a dissenting opinion, questioning the majority's wisdom: "If such 'economic development' takings are for a 'public use,' any taking is, and the Court has erased the Public Use Clause from our Constitution."

THE ROBERTS COURT (2005–PRESENT)

How many and **which justices have served on the Roberts Court**?

Ten justices have served on the Roberts Court as of the summer of 2007. They include Chief Justice John G. Roberts Jr. and Justices John Paul Stevens, Antonin Scalia, Sandra Day O'Connor, Anthony Kennedy, Clarence Thomas, David Souter, Ruth Bader Ginsburg, Stephen Breyer, and Samuel Alito Jr.

What **official positions did John Roberts hold** before becoming the nation's seventeenth chief justice?

John Roberts served as a special assistant to the U.S. attorney general from 1981 to 1982, associate counsel to President Ronald Reagan from 1982 to 1986, principal deputy solicitor general for the U.S. Department of Justice from 1989 to 1993, and as a judge on the U.S. Court of Appeals for the D.C. Circuit from 2003 to 2005.

For what **Supreme Court position was Roberts first nominated**?

President George W. Bush first nominated Roberts to the position of associate justice on July 19, 2005, after Sandra Day O'Connor announced her intention to retire. However, Chief Justice William Rehnquist died on September 3, 2005. Two days later, President Bush announced that he was nominating Roberts for the position of chief justice. Justice O'Connor agreed to continue on the Court until a new nominee was announced and confirmed.

Who was the **first new justice to join the Roberts Court** after the chief?

Samuel A. Alito Jr. became the nation's 110th Supreme Court justice, taking the place of the retired Sandra Day O'Connor. President Bush nominated Alito on October 31, 2005, and the Senate confirmed him on January 31, 2006.

U.S. Supreme Court chief justice John G. Roberts Jr. *AP Images.*

What were the **confirmation votes** of Chief Justice Roberts and Justice Alito?

The Senate confirmed Roberts by a commanding vote of 78–22 and Alito by a vote of 58–42.

Who are the **conservative and liberal justices on the current Roberts Court**?

The terms conservative and liberal mean different things to different people, as the terms themselves have been overused. But Chief Justice John G. Roberts Jr., Antonin Scalia, Clarence Thomas, and Samuel Alito are generally considered to be the conservative wing of the Court. Justices John Paul Stevens, David Souter, and Ruth Bader Ginsburg are considered to be the more liberal justices on the Court. Justices Anthony Kennedy and Stephen Breyer are often the "swing votes" in certain cases.

What was the **political affiliation of the presidents** who appointed the current Roberts Court?

Seven of the justices—Chief Justice John Roberts, John Paul Stevens, Antonin Scalia, Anthony Kennedy, Clarence Thomas, David Souter, and Samuel Alito—were appointed by Republican presidents. President Gerald Ford appointed Stevens, President Ronald Reagan appointed Scalia and Kennedy, President George H. W. Bush appointed Thomas and Souter, and President George W. Bush appointed Roberts and Alito. The only members of the Court to be appointed by a Democratic president are Ruth Bader Ginsburg and Stephen Breyer, both appointed by President Bill Clinton.

What were the **prior occupations of the current justices** before they ascended to the High Court?

Chief Justice John Roberts clerked for then-Justice William Rehnquist in 1980–81 and also argued thirty-nine cases before the U.S. Supreme Court while he was in public service (deputy solicitor general) and in private practice (with a Washington, D.C., law firm). Roberts became the fifth justice (along with Justices Byron White, William Rehnquist, John Paul Stevens, and Stephen Breyer) to have previously served as a law clerk on the U.S. Supreme Court. Before his nomination to the U.S. Supreme Court, Roberts served as a judge on the U.S. Court of Appeals for the District of Columbia Circuit.

Justice John Paul Stevens served as a judge on the Seventh U.S. Circuit Court of Appeals prior to his nomination. Justices Antonin Scalia, Clarence Thomas, and Ruth Bader Ginsburg were all judges on the U.S. Court of Appeals for the District of Columbia Circuit. Anthony Kennedy was a judge on the Ninth U.S. Circuit Court of Appeals for nearly thirteen years before his nomination. David Souter and Stephen Breyer

411

Roberts Court Justices and Their College Degrees

Justice	Undergraduate	Law Degree
John Roberts	Harvard	Harvard
John Paul Stevens	Chicago	Northwestern
Antonin Scalia	Georgetown	Harvard
Anthony Kennedy	Stanford	Harvard
David Souter	Harvard	Harvard
Clarence Thomas	Holy Cross	Yale
Ruth Bader Ginsburg	Cornell	Columbia
Stephen Breyer	Stanford	Harvard
Samuel Alito	Princeton	Yale

were both judges on the First U.S. Circuit Court of Appeals before their nominations. Justice Samuel Alito served as a judge on the Third U.S. Circuit Court of Appeals before his nomination.

What **common thread links** all current members of the Roberts Court?

All the members of the Roberts Court served as judges on the federal courts of appeal before being elevated to the U.S. Supreme Court. The U.S. Court of Appeals is the intermediate appellate court in the U.S. system—above the federal trial courts (federal district courts) and beneath the U.S. Supreme Court.

Which of the current members of the Roberts Court **taught in law school**?

Justices Antonin Scalia, Anthony Kennedy, Ruth Bader Ginsburg, and Stephen Breyer all taught at law schools in their careers before becoming associate justices on the U.S. Supreme Court. Scalia taught at the University of Virginia from 1967 to 1971 and at the University of Chicago from 1977 to 1982. Kennedy taught constitutional law at the McGeorge School of Law, Pacific University, from 1975 to 1988. Ginsburg taught at the Rutgers University School of Law from 1963 to 1972 and at the Columbia Law School from 1972 to 1980. Breyer taught at the Harvard Law School from 1967 to 1994.

Which justice is a former **Rhodes Scholar**?

Justice David Souter spent two years as a Rhodes Scholar at Magdalen College, Oxford. Interestingly, Justice Stephen Breyer was a Marshall Scholar at Magdalen College, Oxford. These scholarships finance high-achieving young Americans, giving them the ability to study for degrees in the United Kingdom.

> ## CourtSpeak: *Martin v. Franklin Capital Corporation* Attorney Fee Case (2005)
>
> Chief Justice John Roberts (unanimous): "Discretion is not a whim, and limiting discretion according to legal standards helps promote the basic principle of justice that like cases should be decided alike."

Which justices earned their **law degrees from Harvard**?

Chief Justice John G. Roberts Jr. and Justices Antonin Scalia, Anthony Kennedy, David Souter, and Stephen Breyer all earned LLBs from Harvard Law School. Justice Ruth Bader Ginsburg attended Harvard Law School, but earned her degree from Columbia.

DECISIONS

In what decision did Chief Justice **Roberts write his first opinion** for the Court?

Chief Justice Roberts wrote his first opinion in *Martin v. Franklin Capital Corporation* (2005), an attorney fee case. The issue concerned the proper legal standard for when a plaintiff in a civil suit could recover attorney's fees when a lawsuit is sent back to state court.

Often, plaintiffs file lawsuits in state courts and then defendants remove those cases to federal courts for different reasons. However, sometimes the federal courts then order the cases removed back to state court. That is what happened in *Martin v. Franklin Capital Corporation.* The plaintiffs filed a class-action suit in state court, the defendants removed to federal court, and then the federal court sent it back to state court. The Martins then sought attorney fees for the time and legal costs it took in removing the case to federal court and then back to state court.

The federal law dealing with removal costs provides that a federal judge "may" award attorney fees for removal costs. Roberts reasoned that "absent unusual circumstances, courts may award attorney's fees under [the removal statute] only where the removing party lacked an objectively reasonable basis for seeking removal." The Court concluded that the Martins were not allowed attorney's fees because the defendant had a reasonable basis for thinking the federal court had jurisdiction.

In what decision did Justice Samuel **Alito write his first opinion**?

Justice Samuel Alito wrote his first opinion for the U.S. Supreme Court in *Holmes v. South Carolina* (2006). Ironically, Alito, a former federal prosecutor, wrote an opinion that protected the constitutional rights of Bobby Lee Holmes, a criminal defendant

413

President George W. Bush (right) applauds as U.S. Supreme Court justice Samuel Alito speaks following his swearing-in ceremony on February 1, 2006. *Getty Images.*

who was prevented by South Carolina state courts from introducing evidence that another person committed the crime.

The South Carolina Supreme Court had ruled that the trial judge did not need to allow the defendant to present evidence of third-party guilt if the prosecution had strong forensic evidence showing the defendant's guilt.

Alito and the rest of the U.S. Supreme Court disagreed, writing that it violated the defendant's right to present a complete defense. "The true strength of the prosecution's proof cannot be assessed without considering challenges to the reliability of the prosecution's evidence," he wrote.

In what decision did the Roberts Court invalidate the president's **creation of military commissions** in the War on Terror?

The Roberts Court ruled 5–3 in *Hamdan v. Rumsfeld* (2006) that the executive branch (the George W. Bush administration) exceeded its constitutional authority in establishing military commissions to try the so-called "enemy combatants" held at the Naval base in Guantanamo Bay, Cuba. The Court determined that such military commissions, created without approval from the U.S. Congress, did not conform to the procedures established by the Uniform Code for Military Justice or the Geneva Conventions, which contain procedures for dealing with prisoners of war. The Court's opinion means that the government must either seek legislation from Congress authorizing such military commissions

---

CourtSpeak: *Hamdan v. Rumsfeld* Military Commissions Case (2006)

Justice John Paul Stevens (plurality): "It bears emphasizing that Hamdan does not challenge, and we do not today address, the Government's power to detain him for the duration of active hostilities in order to prevent such harm. But in undertaking to try Hamdan and subject him to criminal punishment, the Executive is bound to comply with the Rule of Law that prevails in this jurisdiction."

Justice Clarence Thomas (dissenting): "The plurality's willingness to second-guess the determination of the political branches that these conspirators must be brought to justice is both unprecedented and dangerous."

---

or try individuals like Hamdan according to established rules of military justice. In a concurring opinion, Justice Stephen Breyer wrote that there was nothing to stop the president from urging Congress to pass legislation authorizing such military commissions.

Justices Clarence Thomas, Antonin Scalia, and Samuel Alito dissented, arguing that the Court should show more deference to the executive branch during the War on Terror. In his dissenting opinion, Justice Thomas termed the Court's opinion "dangerous."

Who is **Hamdan**?

Hamdan refers to Salim Ahmed Hamdan, who allegedly served as Al-Qaeda leader Osama bin Laden's personal bodyguard and driver from 1996 until his capture in November 2001.

Why did Chief Justice **Roberts not participate in the *Hamdan* case**?

Chief Justice John Roberts did not participate because he ruled on the very same case when it was before the U.S. Court of Appeals for the D.C. Circuit. Roberts had ruled for the government at the D.C. Circuit level.

In what decision did the Roberts Court uphold a state's **assisted-suicide law**?

The Roberts Court ruled 6–3 in *Oregon v. Gonzales* (2006) that the U.S. attorney general could not prohibit the operation of a state medical law that allowed for assisted suicide. In 1994, Oregon passed the Oregon Death with Dignity Act, which allows physicians to assist terminally ill patients six months from death by prescribing lethal doses. In 2001, then-U.S. Attorney General John Ashcroft announced a rule that "assisting suicide is not a 'legitimate medical purpose'" and could be prohibited under the Controlled Substances Act (CSA).

Military personnel transport a detainee at the U.S. naval base in Guantanamo Bay, Cuba. The Roberts Court ruled in *Hamdan v. Rumsfeld* that the George W. Bush administration exceeded its constitutional authority in establishing military commissions to try the so-called "enemy combatants" at Guantanamo Bay. *Brennan Linsley/AP Images.*

The state of Oregon, a physician, a pharmacist, and some terminally ill patients sued, contending that the attorney general's "interpretative rule" was unconstitutional.

The majority of the U.S. Supreme Court agreed, finding that federal law's "prescription requirement does not authorize the Attorney General to bar dispensing controlled substances for assisted suicide in the face of a state medical regime permitting such suicide." Anthony Kennedy, who issued the Court's opinion, wrote that the "structure" of the Controlled Substances Act "conveys unwillingness to cede medical judgments to an Executive official who lacks medical expertise." The majority viewed the CSA requirements as primarily concerned with "illicit drug dealing" and "trafficking."

Chief Justice Roberts and Justices Antonin Scalia and Clarence Thomas dissented, with Scalia and Thomas writing opinions. Scalia wrote that the attorney general's interpretation of federal drug regulations was entitled to substantial deference and questioned whether assisted suicide is medically legitimate. Thomas questioned how the majority could square its decision with the Rehnquist Court's recent 2005 decision in *Raich v. Gonzales,* prohibiting the medical use of marijuana.

How did the Roberts Court change the law of **public employee free-speech rights**?

The Roberts Court changed the Supreme Court's jurisprudence on employee free-speech rights with its ruling in *Garcetti v. Ceballos* (2006). Previously, the U.S.

CourtSpeak: *Gonzales v. Oregon* Assisted Suicide Case (2006)

Justice Anthony Kennedy (majority): "The Government, in the end, maintains that the prescription requirement delegates to a single Executive officer the power to effect a radical shift of authority from the States to the Federal Government to define general standards of medical practice in every locality. The text and structure of the CSA [Controlled Substances Act] show that Congress did not have this far-reaching intent to alter the federal-state balance and the congressional role in maintaining it."

Justice Antonin Scalia (dissenting): "Even if the Directive were entitled to no deference whatever, the most reasonable interpretation of the Regulation and of the statute would produce the same result. Virtually every relevant source of authoritative meaning confirms that the phrase 'legitimate medical purpose' does not include intentionally assisting suicide."

Justice Clarence Thomas (dissenting): "In other words, in stark contrast to *Raich*'s broad conclusions about the scope of the CSA as it pertains to the medicinal use of controlled substances, today this Court concludes that the CSA is merely concerned with fighting 'drug abuse' and only insofar as that abuse leads to 'addiction or abnormal effects on the nervous system.' The majority's newfound understanding of the CSA as a statute of limited reach is all the more puzzling because it rests upon constitutional principles that the majority of the Court rejected in *Raich*."

Supreme Court had applied the following test: Public employees have a First Amendment right to speak on matters of public concern as long as their free-speech rights trump their employer's right to an efficient, disruptive-free workplace.

Under the old rules, it appeared that Los Angeles deputy district attorney Richard Ceballos had a good claim since he spoke out on a matter of extreme public importance—the veracity of law enforcement officials. Ceballos had written a memo in which he questioned the honesty of a sheriff deputy's comments made for a search warrant affidavit. Ceballos eventually claimed that, as a result of exposing this wrongdoing by the law enforcement official and other statements, he was demoted.

The Roberts Court, by a narrow 5–4 vote, carved out an important exception by ruling that public employees do not have First Amendment protection for statements that they make as part of their official job duties. The majority, in an opinion written by Justice Anthony Kennedy, determined that when employees engage in such work-related expression, they are acting as employees subject to discipline, not as citizens entitled to First Amendment protection. Kennedy warned that employers must be able

A group photo of the Roberts Court on March 3, 2006. Seated (left to right) are Anthony Kennedy, John Paul Stevens, Chief Justice John Roberts Jr., Antonin Scalia, and David Souter. Standing (left to right) are Stephen Breyer, Clarence Thomas, Ruth Bader Ginsburg, and Samuel Alito Jr. *J. Scott Applewhite/AP Images.*

to operate and conduct business without turning every dispute in the workplace into a constitutional concern.

The dissenters warned that the Court's decision could have harmful consequences for those employees who blow the whistle on government corruption and could be harmful to the public, who potentially had lost an important source of information.

What did the Roberts Court rule with respect to **religious usage of hallucinogenic tea**?

The Roberts Court unanimously affirmed a preliminary injunction preventing the federal government from enforcing a ban on a church's use of a sacramental tea containing a hallucinogen in *Gonzales v. O Centro Espirita Beneficiente Uniao do Vegetal* (2006).

The case involved a Brazilian-based church (referred to as UDV) with approximately 130 members in the United States who drink hoasca, a tea containing a hallucinogen. The government seized several drums of the tea from a church member, claiming it violated federal drug control laws. The church then filed a lawsuit, saying that the government violated the Religious Freedom Restoration Act (RFRA), which imposes a high burden on government officials when they substantially infringe on a religious group's exercise of their religious liberty rights.

> ## CourtSpeak: *Garcetti v. Ceballos* Employee Free-Speech Case
>
> Justice Anthony Kennedy (majority): "The controlling factor in Ceballos' case is that his expressions were made pursuant to his duties as a calendar deputy. We hold that when public employees make statements pursuant to their official duties, the employees are not speaking as citizens for First Amendment purposes, and the Constitution does not insulate their communications from employer discipline."
>
> Justice John Paul Stevens (dissenting): "The notion that there is a categorical difference between speaking as a citizen and speaking in the course of one's employment is quite wrong."

The Court determined that, at this stage of the litigation, the government had failed to meet the RFRA's high burden. Chief Justice John Roberts, in his second opinion on the Court, noted that Congress had granted a similar exception for religious drug usage in the American Indian Religious Freedom Act Amendments. "If such use is permitted … for hundreds of thousands of Native Americans practicing their faith, it is difficult to see how those same findings alone can preclude any consideration of a similar exception for the 130 or so American members of the UDV who want to practice theirs," he wrote.

In what decision did the Roberts Court consider a claim by a **famous celebrity involving wills and estates**?

The Roberts Court ruled in *Marshall v. Marshall* (2006) that Vickie Lynn Marshall, better known to the world as former Playmate model Anna Nicole Smith, had a right to file a tort claim in federal court against her late husband's son, E. Pierce Marshall. The case involved a dispute over the estate of nanogenarian J. Howard Marshall, who married the much-younger Smith in 1994. When J. Howard Marshall died in 1995, his son and Smith battled over whether Smith should receive substantial monies from his estate. Pierce and Smith sued each other. Smith sued Pierce for interfering with a gift that had been given to her from her late husband. A federal district court in California awarded her more than $400 million in damages. On appeal, a federal appeals court reversed, finding that proper jurisdiction was held by the Texas probate court under the so-called "probate exception." The issue before the U.S. Supreme Court concerned whether a federal court in California (where Smith had filed bankruptcy) had jurisdiction to hear Smith's suit or whether sole jurisdiction rested with the Texas probate court. The Supreme Court ruled that the federal court in California had jurisdiction to hear Smith's claim.

The case is currently on hold following the sudden deaths of both E. Pierce Marshall and Anna Nicole Smith. Marshall died of an aggressive infection in June

Model Anna Nicole Smith. The Roberts Court ruled in *Marshall v. Marshall* that Vickie Lynn Marshall (Smith's real name) had a right to file a tort claim in federal court against her late husband's son, E. Pierce Marshall. *Frank Micelotta/Getty Images.*

2006 and Smith died of an accidental drug overdose in February 2007. Some speculate that much of the estate that was the subject of this protracted litigation will pass to Smith's infant daughter, who was the only surviving Smith heir, following the untimely death of Smith's 20-year-old son, Daniel, in September 2006.

In what **search and seizure case** did the Roberts Court invalidate a warrantless search because the **husband denied consent**?

The Roberts Court ruled 6–3 in *Georgia v. Randolph* (2006) that law enforcement officials violated the Fourth Amendment when they searched an estranged couple's home with the wife's initial consent but without the husband's consent. Writing for the majority, Justice David Souter reasoned that "a warrantless search of a shared dwelling for evidence over the express refusal of consent by a physically present resident cannot be justified as reasonable as to him on the basis of consent given to the police by another resident."

The case began when Janet Randolph called the police and told them that her husband Scott used drugs and there were "items of drug evidence" in the house. Mr. Randolph returned home before the police began their search and explicitly objected to the search.

The officer then received permission from Janet Randolph to search the premises and noticed a cocaine straw. He then went to his car to get an evidence bag and call for a warrant. When the officer returned, Janet Randolph withdrew her consent but the officer took the straw and later returned with a search warrant. Scott Randolph was later charged with possession of cocaine.

Scott Randolph filed a motion to suppress, contending that his Fourth Amendment rights were violated when the officer initially engaged in a warrantless search of his home in the face of his denials of permission. A trial court denied his motion, but the Georgia Court of Appeals and Supreme Court ruled in his favor.

CourtSpeak: *Georgia v. Randolph* Warrantless Search Case (2006)

Justice David Souter (majority): "The consenting tenant may simply not disclose enough information, or information factual enough, to add up to a showing of probable cause, and there may be no exigency to justify fast action. But nothing in social custom or its reflection in private law argues for placing a higher value on delving into private premises to search for evidence in the face of disputed consent, than on requiring clear justification before the government searches private living quarters over a resident's objection. We therefore hold that a warrantless search of a shared dwelling for evidence over the express refusal of consent by a physically present resident cannot be justified as reasonable as to him on the basis of consent given to the police by another resident."

Chief Justice John Roberts (dissenting): "The majority's analysis alters a great deal of established Fourth Amendment law…. Rather than constitutionalize such an arbitrary rule, we should acknowledge that a decision to share a private place, like a decision to share a secret or a confidential document, necessarily entails the risk that those with whom we share may in turn choose to share—for their own protection or for other reasons—with the police."

Why did the majority rule that the **police violated Scott Randolph's Fourth Amendment rights**?

The majority noted that a person has the greatest protection from unreasonable searches and seizures in his or her home. The police searched the premises without a warrant and without the husband's permission. In such a case of "disputed permission," the majority reasoned that social expectations show that the search was unreasonable because a third party would not expect to enter a home when a co-tenant gives express permission not to enter the dwelling. The Court explained: "Since the co-tenant wishing to open the door to a third party has no recognized authority in law or social practice to prevail over a present and objecting co-tenant, his disputed invitation, without more, gives a police officer no better claim to reasonableness in entering than the officer would have in the absence of any consent at all."

Why did Chief Justice **Roberts dissent in the *Randolph* case**?

Chief Justice John G. Roberts Jr. dissented vigorously, believing that the majority opinion had distorted Fourth Amendment law. He called the majority's rule "random" and "arbitrary," offering "a complete lack of practical guidance for the police in the field, let alone for the lower courts." Roberts wrote that a tenant assumes the risk that a co-tenant may give permission to law enforcement to conduct a search.

421

In what decision did the Roberts Court **narrow the exclusionary rule**?

The Roberts Court narrowed the exclusionary rule—which excludes evidence that has been unconstitutionally seized by police—in *Hudson v. Michigan.* The Court narrowed the exclusionary rule by holding that it did not apply when the police failed to "knock and announce" their presence before searching a suspect's home pursuant to a warrant. Justice Antonin Scalia, writing for a five-member majority, reasoned that the "knock and announce" rule "has never protected an individual from the government seeing evidence particularly described in a search warrant." The dissenting justices contended that the majority ignored past Court decisions that protected the sanctity of privacy in the home.

In what decision did the Court explain what statements are "testimonial" subject to a **criminal defendant's Confrontation Clause rights**?

The Roberts Court explained the meaning of "testimonial" statements for constitutional criminal law purposes in the consolidated cases of *Davis v. Washington* and *Hammon v. Indiana* (both 2006). These cases gave the Court a chance to explain its 2004 decision in *Crawford v. Washington.* In that decision, the Court ruled that testimonial statements must satisfy the Sixth Amendment's Confrontation Clause, giving the defendant the right to cross-examine witnesses. This means that if a person gives an accusatory statement to the police, then the defendant generally has a right to confront the speaker or listener of those statements in Court.

Davis v. Washington and *Hammon v. Indiana* involved domestic violence cases in which women either made a 911 call to the police or told police in an interview that their male companions had beaten them. In each case, prosecutors brought criminal charges against the men but the women later refused to testify. The prosecutors in each case sought to introduce the statements under the "excited utterance" exception to the hearsay rule. In the *Davis* case, the police sought to introduce the text of the 911 call and in *Hammon,* the police sought to introduce the woman's statement to the police.

The Roberts Court determined by a vote of 8–1 that the 911 call was not testimonial and, thus, could be freely admitted at trial. However, the Court determined that the statement to the police in the *Hammon* case was testimonial and would violate the defendant's Confrontation Clause rights. Writing for the Court, Justice Antonin Scalia established the following rule:

> Statements are nontestimonial when made in the course of police interrogation under circumstances objectively indicating that the primary purpose of the interrogation is to enable police assistance to meet an ongoing emergency. They are testimonial when the circumstances objectively indicate that there is no such ongoing emergency, and that the primary purpose of the interrogation is to establish or prove past events potentially relevant to later criminal prosecution.

Mayola Williams, whose husband died of lung cancer, leaves the Supreme Court Building on October 31, 2006, following oral arguments against tobacco company Philip Morris. *Dennis Cook/AP Images.*

Applying this standard, Scalia reasoned that the 911 call was nontestimonial because it was part of an "ongoing emergency," while when the woman made the statement to the police in *Hammon* there was no such emergency.

Who was the Court's **lone dissenter in the *Hammon* case**?

Justice Clarence Thomas was the only dissenter in the case. Thomas believed that both the 911 call and the statement to police should be admissible in court and not violative of a defendant's Confrontation Clause rights. He criticized the Court's test as "unpredictable" and one that would force police and prosecutors to guess which statements would be considered testimonial or nontestimonial.

In what decision did the Roberts Court examine a **large punitive damage award imposed on a tobacco company**?

The Roberts Court ruled 5–4 in *Philip Morris USA v. Williams* (2007) that $79.5 million in punitive damages against a tobacco company must be set aside because the Oregon courts allowed for consideration of damages to other smokers who were not parties to the actual litigation. Following the death of lifelong smoker Jesse Williams, his widow, Mayola, filed a lawsuit against Philip Morris, the maker of Marlboro cigarettes, the brand her late husband had smoked. She alleged that the company knowingly and falsely deceived her husband into believing that smoking cigarettes was not harmful. A jury awarded her $821,000 in compensatory damages (damages designed to compensate a plaintiff for the actual harm they have suffered) and $79.5 million in punitive damages (damages designed to harm the wrongdoer).

Philip Morris argued that the damage award was so excessive that it violated its rights under the Due Process Clause. One of Philip Morris's arguments was that allow-

Nebraska physician LeRoy Carhart, founder of Abortion and Contraception Clinic of Nebraska, was involved in two Supreme Court cases involving restrictions on abortion. *Steve Liss/Getty Images.*

ing the jury to take into consideration damages to other people amounted to a "taking of property" from the company without due process. It pointed out that it could not argue applicable defenses that may have been appropriate in possible claims asserted by nonparties (other smokers). The Oregon Supreme Court ruled that the $79.5-million award was within the province of the jury and was not unconstitutional.

Writing for the majority, Justice Stephen Breyer said that "the Constitution's Due Process Clause forbids a State to use a punitive damage award to punish a defendant for injury upon nonparties or those whom they directly represent." The majority said that trial courts must issue instructions to ensure that in determining punitive damages, jurors not punish defendants for harm caused "strangers to the litigation." A jury can take into account the fact that the defendant's conduct hurt other people in determining reprehensibility, but the majority viewed this as different from actually awarding damages based on harm caused other people. Four justices dissented, with three of them—John Paul Stevens, Clarence Thomas, and Ruth Bader Ginsburg—writing their own opinions.

How did the Roberts Court rule with respect to **partial-birth abortion**?

In one of its most highly anticipated decisions, a sharply divided Roberts Court ruled 5–4 in *Gonzales v. Carhart* (2007), in favor of a federal law known as the Partial-Birth Abortion Ban Act of 2003, which outlawed a particular type of abortion procedure during the second trimester of pregnancy. In this procedure, called intact dilation and

425

extraction (D&E), the physician pulls the fetus partially outside the cervix before terminating the fetus—often by crushing the skull. It is called partial birth because the physician initiates delivery and then aborts the fetus's life. The law flatly banned the procedure and critics pointed out that the law did not even contain a health exception to allow use of the procedure if medically necessary for the woman's health.

The majority of the Court, in an opinion written by Justice Anthony Kennedy, distinguished the federal law from a Nebraska law invalidated by the Rehnquist Court in *Stenberg v. Carhart* (in both cases, Nebraska physician LeRoy Carhart was one of the challengers to the restrictions on abortion), noting that the federal law "is more specific concerning the instances to which it applies and in this respect more precise in its coverage."

Cynics said the decision was more about the changed composition of the Court since 2000, noting that Justice Samuel Alito, who replaced the retiring Justice Sandra Day O'Connor, may have accounted for the different ruling.

Both proponents and opponents of the decision recognize the importance of the decision, calling it one of the most significant rulings in the area since *Roe v. Wade.*

Did the Roberts Court rule on **global warming**?

The Roberts Court ruled in *Massachusetts v. Environmental Protection Agency* (2006) that several states, local governments, and private organizations had the standing to challenge the controversial decision made by the federal Environmental Protection

<table>
<tr><td>

CourtSpeak: *Massachusetts v. Environmental Protection Agency*
Global Warming Case (2006)

Justice John Paul Stevens (majority): "In sum—at least according to petitioners' uncontested affidavits—the rise in sea levels associated with global warming has already harmed and will continue to harm Massachusetts. The risk of catastrophic harm, though remote, is nevertheless real. That risk would be reduced to some extent if petitioners received the relief they seek. We therefore hold that petitioners have standing to challenge the EPA's denial of their rulemaking petition."

Chief Justice John Roberts (dissenting): "I would reject these challenges as nonjusticiable. Such a conclusion involves no judgment on whether global warming exists, what causes it, or the extent of the problem. Nor does it render petitioners without recourse. This Court's standing jurisprudence simply recognizes that redress of grievances of the sort at issue here 'is the function of Congress and the Chief Executive.'"

</td></tr>
</table>

Agency (EPA) to not exercise its powers under the federal Clean Air Act to determine whether emissions of gases such as carbon dioxide contribute to global warming. The EPA had declined to regulate the emissions of such gases, saying that such a course of action may hamper the president's "comprehensive approach" to the problem.

A sharply divided Supreme Court ruled 5–4 that the state of Massachusetts and the other plaintiffs had the standing to challenge the EPA's inaction. "EPA's steadfast refusal to regulate greenhouse gas emissions presents a risk of harm to Massachusetts that is both 'actual' and 'imminent,'" wrote Justice John Paul Stevens for the majority. Stevens reasoned that the challengers certainly had the legal right to challenge the EPA's decision to terminate the rulemaking process on this important issue of global warming.

In what decision did the Roberts Court examine the message "Bong Hits 4 Jesus"?

The Roberts Court ruled in *Morse v. Frederick* (2007) that a high school principal in Alaska did not violate the First Amendment rights of one of her students when she punished him for his "Bong Hits 4 Jesus" banner. Student Joe Frederick displayed the banner, as the Olympic Torch Relay passed down a public street across from Juneau-Douglas High School. Frederick skipped school that day and sought to make a statement about his First Amendment rights. He claimed that the message was not a pro-drug message, but principal Deborah Morse claimed that the message contradicted the school's anti-drug policies.

Chief Justice John Roberts, in his majority opinion, created an exception to the famous Warren Court *Tinker v. Des Moines Independent Community School District*

(1969) precedent that established that students do not lose their free-speech rights at school. Roberts rejected the argument that Frederick's speech was sufficiently off-campus. He then ruled that school officials can censor student expression that they reasonably believe promotes illegal drug use.

What justice in his concurring opinion **believed public secondary school students have no First Amendment rights**?

Justice Clarence Thomas, the most staunch originalist (one who interprets the Constitution on the beliefs of the Founding Fathers who created the Constitution) on the Roberts Court, wrote a concurring opinion in which he advocated for the overruling of the *Tinker* decision. Thomas cited several nineteenth-century cases in which courts rejected students' free-expression claims. He believed that the federal courts should not intervene in the day-to-day operations of school officials.

What **famous attorney argued the case** before the Supreme Court on behalf of the principal and the school officials?

Kenneth Starr, the dean of the Pepperdine Law School, argued the case pro bono for the school officials. Starr was a former federal appeals court judge best known for his role as the independent counsel that investigated President Bill Clinton and produced the so-called "Starr Report." Starr has had a successful career as an advocate, arguing several cases before the U.S. Supreme Court.

Chief Justice John Roberts Jr. recently had a seizure from which he fortunately recovered, but **what happens when a justice becomes incapacitated**?

Unfortunately, this has happened from time to time in the Court's history, particularly given the advanced age of many of the justices. There is no particular rule that comes into play when a justice becomes incapacitated. No rule forces a justice to resign. Periodically, measures have been introduced in Congress to try to pass legislation forcing the involuntary retirement of justices when they have become mentally incapacitated. U.S. senator Sam Nunn of Georgia introduced such a measure in the 1970s.

Sometimes, a justice's colleagues may try to suggest that the justice take time off or even step down. Toward the end of their careers, some justices allegedly have lost much of their effectiveness. Reportedly, Justices William O. Douglas and Thurgood Marshall, for example, were ineffective and shadows of their former selves.

Most often, the justice may take a break and hopefully recover. For example, when Chief Justice William Rehnquist had cancer surgery, Justice John Paul Stevens—the most senior associate justice—presided over the Court.

Justices of the
U.S. Supreme Court

Name	Position(s)	Years of Service	Chief Justice(s)	President Who Appointed
John Jay	Chief Justice	1789–1795	Jay	Washington
John Rutledge	Associate Justice	1789–1791	Jay	Washington
	Chief Justice	1795–1795	Rutledge	Washington
William Cushing	Associate Justice	1789–1810	Jay Rutledge Ellsworth Marshall	Washington
James Wilson	Associate Justice	1789–1798	Jay Rutledge Ellsworth	Washington
John Blair	Associate Justice	1790–1796	Jay Rutledge	Washington
James Iredell	Associate Justice	1790–1799	Jay Rutledge Ellsworth	Washington
Thomas Johnson	Associate Justice	1792–1793	Jay	Washington
William Paterson	Associate Justice	1793–1806	Jay Rutledge Ellsworth Marshall	Washington
Samuel Chase	Associate Justice	1796–1811	Rutledge Ellsworth Marshall	Washington
Oliver Ellsworth	Chief Justice	1796–1800	Ellsworth	Washington
Bushrod Washington	Associate Justice	1799–1829	Ellsworth Marshall	J. Adams
Alfred Moore	Associate Justice	1800–1804	Ellsworth Marshall	J. Adams
John Marshall	Chief Justice	1801–1835	Marshall	J. Adams
William Johnson	Associate Justice	1804–1834	Marshall	Jefferson
Henry B. Livingston	Associate Justice	1807–1823	Marshall	Jefferson
Thomas Todd	Associate Justice	1807–1826	Marshall	Jefferson

Name	Position(s)	Years of Service	Chief Justice(s)	President Who Appointed
Gabriel Duvall	Associate Justice	1811–1835	Marshall	Madison
Joseph Story	Associate Justice	1812–1845	Marshall Taney	Madison
Smith Thompson	Associate Justice	1823–1845	Marshall Taney	Monroe
Robert Trimble	Associate Justice	1826–1828	Marshall	J. Q. Adams
John McLean	Associate Justice	1830–1861	Marshall Taney	Jackson
Henry Baldwin	Associate Justice	1830–1844	Marshall Taney	Jackson
James Moore Wayne	Associate Justice	1835–1867	Marshall Taney Chase	Jackson
Roger Taney	Chief Justice	1836–1864	Taney	Jackson
Philip Pendleton Barbour	Associate Justice	1836–1841	Taney	Jackson
John Catron	Associate Justice	1837–1865	Taney Chase	Jackson
John McKinley	Associate Justice	1838–1852	Taney	Van Buren
Peter Vivian Daniel	Associate Justice	1841–1860	Taney	Van Buren
Samuel Nelson	Associate Justice	1845–1872	Taney Chase	Tyler
Levi Woodbury	Associate Justice	1845–1851	Taney	Polk
Robert Cooper Grier	Associate Justice	1846–1870	Taney Chase	Polk
Benjamin R. Curtis	Associate Justice	1851–1857	Taney	Fillmore
John Campbell	Associate Justice	1853–1861	Taney	Pierce
Nathan Clifford	Associate Justice	1858–1881	Taney Chase Waite	Buchanan
Noah Haynes Swayne	Associate Justice	1862–1881	Taney Chase Waite	Lincoln
Samuel Miller	Associate Justice	1862–1890	Taney Chase Waite Fuller	Lincoln
David Davis	Associate Justice	1862–1877	Taney Chase	Lincoln
Stephen J. Field	Associate Justice	1863–1897	Taney Chase Waite Fuller	Lincoln
Salmon P. Chase	Chief Justice	1864–1873	Chase	Lincoln
William Strong	Associate Justice	1870–1880	Chase Waite	Grant

Name	Position(s)	Years of Service	Chief Justice(s)	President Who Appointed
Joseph Bradley	Associate Justice	1870–1892	Chase Waite Fuller	Grant
Ward Hunt	Associate Justice	1873–1882	Chase Waite	Grant
Morrison Waite	Chief Justice	1874–1888	Waite	Grant
John Marshall Harlan	Associate Justice	1877–1911	Waite Fuller White	Hayes
William B. Woods	Associate Justice	1881–1887	Waite	Hayes
Stanley Matthews	Associate Justice	1881–1889	Waite Fuller	Garfield
Horace Gray	Associate Justice	1882–1902	Waite Fuller	Arthur
Samuel Blatchford	Associate Justice	1882–1893	Waite Fuller	Arthur
Lucius Q. C. Lamar	Associate Justice	1888–1893	Waite Fuller	Cleveland (1st term)
Melville W. Fuller	Chief Justice	1888–1910	Fuller	Cleveland (1st term)
David Brewer	Associate Justice	1890–1910	Fuller	B. Harrison
Henry Billings Brown	Associate Justice	1891–1906	Fuller	B. Harrison
George Shiras Jr.	Associate Justice	1892–1903	Fuller	B. Harrison
Howell Edmunds Jackson	Associate Justice	1893–1895	Fuller	B. Harrison
Edward White	Associate Justice	1894–1910	Fuller	Cleveland (2nd term)
	Chief Justice	1910–1921	White	Taft
Rufus Peckham	Associate Justice	1896–1909	Fuller	Cleveland (2nd term)
Joseph McKenna	Associate Justice	1898–1925	Fuller White Taft	McKinley
Oliver Wendell Holmes Jr.	Associate Justice	1902–1932	Fuller White Taft Hughes	T. Roosevelt
William R. Day	Associate Justice	1903–1922	Fuller White Taft	T. Roosevelt
William Moody	Associate Justice	1906–1910	Fuller	T. Roosevelt
Horace Lurton	Associate Justice	1910–1914	Fuller White	Taft
Charles Evans Hughes	Associate Justice	1910–1916	White	Taft
	Chief Justice	1930–1941	Hughes	Taft
Willis Van Devanter	Associate Justice	1911–1937	White Taft Hughes	Taft
Joseph Lamar	Associate Justice	1911–1916	White	Taft
Mahlon Pitney	Associate Justice	1912–1922	White Taft	Taft

431

Name	Position(s)	Years of Service	Chief Justice(s)	President Who Appointed
James C. McReynolds	Associate Justice	1914–1941	White Taft Hughes	Wilson
Louis Brandeis	Associate Justice	1916–1939	White Taft	Wilson
John H. Clarke	Associate Justice	1916–1922	White Taft	Wilson
William Howard Taft	Chief Justice	1921–1930	Taft	Harding
George Sutherland	Associate Justice	1922–1938	Taft Hughes	Harding
Pierce Butler	Associate Justice	1923–1939	Taft Hughes	Harding
Edward Sanford	Associate Justice	1923–1930	Taft Hughes	Harding
Harlan Fiske Stone	Associate Justice	1925–1941	Taft Hughes	Coolidge
	Chief Justice	1941–1946	Stone	F. Roosevelt
Owen J. Roberts	Associate Justice	1930–1945	Hughes Stone	Hoover
Benjamin Cardozo	Associate Justice	1932–1938	Hughes	Hoover
Hugo Black	Associate Justice	1937–1971	Hughes Stone Vinson Warren Burger	F. Roosevelt
Stanley Reed	Associate Justice	1938–1957	Hughes Stone Vinson Warren	F. Roosevelt
Felix Frankfurter	Associate Justice	1939–1962	Hughes Stone Vinson Warren	F. Roosevelt
William O. Douglas	Associate Justice	1939–1975	Hughes Stone Vinson Warren Burger	F. Roosevelt
Frank W. Murphy	Associate Justice	1940–1949	Hughes Stone Vinson	F. Roosevelt
James Byrnes	Associate Justice	1941–1942	Stone	F. Roosevelt
Robert Jackson	Associate Justice	1941–1954	Stone Vinson Warren	F. Roosevelt
Wiley Rutledge	Associate Justice	1943–1949	Stone Vinson	F. Roosevelt

Name	Position(s)	Years of Service	Chief Justice(s)	President Who Appointed
Harold Burton	Associate Justice	1945–1958	Stone Vinson Warren	Truman
Fred Vinson	Chief Justice	1946–1953	Vinson	Truman
Tom C. Clark	Associate Justice	1949–1967	Vinson Warren	Truman
Sherman Minton	Associate Justice	1949–1956	Vinson Warren	Truman
Earl Warren	Chief Justice	1953–1969	Warren	Eisenhower
John Marshall Harlan	Associate Justice	1955–1971	Warren Burger	Eisenhower
William Brennan	Associate Justice	1956–1990	Warren Burger Rehnquist	Eisenhower
Charles Whittaker	Associate Justice	1957–1962	Warren	Eisenhower
Potter Stewart	Associate Justice	1958–1981	Warren Burger	Eisenhower
Byron White	Associate Justice	1962–1993	Warren Burger Rehnquist	Kennedy
Arthur Goldberg	Associate Justice	1962–1965	Warren	Kennedy
Abe Fortas	Associate Justice	1965–1969	Warren	L. Johnson
Thurgood Marshall	Associate Justice	1967–1991	Warren Burger Rehnquist	L. Johnson
Warren Burger	Chief Justice	1969–1986	Burger	Nixon
Harry Blackmun	Associate Justice	1970–1994	Burger Rehnquist	Nixon
Lewis Powell	Associate Justice	1972–1987	Burger Rehnquist	Nixon
William Rehnquist	Associate Justice	1972–1986	Burger	Nixon
	Chief Justice	1986–2005	Rehnquist	Reagan
John Paul Stevens	Associate Justice	1975–present	Burger Rehnquist Roberts	Ford
Sandra Day O'Connor	Associate Justice	1981–2006	Burger Rehnquist Roberts	Reagan
Antonin Scalia	Associate Justice	1986–present	Rehnquist Roberts	Reagan
Anthony Kennedy	Associate Justice	1988–present	Rehnquist Roberts	Reagan
David Souter	Associate Justice	1990–present	Rehnquist Roberts	G. H. W. Bush
Clarence Thomas	Associate Justice	1991–present	Rehnquist Roberts	G. H. W. Bush

Name	Position(s)	Years of Service	Chief Justice(s)	President Who Appointed
Ruth Bader Ginsburg	Associate Justice	1993–present	Rehnquist Roberts	Clinton
Stephen Breyer	Associate Justice	1994–present	Rehnquist Roberts	Clinton
John G. Roberts Jr.	Chief Justice	2005–present	Roberts	G. W. Bush
Samuel A. Alito Jr.	Associate Justice	2006–present	Roberts	G. W. Bush

The Constitution of the United States

We the People of the United States, in Order to form a more perfect Union, establish Justice, insure domestic Tranquility, provide for the common defence, promote the general Welfare, and secure the Blessings of Liberty to ourselves and our Posterity, do ordain and establish this Constitution for the United States of America.

ARTICLE I.

SECTION 1. All legislative Powers herein granted shall be vested in a Congress of the United States, which shall consist of a Senate and House of Representatives.

SECTION 2. The House of Representatives shall be composed of Members chosen every second Year by the People of the several States, and the Electors in each State shall have the Qualifications requisite for Electors of the most numerous Branch of the State Legislature.

No Person shall be a Representative who shall not have attained to the Age of twenty five Years, and been seven Years a Citizen of the United States, and who shall not, when elected, be an Inhabitant of that State in which he shall be chosen.

Representatives and direct Taxes shall be apportioned among the several States which may be included within this Union, according to their respective Numbers, which shall be determined by adding to the whole Number of free Persons, including those bound to Service for a Term of Years, and excluding Indians not taxed, three fifths of all other Persons.

The actual Enumeration shall be made within three Years after the first Meeting of the Congress of the United States, and within every subsequent Term of ten Years, in such Manner as they shall by Law direct. The Number of Representatives shall not exceed one for every thirty Thousand, but each State shall have at Least one Representative; and until such enumeration shall be made, the State of New Hampshire shall be entitled to chuse three, Massachusetts eight, Rhode Island and Providence Plantations one, Connecticut five, New York six, New Jersey four, Pennsylvania eight,

Delaware one, Maryland six, Virginia ten, North Carolina five, South Carolina five and Georgia three.

When vacancies happen in the Representation from any State, the Executive Authority thereof shall issue Writs of Election to fill such Vacancies.

The House of Representatives shall chuse their Speaker and other Officers; and shall have the sole Power of Impeachment.

SECTION 3. The Senate of the United States shall be composed of two Senators from each State, chosen by the Legislature thereof, for six Years; and each Senator shall have one Vote.

Immediately after they shall be assembled in Consequence of the first Election, they shall be divided as equally as may be into three Classes. The Seats of the Senators of the first Class shall be vacated at the Expiration of the second Year, of the second Class at the Expiration of the fourth Year, and of the third Class at the Expiration of the sixth Year, so that one third may be chosen every second Year; and if Vacancies happen by Resignation, or otherwise, during the Recess of the Legislature of any State, the Executive thereof may make temporary Appointments until the next Meeting of the Legislature, which shall then fill such Vacancies.

No person shall be a Senator who shall not have attained to the Age of thirty Years, and been nine Years a Citizen of the United States, and who shall not, when elected, be an Inhabitant of that State for which he shall be chosen.

The Vice President of the United States shall be President of the Senate, but shall have no Vote, unless they be equally divided.

The Senate shall chuse their other Officers, and also a President pro tempore, in the absence of the Vice President, or when he shall exercise the Office of President of the United States.

The Senate shall have the sole Power to try all Impeachments. When sitting for that Purpose, they shall be on Oath or Affirmation. When the President of the United States is tried, the Chief Justice shall preside: And no Person shall be convicted without the Concurrence of two thirds of the Members present.

Judgment in Cases of Impeachment shall not extend further than to removal from Office, and disqualification to hold and enjoy any Office of honor, Trust or Profit under the United States: but the Party convicted shall nevertheless be liable and subject to Indictment, Trial, Judgment and Punishment, according to Law.

SECTION 4. The Times, Places and Manner of holding Elections for Senators and Representatives, shall be prescribed in each State by the Legislature thereof; but the Congress may at any time by Law make or alter such Regulations, except as to the Place of Chusing Senators.

The Congress shall assemble at least once in every Year, and such Meeting shall be on the first Monday in December, unless they shall by Law appoint a different Day.

SECTION 5. Each House shall be the Judge of the Elections, Returns and Qualifications of its own Members, and a Majority of each shall constitute a Quorum to do Business; but a smaller number may adjourn from day to day, and may be authorized to compel the Attendance of absent Members, in such Manner, and under such Penalties as each House may provide.

Each House may determine the Rules of its Proceedings, punish its Members for disorderly Behavior, and, with the Concurrence of two-thirds, expel a Member.

Each House shall keep a Journal of its Proceedings, and from time to time publish the same, excepting such Parts as may in their Judgment require Secrecy; and the Yeas and Nays of the Members of either House on any question shall, at the Desire of one fifth of those Present, be entered on the Journal.

Neither House, during the Session of Congress, shall, without the Consent of the other, adjourn for more than three days, nor to any other Place than that in which the two Houses shall be sitting.

SECTION 6. The Senators and Representatives shall receive a Compensation for their Services, to be ascertained by Law, and paid out of the Treasury of the United States. They shall in all Cases, except Treason, Felony and Breach of the Peace, be privileged from Arrest during their Attendance at the Session of their respective Houses, and in going to and returning from the same; and for any Speech or Debate in either House, they shall not be questioned in any other Place.

No Senator or Representative shall, during the Time for which he was elected, be appointed to any civil Office under the Authority of the United States which shall have been created, or the Emoluments whereof shall have been increased during such time; and no Person holding any Office under the United States, shall be a Member of either House during his Continuance in Office.

SECTION 7. All bills for raising Revenue shall originate in the House of Representatives; but the Senate may propose or concur with Amendments as on other bills.

Every Bill which shall have passed the House of Representatives and the Senate, shall, before it become a Law, be presented to the President of the United States; If he approve he shall sign it, but if not he shall return it, with his Objections to that House in which it shall have originated, who shall enter the Objections at large on their Journal, and proceed to reconsider it. If after such Reconsideration two thirds of that House shall agree to pass the Bill, it shall be sent, together with the Objections, to the other House, by which it shall likewise be reconsidered, and if approved by two thirds of that House, it shall become a Law. But in all such Cases the Votes of both Houses shall be determined by Yeas and Nays, and the Names of the Persons voting for and against the Bill shall be entered on the Journal of each House respectively. If any Bill shall not be returned by the President within ten Days (Sundays excepted) after it shall have been presented to him, the Same shall be a Law, in like Manner as if he had signed it, unless the Congress by their Adjournment prevent its Return, in which Case it shall not be a Law.

437

Every Order, Resolution, or Vote to which the Concurrence of the Senate and House of Representatives may be necessary (except on a question of Adjournment) shall be presented to the President of the United States; and before the Same shall take Effect, shall be approved by him, or being disapproved by him, shall be repassed by two thirds of the Senate and House of Representatives, according to the Rules and Limitations prescribed in the Case of a Bill.

SECTION 8. The Congress shall have Power To lay and collect Taxes, Duties, Imposts and Excises, to pay the Debts and provide for the common Defence and general Welfare of the United States; but all Duties, Imposts and Excises shall be uniform throughout the United States;

To borrow money on the credit of the United States;

To regulate Commerce with foreign Nations, and among the several States, and with the Indian Tribes;

To establish an uniform Rule of Naturalization, and uniform Laws on the subject of Bankruptcies throughout the United States;

To coin Money, regulate the Value thereof, and of foreign Coin, and fix the Standard of Weights and Measures;

To provide for the Punishment of counterfeiting the Securities and current Coin of the United States;

To establish Post Offices and Post Roads;

To promote the Progress of Science and useful Arts, by securing for limited Times to Authors and Inventors the exclusive Right to their respective Writings and Discoveries;

To constitute Tribunals inferior to the supreme Court;

To define and punish Piracies and Felonies committed on the high Seas, and Offenses against the Law of Nations;

To declare War, grant Letters of Marque and Reprisal, and make Rules concerning Captures on Land and Water;

To raise and support Armies, but no Appropriation of Money to that Use shall be for a longer Term than two Years;

To provide and maintain a Navy;

To make Rules for the Government and Regulation of the land and naval Forces;

To provide for calling forth the Militia to execute the Laws of the Union, suppress Insurrections and repel Invasions;

To provide for organizing, arming, and disciplining the Militia, and for governing such Part of them as may be employed in the Service of the United States, reserving to the States respectively, the Appointment of the Officers, and the Authority of training the Militia according to the discipline prescribed by Congress;

To exercise exclusive Legislation in all Cases whatsoever, over such District (not exceeding ten Miles square) as may, by Cession of particular States, and the acceptance of Congress, become the Seat of the Government of the United States, and to exercise like Authority over all Places purchased by the Consent of the Legislature of the State in which the same shall be, for the Erection of Forts, Magazines, Arsenals, dock-Yards, and other needful Buildings; And

To make all Laws which shall be necessary and proper for carrying into Execution the foregoing Powers, and all other Powers vested by this Constitution in the Government of the United States, or in any Department or Officer thereof.

SECTION 9. The Migration or Importation of such Persons as any of the States now existing shall think proper to admit, shall not be prohibited by the Congress prior to the Year one thousand eight hundred and eight, but a tax or duty may be imposed on such Importation, not exceeding ten dollars for each Person.

The privilege of the Writ of Habeas Corpus shall not be suspended, unless when in Cases of Rebellion or Invasion the public Safety may require it.

No Bill of Attainder or ex post facto Law shall be passed. No capitation, or other direct, Tax shall be laid, unless in Proportion to the Census or Enumeration herein before directed to be taken.

No Tax or Duty shall be laid on Articles exported from any State.

No Preference shall be given by any Regulation of Commerce or Revenue to the Ports of one State over those of another: nor shall Vessels bound to, or from, one State, be obliged to enter, clear, or pay Duties in another.

No Money shall be drawn from the Treasury, but in Consequence of Appropriations made by Law; and a regular Statement and Account of the Receipts and Expenditures of all public Money shall be published from time to time.

No Title of Nobility shall be granted by the United States: And no Person holding any Office of Profit or Trust under them, shall, without the Consent of the Congress, accept of any present, Emolument, Office, or Title, of any kind whatever, from any King, Prince or foreign State.

SECTION 10. No State shall enter into any Treaty, Alliance, or Confederation; grant Letters of Marque and Reprisal; coin Money; emit Bills of Credit; make any Thing but gold and silver Coin a Tender in Payment of Debts; pass any Bill of Attainder, ex post facto Law, or Law impairing the Obligation of Contracts, or grant any Title of Nobility.

No State shall, without the Consent of the Congress, lay any Imposts or Duties on Imports or Exports, except what may be absolutely necessary for executing its inspection Laws: and the net Produce of all Duties and Imposts, laid by any State on Imports or Exports, shall be for the Use of the Treasury of the United States; and all such Laws shall be subject to the Revision and Controul of the Congress.

No State shall, without the Consent of Congress, lay any duty of Tonnage, keep Troops, or Ships of War in time of Peace, enter into any Agreement or Compact with another State, or with a foreign Power, or engage in War, unless actually invaded, or in such imminent Danger as will not admit of delay.

ARTICLE II.

SECTION 1. The executive Power shall be vested in a President of the United States of America. He shall hold his Office during the Term of four Years, and, together with the Vice-President chosen for the same Term, be elected, as follows:

Each State shall appoint, in such Manner as the Legislature thereof may direct, a Number of Electors, equal to the whole Number of Senators and Representatives to which the State may be entitled in the Congress: but no Senator or Representative, or Person holding an Office of Trust or Profit under the United States, shall be appointed an Elector.

The Electors shall meet in their respective States, and vote by Ballot for two persons, of whom one at least shall not lie an Inhabitant of the same State with themselves. And they shall make a List of all the Persons voted for, and of the Number of Votes for each; which List they shall sign and certify, and transmit sealed to the Seat of the Government of the United States, directed to the President of the Senate. The President of the Senate shall, in the Presence of the Senate and House of Representatives, open all the Certificates, and the Votes shall then be counted. The Person having the greatest Number of Votes shall be the President, if such Number be a Majority of the whole Number of Electors appointed; and if there be more than one who have such Majority, and have an equal Number of Votes, then the House of Representatives shall immediately chuse by Ballot one of them for President; and if no Person have a Majority, then from the five highest on the List the said House shall in like Manner chuse the President. But in chusing the President, the Votes shall be taken by States, the Representation from each State having one Vote; a quorum for this Purpose shall consist of a Member or Members from two-thirds of the States, and a Majority of all the States shall be necessary to a Choice. In every Case, after the Choice of the President, the Person having the greatest Number of Votes of the Electors shall be the Vice President. But if there should remain two or more who have equal Votes, the Senate shall chuse from them by Ballot the Vice President.

The Congress may determine the Time of chusing the Electors, and the Day on which they shall give their Votes; which Day shall be the same throughout the United States.

No person except a natural born Citizen, or a Citizen of the United States, at the time of the Adoption of this Constitution, shall be eligible to the Office of President; neither shall any Person be eligible to that Office who shall not have attained to the Age of thirty-five Years, and been fourteen Years a Resident within the United States.

In Case of the Removal of the President from Office, or of his Death, Resignation, or Inability to discharge the Powers and Duties of the said Office, the same shall devolve on the Vice President, and the Congress may by Law provide for the Case of Removal, Death, Resignation or Inability, both of the President and Vice President, declaring what Officer shall then act as President, and such Officer shall act accordingly, until the Disability be removed, or a President shall be elected.

The President shall, at stated Times, receive for his Services, a Compensation, which shall neither be increased nor diminished during the Period for which he shall have been elected, and he shall not receive within that Period any other Emolument from the United States, or any of them.

Before he enter on the Execution of his Office, he shall take the following Oath or Affirmation: "I do solemnly swear (or affirm) that I will faithfully execute the Office of President of the United States, and will to the best of my Ability, preserve, protect and defend the Constitution of the United States."

SECTION 2. The President shall be Commander in Chief of the Army and Navy of the United States, and of the Militia of the several States, when called into the actual Service of the United States; he may require the Opinion, in writing, of the principal Officer in each of the executive Departments, upon any subject relating to the Duties of their respective Offices, and he shall have Power to Grant Reprieves and Pardons for Offenses against the United States, except in Cases of Impeachment.

He shall have Power, by and with the Advice and Consent of the Senate, to make Treaties, provided two thirds of the Senators present concur; and he shall nominate, and by and with the Advice and Consent of the Senate, shall appoint Ambassadors, other public Ministers and Consuls, Judges of the supreme Court, and all other Officers of the United States, whose Appointments are not herein otherwise provided for, and which shall be established by Law: but the Congress may by Law vest the Appointment of such inferior Officers, as they think proper, in the President alone, in the Courts of Law, or in the Heads of Departments.

The President shall have Power to fill up all Vacancies that may happen during the Recess of the Senate, by granting Commissions which shall expire at the End of their next Session.

SECTION 3. He shall from time to time give to the Congress Information of the State of the Union, and recommend to their Consideration such Measures as he shall judge necessary and expedient; he may, on extraordinary Occasions, convene both Houses, or either of them, and in Case of Disagreement between them, with Respect to the Time of Adjournment, he may adjourn them to such Time as he shall think proper; he shall receive Ambassadors and other public Ministers; he shall take Care that the Laws be faithfully executed, and shall Commission all the Officers of the United States.

SECTION 4. The President, Vice President and all civil Officers of the United States, shall be removed from Office on Impeachment for, and Conviction of, Treason, Bribery, or other high Crimes and Misdemeanors.

ARTICLE III.

SECTION 1. The judicial Power of the United States, shall be vested in one supreme Court, and in such inferior Courts as the Congress may from time to time ordain and establish. The Judges, both of the supreme and inferior Courts, shall hold their Offices during good Behavior, and shall, at stated Times, receive for their Services a Compensation which shall not be diminished during their Continuance in Office.

SECTION 2. The judicial Power shall extend to all Cases, in Law and Equity, arising under this Constitution, the Laws of the United States, and Treaties made, or which shall be made, under their Authority; to all Cases affecting Ambassadors, other public Ministers and Consuls; to all Cases of admiralty and maritime Jurisdiction; to Controversies to which the United States shall be a Party; to Controversies between two or more States; between a State and Citizens of another State; between Citizens of different States; between Citizens of the same State claiming Lands under Grants of different States, and between a State, or the Citizens thereof, and foreign States, Citizens or Subjects.

In all Cases affecting Ambassadors, other public Ministers and Consuls, and those in which a State shall be Party, the supreme Court shall have original Jurisdiction. In all the other Cases before mentioned, the supreme Court shall have appellate Jurisdiction, both as to Law and Fact, with such Exceptions, and under such Regulations as the Congress shall make.

Trial of all Crimes, except in Cases of Impeachment, shall be by Jury; and such Trial shall be held in the State where the said Crimes shall have been committed; but when not committed within any State, the Trial shall be at such Place or Places as the Congress may by Law have directed.

SECTION 3. Treason against the United States, shall consist only in levying War against them, or in adhering to their Enemies, giving them Aid and Comfort. No Person shall be convicted of Treason unless on the Testimony of two Witnesses to the same overt Act, or on Confession in open Court.

The Congress shall have power to declare the Punishment of Treason, but no Attainder of Treason shall work Corruption of Blood, or Forfeiture except during the Life of the Person attainted.

ARTICLE IV.

SECTION 1. Full Faith and Credit shall be given in each State to the public Acts, Records, and judicial Proceedings of every other State. And the Congress may by general Laws prescribe the Manner in which such Acts, Records and Proceedings shall be proved, and the Effect thereof.

SECTION 2. The Citizens of each State shall be entitled to all Privileges and Immunities of Citizens in the several States.

A Person charged in any State with Treason, Felony, or other Crime, who shall flee from Justice, and be found in another State, shall on demand of the executive Authority of the State from which he fled, be delivered up, to be removed to the State having Jurisdiction of the Crime.

No Person held to Service or Labour in one State, under the Laws thereof, escaping into another, shall, in Consequence of any Law or Regulation therein, be discharged from such Service or Labour, But shall be delivered up on Claim of the Party to whom such Service or Labour may be due.

SECTION 3. New States may be admitted by the Congress into this Union; but no new States shall be formed or erected within the Jurisdiction of any other State; nor any State be formed by the Junction of two or more States, or parts of States, without the Consent of the Legislatures of the States concerned as well as of the Congress.

The Congress shall have Power to dispose of and make all needful Rules and Regulations respecting the Territory or other Property belonging to the United States; and nothing in this Constitution shall be so construed as to Prejudice any Claims of the United States, or of any particular State.

SECTION 4. The United States shall guarantee to every State in this Union a Republican Form of Government, and shall protect each of them against Invasion; and on Application of the Legislature, or of the Executive (when the Legislature cannot be convened) against domestic Violence.

ARTICLE V.

The Congress, whenever two thirds of both Houses shall deem it necessary, shall propose

Amendments to this Constitution, or, on the Application of the Legislatures of two thirds of the several States, shall call a Convention for proposing Amendments, which, in either Case, shall be valid to all Intents and Purposes, as part of this Constitution, when ratified by the Legislatures of three fourths of the several States, or by Conventions in three fourths thereof, as the one or the other Mode of Ratification may be proposed by the Congress; Provided that no Amendment which may be made prior to the Year One thousand eight hundred and eight shall in any Manner affect the first and fourth Clauses in the Ninth Section of the first Article; and that no State, without its Consent, shall be deprived of its equal Suffrage in the Senate.

ARTICLE VI.

All Debts contracted and Engagements entered into, before the Adoption of this Constitution, shall be as valid against the United States under this Constitution, as under the Confederation.

This Constitution, and the Laws of the United States which shall be made in Pursuance thereof; and all Treaties made, or which shall be made, under the Authority of the United States, shall be the supreme Law of the Land; and the Judges in every State shall be bound thereby, any Thing in the Constitution or Laws of any State to the Contrary notwithstanding.

The Senators and Representatives before mentioned, and the Members of the several State Legislatures, and all executive and judicial Officers, both of the United States and of the several States, shall be bound by Oath or Affirmation, to support this Constitution; but no religious Test shall ever be required as a Qualification to any Office or public Trust under the United States.

ARTICLE VII.

The Ratification of the Conventions of nine States, shall be sufficient for the Establishment of this Constitution between the States so ratifying the Same.

DONE in Convention by the Unanimous Consent of the States present the Seventeenth Day of September in the Year of our Lord one thousand seven hundred and Eighty seven and of the Independence of the United States of America the Twelfth. In Witness whereof We have hereunto subscribed our Names.

Go. Washington
President and deputy from Virginia

New Hampshire
John Langdon
Nicholas Gilman

Massachusetts
Nathaniel Gorham
Rufus King

Connecticut
Wm Saml Johnson
Roger Sherman

New York
Alexander Hamilton

New Jersey
Wil Livingston
David Brearley
Wm Paterson
Jona. Dayton

Pennsylvania
B Franklin
Thomas Mifflin
Robt Morris
Geo. Clymer
Thos FitzSimons
Jared Ingersoll
James Wilson
Gouv Morris

Delaware
Geo. Read
Gunning Bedford jun
John Dickinson
Richard Bassett
Jaco. Broom

Maryland
James McHenry
Dan of St Tho Jenifer
Danl Carroll

Virginia	Charles Cotesworth Pinckney
John Blair	Charles Pinckney
James Madison Jr.	Pierce Butler
North Carolina	**Georgia**
Wm Blount	William Few
Richd Dobbs Spaight	Abr Baldwin
Hu Williamson	
South Carolina	Attest: William Jackson, Secretary
J. Rutledge	

AMENDMENT I.

Congress shall make no law respecting an establishment of religion, or prohibiting the free exercise thereof; or abridging the freedom of speech, or of the press; or the right of the people peaceably to assemble, and to petition the Government for a redress of grievances.

AMENDMENT II.

A well regulated Militia, being necessary to the security of a free State, the right of the people to keep and bear Arms, shall not be infringed.

AMENDMENT III.

No Soldier shall, in time of peace be quartered in any house, without the consent of the Owner, nor in time of war, but in a manner to be prescribed by law.

AMENDMENT IV.

The right of the people to be secure in their persons, houses, papers, and effects, against unreasonable searches and seizures, shall not be violated, and no Warrants shall issue, but upon probable cause, supported by Oath or affirmation, and particularly describing the place to be searched, and the persons or things to be seized.

AMENDMENT V.

No person shall be held to answer for a capital, or otherwise infamous crime, unless on a presentment or indictment of a Grand Jury, except in cases arising in the land or naval forces, or in the Militia, when in actual service in time of War or public danger; nor shall any person be subject for the same offense to be twice put in jeopardy of life or limb; nor shall be compelled in any criminal case to be a witness against himself, nor be deprived of life, liberty, or property, without due process of law; nor shall private property be taken for public use, without just compensation.

AMENDMENT VI.

In all criminal prosecutions, the accused shall enjoy the right to a speedy and public trial, by an impartial jury of the State and district wherein the crime shall have been committed, which district shall have been previously ascertained by law, and to be informed of the nature and cause of the accusation; to be confronted with the witnesses against him; to have compulsory process for obtaining witnesses in his favor, and to have the Assistance of Counsel for his defence.

AMENDMENT VII.

In Suits at common law, where the value in controversy shall exceed twenty dollars, the right of trial by jury shall be preserved, and no fact tried by a jury, shall be otherwise re-examined in any Court of the United States, than according to the rules of the common law.

AMENDMENT VIII.

Excessive bail shall not be required, nor excessive fines imposed, nor cruel and unusual punishments inflicted.

AMENDMENT IX.

The enumeration in the Constitution, of certain rights, shall not be construed to deny or disparage others retained by the people.

AMENDMENT X.

The powers not delegated to the United States by the Constitution, nor prohibited by it to the States, are reserved to the States espectively, or to the people.

AMENDMENT XI.

The Judicial power of the United States shall not be construed to extend to any suit in law or equity, commenced or prosecuted against one of the United States by Citizens of another State, or by Citizens or Subjects of any Foreign State.

AMENDMENT XII.

The Electors shall meet in their respective states, and vote by ballot for President and Vice-President, one of whom, at least, shall not be an inhabitant of the same state with themselves; they shall name in their ballots the person voted for as President, and in distinct ballots the person voted for as Vice-President, and they shall make distinct lists of all persons voted for as President, and of all persons voted for as Vice-President and of the number of votes for each, which lists they shall sign and certify, and transmit sealed to the seat of the government of the United States, directed to the President of the Senate;

The President of the Senate shall, in the presence of the Senate and House of Representatives, open all the certificates and the votes shall then be counted;

The person having the greatest Number of votes for President, shall be the President, if such number be a majority of the whole number of Electors appointed; and if no person have such majority, then from the persons having the highest numbers not exceeding three on the list of those voted for as President, the House of Representatives shall choose immediately, by ballot, the President. But in choosing the President, the votes shall be taken by states, the representation from each state having one vote; a quorum for this purpose shall consist of a member or members from two-thirds of the states, and a majority of all the states shall be necessary to a choice. And if the House of Representatives shall not choose a President whenever the right of choice shall devolve upon them, before the fourth day of March next following, then the Vice-President shall act as President, as in the case of the death or other constitutional disability of the President.

The person having the greatest number of votes as Vice-President, shall be the Vice-President, if such number be a majority of the whole number of Electors appointed, and if no person have a majority, then from the two highest numbers on the list, the Senate shall choose the Vice-President; a quorum for the purpose shall consist of two-thirds of the whole number of Senators, and a majority of the whole number shall be necessary to a choice. But no person constitutionally ineligible to the office of President shall be eligible to that of Vice-President of the United States.

AMENDMENT XIII.

1. Neither slavery nor involuntary servitude, except as a punishment for crime whereof the party shall have been duly convicted, shall exist within the United States, or any place subject to their jurisdiction.

2. Congress shall have power to enforce this article by appropriate legislation.

AMENDMENT XIV.

1. All persons born or naturalized in the United States, and subject to the jurisdiction thereof, are citizens of the United States and of the State wherein they reside. No State shall make or enforce any law which shall abridge the privileges or immunities of citizens of the United States; nor shall any State deprive any person of life, liberty, or property, without due process of law; nor deny to any person within its jurisdiction the equal protection of the laws.

2. Representatives shall be apportioned among the several States according to their respective numbers, counting the whole number of persons in each State, excluding Indians not taxed. But when the right to vote at any election for the choice of electors for President and Vice-President of the United States, Representatives in Congress, the Executive and Judicial officers of a State, or the members of the Legislature thereof, is

denied to any of the male inhabitants of such State, being twenty-one years of age, and citizens of the United States, or in any way abridged, except for participation in rebellion, or other crime, the basis of representation therein shall be reduced in the proportion which the number of such male citizens shall bear to the whole number of male citizens twenty-one years of age in such State.

3. No person shall be a Senator or Representative in Congress, or elector of President and Vice-President, or hold any office, civil or military, under the United States, or under any State, who, having previously taken an oath, as a member of Congress, or as an officer of the United States, or as a member of any State legislature, or as an executive or judicial officer of any State, to support the Constitution of the United States, shall have engaged in insurrection or rebellion against the same, or given aid or comfort to the enemies thereof. But Congress may by a vote of two-thirds of each House, remove such disability.

4. The validity of the public debt of the United States, authorized by law, including debts incurred for payment of pensions and bounties for services in suppressing insurrection or rebellion, shall not be questioned. But neither the United States nor any State shall assume or pay any debt or obligation incurred in aid of insurrection or rebellion against the United States, or any claim for the loss or emancipation of any slave; but all such debts, obligations and claims shall be held illegal and void.

5. The Congress shall have power to enforce, by appropriate legislation, the provisions of this article.

AMENDMENT XV.

1. The right of citizens of the United States to vote shall not be denied or abridged by the United States or by any State on account of race, color, or previous condition of servitude.

2. The Congress shall have power to enforce this article by appropriate legislation.

AMENDMENT XVI.

The Congress shall have power to lay and collect taxes on incomes, from whatever source derived, without apportionment among the several States, and without regard to any census or enumeration.

AMENDMENT XVII.

The Senate of the United States shall be composed of two Senators from each State, elected by the people thereof, for six years; and each Senator shall have one vote. The electors in each State shall have the qualifications requisite for electors of the most numerous branch of the State legislatures.

When vacancies happen in the representation of any State in the Senate, the executive authority of such State shall issue writs of election to fill such vacancies: Provided, That the legislature of any State may empower the executive thereof to make temporary appointments until the people fill the vacancies by election as the legislature may direct.

This Amendment shall not be so construed as to affect the election or term of any Senator chosen before it becomes valid as part of the Constitution.

AMENDMENT XVIII.

1. After one year from the ratification of this article the manufacture, sale, or transportation of intoxicating liquors within, the importation thereof into, or the exportation thereof from the United States and all territory subject to the jurisdiction thereof for beverage purposes is hereby prohibited.

2. The Congress and the several States shall have concurrent power to enforce this article by appropriate legislation.

3. This article shall be inoperative unless it shall have been ratified as an Amendment to the Constitution by the legislatures of the several States, as provided in the Constitution, within seven years from the date of the submission hereof to the States by the Congress.

AMENDMENT XIX.

The right of citizens of the United States to vote shall not be denied or abridged by the United States or by any State on account of sex.

Congress shall have power to enforce this article by appropriate legislation.

AMENDMENT XX.

1. The terms of the President and Vice President shall end at noon on the 20th day of January, and the terms of Senators and Representatives at noon on the 3d day of January, of the years in which such terms would have ended if this article had not been ratified; and the terms of their successors shall then begin.

2. The Congress shall assemble at least once in every year, and such meeting shall begin at noon on the 3d day of January, unless they shall by law appoint a different day.

3. If, at the time fixed for the beginning of the term of the President, the President elect shall have died, the Vice President elect shall become President. If a President shall not have been chosen before the time fixed for the beginning of his term, or if the President elect shall have failed to qualify, then the Vice President elect shall act as

President until a President shall have qualified; and the Congress may by law provide for the case wherein neither a President elect nor a Vice President elect shall have qualified, declaring who shall then act as President, or the manner in which one who is to act shall be selected, and such person shall act accordingly until a President or Vice President shall have qualified.

4. The Congress may by law provide for the case of the death of any of the persons from whom the House of Representatives may choose a President whenever the right of choice shall have devolved upon them, and for the case of the death of any of the persons from whom the Senate may choose a Vice President whenever the right of choice shall have devolved upon them.

5. Sections 1 and 2 shall take effect on the 15th day of October following the ratification of this article.

6. This article shall be inoperative unless it shall have been ratified as an Amendment to the Constitution by the legislatures of three-fourths of the several States within seven years from the date of its submission.

AMENDMENT XXI.

1. The eighteenth article of Amendment to the Constitution of the United States is hereby repealed.

2. The transportation or importation into any State, Territory, or possession of the United States for delivery or use therein of intoxicating liquors, in violation of the laws thereof, is hereby prohibited.

3. The article shall be inoperative unless it shall have been ratified as an Amendment to the Constitution by conventions in the several States, as provided in the Constitution, within seven years from the date of the submission hereof to the States by the Congress.

AMENDMENT XXII.

1. No person shall be elected to the office of the President more than twice, and no person who has held the office of President, or acted as President, for more than two years of a term to which some other person was elected President shall be elected to the office of the President more than once. But this Article shall not apply to any person holding the office of President, when this Article was proposed by the Congress, and shall not prevent any person who may be holding the office of President, or acting as President, during the term within which this Article becomes operative from holding the office of President or acting as President during the remainder of such term.

2. This article shall be inoperative unless it shall have been ratified as an Amendment to the Constitution by the legislatures of three-fourths of the several States within seven years from the date of its submission to the States by the Congress.

AMENDMENT XXIII.

1. The District constituting the seat of Government of the United States shall appoint in such manner as the Congress may direct: A number of electors of President and Vice President equal to the whole number of Senators and Representatives in Congress to which the District would be entitled if it were a State, but in no event more than the least populous State; they shall be in addition to those appointed by the States, but they shall be considered, for the purposes of the election of President and Vice President, to be electors

appointed by a State; and they shall meet in the District and perform such duties as provided by the twelfth article of Amendment.

2. The Congress shall have power to enforce this article by appropriate legislation.

AMENDMENT XXIV.

1. The right of citizens of the United States to vote in any primary or other election for President or Vice President, for electors for President or Vice President, or for Senator or Representative in Congress, shall not be denied or abridged by the United States or any State by reason of failure to pay any poll tax or other tax.

2. The Congress shall have power to enforce this article by appropriate legislation.

AMENDMENT XXV.

1. In case of the removal of the President from office or of his death or resignation, the Vice President shall become President.

2. Whenever there is a vacancy in the office of the Vice President, the President shall nominate a Vice President who shall take office upon confirmation by a majority vote of both Houses of Congress.

3. Whenever the President transmits to the President pro tempore of the Senate and the Speaker of the House of Representatives his written declaration that he is unable to discharge the powers and duties of his office, and until he transmits to them a written declaration to the contrary, such powers and duties shall be discharged by the Vice President as Acting President.

4. Whenever the Vice President and a majority of either the principal officers of the executive departments or of such other body as Congress may by law provide, transmit to the President pro tempore of the Senate and the Speaker of the House of Representatives their written declaration that the President is unable to discharge the powers and duties of his office, the Vice President shall immediately assume the powers and duties of the office as Acting President.

Thereafter, when the President transmits to the President pro tempore of the Senate and the Speaker of the House of Representatives his written declaration that no inability exists, he shall resume the powers and duties of his office unless the Vice President and a majority of either the principal officers of the executive department or of such other body as Congress may by law provide, transmit within four days to the President pro tempore of the Senate and the Speaker of the House of Representatives their written declaration that the President is unable to discharge the powers and duties of his office. Thereupon Congress shall decide the issue, assembling within forty eight hours for that purpose if not in session. If the Congress, within twenty one days after receipt of the latter written declaration, or, if Congress is not in session, within twenty one days after Congress is required to assemble, determines by two thirds vote of both Houses that the President is unable to discharge the powers and duties of his office, the Vice President shall continue to discharge the same as Acting President; otherwise, the President shall resume the powers and duties of his office.

AMENDMENT XXVI.

1. The right of citizens of the United States, who are eighteen years of age or older, to vote shall not be denied or abridged by the United States or by any State on account of age.

2. The Congress shall have power to enforce this article by appropriate legislation.

AMENDMENT XXVII.

No law, varying the compensation for the services of the Senators and Representatives, shall take effect, until an election of Representatives shall have intervened.

Resources

Books

Abraham, Henry J. *Justices, Presidents and Senators: A History of U.S. Supreme Court Appointments from Washington to Clinton.* 4th ed. Lanham, MD: Rowman & Littlefield Publishers, 1999.

Amar, Akhil Reed. *America's Constitution: A Biography.* New York: Random House, 2005.

Asch, Sidney H. *The Supreme Court and Its Great Justices.* New York: Arco, 1971.

Baum, Lawrence. *The Supreme Court.* 9th ed. Washington, DC: CQ Press, 2007.

Bickel, Alexander. *The Least Dangerous Branch: The Supreme Court at the Bar of Politics.* 2nd ed. New Haven, CT: Yale University Press, 1986.

Biskupic, Joan. *Sandra Day O'Connor: How the First Woman on the Supreme Court Became Its Most Influential Justice.* New York: ECCO, 2005.

Biskupic, Joan, and Elder Witt. *The Supreme Court at Work.* 2nd ed. Washington, DC: CQ Press, 1997.

Blasi, Vincent, ed. *The Burger Court: The CounterRevolution That Wasn't.* New Haven, CT: Yale University Press, 1983.

Blaustein, Albert P., and Roy M. Mersky. *The First One Hundred Justices.* Hamden, CT: Archon Books, 1978.

Brenner, Saul, and Harold Spaeth. *Stare Indecisis: The Alteration of Precedent on the Supreme Court, 1946–1992.* New York: Cambridge University Press, 1995.

Breyer, Stephen G. *Active Liberty: Interpreting Our Democratic Constitution.* New York: Knopf, 2005.

Brisbin, Richard A. Jr. *Justice Antonin Scalia and the Conservative Revival.* Baltimore: John Hopkins University Press, 1997.

Casto, William R. *The Supreme Court in the Early Republic: The Chief Justiceships of John Jay and Oliver Ellsworth.* Columbia: University of South Carolina Press, 1995.

Choper, Jesse, ed. *The Supreme Court and Its Justices.* 2nd ed. Chicago: American Bar Association, 2001.

Comiskey, Michael. *Seeking Justices: The Judging of Supreme Court Nominees.* Lawrence: University Press of Kansas, 2004.

Cooper, Phillip J. *Battles on the Bench: Conflict Inside the Supreme Court.* Lawrence: University Press of Kansas, 1995.

Cox, Archibald. *The Court and the Constitution.* Boston: Houghton Mifflin, 1987.

Cray, Ed. *Chief Justice: A Biography of Earl Warren.* New York: Simon & Schuster, 1997.

Currie, David P. *The Constitution in the Supreme Court: The Second Century, 1888–1986.* Chicago: University of Chicago Press, 1990.

Cushman, Claire, ed. *The Supreme Court Justices: Illustrated Biographies, 1789–1995.* 2nd ed. Washington, DC: Congressional Quarterly, 1995.

Domnarski, William. *The Great Justices, 1941–54 : Black, Douglas, Frankfurter & Jackson in Chambers.* Ann Arbor: University of Michigan Press, 2006.

Flynn, James J. *Famous Justices of the Supreme Court.* New York: Dodd Mead, 1968.

Frank, John P. *Marble Palace: The Supreme Court in American Life.* New York: Knopf, 1958.

Friedman, Leon, and Fred Israel, eds. *The Justices of the United States Supreme Court: Their Lives and Major Opinions.* 5 vols. New York: Chelsea House Publishers, 1997.

Greenhouse, Linda. *Becoming Justice Blackmun: Harry Blackmun's Supreme Court Journey.* New York: Times Books, 2005.

Hall, Kermit, ed. *The Oxford Companion to the Supreme Court of the United States.* 2nd ed. New York: Oxford University Press, 2005.

Hutchinson, Dennis. *The Man Who Once Was Whizzer White: A Portrait of Justice Byron R. White.* New York: Free Press, 1998.

Irons, Peter. *A People's History of the Supreme Court.* Rev. ed. New York: Penguin Books, 2006.

Irons, Peter, and Stephanie Guitton, eds. *May It Please the Court: The Most Significant Oral Arguments Made before the Supreme Court since 1955.* New York: The New Press, 1993.

Jeffries, John C. Jr. *Justice Lewis F. Powell, Jr.* New York: Fordham University Press, 2001.

Kaufman, Andrew L. *Cardozo.* Boston: Harvard University Press, 1998.

Lazarus, Edward. *Closed Chambers: The Rise, Fall, and Future of the Modern Supreme Court.* Rev. ed. New York: Penguin Books, 2005.

Lieberman, Jethro K. *A Practical Companion to the Constitution: How the Supreme Court Has Ruled on Issues from Abortion to Zoning.* Rev. ed. Berkeley: University of California Press, 1999.

Mason, Alpheus Thomas. *The Supreme Court from Taft to Burger.* 3rd ed. Baton Rouge: Louisiana State University Press, 1979.

Nelson, William E. *Marbury v. Madison: The Origins and Legacy of Judicial Review.* Lawrence: University Press of Kansas, 2000.

Newman, Roger K. *Hugo Black: A Biography.* 2nd ed. New York: Fordham University Press, 1997.

O'Brien, David M. *Storm Center: The Supreme Court in American Politics.* 7th ed. New York: W. W. Norton, 2005.

O'Connor, Sandra Day. *The Majesty of the Law: Reflections of a Supreme Court Justice.* Edited by Craig Joyce. New York: Random House, 2003.

Pacelle, Richard. *The Role of the U.S. Supreme Court in Politics: The Least Dangerous Branch.* Boulder, CO: Westview Press, 2002.

Paddock, Lisa. *Facts About the Supreme Court of the United States.* New York: H. W. Wilson, 1996.

Pearson, Drew. *The Nine Old Men.* Garden City, NY: Doubleday Doran & Co., 1937.

Perry, Barbara A. *The Priestly Tribe: The Supreme Court's Image in the American Mind.* Westport, CT: Praeger, 1999.

Rehnquist, William H. *All the Laws but One: Civil Liberties in Wartime.* New York: Knopf, 1998.

Rehnquist, William H. *The Supreme Court.* Rev. ed. New York: Vintage Books, 2002.

Rodell, Fred. *Nine Men: A Political History of the Supreme Court from 1790 to 1955.* New York: Random House, 1955.

Savage, David G. *Turning Right: The Making of the Rehnquist Court.* New York: Wiley, 1992.

Scalia, Antonin. *A Matter of Interpretation: Federal Courts and the Law.* Princeton, NJ: Princeton University Press, 1997.

Schwartz, Bernard. *A History of the Supreme Court.* New York: Oxford University Press, 1993.

Smith, Jean Edward. *John Marshall: Definer of a Nation.* New York: Henry Holt, 1996.

Stahr, Walter. *John Jay: Founding Father.* New York: Hambledon & London, 2005.

Starr, Kenneth W. *First Among Equals: The Supreme Court in American Life.* New York: Warner Books, 2002.

Tomlins, Christopher, ed. *The United States Supreme Court: The Pursuit of Justice.* Boston: Houghton Mifflin Company, 2005.

Tribe, Laurence H. *God Save This Honorable Court: How the Choice of Supreme Court Justices Shapes Our History.* New York: Random House, 1985.

Tushnet, Mark. *A Court Divided: The Rehnquist Court and the Future of Constitutional Law.* New York: W. W. Norton & Co., 2005.

Urofsky, Melvin. *Division and Discord: The Supreme Court under Stone and Vinson, 1941–1953.* Columbia: University of South Carolina Press, 1997.

Urofksy, Melvin I., ed. *The Supreme Court Justices: A Biographical Dictionary.* New York: Garland Publishing, 1994.

Wagman, Robert J. *The Supreme Court: A Citizen's Guide.* New York: Pharos Books, 1993.

Warren, Charles. *The Supreme Court in United States History.* Rev. ed. Littleton, CO: F. B. Rothman, 1987.

Williams, Juan. *Thurgood Marshall: American Revolutionary.* New York: Times Books, 1998.

Woodward, Bob, and Scott Armstrong. *The Brethren.* New York: Simon & Schuster, 1979.

Yalof, David Alistair. *Pursuit of Justices: Presidential Politics and the Selection of Supreme Court Nominees.* Chicago: University of Chicago Press, 1999.

Yarbrough, Tinsley E. *David Hackett Souter: Traditional Republican on the Rehnquist Court.* Oxford: Oxford University Press, 2005.

Online Resources

Administrative Office of the U.S. Courts. *U.S. Courts.* http://www.uscourts.gov/. This site contains links to all of the federal court's websites.

American Bar Association. *Standing Committee on the Federal Judiciary.* http://www.abanet.org/scfedjud/. This site reviews federal court nominees. It includes the ABA's publication on the Standing Committee at http://www.abanet.org/scfedjud/Federal_Judiciary%20(2).pdf.

American Bar Association. *Supreme Court Preview.* http://www.abanet.org/publiced/preview/home.html. This is a link to a publication that summarizes cases before the U.S. Supreme Court.

Cornell University Law School. *Supreme Court Collection.* http://www.law.cornell.edu/supct/index.html. This site enables researchers to find U.S. Supreme Court opinions.

Federal Judicial Center. http://www.fjc.gov/. This site contains historical information on the justices as well as a biographical dictionary of federal judges.

Findlaw. *US Supreme Court Center.* http://supreme.lp.findlaw.com/. This helpful site contains links to just about everything on the Court.

LLRX. *Web Guide to U.S. Supreme Court Research.* http://www.llrx.com/features/supremectwebguide.htm. This publication by law librarian Gail Partin contains hundreds of helpful links and information about the Court.

Street Law and the Supreme Court Historical Society. *Landmark Supreme Court Cases.* http://www.landmarkcases.org/. This site has information about many important Supreme Court opinions.

Supreme Court of the United States. http://www.supremecourtus.gov. The Supreme Court's own website contains the justices' opinions, their biographies, the Court's docket, and a wealth of other useful information.

Index

Notes: (ill.) indicates photos and illustrations.

A

457

462

470

473

478

479

S